GRAND INQUEST

THE STORY OF CONGRESSIONAL INVESTIGATIONS

BY

Telford Taylor

SIMON AND SCHUSTER
NEW YORK

WGE

PUBLISHED BY SIMON AND SCHUSTER, INC.
ROCKEFELLER CENTER, 630 FIFTH AVENUE
NEW YORK 20, N. Y.

AUTHOR'S NOTE

This book is an expansion of an address on the powers of legislative investigating committees presented in December, 1953, at a symposium at Notre Dame University and printed as an article in the following issue of the *Notre Dame Lawyer*, and of other addresses and lectures on the same subject delivered in 1953 under various auspices including the Graduate College of Princeton University, the Essex County (N. J.) Bar Association, Sarah Lawrence College, the *Columbia Law Review*, the New York Young Republican Club, and the Cadet Forum of the United States Military Academy at West Point.

SECOND PRINTING
LIBRARY OF CONGRESS CATALOG CARD NUMBER: 54-9803
DEWEY DECIMAL CLASSIFICATION NUMBER: 328.739
MANUFACTURED IN THE UNITED STATES OF AMERICA
BY AMERICAN BOOK–STRATFORD PRESS, INC., NEW YORK

TO THE MEMORY OF

JUSTICE ROBERT H. JACKSON

CONTENTS

	FOREWORD	xi
I	HOW IT ALL BEGAN	1
II	THE ORDEAL OF MAJOR GENERAL ARTHUR ST. CLAIR	17
III	CONSTITUTIONS, COURTS AND INVESTIGATIONS	30
	The First Sixty-five Years	32
	The State Courts and the "Know-Nothing" Investigations of 1855	35
	The Supreme Court Steps In	45
	Adjustment and Balance: "The Least Possible Power"	50
IV	THE ILLUSION OF INVESTIGATIVE OMNIPOTENCE	58
	Money Trust, Teapot Dome, and New Deal	60
	The Wind Shifts: Loyalty and Subversion	70
	Illusion and Dilemma	79
	Dispelling the Illusion: The General Nature and Limits of Investigative Power	83

V INVESTIGATIONS AND THE SEPARATION OF POWERS 89

Congress vs. the Courts 90

Congress vs. the Executive 97

Senator vs. Commander-in-Chief 109

VI INVESTIGATIONS AND INDIVIDUAL LIBERTIES 136

Mr. Rumely, the Lady from Toledo, and the Supreme Court 140

"Are You or Have You Ever Been a Communist?" 147

Investigation, Identification, and Inquisition 159

The Interdependence of Freedom and Security 173

VII THE PRIVILEGE AGAINST SELF-ACCUSATION 184

The Origins of the Privilege 186

The Privilege in Investigations 191

"Fifth Amendment Communists" 196

Use and Abuse of the Privilege 199

Other People's Names 205

Inferences and Consequences 210

Immunity Grants and Baths 215

VIII OTHER LIMITATIONS AND PRIVILEGES 222

Delegated Powers and States' Rights 223

Vagueness: "Call it Un-American!" 229

Safety Valve: Pertinence and Impertinence 233

Doctor, Lawyer 235

IX INVESTIGATING COMMITTEE PROCEDURES 240

Lo! The Poor Witness 242

Secret and Not-So-Secret Hearings 244

With Gun and Camera 247

Codes of Fair Practices 252
Two Suggestions: Starting and Stopping Investigations 257

X THE COLD CIVIL WAR 263
How to Hunt a Skunk 264
Freedom and Security Under Law 276

APPENDIX I: A NOTE FOR LAYMEN ON BRITISH PARLIAMENTARY INVESTIGATIVE PRACTICE 285

APPENDIX II: A NOTE FOR LAWYERS ON THE NEW FEDERAL "IMMUNITY" STATUTE 296

APPENDIX III: AN HISTORICAL NOTE ON OUTLAWRY 301

NOTES TO THE TEXT AND APPENDICES 307

SOURCES AND ACKNOWLEDGMENTS 343

INDEX 345

FOREWORD

As THE CHOSEN instrument of a new and potent combination of domestic political forces, Congressional investigations are an immediate and major cause of the internal crisis of confidence in which the United States is presently gripped. The purpose of this book is to describe the origin and growth of the investigations, to explore their purposes and powers, and to trace the process by which they have now arrived at the center of the political stage, where they are playing so controversial a role.

All human institutions, no matter how beneficent, can be perverted and abused, and investigations have had their full measure of misuse during the past hundred years. Nevertheless, in the Britain of their birth as well as in this country, investigations are an accepted and important part of democracy's governmental machinery. The excesses to which they are susceptible have marred but not destroyed their solid and enduring value in exposing official corruption or inefficiency, and illuminating the facts and circumstances with which the law-making process is concerned.

But with the increasing participation of investigating committees in matters of loyalty and subversion, their activities have raised new and much more searching issues. The problem is no longer merely one of partisan distortions and procedural crudities—of regrettable excrescences on a basically sound political organism. The question is whether this relatively new instrumentality, the Congressional loyalty investigation, has not been captured lock, stock, and barrel for exploitation, not for the benefit of Congress as a representative body, but under the domination of a particular conglomeration of political forces and interests.

To apprehend this danger it is necessary only to scan the names of those who have been most prominently identified with these investigations. Martin Dies, Jack Tenney, J. Parnell Thomas, Patrick McCarran, Eugene Cox, William Jenner, Joseph R. McCarthy, Harold Velde, Carroll Reece—whatever one's personal estimate of these men, one thing is clear: they are not a representative group of American legislators. They are clustered at the extreme right end of the political color spectrum, where purple deepens into black. Largely for this reason, the Congressional loyalty investigations have been like a baseball game in which only one team ever comes to bat.

Under these circumstances, it would be worse than futile to essay a "pure" analysis of investigations, divorced from the political conflicts in which they are so deeply involved. I have made no such effort, and on the contrary have endeavored throughout to sketch in the setting, the better to portray the subject. In fact, and as is hardly surprising, the investigative process itself has been powerfully affected by the uses to which it has recently been put and the objectives of those who have controlled the principal committees inquiring into subversion.

Largely because of these changes in their scope and effect, the investigations have ceased to be a subject of interest chiefly to lawyers, politicians, and social scientists, and have become a matter of increasing personal concern to all citizens. It is not only that investigations are bigger and much more numerous than ever before. Rather it is the intrinsic nature of the loyalty inquiries that greatly broadens their impact on the general public.

The traditional investigations of government agencies, or inquiries into a particular subject of legislation, were generally confined to official Washington and to a few spectacular and powerful locales such as the Wall Street financial community. They sometimes made headlines, but touched the average citizen chiefly through the press and radio, and rarely in his own community, much less in his neighborhood or his home. The witnesses summoned before the committees were generally government officials, financiers, corporation officials, labor leaders, and economic experts—prominent and powerful or intellectually sophisticated individuals whose problems and opinions seemed remote from the life of plain people.

Today the net of the loyalty investigations is far more widely cast. Since 1946 three permanent Congressional committees or subcommittees—the House Un-American Activities Committee, the Senate Internal Security Subcommittee, and the Senate Permanent Investigating Subcommittee—have been busily exploring and exposing the political activities, associations, and attitudes of American citizens. They have penetrated the most diverse surroundings and occupations, among others the Hollywood motion picture industry, philanthropic foundations, public and private education at all levels, and industrial labor, with side glances into journalism, publishing, radio-television, and the clergy.

Thus the teacher and the workman are now under Congressional scrutiny, and the end is not yet in sight. Eleven residents of the District of Columbia recently summoned before the House Un-American Activities Committee included a doctor, an optometrist, a commercial artist, a magazine writer, an electrician, an automobile mechanic, a piano tuner, a public relations consultant, a commercial photographer and two housewives. This is a measure of how deeply the investigations are biting into the everyday life of the average citizen. Even if his own loyalty is not in question, the lightning may strike the teacher at his daughter's school, or the man working beside him at the shop.

There is another and even more significant change to be remarked. The historic function of legislative inquiries—to obtain information—is secondary or even completely lacking in many of the loyalty proceedings. At times it almost seems that Congress' primary function of law-making is being submerged by the supposedly auxiliary function of investigating, and indeed this was one of the criticisms most commonly raised against the recent Army-McCarthy hearings.

In part, of course, this is a sheer matter of publicity. Congressional debates and committee sessions devoted to legislation cannot compete with all-star casts such as Messrs. Jenkins, Welch, McCarthy and Cohn. Charge and counter-charge, the breath of scandal and the clash of personalities, make a better show than knotty problems of public policy. Most of our leading inquisitors yield readily to the lure of television screen and newspaper headlines, and publicity thus becomes the core rather than the setting of the investigation.

But there is a more sinister aspect to this withering away of the information-gathering purpose. Often the loyalty hearings are nothing other than a method, outside the law, of inflicting punishment on individuals. Of course, incidental injury to persons or institutions in the course of searching legislative inquiries is sometimes unavoidable. But committee proceedings that have no purpose or effect other than to expose individuals to public contumely, and to the loss of their jobs and perhaps of their livelihoods, are a new and dangerous political device, never authorized by law or contemplated during the evolution of legislative investigations.

The phenomenon of extra-legal condemnation on suspicion of political unreliability has spread from the investigations into many other areas. A wide assortment of "Fifth Amendment Communists," "left wingers," and others face the prospect of dismissal from their positions, disbarment, revocation of licenses as physicians, dentists, or veterinarians, denial of passports, income-tax exemptions, access to public housing, and civic if not social ostracism. In Indiana, the loyalty of professional boxers is now a matter of official scrutiny, and another curious manifestation of this trend is a Massachusetts statute which forbids the appearance on educational television programs of persons who have refused "for any reason" to answer any question put to them by Congressional investigating committees. This remarkable provision bars from the television screen ex-President Truman, Supreme Court Justice Tom Clark, Generals Omar Bradley, Kirke Lawton, and Ralph Zwicker, Secretary of the Army Stevens, Senator Joseph R. McCarthy, and Walter Winchell, all of whom have, for one reason or another, declined to answer certain committee questions.

Now, there is a word which describes, better than any other, the status toward which these miscellaneous and cumulative pains and penalties are tending. That word is "outlawry." The investigations are creating and constantly enlarging a category of citizens effectively stigmatized though never convicted of any offense, who are finding life in the United States increasingly difficult and who cannot, under twentieth century conditions, emulate that famous outlaw Robin Hood by taking to the forest to live under the greenwood tree.

In short, we are approaching a condition in which political orthodoxy is scrutinized by roving inquisitions, which punish heresy by a sort of outlawry. This is a strange vocabulary for twentieth-century democracy; inquisition and outlawry are medieval concepts, long since discarded in modern law and morals, and thoroughly repugnant to our Constitutional system. Their revival is an eloquent measure of the depth and bitterness of America's crisis of confidence. In a very real sense, we are living in a state of cold civil war.

The elements of this conflict are diverse and tangled. In general and certainly inadequate terms, it may be described as a nationalist, "native-American" challenge to the middle-class liberalism and internationalism which have been the prevailing (though often-disturbed) political climate of the United States, Britain, and the democracies of Western Europe.

The fears and forces of which this challenge is compounded long antedate the Communist menace. In cultural terms, it involves the rejection of cultural affinities with Europe, together with derivative regional mistrust of the Atlantic seaboard, where European ties are closest. In political terms, it displays indifference if not hostility toward the Anglo-American-French libertarianism of Locke, Bentham, Montesquieu, Franklin and Jefferson, which the Bill of Rights embodies. In terms of world outlook, it embraces a combination of isolationism toward Europe, signalized by profound distrust of involvement in European problems or in international organizations thought to be dominated by European interests, and, in the Orient, a strident, but strangely flaccid, papier-mâché imperialism.

While these amorphous and overlapping attitudes have been sharpening into an American nationalist alignment, Communism has sprung from its tiny dialectical seed and emerged as an enormous and dynamic world force. A mere handful of revolutionaries at the outbreak of the First World War, less than forty years later Communism dominates the heartland of Eurasia and is the way of life for some 800 million people.

An accident of the European parliamentary vocabulary is originally responsible for the notion, sedulously fostered by the nationalists, that the politics of liberalism and social democracy are closely akin to Communism. In the multi-party European legislatures, unlike both Parliament and Congress, the parties are ranged in a political spectrum from right to left, with the Social Democrats next to the Communists on the extreme left. This is why "leftist" politics have fallen in the popular mind, quite undeservedly, into the pink shadow of Communism—a preconception which quite overlooks the fact that the Communists are usually found making common cause with the extremists of the right, and that the physical proximity of the Socialists and Communists does nothing to alleviate the implacable enmity between them. Indeed, the Communist *Weltanschauung* and conception of the individual's relation to the State have much more in common with the nationalism of the radical right than with the liberal internationalism of the left.

Accordingly, it is quite wrong to suppose that Communism is an issue in America's cold civil war, in the sense that either side is favorably disposed toward it. But Communism is, of course, a factor of enormous importance in this domestic struggle. The Communist menace takes quite different shapes, depending upon the lenses through which it is viewed. Counter measures advocated by some may and, indeed, do seem suicidal to others. Furthermore—and this is what has made our internal conflict so venomously lethal that it deserves to be called the cold civil war—the nationalist alignment has succeeded, beyond all prior imagining, in saddling the democratic-liberal groups with the onus of Communist advances whether in China or Czechoslovakia, in labeling their leaders with derogatory epithets such as "left-winger," "soft-headed liberal," "anti-anti-Communist," and "egghead," and in portraying Eisenhower Republicans and Fair Deal Democrats alike as "soft" toward Communism.

Congressional investigations have been the principal instrumentality in accomplishing these results. They are, in fact, the greatest single arena of the cold civil war, and it is easy to see how this has come about. From 1933 to 1953 the White House was the citadel of liberal democracy, and its present tenant is of a subdued political hue and by no means an extreme nationalist. Executive power, except in rare instances, has been beyond the grasp of the nationalist alignment; Congressional power has proved attainable. At the Capitol, too, the nationalists have been able to exploit the jealous Congressional reaction awakened by the "strong" presidencies of Roosevelt and Truman and exacerbated by Congress' necessarily secondary role during the war years.

To discredit the executive branch, upset the *status quo*, and destroy their opponents, the investigative power has proved the nationalists' most effective weapon—much better adapted to these purposes than the law-making power. A statute must be drawn in general terms and is not self-executing. It is enforced by the executive and interpreted by the judicial branches. The President may veto the bill, or the courts may declare the law unconstitutional.

Investigations are confined within no such limits, and are under direct Congressional control. The most sensational charges can be made and the most damning reports of "findings" written, whether or not there is the slightest basis for them. The hearings can readily be arranged for maximum exploitation by way of publicity. Dossiers on many thousands of individuals can be compiled and made available to journalists, radio commentators, and others sympathetic to the aims of the committees. In skillful and unscrupulous hands, a legislative investigation is truly a most potent and versatile engine of destruction.

Where will it all end? The courts have been notably and rightly reluctant to interfere with the exercise of legislative prerogative. Nevertheless investigations, like statutes, regulations, and all other legislative and executive actions, are subject to the Constitution as the supreme law of the land.

Judicial restraint in the face of investigative excesses and abuses is, on the whole, a desirable lubricant of the governmental machinery. But now our basic system of law and tradition of individual freedom are gravely threatened by the investigative assault, and the consequent emergence of inquisition and outlawry. If the courts shut their eyes to this peril, they may never again be opened at all. Therefore, I have dealt at length herein with the Constitutional and legal limits on the investigative power, for the time is at hand when their observance must be enforced if the framework of the Republic is to endure.

In broader terms, however, the future of Congressional investigations will be largely governed by the course of the cold civil war, of which they have become so important a part. In a democratic society, the people must understand what is happening if a public evil is to be mastered. That, indeed, is precisely what investigations are for. In responsible and representative hands, they could do much to illuminate the causes and allay the passions of this internecine strife, and restore the mutual trust and unity that we so desperately need to meet the terrible challenge of might and morals that confronts our nation and the world.

Unless something like this happens, we are all likely to become so preoccupied with right and left that we can no longer distinguish right from wrong.

TELFORD TAYLOR

New York City
December 5, 1954

GRAND INQUEST

CHAPTER I

HOW IT ALL BEGAN

"We are called the Grand Inquest of the Nation, and as such it is our duty to inquire into every Step of publick management, either Abroad or at Home, in order to see that nothing has been done amiss."

—William Pitt in the House of Commons, 1742

ONE DAY EARLY IN 1954, *The New York Times* carried a front-page picture of a man drinking from a glass of water. Few readers recognized Wendell H. Furry, Associate Professor of Physics at Harvard University, whose professional attainments are respectable but not widely noted. His prominence in the news was indeed greatness thrust upon him, for its occasion was his testimony, given in a Boston courthouse under the compulsion of subpoena and the eye of a television camera, before the Permanent Subcommittee on Investigations of the Committee on Government Operations of the United States Senate.

This was not the first time that Professor Furry had been summoned for Congressional questioning. Some weeks earlier [1] he had been asked "whether he had indoctrinated students in Communist philosophy" and whether he had turned over to Communists any secret scientific information obtained during his wartime work for the Army Signal Corps. But the Harvard scientist had claimed the protection of the Fifth Amendment to the Constitution and declined to answer these and other questions because, he said, the answers might tend to incriminate him.

At his second appearance, however, the witness abandoned reliance on the Fifth Amendment. Through "misrepresentations" about that Amendment, he declared, "although its real purpose has been to shield the innocent, many people have been misled into feeling that the exercise of the privilege is an admission of guilt." Therefore, and in order to avoid "undue harm to me and the great institution with which I am connected," Professor Furry replied to questions which he had previously refused to answer, and testified that, although he was no longer, he had indeed been a member of the Communist Party while employed by the Signal Corps,[2] as were five of his co-workers.

To this change of front the chairman of the Subcommittee reacted with some surprise but no satisfaction. Immediately he asked for the names of the five wartime fellow-members. At this the professor balked again, stating that he was "not seeking to protect the guilty from prosecution," but wished rather "to secure the innocent from persecution." Pressed by the chairman who, in default of names, referred to the five by numbers, the witness testified that No. 1 was at a British university, No. 2 at an American university, and Nos. 3 and 4 in Western Europe; he had lost track of No. 5.

Opinions may differ on the justifiability of Professor Furry's refusal to identify one-time Party members by name. Certainly his wish "to secure the innocent from persecution"—if by that he meant protection of their identities—was not the father of clear thought. It may safely be assumed that *all* of the professor's wartime colleagues in the Signal Corps have by now been under investigation and, with the aid of the geographical information he furnished at the hearing, the Federal Bureau of Investigation should have had little difficulty in soon identifying the five fellow members.

The behavior of the chairman of the Subcommittee, Senator Joseph R. McCarthy of Wisconsin, made it plain that nothing could be of less importance to his larger aims than the person of Professor Furry. True, the Senator threatened contempt proceedings to punish the witness for refusing to name his "Communist associates," and opined that he ought to "serve time." But it was abundantly apparent that Senator McCarthy's real target lay on the opposite bank of the Charles River, in Cambridge.

Sitting in the Boston courtroom under emblematic wall inscriptions bearing the names of the great jurists of Massachusetts and of

Harvard—Brandeis, Cushing, Frankfurter, Gray, Holmes, and Story—the one-time Wisconsin circuit judge took dead aim at the venerable and hallowed university and its new president, Nathan M. Pusey. He referred to Professor Furry as one of "Pusey's Fifth Amendment Communists," and suggested that the removal of all Communists would "decimate Harvard's faculty." The University was a "smelly mess," and he found it "inconceivable that a university that has had [*sic*] the reputation of a great university should keep this kind of [Furry] creature teaching young Americans." Federal tax exemptions, the Senator declared, should be withdrawn from educational institutions such as Harvard that harbor "Fifth Amendment Communists."

The following day when the Subcommittee—i.e., Senator McCarthy, who as chairman had convened himself as a one-man Subcommittee—met again, the atmosphere was less intellectual and more physical.[3] On the chairman's orders, five federal marshals ejected Theodore Pappas, an employee of General Electric's Lynn plant, and his attorney, when the latter endeavored to read a statement for the record explaining the reason for his client's invocation of the Fifth Amendment. But Professor Furry's replacement in the witness box by Mr. Pappas did not affect the chairman's preoccupation with Harvard. As soon as Mr. Pappas disclosed that he had attended Harvard Law School he became the object of scoffs and jeers. Surely a Harvard law school graduate ought to be able "to understand a simple question"! And here was another of the institution's "Fifth Amendment Communists"! Clearly, the Senator was intent on giving new and sinister meaning to the "Crimson Tide."

While Senator McCarthy was mingling philippics with Donnybrooks in Boston, a very different and yet related convocation was under way at the Association of the Bar of the City of New York, where Sir Hartley Shawcross—former Attorney General of the United Kingdom and Chairman of the Council of the Bar of England—was describing the British attitude toward internal security problems. Sir Hartley asserted [4] that "public opinion in England would never tolerate . . . public inquisition save in a particular and exceptional case of great gravity . . . certainly never with a roving commission to inquire into people's political or other beliefs." Far too much the diplomat to mention any American political figure by name, Sir

Hartley brought to bear his front-bencher's ineluctable blend of humor and hauteur, nonchalance and gravity:

> There are now and again in my country, as for all I know there may sometimes be in yours, those factious and self-seeking persons who propound policies and express views which are inimical to mutual cooperation and confidence between us. When we hear these harsh and strident tones—in whatever brief authority their speakers may be dressed—we must not be misled into believing them to be the authentic voices of our respective peoples.

The other foreign savants at the Bar Association were equally considerate of American susceptibilities. Some Congressional inquisitors, however, might well have winced at the words of Justice Ivan C. Rand of the Supreme Court of Canada:

> Although in vital activities [in Canada] men cannot be suffered whose minds may be tainted with hostile purposes, there is no intention or desire that they should be treated as outcasts. . . .
>
> The individual is not subjected to a public exposure which, whatever his guilt or innocence, might destroy his standing in the community; and when the case is intelligently dealt with, as by transferring him to other departmental work, he may be enabled to give to the country, in purely civil activities, service of high value.

It is a strangely assorted harvest of men, named and unnamed, that this two-day selection of press cuttings has yielded up—President Pusey; Professor Furry and his five unidentified former colleagues; Mr. Pappas, his lawyer, and five federal marshals; a Canadian judge and a leading British barrister; the junior Senator from Wisconsin. The geographical and cultural spread within this group is enormous, yet all were caught up in a conglomeration of issues that has bitten deep into the political and social consciousness of America in mid-century.

Is it the purpose of the Fifth Amendment, as Professor Furry contended, "to shield the innocent"? Or should President Pusey have sacked him from the Harvard faculty for invoking the Amendment in the first place? Should General Electric discharge Mr. Pappas for the same reason? And why should Mr. Pappas and his attorney have been given the bum's rush for endeavoring to make an explanation? What, if anything, is a "Fifth Amendment Communist"?

Senator McCarthy's Subcommittee is supposedly concerned with "government operations"; does this include Harvard University and the General Electric Company? If so, what is *not* included? Can Professor Furry's refusal to name his five colleagues be justified, legally or morally?

These and many other such questions start like hares from nearly every line of the press accounts of these doings. But far broader problems are equally apparent. Senator McCarthy has interested himself only sporadically in subversion on the campus, but Senator William Jenner's Subcommittee on Internal Security has been continuously active in this field. Is there cause for alarm here, and, if so, what should we be alarmed about? Would the exposure of all "Fifth Amendment Communists" really decimate the faculties of Harvard and other educational institutions, or are Congressional investigations themselves the greater danger to educational values?

Are academic freedom and national security incompatible or complementary? It has often been said during recent years that Americans are living in a state of fear. But it is by no means clear that we all fear the same things. Rather it appears that the nation's political outlook is being fragmentized, and its will paralyzed, by inability to agree on what is rightly to be feared, and how much.

I have selected these events of a mere forty-eight hours as a point of departure because they precipitated, in close conjunction, so many of the elements of which this book is compounded. Despite the contemporary flavor of the questions just posed, they cannot be well understood—much less answered—without some knowledge of legal and political principles that are several centuries old. And so, in seeking an answer to these and other issues raised by the investigations that are so constantly in the public eye, we must start a long way back.

Sir Hartley Shawcross told his learned audience that Britons regard public inquisition as intolerable. Nevertheless, the legislative investigation was born in Merrie England, centuries ago but under circumstances which truly reflect its contemporary nature and purpose. And that purpose can be stated in a single sentence. A legislative body—be it the British House of Commons, or either house of Congress, or a state legislature—is endowed with the investigative power *in order to obtain information,* so that its legislative functions may be discharged on an enlightened rather than a benighted basis. In fact Woodrow Wilson, no mean political scholar, described Congressional investigations as performing the "informing function." [5]

A legislative body, after all, does not operate in a vacuum or an ivory tower. Like any other human institution, it must have eyes, ears, and feelers. It must also have means of self-defense, particularly since it is the forum in which great political forces clash, and grind out conquest and compromise. If it is to deliberate, it must be enabled to discipline those who disturb its deliberations and assail its dignity. If men are to lay store by the outcome of the deliberations, their integrity must be protected against bribery and similar assaults. And since the upshot of the deliberations is generally affected by facts and circumstances, the legislature must be able to find out what it needs to know.

All these things, which are so apparent today, were learned only gradually and painfully during the evolution of Parliamentary government in England. The House of Commons did not spring into being full-panoplied like Athena; it had to forge its own arms in the course of a bitter and often bloody struggle for political supremacy against the monarchs, lords and bishops of the Tudor and Stuart periods. At least as early as Elizabethan times, the House of Commons successfully asserted the power to punish those who disturbed its proceedings by boisterous or threatening conduct, or by insults and libels.[6] Attempts to bribe Members of Parliament were soon treated as similarly punishable. Individuals found guilty of bribery or aggressive conduct were jailed by the House itself, without resort to the courts. The authority of the House to deal with these threats and hostile acts was regarded as its own inherent power, necessary for its own protection and for the integrity of its proceedings. It became known as the power to punish *contempt* * of the House, and this is the root of the power exercised by Congressional committees today.

The English courts also exercised the power to punish contempts. Assaults or insults directed against the judges, refusals to testify, or

---

* In its legal sense, "contempt" means willful disregard of the authority of a court or legislative body, by disobedience or by acts or attitudes calculated to undermine its dignity and authority.

other actions which obstructed or denigrated the judicial process were summarily dealt with by the courts, by imprisoning offenders and compelling them to "purge" themselves of the contempt by apology, giving testimony, or other appropriate amends. In court as in the Commons, the power to punish contempts was developed not to reform the offender, but to enable the basic governmental functions, legislative or judicial as the case might be, to be effectively discharged.

Early in the seventeenth century, the House of Commons became aware of its need for some kind of process for the determination of facts. The necessity first became apparent in connection with contested elections of its own members.[7] Decisions as between rival candidates often depended upon disputed facts, and the House took to appointing committees and giving them the power to summon witnesses and examine documents—in the words of the times "to send for persons and papers"—in order to establish the truth. If a person refused to testify or produce his records, or if he testified falsely, his conduct was treated as a contempt, and the Commons could, and often did, punish him by imprisonment.[8]

Thus legislative investigations were born of the Commons' desire to determine rightly its own membership. Very soon thereafter, however, they were put to two other and broader uses, identical to those which comprise their principal employment today. These were the ascertainment of facts (1) to assist in the wise formulation of laws, and (2) to enable Parliament to exercise a measure of surveillance of the activities of the civil and military officials who carried the laws into effect and spent the moneys made available by Parliament for governmental purposes. As an early example of the first type, we may note that in 1664 the House of Commons empowered one of its committees to compel the attendance and testimony of a witness, in aid of its consideration of a bill to regulate navigation on the River Wye. Two years later an investigation of the second type was authorized, in order to inspect "the several Accompts of the Officers of the Navy, Ordnance and Stores."[9]

However, one important limitation on the Commons' power to imprison witnesses for contempt must be remarked. The House could exercise it only when in session, and the imprisonment could not endure beyond its end. This situation reflects the ancient conception of contempt as being a weapon against interference with the *functioning* of Parliament. When the House was not in session, there were no functions to be interfered with, and no basis for exercise of the power. And so, once the session had ended, "every court in Westminster Hall and every judge of all the courts would be bound to discharge . . . by *habeas corpus*" any person still in confinement on the order of the House, no matter how grave his offense.[10]

The expulsion of the Stuarts and the dawn of decisive Parliamentary supremacy led to an ever more frequent employment of Parliamentary investigating committees. In wartime, dissatisfaction with the conduct of military affairs often led to such inquiries. Thus in 1689 the House established a committee to examine "By what means the Intelligence came to be given to their Majesties Enemies, concerning the several Stations of Winter Guards of their Majesties Navy; and likewise into the Miscarriage in the Victualing of the Navy; and the Transportation of the Army; and all and other things relating to the War, both by Sea and Land, [during] the last Year." Over a century and a half later, a similar inquiry was ordered into the handling of the British forces before Sebastopol in the Crimean War.

But the area of customary Parliamentary scrutiny was by no means exclusively military; it rapidly came to include such diverse topics as the poor laws, prison administration, operations of the East India Company, sending of children out of the country for instruction in Catholicism, and revision of the laws pertaining to bankruptcy. Resistance or prevarication was summarily dealt with by warrants of arrest and the imprisonment of recalcitrant witnesses in custody of the Serjeant-at-Arms of the House of Commons. Well might the famous British jurist, Sir Edward Coke, describe the Commons as the "generall inquisitors of the realm." [11]

Nevertheless, the Commons' investigative supremacy was established only after bitter struggles and setbacks. Many harbingers of the contemporary American scene may be observed in the great political crisis which attended the fall from power in 1742 of Sir Robert Walpole, after years of mounting opposition to his regime. Immediately after his resignation as Prime Minister, his opponents in the Commons introduced a motion for a committee "to enquire into the Conduct of our Affairs at home and abroad, during the last 20 years." A "great debate ensued" on this ancient version of "twenty years of treason," in the course of which it was argued that there was no such proof of mishandling the realm's affairs as warranted inquiry, that its intended scope was far too broad, and that it would expose State secrets to the gaze of foreign enemies. In response, William Pitt the Elder declared that the investigation could be so conducted as not to disclose secret matters, and claimed for Parliament a sweeping power of review of ministerial affairs: [12]

> I have no great occasion to answer what has been said, that no Parliamentary inquiry ought ever to be set up, unless we are convinced that something has been done amiss. Sir, the very name given to this House of Parliament shews the contrary. We are called the Grand Inquest of the Nation, and as such it is our duty to inquire into every Step of publick management, either Abroad or at Home, in order to see that nothing has been done amiss.

In the upshot, a more limited inquiry was approved, calling for an investigation by a Secret Committee of Walpole's conduct as Chancellor of the Exchequer during the preceding ten years. But as soon as the Committee embarked upon its proceedings, issues arose which today, over two centuries later, are rife in the halls of Congress. The Solicitor of the Treasury, Nicholas Paxton, when asked whether he had advanced state moneys to a friend during an election, declined to answer on the ground that "it may tend to accuse myself"—the ancestor of the plea of self-incrimination under the Fifth Amendment. Confinement in Newgate prison did not loosen Paxton's tongue, and by a close vote the Commons approved a bill to grant "indemnity" to persons examined by the Secret Committee on questions pertaining to the public funds. But the House of Lords rejected this precursor of the recently enacted and highly controversial statute authorizing grants of "immunity" to Congressional witnesses pleading the Fifth Amendment, and Paxton's lips remained sealed.

Later it appeared that large sums had been disbursed by the Crown to one John Scrope "for secret services." Summoned before the Committee, Scrope declared that he could not account for the funds without royal leave, and a few days later he informed his inquisitors that he "had laid his case before the King, and was authorized to say, 'That the disposal of Money issu'd for Secret Service, by the Nature of it, requires the utmost secrecy, and is accounted for to His

Majesty only, and therefore His Majesty cou'd not permit him to disclose anything on that subject.'"

At this the Committee was "surpriz'd," but it appears to have made no effort, in the face of King George II's mandate, to coerce Scrope by exercise of the contempt power. These issues, later resolved by Parliamentary supremacy, were not then fought to a finish, and it might fairly be said that the reach of the Commons' investigative power vis-à-vis the King in 1742 was not far removed from that of Congress vis-à-vis the President today.

The American colonies were settled during the very period in which Parliament asserted and consolidated its supremacy in England. The early colonial legislatures included lawyers and others attuned to Parliamentary practices, and it is hardly surprising that the power to punish contempts, and to use that power in aid of investigations, was soon asserted by the colonial assemblies.[13]

As in England, the earliest contempt cases involved libels, assaults, and bribes. In 1693, the Virginia House of Burgesses ordered that an unhappy gentleman named Thomas Rooke "on his bended knees acknowledge his offense, and beg the pardon of the house in such words as shall be appointed and that for the personal abuse given Mr. Kemp, a member of the house, he ask his forgiveness in particular." The Virginian legislators appear to have set great store by the symbols of abject and public apology, for in 1727 one Edward West was bending his knees for similar reasons. A few years earlier William Hopkins refused to kneel or apologize to a Burgess whom he had insulted, and as a result it was ordered:

> That said Wm. Hopkins be led thro' the Town . . . from the Capital Gate to the College Gate and back again with an Inscription in Great Letters pind upon his Breast in the following words—"For Insolent Behavior at the Bar of the House of Burgesses when he was there as an offender and with obstinacy and Contempt disobeying their Order"—And in case he shall refuse to walk that he be Tied to a Cart and Drawn thro' the Town, And that he be afterwards committed to the public gaol in Williamsburg The Keeper whereof is hereby required to receive and there safely to keep him during the pleasure of this House.

Yankee legislators contented themselves with less spectacular reprisals, but were just as quick as the Virginia Burgesses to chastise offenders against the legislative dignities. So were those of New York and Pennsylvania. Echoes of the Revolution resound in the story of Captain Alexander McDougall, who in 1769 labeled as "base inglorious conduct" the action of the New York General Assembly in voting to supply British troops then stationed in New York. Arrested and arraigned before the Assembly, his words were declared a "high contempt." Imprisoned on the Speaker's warrant, the courts refused his application for *habeas corpus.* He languished in jail for eighty-one days, but was discharged, according to the English practice, when the General Assembly adjourned. Happier days were in store for the stubborn Scot, who became a major general during the War of Independence, and thereafter—poetic justice—a prominent member of the New York State Senate.

Investigations by colonial legislatures date back at least to 1691, when the New York Assembly committed a Mr. Dally, who had refused to answer the Assembly's questions, "to the custody of the Sergeant-at-Arms, and there to remain until he shall make Answer, or be discharged by the House." Thirty years later, dissatisfaction with the progress of Indian hostilities caused the Massachusetts House of Representatives, over the Governor's objections, to summon for questioning the two officers commanding the colonial forces in Maine, and the testimony led to their retirement from service.

In Pennsylvania, the colonial Assembly asserted investigative authority beyond the bounds of English practice. A standing committee to audit the public accounts was empowered to sit even when the Assembly was in recess, "with full power to send for Persons, Papers and Records by the Sergeant-at-Arms of this House . . ." Even the judges in Pennsylvania felt the reach and squeeze of the contempt power. In 1758 Judge William Moore of the Court of Common Pleas was found guilty of contemptuous and slanderous "Aspersions against the Conduct of the late Assembly," and was confined in the "common Gaol of the County of Philadelphia, there to remain until he shall make such a retraction . . . as this House shall approve of." On this occasion, the English rule was respected; a court discharged Judge Moore on *habeas corpus* when the Assembly recessed. But he was rearrested when the House met again, released at the end of the session, and then, no doubt surfeit with contempt, he absconded.

With independence came our great wave of written constitutions. They were drawn by men who regarded the investigative function, and the contempt power which gives it teeth, as normal and necessary attributes of a legislative assembly. Indeed, the existence and validity of the power were taken for granted, so that it was rarely mentioned in the new constitutions. Only in a few instances, notably in Maryland and Massachusetts, was it expressly dealt with. The Maryland Constitution of 1776 was the most specific; it contained a very broad grant to both the House of Delegates and the Senate to punish contempts of the most varied kinds, and made express provision (in Article X) for investigations by the House, which: "... may inquire on the oath of witnesses, into all complaints, grievances, and offenses, as the grand inquest of this state; and . . . may call for all public or official papers and records, and send for persons, whom they may judge necessary in the course of inquiries concerning affairs relating to the public interest. . . ." [14]

Extensive as they were, similar powers were exercised quite as freely, and equally without objection, in the states with constitutions which were silent on the subject. In Virginia, as early as 1781 the House of Delegates gave power to "send for persons, papers, and records for their information" to its standing committees on religion, privileges and elections, courts of justice, and trade. In New York and Pennsylvania, as well as Virginia, there were early episodes in which contumacious witnesses and others were imprisoned for contempt by the state legislatures.

As it was in the newborn states, so it was in the federal government. Even before the Declaration of Independence was signed, the President of the Continental Congress was treated with "great rudeness" by one Isaac Melchior, who was thereupon ordered to appear before the Congress the following morning "to answer for his conduct." It is perhaps not too rash to infer that Isaac had been hitting the bottle, for he denied any recollection of what he had done "owing to the particular circumstances he happened to be under"; at all events, he apologized and was then allowed to go his way.

Like most of the state constitutions, the federal Constitution nowhere mentions contempts or investigations, and this omission reflects the general acceptance of both as natural attributes of the Congress.* The first Congressional investigation was initiated in 1792, and in 1795 one Robert Randall, who in order to obtain a grant of western lands had attempted to bribe three members of the House of Representatives, was haled before the bar of the House and, for his contempt, was committed to the custody of the Sergeant-at-Arms, where he remained for eight days and then, upon his humble petition, was discharged.

Before proceeding with the development of Congressional investigations under the federal Constitution—the mainstream of our story—it may be useful to take a second look at Parliamentary inquiries, and a side glance at legislative investigations in other countries.

So far as Britain is concerned, there is little in the modern history of the Parliamentary committees of inquiry that bears directly on the issues with which we are now concerned. This is because in Britain, unlike the United States, the struggle for legislative supremacy was carried through to full victory, and the House of Commons eventually emerged as the repository of supreme government authority, unrivaled by the executive and judicial branches. The executive functions are reposed in the several ministries, but these derive their powers from and are creatures of the Parliamentary majority. Neither have the British courts assumed the power of reviewing the "constitutionality" of Parliamentary action. A British judge, shocked by the apparent injustice or despotic reach of a statute, might draw its claws by an artificially narrow construction of its language, but he would never dream of openly setting it aside as unconstitutional. No more will he review the validity of a duly issued Parliamentary warrant of arrest for contempt, so long as the Commons are in session.

In summary it may be said that the Parliamentary power to compel individuals to testify before its committees of inquiry knows no limits in legal theory and will not be reviewed or restricted by the courts. In 1845 Lord Justice Coleridge wrote that "it would be difficult to define any limits by which the subject matter of their [the Commons'] inquiry can be bounded . . . I would be content to state

* Especially of the House of Representatives. Lecturing in Philadelphia in 1791, Justice James Wilson (of the Supreme Court, and a close friend of President Washington) declared [14a]: "The house of representatives . . . form the grand inquest of the state. They will diligently inquire into grievances, arising both from men and things."

that they may inquire into everything which it concerns the public weal for them to know; and they themselves, I think, are entrusted with the determination of what falls within that category." [15] Public opinion, as Sir Hartley Shawcross said, would not tolerate inquisition, but the restraint is exerted by public opinion itself, not the courts.

Over a century has passed since the last serious attempt was made to challenge the investigative authority of the House of Commons.[16] Short of revolutionary political changes in Britain, it is unlikely again to be called in question. This general acceptance is due not only to Parliament's supremacy, but also to its moderation. The investigative power has been truly used to inform; it has rarely been turned to partisan ends, has never been captured by passionate protagonists, and its exercise has not raised notable public controversy within the memory of living man.* All of which may be admirable, but gives us no gauge of the smoking issues with which we are now concerned.

For nearly opposite reasons, the role of legislative inquiries among the nations of continental Europe is equally unilluminating. Investigations are, as we have seen, an attribute of legislative power, and are therefore unlikely to flourish unless the legislature asserts sovereign authority. Only in Britain and America was decisive legislative power vested in elected deliberative assemblies, prior to the nineteenth century.[17] At no time have the French Chamber of Deputies, the German Reichstag, or other continental legislatures attained the stable traditions and prerogatives of Congress and Parliament. Furthermore, the summary punishment of contempt—whether by a court or a legislative assembly—is unknown in continental law.

In France, throughout the nineteenth century, investigations with power to compel testimony were authorized only in years of revolution and war—1830, 1848, and 1871. Under the Third Republic, the powerlessness of investigating committees became the object of public ridicule. In 1879, the Court of Appeals of Bordeaux held that the committees had no power to compel the giving of testimony. The president of a committee bewailed the "utterly disgraceful" answers

* *See* Appendix I: A Note for Laymen on British Investigative Practice, *infra*, pp. 285-295.

which his "polite letters" of invitation to testify had elicited.[18] As a result of the Rochette-Caillaux scandal, a statute was finally enacted in 1914 under which fines could be imposed on recalcitrant witnesses, but it proved largely ineffective. The French simply do not like legislative investigations, and eminent scholars and statesmen—Duguit, Berthélémy, and Paul Reynaud—have declared that they encroach on the domain of the courts and endanger civil liberties. In 1925, while regretfully prosecuting contumacious witnesses under the 1914 law, the Attorney General expressed his admiration for their conduct; the wealthy defendants were fined each 300 francs. *Quel dommage!*

In the Prussian constitution of 1848, the power of British example led to the inclusion of a provision for parliamentary investigations, but efforts to use it foundered in 1863 on the rock of Bismarck's ruthless opposition, and were never renewed during Imperial times. The Weimar Constitution (Article 34) gave the Reichstag broad investigative powers, but their first exercise proved unfortunate. The 1919 Commission of Inquiry into war-responsibility and war-guilt "proved to be a process of unrelieved humiliation and defeat for the Government."[19] Its dignity was openly flouted by Ludendorff and Hindenburg, and the latter used his appearance before the Commission as a sounding board for his famous "stab-in-the-back" (*Dolchstoss*) statement, by which the prestige of the army was rescued from the welter of defeat and revolution. In the later years of the Weimar Republic, legislative investigations began to raise problems similar to those currently debated in the United States, such as the privilege against self-incrimination and the need for a uniform code of investigative procedures. But the advent of Hitler put an end to the power of the Reichstag before the fruits of its investigative experience had a chance to ripen.

Internationally viewed, the pattern of legislative investigation is indeed paradoxical. On the European continent, although there is no well-defined separation of executive, judicial, and legislative powers, the attitude that individuals should be investigated by the police and tried by courts, rather than by committees of politicians, has stunted the growth of investigative power. In Great Britain, where the Commons' power of inquiry knows no legal limits, it is used freely and effectively, but only within well-recognized bounds determined by a stable public temper. In the United States, where the Constitution imposes judicially enforceable limits on the power of Congress, its investigative activities have proliferated and expanded and become the vortex of tension and passion.* And we will now turn to the story of how that has come about.

---

* It might be useful for some political scholar to study the history and present status of legislative investigative power in the South and Central American republics, where our form of government has been widely copied, but where the Continental system of law prevails. In the Argentina of Peron, as we will see later,[20] congressional investigative power has been used virtually as a police arm of presidential suppression of freedom of the press.

CHAPTER II

THE ORDEAL OF MAJOR GENERAL ARTHUR ST. CLAIR

"'Twas November the fourth in the year of ninety-one
We had a sore engagement near to Fort Jefferson;
Sinclaire was our commander, which may remembered be,
For there we left nine hundred men in the Western ter'tory!"
—Anonymous

EARLY IN NOVEMBER, 1791, some 1500 American soldiers were pushing north through the wilderness along the future Ohio-Indiana line, toward the headwaters of the Wabash River. The weather was wet and cold, and the troops—a mixed group of regulars, raw levies, and Kentucky militia—were drenched, tired, and hungry. On the last day of October, sixty of the levies had declared that their term of enlistment was up, and had taken off to the rear. Fearing they would plunder the supply wagons, the commander, Major General Arthur St. Clair, sent his best-disciplined unit (the First Regiment of United States regulars) back to round up the deserters and protect his train, and then pushed on with his depleted forces. His mission was to cut a road and build fortifications north from Fort Washington (now Cincinnati) to the Indian villages at the Maumee River forks, in order to awe and subdue the Miamis and Shawnees who, at the instigation and with the support of the British, had refused to make peace with the infant United States government, and were preying on the scattered settlers of the Ohio frontier.

At the end of a hard day's march on November 3, the army came upon a stretch of high, dry ground on the eastern branch of the upper Wabash, at the present site of Fort Recovery, Ohio. Here St. Clair determined to pass the night, thinking to throw up earthworks the following morning. At daybreak, however, his army was suddenly attacked by a numerous and determined band of Miamis, Shawnees, and Delawares, supported by a few Canadians and other whites, among them the notorious renegade Simon Girty. In discipline and leadership this group probably excelled any other the red men ever assembled. Blue Jacket and Buckongahelas, chiefs respectively of the Shawnees and Delawares, were there, and the entire force was led by the redoubtable and once famous Me-She-Kin-No-Quah or Little Turtle, chief of the Miamis, who, the previous year, had trapped Major General Harmar's regulars at the Maumee forks and taken two hundred scalps.

For all their lack of training the soldiers fought bravely, but they were no match for the Indians in marksmanship or forest warfare. Indian sharpshooters soon finished off every artilleryman, and the cannon had to be spiked. The second-in-command, Major General Richard Butler, was mortally wounded, and the raw troops gave way as most of the other officers were picked off. General St. Clair, nearing sixty and tortured with gout, had three horses shot from under him as he was being assisted to the saddle.

In three hours' time half the army had been lost, and the commander gave the order to break through to the road and retreat to Fort Jefferson, some thirty miles to the south. Astride a pack horse which barely could be pricked to a trot, his white hair streaming wildly, St. Clair miraculously escaped injury * as he remained on the field in a gallant but futile effort to organize the retreat. Soon it was a rout, and the men threw away their arms in panic as they ran, but fortunately the Indians were diverted by captured liquor and spoils, and gave up the pursuit.

It was after sundown when the remnants of the army reached Fort Jefferson, where they rejoined the First Regiment. In concert with his officers, and in view of the losses of men and supplies and the apparent strength of the enemy, St. Clair decided that it would be

* There is a story that St. Clair's life was spared by order of the famous Mohawk chief Joseph Brant, who had once fallen in love with St. Clair's glamorous and courageous daughter, Louisa.

foolhardy to risk another advance. He returned to Fort Washington, whence he despatched to the Secretary of War his report of "as warm and as unfortunate an action as almost any that has ever been fought," and then set off with heavy heart and aching flesh to the capital at Philadelphia.

In its eighteenth-century setting, St. Clair's description of the magnitude of his defeat was no great exaggeration. Over 600 officers and men fell, and half as many were wounded, while fewer than 70 Indians were slain. Little Turtle's triumph on the Wabash was one of the three greatest Indian victories over white men in the history of the North American continent; St. Clair's losses matched those of Braddock and far exceeded the massacre of Custer and his men on the Little Big Horn. Pacification and settlement of the Northwest Territory were set back by several years. The British continued to maintain posts south of the Great Lakes, and Little Turtle and his Miamis roamed the frontier unchecked, until their defeat in August, 1794, by General "Mad Anthony" Wayne at the Battle of Fallen Timbers.* Not until 1795, when Wayne and Little Turtle signed the Treaty of Greenville, did lasting peace descend on the Northwest Territory.[1]

Arthur St. Clair, whose misfortune it is to be remembered chiefly for the disaster on the Wabash, was one of the most versatile and adventurous men of his time. He was born in Caithness of an old Norman family collaterally descended from William the Conqueror—the "lordly line of high St. Clair," as Scott calls it in the *Lay of the Last Minstrel*—and studied at the University of Edinburgh. A commission in the Duke of Cumberland's regiment brought St. Clair to America, where he fought under Jeffrey Amherst at Louisburg in 1758, and a year later under Wolfe on the Plains of Abraham. In 1762 he resigned his British Army commission after marrying in Boston a wealthy niece of Governor Bowdoin, but again fell victim to wanderlust and took an appointment as commandant of Fort Ligonier in southwestern Pennsylvania, where he settled with his family, held

* So called because the battlefield was strewn with trees recently felled by a tornado. Little Turtle had favored making peace with Wayne, whom he called "The Chief that Never Sleeps," but was outvoted by Blue Jacket and the other chiefs in council.

various public offices, and became the foremost man in those parts.

Despite his Scottish birth and military-aristocratic background, St. Clair early threw in his lot with the patriots. When war came he was commissioned as a colonel in the Continental Army, and raised a regiment which he led to Quebec and back to Ticonderoga. In August, 1776, he was promoted to brigadier general and attached to Washington's staff; with Washington he crossed the Delaware (a maneuver which St. Clair himself is said to have suggested) and fought at Trenton. An enduring attachment was formed, and early in 1777 Washington promoted him to major general and sent him to command at Fort Ticonderoga, then threatened by Burgoyne's advance from the north. Finding himself hopelessly outnumbered,* St. Clair wisely evacuated the Fort, but his prudence was mistaken for timidity, and reaped much public criticism after Burgoyne's surrender at Saratoga. However, the court martial which St. Clair demanded cleared him "with highest honor," and he served out the war with distinction at Brandywine, Valley Forge, and Yorktown, and under Nathanael Greene in the Carolinas.

Finding his Ligonier properties run down after the war—he had also mortgaged or advanced much of his personal fortune to aid the Revolutionary cause—St. Clair remained in Philadelphia in various public capacities. In 1787 he was elected to the Congress, and was then chosen as its President, the highest office in the Confederation. Under his presidency Congress enacted the Ordinance of 1787 establishing the Northwest Territory, and St. Clair himself was chosen as its first Governor.

By now in his fifties, St. Clair for the third time plunged into primitive wilderness. He established his headquarters at Fort Washington, to which he gave the name of Cincinnati, and negotiated peace treaties with the Six Nations and other tribes. But the British had not yet realized that Independence had come to stay, and fomented continued hostility among the Shawnees and Miamis. General Harmar's punitive expedition of 1790 came to grief at Little Turtle's hands, and in March of 1791 Washington called St. Clair to Philadelphia, renewed his commission as a major general, and entrusted

---

* It is said that Little Turtle, then a young brave, was with the Indians that advanced with Burgoyne to Ticonderoga and Saratoga.

him with command of the forces which Congress had authorized to put an end to the mischief.

In proffering and accepting this task, it is now clear that both Washington and St. Clair erred. Courageous and experienced a fighter as he was, St. Clair was fifty-eight, partly disabled by illness, and already burdened with grave and taxing responsibilities as Governor. These drawbacks, however, might not have proved fatal had the raising and fitting out of the new army been handled with efficiency and dispatch. But the logistics were badly bungled by the War Department and the responsible quartermaster, Samuel Hodgdon. The levies were swept off the streets and out of the jails of eastern cities; they were poor enough as raw material, and were sent on to Fort Washington with little or no training. The equipment was shoddy and the powder defective. St. Clair was helpless to take corrective action; at Fort Washington he was a two weeks' journey from Fort Pitt, where General Richard Butler assembled the men and material and dispatched them westward on Ohio River flatboats.

The expedition was supposed to have set off in early summer, but Hodgdon's incompetence delayed everything, and General Butler did not even arrive at Fort Washington until September 7. Their absence throughout the summer added to the harassments of the already overburdened St. Clair, who was obliged personally to endorse promissory notes, to the tune of several thousands of dollars, to procure horses and supplies. The army did not move north until September 17, by which time the good weather was near its end and the campaign should already have been concluded. No doubt St. Clair would have been well advised to postpone his advance until the following spring, but the limited enlistments of the levies would have expired, and he was under firm orders from President Washington to act with the utmost expedition.

Accordingly, Arthur St. Clair had abundant cause for bitter remonstrance as he sat at Fort Washington and penned his report of the slaughter on the Wabash to the Secretary of War. It is much to his credit that so little of his emotions escaped through the quill: "I have nothing, sir, to lay to the charge of the troops but their want of discipline," he wrote, and allowed that their training had been so short that better behavior could hardly have been expected in such dire straits.

On his long journey to Philadelphia, St. Clair had opportunity to discover how the misfortune had inflamed against him the popular temper. Recalling his similar experience in 1777 after the retreat from Ticonderoga, he requested Washington to appoint a military court of inquiry, but this the President was obliged to decline for want of enough officers of sufficient rank to form a competent military court. And before any other solution could be found the pressure of public opinion had so mounted that on March 27, 1792, the House of Representatives took matters into its own hands by appointing a select committee "to inquire into the failure of the late expedition under General St. Clair" and empowering it "to call for such persons, papers and records as may be necessary to assist in their inquiries." [2]

Such were the events that led to the first Congressional investigation in the history of the United States. This action was, as we have seen, entirely in accordance with Parliamentary and colonial governmental traditions. Nevertheless, the circumstances surrounding the initiation of the inquiry plainly bespoke the impact of the newly adopted Constitution, and foreshadowed conflicts and tensions which besiege our government today as never before.

The proposal as first brought up for debate in the House [3] did not provide for a Congressional investigation; rather it called upon the President to institute and carry out the inquiry. This was immediately opposed by some members as an improper mode of procedure in view of the constitutional separation of powers, as it amounted to an effort to instruct the President in the conduct of the Executive branch. Soon Williamson of North Carolina proposed that a select committee of the House be established to prosecute the inquiry, and this suggestion was strongly supported by James Madison as well as by Fitzsimmons of Pennsylvania, who brought the debate into line with traditional Parliamentary and colonial practice by calling for a committee "to inquire relative to such objects as come properly under the cognizance of this House, particularly respecting the expenditures of public money . . ." In the upshot the originally proposed Presidential inquiry was defeated 35 to 21, and thereupon, by a vote of 44 to 10, the resolution for a select investigation committee, with power to send for persons and papers, was approved.

The committee's first action was to write directly to the Secretary of War, General Henry Knox, requesting that he turn over all the original letters, orders, and other records relating to St. Clair's expedition. Knox laid the matter before President Washington who promptly called a full Cabinet meeting—Jefferson, Hamilton, Knox and Edmund Randolph (the Attorney General)—to consider the matter. From Thomas Jefferson's record of the meeting [4] we learn that:

> The President had called us to consult, merely because it was the first example, and he wished that so far as it should become a precedent, it should be rightly conducted. He neither acknowledged nor denied, nor even doubted the propriety of what the House was doing, for he had not thought upon it, nor was acquainted with subjects of this kind: he could readily conceive there might be papers of so secret a nature, as that they ought not to be given up.

How seriously the matter was regarded may be seen from the Cabinet's conclusion that they "were not prepared and wished time to think and enquire." When they met again on April 2, Jefferson recorded that they "had principally consulted the proceedings of the Commons in the case of Sir Robert Walpole," including the expressions both of those who had supported and those who had opposed the investigation of Walpole. Nevertheless, Washington's advisors by now "were of one mind," and it was unanimously * determined:

> First, that the House was an inquest and therefore might institute inquiries. Second, that they might call for papers generally. Third, that the Executive ought to communicate such papers as the public good would permit, and ought to refuse those, the disclosure of which would endanger the public. Consequently were to exercise a discretion. Fourth, that neither the committee nor House had a right to call on the Head of a department, who and whose papers were under the President alone,

---

* Jefferson noted, however, that "Hamilton agreed with us in all these points, except as to the power of the House to call on Heads of Departments. He observed that as to his department, the act constituting it had made it subject to Congress in some points, but he thought he himself not so far subject, as to be obliged to produce all the papers they might call for. They might demand secrets of a very mischievous nature." Jefferson recorded his private opinion that Hamilton was concerned about inquiries into speculations by government officials, and concluded acidly: ". . . in short, he endeavored to place himself subject to the House, when the Executive should propose what he did not like, and subject to the Executive, when the House should propose something disagreeable."

but that the committee should instruct their chairman to move the House to address the President.*

Jefferson's own explanation of the theoretical basis for these conclusions is especially significant because it reveals his keen awareness that Congress, unlike Parliament, was limited by the Constitution to legislative functions:

> I observed here a difference between the British Parliament and our Congress, that the former was a legislature, an inquest and a council for the King. The latter was, by the Constitution, a legislature and an inquest but not a council.

We will soon have occasion to remark the pertinence, to several issues precipitated by contemporary Congressional "inquests," of these determinations by Washington's Cabinet. At the time, they aroused no controversy, for the Cabinet agreed that, so far as the St. Clair records were concerned, "there was not a paper which might not properly be produced." Accordingly, on April 4 the President directed the Secretary of War to lay before the House committee the records it desired.

"General St. Clair shall have justice," Washington had declared, after recovering from his initial anger at the news of the defeat. Certainly the select committee conducted itself with a decorum and dispassionateness which was the more remarkable in that the Jeffersonians were already using the disaster as a stick with which to beat the incumbent Federalists. It promptly set about reviewing the records and examining St. Clair, Secretary Knox, Hodgdon, and others called to testify upon the request of the committee or of the principal individuals under investigation.

On May 8, 1792, the last day of the session, the committee made a unanimous report to the House. It was extremely critical of the War Department and especially of the quartermaster and the contractors, whose "gross and various mismanagements and neglects" were found to have been the principal cause of the disaster. General St. Clair was completely vindicated: [6]

---

* As a result, two days later (April 4, 1792) the House addressed a resolution to the President asking him to "cause the proper officers" to make available the pertinent documents.[5]

> The committee conceive it but justice to the commander in chief, to say, that in their opinion, the failure of the late expedition can in no respect be imputed to his conduct, either at any time before or during the action; but that, as his conduct, in all the preparatory arrangements, was marked with peculiar ability and zeal, so his conduct, during the action, furnished strong testimonies of his coolness and intrepidity.

Early in the next session of Congress (November, 1792) the committee's report was taken up by the House. By that time friends of Knox and Hamilton (who thought himself somewhat implicated) had stirred up considerable opposition to the report, and a motion was made to invite Hamilton and Knox to be present in the House, and available to give information, when the report was to be considered. So for the second time St. Clair's case became the focus of a fundamental constitutional question, since the attendance of Cabinet members in the House would have been a long step in the direction of Parliamentary government on the British model. It was a situation made to order for James Madison, who "objected to the motion on constitutional grounds as being contrary to the practice of the house" because "it would . . . introduce a precedent which would lead to perplexing and embarrassing consequences; as it involved a conclusion, in respect to the principles of the government, which at an earlier day would have been revolted from."

The House was convinced; it rejected the motion to invite the Secretaries, "and thereby cut off the possible rise of Cabinet government in the United States." [7] However, the report itself was recommitted for further consideration by the select committee.[8] Knox and Hodgdon submitted voluminous *critiques,* to which St. Clair responded with written "observations." On February 15, 1793, the committee brought in a supplementary report, which in certain details mitigated the severity, but confirmed the conclusions, of the original report.

Once again the friends of Hamilton and Knox succeeded in preventing any action by the House. On February 26 it was formally laid aside and upon the expiration of the Second Congress, St. Clair's hope for public vindication perished. Twenty years later he wrote: [9]

> Thus it appears that, although the House had resolved to inquire into the causes of the failure of that expedition, and the inquiry had been pursued with great assiduity by the committees to whom it was referred,

and a report had been made from each of them, they were determined that neither themselves or the public should be informed; the ill consequences of which I have severely felt, and still continue to feel, though twenty-one years have elapsed since the event that gave rise to the inquiry.

Grievously as Arthur St. Clair had suffered mortification on account of the disaster on the Wabash, his ordeal had only begun, and was to endure a full quarter century. He retained his post as Governor of the Northwest Territory—for which he was paid the munificent stipend of $1500 a year—throughout the administrations of Washington and John Adams. But he was a Federalist of the old school, and the advent of Jefferson spelled his official doom. In November, 1802, he was given his walking papers in a thankless and insulting manner,* and St. Clair, by then in his sixty-ninth year, returned to his home in Ligonier, burdened with debts and dependents.

The debts had been contracted in the service of his country, and arose from his personal endorsement of notes issued for supplies needed by the Territorial Government. Alexander Hamilton had promised that the Treasury would take them up, but technicalities were interposed, Hamilton left the Treasury, and in 1796 the official records were destroyed in a fire. The government never honored the notes, and in 1805 the holder obtained a judgment against St. Clair. Five years later, at a time when the embargo had caused an acute money shortage, his Ligonier estate and all of his other properties were sold at a foreclosure sale. The proceeds of the sale did not even cover the debt, and St. Clair was left penniless. "They left me a few books of my classical library, and the bust of Paul Jones, which he sent me from Europe, for which I was very grateful," he noted sadly, after he had moved to a rude log cabin a few miles from his lost estates, where he lived in poverty.

* The letter of dismissal, written by James Madison as Secretary of State, was grounded on an unwarranted charge that St. Clair had been guilty of "intemperance and indecorum of language." Madison's least attractive side was manifest in that he despatched the letter to one of St. Clair's bitterest opponents in the Territorial Government, instead of directly. This slight dislodged St. Clair from his customary magisterial diction, and so provoked him that he informed Madison that the manner of dismissal "produced . . . no other emotion in me but that kind of derision which physiognomists tell us is 'the involuntary expression on the countenance of a certain mental sensation,' which I do not choose to name, and never fails to produce it."

A few years earlier when sorely pressed for funds, St. Clair had presented a petition to Congress praying reimbursement of $1800 which he had personally advanced in 1776 to recruit men into the Continental Army. There was no doubt that the claim was founded on fact, but it was long since barred by limitations. From 1808 to 1812 the claim was considered and reconsidered, in committees and in the House and Senate, but every time it was brought up for action it failed, chiefly because of charges that St. Clair had been to blame for the disaster of 1791. In vain St. Clair besought Congress to print the committee reports of 1792 exonerating him. In 1812 the reports and his own account of the action on the Wabash were published by private subscription,[10] but however this may have salved his feelings, it was without effect on the Congress, which took no further action until 1818.

In that year, St. Clair's eighty-fourth, the 1776 claim was once again presented to the House. Incredible as it may seem, the bill was debated "until sunset" on February 2, and again extensively the next day, as all the old accusations were revived. At length Henry Clay proposed as a compromise that St. Clair be awarded a monthly pension. While the aged soldier, statesman, and scion of the "lordly line of high St. Clair" eked out a living selling supplies to wayfaring strangers who passed his humble door, the House haggled over the size of his pension. Eighty dollars was too high; seventy-five dollars likewise; seventy dollars the same. Eventually sixty dollars was agreed to, and the Senate promptly concurred.[11]

But it was too late to be of much use to Arthur St. Clair. Six months after this grudging and niggardly amend, he was thrown from his wagon on a lonely stretch of rough mountain road, lay unconscious for many hours, and died soon after he was discovered. In 1857 Congress made a substantial appropriation for his heirs.

I have set forth the causes, conduct, and consequences of the St. Clair investigation in some detail not only because it was the first such inquiry, but also because it strikingly demonstrates that some of the most hotly debated issues of the present day are far from new. To be sure, we cannot solve these issues by simply lapping up the wisdom of Washington, Jefferson and Madison. They themselves did not and could not finally "solve the problem" of Congressional investigations, because the legislative investigation is a piece of governmental machinery, the workings of which from time to time generate conflicts and questions which are variants of old ones, and must be handled (rather than "solved") not by historical rote but in accord with the needs of the times. Nevertheless, purposeful and wise handling will be much assisted by comprehension of the theories and methods employed by able and devoted men on earlier occasions, and by awareness of the results which were achieved.

In its primary purpose of *informing the Congress*, it would appear that the St. Clair investigation was highly successful. The lawmakers wanted to know what had been "done amiss," as William Pitt had put it, and they found out. Part of the fault was their own, in delaying the appropriations for the expedition while demanding haste in its consummation; the army could not be mobilized, trained, and put into the field as an effective force in a single year. Part was lack of both diligence and experience in supplying the army, and part was the decision, in which both Washington and St. Clair participated, to proceed with the expedition under these unfavorable circumstances. Whether or not owing to the revelations of the investigation, these errors were not repeated. General Wayne's army was larger, better trained, and better equipped. Nor did "Mad Anthony" indulge his storied impetuosity. He and his army arrived at Fort Washington in April, 1793, but he spent a year and a half building forts and training his troops, and did not move aggressively against Little Turtle until the late summer of 1794.

But Congress' attempt by means of the investigation to determine *who was to blame* for St. Clair's defeat was conspicuously unsuccessful. True, the committee came to a clear and forthright conclusion in its report, but this very clarity roused the partisans of Hamilton and Knox to violent opposition to its conclusions, and the factual issues became enmeshed with political strife between Federalists and Anti-Federalists. The result was a total paralysis of Congressional judgment. The House was unable to take any action on the report whatever. St. Clair was left accused but unjudged; the tensions generated by the issue persisted, and prevented even acts of simple justice, such as reimbursing him for his advances at a time of critical urgency to the cause of Independence, or honoring the obligations which eventually bore him into bankruptcy and poverty. All this suggests that legislative investigations are less than perfect devices for appraising guilt or innocence, at least where there are heavy political stakes on the verdict—in other words, that they are more suitable for the informing function than for the judicial function.

In retrospect, however, the most remarkable feature of the St. Clair investigation was the prompt realization, both in the executive branch and in Congress, that deep constitutional issues had been raised. Eighty-eight years before the Supreme Court ruled that Congressional investigations are limited to the legislative field,[12] Washington and his Cabinet members clearly recognized that exercise of the investigative power, beyond the limits of legislative power specified or implied in the Constitution, would seriously endanger the effective authority of the executive branch, and declared that encroachment would be resisted. And, as we will now see, their concept of the limited nature of Congress' investigative power, despite many challenges over the course of years, has endured to this day.

CHAPTER III

CONSTITUTIONS, COURTS AND INVESTIGATIONS

". . . few if any of the rights of the people guarded by fundamental law are of greater importance to their happiness and safety than the right to be exempt from all unauthorized, arbitrary or unreasonable inquiries and disclosures in respect of their personal and private affairs."

—Justice Pierce Butler (1929)

RIGHTLY OR WRONGLY but enduringly, the Founding Fathers shaped the government of the United States by means of a written Constitution, to which the acts of all three branches of government—legislative, executive, and judicial—are bound to conform. The Constitution itself, however, nowhere states how its provisions are to be enforced.

Despite this lack of precision within the four corners of the document, the Fathers were well aware of the danger that the federal government or the states might assert authority denied them by the Constitution. To meet this danger, Alexander Hamilton, James Madison, and others among the framers of the Constitution clearly stated and vigorously supported the doctrine of *judicial review,* in order that federal or state acts which were in violation of the Constitution could be judicially declared invalid and of no effect.[1]

In line with these contemporaneous views, as early as 1795 Supreme Court Justice Paterson rejected a Pennsylvania statute on the ground that it was in conflict with the Constitution. His opinion set forth in striking language the sharp contrast between the omnipotence of the British Parliament and the limited powers of American legislatures under written constitutions: [2]

> The power of Parliament is absolute and transcendent; it is omnipotent in the scale of political existence. . . . In America the case is widely different; every State in the Union has its constitution reduced to written exactitude and precision. . . . I take it to be a clear position; that if a legislative act oppugns a constitutional principle, the former must give way, and be rejected on the score of repugnance. I hold it to be a position equally clear and sound, that, in such case, it will be the duty of the Court to adhere to the Constitution, and to declare the act null and void.

Such reasoning applied equally to Congressional acts, and in 1803 the Supreme Court so declared. "It is, emphatically, the province and duty of the judicial department to say what the law is," wrote Chief Justice John Marshall in an historic opinion, as he nailed down the proposition that the constitutional limits on Congressional power must be observed and enforced by the federal courts: [3]

> The question, whether an act, repugnant to the constitution, can become the law of the land, is a question deeply interesting to the United States; but, happily, not of an intricacy proportioned to its interest. It seems only necessary to recognize certain principles, supposed to have been long and well established, to decide it. . . . The powers of the legislature are defined and limited; and that those limits may not be mistaken, or forgotten, the constitution is written. To what purpose are powers limited, and to what purpose is that limitation committed to writing, if these limits may, at any time, be passed by those intended to be restrained? The distinction between a government with limited and unlimited powers is abolished, if those limits do not confine the persons on whom they are imposed, and if acts prohibited and acts allowed are of equal obligation. It is a proposition too plain to be contested, that the constitution controls any legislative act repugnant to it . . .

Now, as we have seen, the investigative power of Parliament and the colonial legislatures did not spring up independently, but rather as an adjunct to the functions of lawmaking and appropriating public moneys for the conduct of governmental affairs. If these basic legislative powers were subject to constitutional limitations, certainly ancillary powers such as the investigative function were likewise so limited. In other words, the Constitution controlled not only statutes but (in Marshall's words, as quoted above) "any legislative act," and Congressional investigations are legislative acts. If a Congressional committee of investigation should endeavor to compel a witness to furnish information for a purpose not authorized or in a manner prohibited by the Constitution, the courts would be bound to hold that the committee's demand was unenforceable, and to uphold the witness' right to withhold the information.

This logic was inexorable, but after the adoption of the Constitution over sixty-five years elapsed before any court, and ninety years before the United States Supreme Court, had occasion to draw that conclusion. If it seems peculiar that the Constitution was in effect for the better part of a century before the Supreme Court was called upon to review Congressional investigative action, it is less so if one recalls that only two statutes of Congress were held unconstitutional during the seventy years preceding the Civil War.* Governmental affairs did not then bulk large in the everyday life of the nation, and few men had the means or need to go to law over such matters.

But if the courts remained silent during the pre-Civil War years, it by no means follows that the Congressional investigative function languished, or that its exercise raised no issues. On the contrary, these were vigorously debated from time to time in Congress, and the St. Clair investigation was soon followed by others.

The First Sixty-five Years

The history of Congressional investigations is in large part the history of American politics. From the earliest times, the burning issues of the day were frequently drawn into the investigative vortex, and there is scarcely a well-remembered name in our political history that does not have some prominent association with the inquiries of the period.

---

* These were the statute (involving the jurisdiction of the Supreme Court) held unconstitutional in Marshall's decision in 1803, and that in the famous *Dred Scott* case in 1857, in which it was held that Congress had no power to ban slavery in the territories.

Many of these early Congressional proceedings were concerned with the traditional "privileges" of a legislature—the scrutiny of charges against a Representative or Senator, or the trial of those accused of libels, physical assaults,* or attempts at bribery.[4] The behavior of the Fourth Estate was a frequent source of irritation and inquiry; enterprising journalists revealed the doings of secret sessions, or "broke" stories reflecting invidiously on the honesty of the members, and were understandably reluctant to divulge their sources of information.[5]

In some of these episodes the political stakes were high, and there were sharp disagreements over the propriety of invoking the contempt power. Indeed, even Congress' right to punish contempts was repeatedly challenged during these debates, and the argument was made that the Constitution had so limited Congress' authority that neither of its houses could claim the ancillary contempt powers which had been exercised by Parliament and the colonial legislatures for over a century.[6] Acting on this premise one John Anderson, who had been arrested and reprimanded by the House of Representatives for attempting to bribe a member, sued the Sergeant-at-Arms for assault and false imprisonment, and carried his suit all the way to the Supreme Court. The Court's decision, announced in 1821, upheld the authority of Congress to punish contempts,[7] and thus laid the question to rest.[8]

Throughout the first hundred years of our history, the great bulk of Congressional investigations were concerned with the civil and military operations of the executive branch. For the most part these were conducted by the House, which scrutinized the Treasury Department (1800 and 1824), the territorial government of Mississippi (1800), the War Department (1809 and 1832), the conduct of General James Wilkinson (1810), government "clerks" generally (1818), the Post Office (1820 and 1822), the Bank of the United States (1832 and 1834), the New York Customs House (1839), the conduct of Captain J. D. Elliott commanding a naval squadron in the Mediterranean (1839), the Commissioner of Indian Affairs (1849), the Sec-

* Examples include the House proceedings in 1832 against Sam Houston for his assault on Representative Stanbery, in reprisal for the latter's statements during a debate, and the Senate and House inquiries in 1856 arising out of Representative Preston Brooks's attack on Senator Sumner in the Senate chamber.

retary of the Interior (1850), and the Smithsonian Institution (1855). In the meantime the Senate had looked into General Andrew Jackson's conduct of the Seminole Wars in Florida (1818), the Internal Revenue Bureau (1828), the Post Office (1830), and John Brown's raid at Harper's Ferry (1859). Soon after the outbreak of the Civil War, the Union disasters at Bull Run and Ball's Bluff led the House and Senate to establish a joint committee (the first such) "to inquire into the conduct of the present war."

It was, accordingly, the suspicion or revelation of executive mismanagement that usually set in motion the investigative machinery during the early years of the Republic. There is a contemporary ring to this description, written seventy years ago, of committee activities: [9]

> Committees instituted inquiries, ran the eye up and down accounts, pointed out little items, snuffed about dark corners, peeped behind curtains and under beds, and exploited every cupboard of the executive household with a mousing alacrity, not so eager it would appear, to correct abuses as to collect campaign material for damaging some candidate and playing the detective in preference to the judge.

But the more general type of investigation in aid of lawmaking was not unknown in pre-Civil War days. In 1827 tariff problems were in the forefront of the legislative mind, and the partisans of northern protection and southern free-trade fell into bitter dispute. To secure accurate commercial information, Representative Mallary of Vermont proposed that the House Committee on Manufactures be empowered to send for persons and papers. "Before I agree to impose this tax on my constituents . . . I want evidence," declared Congressman Edward Livingston, and, despite considerable opposition, the investigation was authorized.[10]

In the course of its practical experience with investigations, Congress twice found it necessary to supplement its inherent authority with statutes, in order to eliminate several inherited shortcomings of the power to punish contempts. For example, it was at first doubted that there was power in the House or Senate to administer oaths, and federal judges were specially called in to swear witnesses.[11] This proved highly inconvenient, and in 1798 Congress enacted a statute authorizing the Vice President, the Speaker, and certain committee chairmen to administer oaths, and providing that false testimony given under oath should be punishable as perjury.[12]

An even more awkward restriction on the power to punish contempts was that imprisonment of the offender could not endure beyond the end of the legislative session.[13] As a practical matter this limited the confinement to a few weeks or months, and left Congress helpless to deal with contempts committed near the close of a session. In 1857 the Washington correspondent of *The New York Times*, who had accused unnamed Congressmen of soliciting bribes in the disposal of public lands, was cited before the House and refused to divulge the members' names. A few days in jail loosened his tongue, but the episode led Congress to pass a statute making it a criminal offense, punishable by imprisonment up to one year, to refuse to furnish information demanded by either house of Congress.[14]

This 1857 statute is the first edition of the law under which the investigative authority of Congress is generally enforced today, by criminal prosecution of those who refuse to answer questions put to them. But at the time of its original enactment and throughout the nineteenth century the new statutory provisions were but little used, as Congress preferred to exercise its own power to imprison for contempt, limited as it was, rather than resort to the courts to punish recalcitrant witnesses. Presumably this preference arose chiefly from a desire to avoid the inevitable delays entailed by judicial proceedings. If there also was some Congressional fear that the courts might be disposed to curb the scope of investigative power, events were about to prove those apprehensions justified.

The State Courts and the "Know-Nothing" Investigations of 1855

In the state legislatures, meanwhile, investigatory methods had been taking much the same course as in Congress. In New York, for example, the State Legislature had made frequent use of committees to explore the administration of the state prisons, the Erie Canal, and other agencies. In 1824, William J. Caldwell was jailed for contempt for refusing to testify during an investigation of corrupt means used in obtaining a state charter for the Chemical Bank, and in 1837 Moses Jacques and Levi Slamm were punished under similar circumstances. In 1853, the Legislature's inherent contempt powers were supplemented by a criminal statute—four years antecedent to the Congressional act just described—which made it a misdemeanor to disregard a committee subpoena, or to refuse "to answer any material and proper question." [15] And two years later, in both New York and Massachusetts and for the first time in our history, investigations were instituted which struck direct and deep into the field of individual liberties.

These investigations of 1855 were manifestations of the virulent nativist and anti-Catholic movement, known as the "Know-Nothing" party, that gripped the United States just a century ago. In large part, this extraordinary outbreak was a reaction to the wave of immigrants, generally of Roman Catholic persuasion, that was then pouring into America. Particularly in the cities of the eastern seaboard these swarms of new arrivals precipitated social and economic conflicts and painful readjustments. Native American resentment against the newcomers, especially the Irish, was frequently intemperate and violent in its manifestations. Catholic church power and resources were greatly increased by the immigrant tide, and in 1850 the militant Archbishop John Hughes of New York City, speaking in St. Patrick's on "The Decline of Protestantism in America," proclaimed a Catholic mission to convert the world, and predicted the day when the President and his Cabinet would all share that faith.[16]

The previous year one Charles B. Allen had founded in New York City the "Order of the Star-Spangled Banner," and from this seed the evil weed of anti-foreign and anti-Catholic hatred sprang and spread with amazing rapidity. Religious feelings were easily inflamed by emerging disputes such as Bible reading in the schools, and the availability of public funds for parochial school use and benefits. Soon Allen's "Order" emerged as a full-blown political party, officially known as the "American" party, but commonly called "Know-Nothing" because it retained many of the trappings of a secret society, and its members professed to know nothing about it when questioned. The initials *K.N.* began to appear as a symbol on books, match-boxes, and candy-wrappings, and in 1854 and 1855 the Know-Nothings scored sweeping and, at the time, frightening successes at the polls.

This was the more remarkable in that the party was almost entirely lacking in any positive program. Northern and southern Know-Nothings were just as far apart on slavery and the other burning issues of the times as other northerners and southerners. Only a few concrete proposals—such as the requirement that all office-holders be native-born citizens, and that twenty-one years of residence be required for naturalization—were ever seriously advanced to carry out the nativist sentiments for which the party stood. "Only one force held members of the Know-Nothing Party together, and that was their hatred of the Catholic Church." [17]

The most overwhelming electoral triumphs were scored in Massachusetts in 1854, when the Know-Nothings elected the governor and all state officers, the entire Senate, and all but three of the 379 members of the House. Once in, however, they had no notion what to do. Most of them were totally lacking in political or civic experience; only 34 of the legislators had ever before served in that capacity. They did, however, manage to take action on petitions which had been addressed to the legislature, calling for an investigation of Catholic nunneries and convents, and which had been stimulated by current suspicion of "popery" and wild rumors that women and girls were being held against their will.

And so, in February, 1855, a joint committee was appointed and authorized to visit "such theological seminaries, boarding schools, academies, nunneries, convents, and other institutions of like character as they may deem necessary" and report their observations.[18] Variously known as the "Nunnery Committee," the "Hiss Committee" (after its chairman, Joseph Hiss of Boston, a "Grand Worthy Instructor" of the Know Nothing Council), and the "Smelling Committee" (because of the members' penchant for poking their noses into closets and cabinets), the inquiry had a colorful but brief existence.

Finding nothing amiss at Holy Cross in Worcester, where the investigation opened, the legislative sleuths next proceeded to the Catholic school at Roxbury. Here, according to accounts: [19]

> The whole party tramped over the school building, frightening the children, treating the nuns with little respect, and peeking into closets and corners to find the dread evidence of popery which propaganda writers had convinced them should be there.* After thoroughly disrupting the

* Another account of the visitation states: "The gentlemen roamed over the whole convent, not a part was spared. The ladies' dresses were tossed over in

school, the whole party adjourned to an elaborate dinner where champagne flowed freely—although sale of the beverage was forbidden in the State. At Lowell members of the Committee and their friends not only imbibed freely of local liquors, but also charged the State expenses incurring from their relationships with a woman "answering to the name of Mrs. Patterson" who was notorious for her easy virtue.

This was too much for even the Know-Nothing legislature to countenance. As a result of public clamor the Hiss Committee was recalled, and the legislature commenced an investigation of its own investigating committee,[21] as a result of which Joseph Hiss was expelled from the legislature. It was the first but not the last occasion when the conduct of a legislative inquiry has drawn the investigators themselves into the witness chair.*

In the meantime, the Know-Nothings had also made considerable headway in New York City, the major port of entry for immigrants and the headquarters of the movement. In 1854 its candidate for Mayor, James W. Barker, lost to Fernando Wood (a Democrat) by a very narrow margin, and Know-Nothing adherents were elected to the Common Council and dominated the Board of Aldermen. For our present purposes, the significant consequence of all this was an investigation of the New York City police, in the course of which the first American judicial decision, dealing with the nature and powers of investigative committees, was rendered.

Although its origins were two centuries older,† the present New York police force was born under the Municipal Police Act of 1844 and shaped by the energetic but controversial George W. Matsell, New York's first Chief of Police.[23] Despite his efforts, ten years later

---

their wardrobes. The party invaded the chapel and showed their respect—as Protestants, we presume—for the One God whom all Christians worship, by talking loudly with their hats on; while the ladies shrank in terror at the desecration of the spot which they hallowed." [20]

* The Senate inquiries into Senator McCarthy's handling of investigations in his capacity as Chairman of the Permanent Investigating Subcommittee of the Government Operations Committee are the most recent example. In July, 1954, Representative Jacob Javits proposed a House investigation of the conduct of the Reece committee, which had terminated its public hearings on educational and philanthropic foundations after hearing only the critical witnesses. Representative Reece completed the circle by calling for an investigation of the sources of criticism of his investigation.[22] Who takes care of the caretaker's daughter?

† A "Burgher guard" was established in New Amsterdam at least as early as 1643.

there was intense public dissatisfaction with the police; while Matsell puffed his men as "the finest police force in the world" (wherefore to this day their *nom d'honneur* is "the Finest"), James W. Gerard (father of the late Ambassador to Germany) was publicly deploring the scandalous crime rate, and comparing the New York force unfavorably with those of European cities generally and of London in particular.[24]

With the advent of the Know-Nothings, the leadership of the police became an issue in a bitter conflict between Mayor Fernando Wood, to whom Matsell was responsible, and the Common Council. In February, 1855, the Council's hand was strengthened when the State Legislature enacted a statute[25] which, in effect, delegated to the Council the Legislature's investigative power in connection with matters pertaining to the city government. By this statute, both boards of the Common Council (the Board of Aldermen and the Board of Councilmen) were authorized to call for testimony or documents under the compulsion of subpoena "in respect to any matter pending" before the Council. In case a witness should refuse to be sworn or to answer any proper question, it was provided that any judge of the New York Supreme Court or of the Court of Common Pleas might issue an order directing the witness to respond, and punish him if he refused to comply with the order.

Within a few days of the passage of this statute, the Know-Nothing-controlled Board of Aldermen adopted a resolution calling upon Chief Matsell to report how many of his force were naturalized or newly arrived in America, and "how many Americans, Irishmen, Scotchmen, Germans, Frenchmen, Englishmen and men of all other nations" were in the Police Department. Matsell's report to the Board of Aldermen revealed that roughly a third of the force had been born in Erin, without regard to the ancestry of the American-born members; the number of non-Irish foreign-born police was negligible.[26]

But the Aldermen felt that Matsell's report understated the size of the Irish component, and that other matters needed looking into. In April of 1855 they adoped another resolution empowering a committee of the Board to investigate "all frauds and corruptions in every branch of the Police Department, and also the manner in which the same is and has been conducted." The inquiry covered not only the nationality question, but also charges such as embezzlement of moneys from the dog pound by Matsell's assistant, one Mackellar, and the theft, allegedly by the Police Department, of the pall (valued at $600) from the coffin of Henry Clay during that illustrious statesman's lying-in-state!

Among the Know-Nothing leaders in the city was a notorious hoodlum and gladiator, of phenomenal physical prowess, by name Bill Poole, who stirred up anti-Irish feeling and collected Know-Nothing votes by harangues and beating up countless individual Irishmen. On the night of February 24, 1855, Poole was fatally shot in a saloon brawl with the followers of John Morrissey, a young Irish-born partisan of Tammany who was generally recognized as the champion prize-fighter of America. Poole lingered eleven days before his death, while national and religious hatreds in the city waxed fiercer than ever; his funeral on March 11 drew enormous crowds, surpassing the demonstrations at the deaths of Clay and Daniel Webster, and the hearse was girdled with a velvet band bearing the legend "I die a true American," said to have been Poole's last words.[27]

Such was the atmosphere in which the Aldermen opened their police inquiry. The committee began by calling a number of witnesses, chiefly elderly ladies, in an effort to establish that Chief Matsell was English-born and unnaturalized, and therefore ineligible by law to hold his office. Thereafter they called Mackellar, to whom they put questions concerning the dog pound and his general duties, and two policemen, Webster and McCann, both of whom were asked about their national origin. All three refused to answer any of the questions; Webster and McCann also declared that they would refuse to answer any other questions the committee might put. Thereupon the committee applied to the Court of Common Pleas for an order directing the witnesses to answer, and the matter came up for argument before the Honorable Charles Patrick Daly of that court.[28]

The ensuing proceedings reflect great credit on the bench and bar of that day. For the Aldermen, William Curtis Noyes and A. Nash—the first American lawyers ever called on to plead in court in behalf of a legislative investigation—spoke forcefully but with great dignity and scholarship. The committee must be allowed great latitude in the breadth of its questioning, Noyes urged: ". . . if the questions are nearly or even remotely relevant to a proper subject for legislative inquiry . . . the court must compel them to be answered." Under

Judge Daly's questioning, however, Noyes was obliged to concede that "if the question is obviously impertinent, if it has nothing to do with any matter which can come before them [the legislature], or in respect to which they can exercise any legislative control, then it is not a proper question" and the witness could not be required to respond.

Assailed as hyper-Hibernian, the Police Department chose as its forensic champion James T. Brady, abundantly endowed with the wit and eloquence of the Emerald Isle. Asked by Judge Daly to describe the object of the investigation, Mr. Brady exhibited magnificent bewilderment. Mostly, the committee had called a lot of "old women" to gossip about Chief Matsell's nativity: "It was like the attempt of the old historians to fix the birthplace of Virgil.* . . . The names of Virgil and Matsell were thus likely to be handed down, in immortal companionship, to a curious and admiring posterity." He then made great play with the questions put to Webster and McCann: "Webster's name . . . had not a very transatlantic sound . . . but about McCann there was, it must be confessed, a little odor of a country that had been proscribed by Great Britain, and was hated a little more by some Americans, just now."

Laying levity aside, Mr. Brady drove to the heart of the problem—whether the committee had the right to put a man to his oath about private matters—and the advocate's Gaelic fire gleams through the archaic diction: [29]

> If a Committee of the Common Council could inquire as to the nativity of a man, why not about his religion also? . . . Had not a man's religion and politics as much to do with the subject of legislative activity as his nativity? Undoubtedly. But fortunately the law stepped in and impeded the progress of weak, designing or evil-minded men, who wanted to elevate themselves to offices of trust or emolument over the ruined reputations and sacrificed private rights of public officers, conspired away in committee rooms, in caucuses, in grog-shops, in porter-houses, and all the places where low and mousing politicians most do congregate.

Truly, Judge Daly had much to ponder and little by way of

* At this point in the notes of Mr. Brady's argument, the scholarly scribe of a century ago noted a query whether it was not "the Chian bard" (Homer) rather than "the Mantuan bard" (Virgil) to whom the learned advocate should properly have made reference.[30]

precedent to guide his thinking. It was indeed fortunate that so potentially explosive an issue came before so stable and dispassionate a judge. Born of Irish Catholic immigrant parents and in humble circumstances, Judge Daly was singularly free from the violent religious and national passions of the times, as well as a highly-respected and, albeit self-educated, scholarly lawyer.*

Caught between bigoted Know-Nothings and resentful Irish policemen, Judge Daly discharged his judicial task with distinction. His opinion, delivered after consulting his brother judges, shows remarkable grasp of the nature of the "informing function" and vision of the problems which its exercise was bound to raise under a government of limited powers: [32]

> The right to pass laws, necessarily implies the right to obtain information upon any matter which may become the subject of a law. It is essential to the full and intelligent exercise of the legislative function . . . If it is essential . . . that each of the two houses composing the legislature of the State should have the right of inquiry, it would seem that both Boards of the Common Council should possess it also, to enable them to act efficiently, within the more limited sphere prescribed for them . . . they should have the means of obtaining full and accurate information respecting every thing of a strictly municipal character relating to the affairs of the city.

Beneficent as was the informing function, it was nevertheless limited, just as the legislature's other powers were limited:

> But the right of either Board of the Common Council to investigate public matters has its limitations; for even the legislature itself can exercise only such powers as have been delegated to it, and is confined strictly within them. . . . It is in the power of either Board to investigate any matter they may think proper; but any inquiry they make must be clearly within the scope and object for which they exist as a political body.

Amplifying these principles, Judge Daly declared that "the examination of the witnesses must be confined to the subject which is under investigation, and they cannot be asked any question not re-

* Judge Daly was a prominent civic and cultural leader, and one of the most notable of New Yorkers during the latter half of the nineteenth century. He achieved an international reputation as a geographer, and was president of the American Geographical Society from 1864 until his death in 1899. His portrait hangs today in the Society's offices in New York City.[31]

lating to it." He then ruled that all the questions put to Mackellar were properly related to the conduct of the Police Department and should have been answered. Not so, however, the questions put to Webster and McCann concerning their national origin:

> These questions were irrelevant. The committee were directed to inquire or investigate as to any frauds or corruptions in any branch of the Police Department, and the manner in which it had been conducted, and they were confined to that subject, and could not enter upon any other. Whether an inquiry as to the nativity of the persons composing the Police Department would or would not be an appropriate subject of inquiry, on the part of the Common Council, it is not necessary to determine. It is sufficient that it was not embraced in the resolution referred to the committee.

However, the two policemen had declared that they would refuse to answer any questions whatsoever; this was "entirely unwarrantable" and rendered them, as well as Mackellar, liable for contempt. And accordingly, on June 18, 1855, Judge Daly signed an order directing the three witnesses to appear before the committee and answer the questions previously put to them, except for those relating to national origin, and all other questions "respecting the matters embraced by the resolution" of the Board of Aldermen.

Despite the relatively humble station of the New York Court of Common Pleas in the judicial hierarchy, Judge Daly's opinion is to be accounted a sound cornerstone and an enduring landmark of the law of legislative investigations.[33] Confronted with a dispute which was both legally novel and politically touchy,* he laid it down firmly and clearly that:

---

* The subsequent history of this municipal imbroglio is in keeping with its origin. Recalled before the committee in September, Messrs. Mackellar, Webster and McCann still declined to answer. Efforts to arrest them for contempt of Judge Daly's order were frustrated on the technical ground that the witnesses had been served with a printed copy, and therefore had never been shown Judge Daly's original signature on the order.[35]

In the meantime, Chief Matsell himself was called and was sworn, whereupon he handed the chairman a note, in which he declined to answer any questions. The committee applied to Judge Ingraham of the Court of Common Pleas for an order, but the redoubtable Mr. Brady pointed out that no questions were actually put to Matsell. How could he be guilty of refusing to answer questions if none were asked? Judge Ingraham found the technical point controlling, and declined to issue the order,[36] so the precise Irish proportion of the force, as well

(1) investigations backed by compulsory process are "essential to the full and intelligent exercise of the legislative function";

(2) unlike in Britain, in the United States the investigative power is limited by the Constitution, for the "legislature . . . can exercise only such powers as have been delegated to it";

(3) legislative committees can require answers only to questions pertinent to the investigation as authorized by the legislature itself;

(4) a witness need not "answer any question that would tend to incriminate him"; [34] and

(5) the courts will, when justiciable controversy arises, review the exercise of the investigative power.

For all that has since been written, the law has not departed far from these principles, enunciated nearly a century ago.

In the course of the twenty-five years following Judge Daly's decision,* the state legislatures instituted investigations with increasing frequency. Upon a very few occasions—and only in New York, Massachusetts, and Wisconsin, so far as the records disclose—witnesses challenged the authority of these committees. Uniformly, the general investigative power of the committees was upheld by the courts.[37] Just as uniformly, they reaffirmed Judge Daly's ruling that the legislatures' investigative powers are subject to constitutional limitations.

In 1859, for example, the Massachusetts House of Representatives launched an inquiry into the State Liquor Agency. When the Commissioner refused to testify, the Supreme Judicial Court upheld his punishment for contempt, but stated: [38]

> The house of representatives is not the final judge of its own powers and privileges in cases in which the rights and liberties of the subject are concerned; but the legality of its action may be examined and determined by this court . . . Especially is it competent and proper for this court to consider whether its proceedings are in conformity with the Constitution and laws, because, living under a written constitution, no branch or department of the government is supreme. . . .

---

as the handling of the dog pound funds and the fate of Henry Clay's funeral pall remained shrouded in mystery.

* The Know-Nothings faded rapidly after 1856, and the party did not survive the War Between the States.

And in 1880, twenty-five years after Judge Daly's order in the New York City police investigation, the Supreme Court of the United States was finally called upon to review the exercise of Congressional investigative power.

The Supreme Court Steps In

The period following the War Between the States, like the post-World War II years, was one in which Congress was restless, vehemently assertive of its prerogatives, and frequently at odds with the executive branch. The impeachment of President Andrew Johnson in 1868 did nothing to re-establish harmony between Capitol and White House, and the seventies proved to be halcyon years for Congressional sleuths. Joint investigating committees of House and Senate, first employed during the Civil War, were established to inquire into the "Condition of the Late Insurrectionary States" (1871), the governance of the District of Columbia (1874), and the Indian Bureau (1878). Financial morality in public affairs was at a low ebb; two separate inquiries into the Credit Mobilier and the construction and financing of the Union Pacific Railroad were instituted by the House in 1873, and another into corruption in the procurement of subsidies for the Pacific Mail Steamship Company was put under way in 1874.[39]

The Credit Mobilier and Pacific Mail inquiries led to episodes which, for the first time, drew Congressional investigations within the purview of the federal courts. During the former, Joseph B. Stewart, counsel for the Union Pacific, declined to answer the committee's questions on the ground that to do so would violate the confidential relationship between himself and his client, the railroad. Unimpressed, the House locked him up in a room at the Capitol, where he lived on the fat of the land and was lionized by partisans of the Union Pacific. After his release he sued the Speaker of the House, James G. Blaine, for damages for false imprisonment, but the District of Columbia court threw out the suit on the ground that Blaine could not be held personally liable for an action directed by the House, irrespective of the legality or illegality of Stewart's imprisonment.[40]

Two years later the Washington agent of the Pacific Mail Steamship Company, R. B. Irwin, refused to answer the House committee's questions. This time the House denied the witness lodging in the Capitol, and committed him to the common jail. Judge McArthur of the District of Columbia bench denied Irwin's petition for a writ of *habeas corpus* and upheld the power of the House to punish him for contempt. In so doing, however, he asserted that [41] ". . . it is entirely competent for any court of justice to inquire into the privilege of Congress . . . the doctrine that Congress is the sole judge of its own privileges can never be the rule in a court of justice and can never be sustained."

These two minor skirmishes set the stage for the big test. It grew out of the financial crisis of 1873, and was precipitated by the failure of Jay Cooke's banking firm, which was a depositary of federal funds. Early in 1876 the House authorized a select committee to investigate financial dealings between Cooke and a "real estate pool" in the District of Columbia in which he was interested, on the ostensible theory that the government's interests as a creditor of Cooke's bank had been injured thereby. This "Real Estate Pool and Jay Cooke Financial Indebtedness Committee" subpoenaed the manager of the pool, Hallett Kilbourn, who refused to answer questions or produce documents, asserting that the House had no authority "to investigate private business in which nobody but me and my customers have any concern." [42]

The ensuing proceedings were tortuous indeed. The House cited Kilbourn for contempt and committed him to the District jail; Kilbourn's friends brought him his meals and "the most sumptuous wines," whereupon the House solemnly instructed the jailor to give Kilbourn "the same prison fare as is furnished to other prisoners in the jail." Upon request of the Speaker, the District grand jury indicted Kilbourn under the criminal statute of 1857,[43] and the District marshall endeavored to take custody of Kilbourn from the Sergeant-at-Arms. After long debate, the House decided to keep Kilbourn in custody for contempt, and not turn him over to the District criminal authorities.

Kilbourn then sued out a writ of *habeas corpus,* and the District Court ordered that he be brought to court. Some of the Representatives urged that the writ should be disregarded, but cooler counsels prevailed, and the House honored the writ by directing the Sergeant-at-Arms to produce "the body of said Kilbourn before said court." Chief Justice Cartter of the District of Columbia court ruled that, by passing the 1857 statute, Congress had deprived itself of the power to punish contempts by imprisonment, and that prosecution under that statute was the only way that recalcitrant witnesses could be dealt with. Accordingly, he ordered Kilbourn's release.[44]

Immediately Kilbourn seized the initiative by suing the Speaker, the members of the investigating committee, and the Sergeant-at-Arms for false imprisonment, thereby also forestalling his trial under the criminal indictment. He carried his suit to the Supreme Court of the United States, where it was decided in 1880. The congressmen, it was held, were constitutionally immune from suit, but the Sergeant-at-Arms was not; the Court declared that Kilbourn's imprisonment had been unlawful, and that the Sergeant-at-Arms was liable to him for damages.[45]

The Court's judgment, known as *Kilbourn* v. *Thompson* and embodied in Mr. Justice Miller's opinion, has proved one of the most controversial in the history of the nation.* But the heart of the decision is sound, and has never been seriously challenged. In essence, the Court ruled that the investigating function and contempt powers of Congress, like its law-making and other powers, are subject to the limitations of the Constitution, and that the courts will review Congress' exercise of all these powers. This was a logical and inevitable extension of Marshall's famous decision in 1803 [48] and was, as has been seen, entirely in line with what had already been decided in the New York and Massachusetts state courts.[49] In Mr. Justice Miller's words:

> The powers of Congress itself, when acting through the concurrence of both branches, are dependent solely on the Constitution . . . Of course, neither branch of Congress, when acting separately, can lawfully exer-

* Unfortunately, Mr. Justice Miller devoted a large part of his opinion to the argument that Parliament's power to punish contempts grew out of its ancient functions as a court rather than a legislature, and therefore, offered no historical precedent for holding that Congress, which is not a court, had inherited the Parliamentary contempt powers. In this the learned Justice was sadly in error since, as we have seen,[46] it was specifically to protect and aid the exercise of *legislative* actions that the contempt and investigative powers grew up. Because of this faulty scholarship, Justice Miller's opinion and the Court's judgment have since been widely criticized.[47]

cise more power than is conferred by the Constitution on the whole body . . . the resolution of the House of Representatives finding Kilbourn guilty of contempt, and the warrant of its speaker for his commitment to prison, are not conclusive in this case. . . .

The question, therefore, was whether Congress had power under the Constitution to force Kilbourn to disclose the operations of a private real estate pool, in which the federal government might have an indirect financial interest through having deposited funds with Jay Cooke, a bankrupt participant in the pool. Under the constitutional separation of powers it is the courts, not Congress, that exercise judicial power. Was such a matter truly related to the legislative power of the House, or was not the government's financial claim a matter for the bankruptcy court rather than Congress? Doubts of this character had assailed members of the House long before the issue reached the Court; Representative Hoar of Massachusetts had pointed to "the grave question of constitutional liberty, which lies at the foundation of this particular inquiry," and Representative Kasson of Iowa put his finger on the core of the matter: [50]

. . . under what class of subjects pertaining to the clear jurisdiction of this House does this inquiry come . . . Shall the House of Representatives take from the court its jurisdiction in a case of bankruptcy, because of an alleged interest of the United States? . . . This case has gone to the extremest verge to which I have known the power of the House extended in making inquiries as to matters before the courts. . . .

The Supreme Court decided that the House had gone beyond the verge, in that "the investigation which the committee was directed to make was judicial . . . and could only be properly and successfully made by a court of justice." Therefore, the House was engaged in "a fruitless investigation into the personal affairs of individuals" —fruitless in the sense "that it could result in no valid legislation on the subject" of the inquiry. "What was the committee charged to do?" asked Justice Miller, and answered his own question somewhat explosively: [51]

To inquire in the nature and history of the real-estate pool. How indefinite! What was the real-estate pool? Is it charged with any crime or offence? If so, the courts alone can punish the members of it. Is it charged with a fraud against the government? Here, again, the courts,

> and they alone, can afford a remedy . . . the *gravamen* of the whole proceeding is that a debtor of the United States may be found to have an interest in the pool. Can the rights of the pool, or of its members, and the rights of the debtor, and of the creditor of the debtor, be determined by the report of a committee or by an act of Congress? If they cannot, what authority has the House to enter upon this investigation into the private affairs of individuals who hold no office under the government.

And so the case was sent back to the District Court to determine the amount of Kilbourn's damages from the false imprisonment. His victory was no empty one; the jury first awarded him $60,000 and, when this was set aside as excessive, at a second trial the verdict was $37,500. Ultimately the matter was settled by the payment of $20,000, not from the pocket of the Sergeant-at-Arms but by special Congressional appropriation.[52]

Quite apart from the result arrived at in the *Kilbourn* case,[53] Justice Miller's opinion compares unfavorably, in clarity and dispassionateness, with that of Judge Daly in the humble New York Court of Common Pleas. Holding the particular inquiry unauthorized by the Constitution, Justice Miller failed to acknowledge the general power of Congress, *within* its constitutional sphere, to conduct investigations in aid of its legislative tasks, and thus raised doubts which lingered for nearly fifty years.[54]

In its peppery phraseology, too, Justice Miller's opinion reflects the political tensions of the post-Civil War era. In a private letter he had expressed apprehension that[55] "the House is gradually absorbing all the powers of the government." Another of his letters, written shortly after the *Kilbourn* decision, reveals that a majority of the Court, including Miller himself, were of the opinion that neither House nor Senate had power to punish for contempt witnesses who refused to testify before investigating committees! Unanimity of the Court was achieved only by passing over that fundamental question; as Justice Miller explained, "It was partly due to my conservative habit of deciding no more than is necessary in any case, that I was selected to write the opinion." The resulting uncertainty was unfortunate, but a decision that the contempt power did not embrace investigations would have had much more serious consequences.

Summarizing his views on the investigations of his day, and the scope of the power, Justice Miller wrote in the same letter:

> I think the public has been much abused, the time of legislative bodies uselessly consumed and rights of the citizen ruthlessly invaded under the now familiar pretext of legislative investigation and that it is time that it was understood that courts and grand juries are the only inquisitions into crime in this country. I do not recognize the doctrine that Congress is *the grand inquest* of the nation, or has any such function to perform, nor that it can by the name of a report slander the citizen so as to protect the newspaper which publishes such slander. If the whole body cannot do this much less can one house do it. . . .
>
> As regards needed information on subjects purely legislative no doubt committees can be raised to inquire and report, money can be used to pay for such information and laws may be made to compel reluctant witnesses to give it under proper guaranty of their personal rights. This is sufficient, without subjecting a witness to the unlimited power of a legislative committee or a single branch of the legislative body.

In these words there is more than a whiff of issues which are crucial today. Admittedly, Congress ought to be able to get information needed in the course of lawmaking. Admittedly too, Congress should "have the means of examining in what manner its laws have been executed" by government officials, as Montesquieu declared two hundred years ago. But to what extent does this justify Congressional scrutiny of the individual conduct of private persons, especially where questions of civil liability, criminal guilt, or public opprobrium may be involved?

In 1880, when Mr. Justice Miller wrote, America was on the verge of the great expansion of governmental power and activity that followed in the wake of the industrial revolution. In this process Congressional investigations were to play a major role, and the questions discussed in Justice Miller's opinion and his contemporaneous letters were to arise time and time again.

Adjustment and Balance: "The Least Possible Power"

The settling of the West, the industrialization of the country and the resultant economic complexities especially of transportation and tariff, the Spanish-American war and the acquisition of a colonial empire—all these things precipitated a host of new issues, legislative and administrative, upon which Congress found itself in need of investigative enlightenment.

In scrutinizing the conduct of the executive departments, the Senate now took the lead away from the House. Between 1880 and the beginning of the First World War, the Senate instituted investigations, backed by the subpoena power, into federal tax collections in North Carolina (1883) and customs collections in New York (1885), the administration of Indian affairs (1886, 1888, 1896, 1906), the civil service (1888 and 1897), the General Land Office (1897), the Army's occupational activities in the Philippines (1901), the use of the "third degree" by government officials (1910), and the failure of the Washington police to maintain order during the women's suffrage parade in 1913. The House, in contrast, conducted very few inquiries into the executive branch after 1885. At least in part this appears to have been due to a decline in the general prestige of the House as compared to the Senate; then, too, the majority leadership dominated the House, and disgruntled groups could not, as was possible in the Senate, combine with the minority party (usually the Democrats) to force an inquiry distasteful to the Administration.

By far the most important development of these years was the greatly increased use of investigations, outside the immediate sphere of government operations, to inquire into and report on economic and social problems. We have noted one such instance as early as 1827,[56] but after 1880 they recurred with ever-increasing frequency. In that year, for example, the Senate inquired into the causes of Negro migration from South to North, and in 1888 the House concerned itself with the immigration of foreign contract labor. In 1892 both houses launched investigations of the railroads' use of the Pinkerton Detective Agency for strike-breaking, and in 1909 the Senate authorized its Standing Committee on Irrigation to study the need for legislation to promote the reclamation of arid lands in the West. With the advent of the Wilson administration and the return to power of the Democrats, the House embarked in 1912 on by far the most ambitious and farflung inquiry up to that time—the so-called "Money Trust" investigation of banking and finance.

Indeed, when it came to the railroads, there was far too much investigating for Congress to handle by itself. The economic power of the railroad managements was fabulous. Their friendship or enmity in the matter of rates and routes could make or break a man, an enterprise, a city, or even an entire region, and railroad securities dominated the financial markets. Rebates and other forms of discrimination, however, aroused bitter antipathy, and the pressure for government regulation of railroad practices led to the establishment in 1887 of the Interstate Commerce Commission. This was the beginning of the trend toward expanded governmental participation in economic matters which was to continue for over fifty years, until the outbreak of the Second World War.

In establishing the Commission, Congress had in mind investigation as well as regulation. Section 12 of the Interstate Commerce Act authorized the Commission to "require the attendance and testimony of witnesses and the production of all books, papers and tariffs. . . ." Another statute, passed a month later, established a special temporary Pacific Railway Commission to investigate the records and activities of all railroads that had received federal assistance, such as by land grants to aid in construction.

By these provisions, Congress in effect delegated investigative power over the railroads to the Commissions, just as in 1855 the New York Legislature had delegated the power to the New York City Common Council in the field of municipal affairs. Neither the Common Council nor the federal Commissions, however, were legislatures, and they had no power to punish recalcitrant witnesses for contempt. As we have already seen in the case of the Common Council,[57] the Legislature resolved the problem by providing that the Council could request a court order directing the witness to testify. Substantially the same course was followed by Congress in 1887; both Commissions were authorized to obtain orders from the federal circuit courts compelling obedience to Commission subpoenas.*

* At first there was some doubt of the constitutionality of this procedure,[58] but in 1894 the Supreme Court gave its approval,[59] while firmly declaring that the federal courts would not automatically issue orders requested by the Interstate Commerce Commission but could, just as did Judge Daly in the New York situation, review the Commission's authority to require the particular testimony, and grant the order only in a proper case. After this decision, it was clear that Congress could exercise its investigative authority not only by resolutions vesting the power in its own committees, but also by statutes delegating it to commissions or other executive agencies.

In 1914, when creating the Federal Trade Commission, Congress again delegated extensive investigative functions, this time in the area of monopoly, competition, and trade practices.[60] But during the First World War and the "back-to-normalcy" twenties, and until the great series of regulatory enactments stimulated by the depression of the early thirties, there was little additional legislation of this type, and Congress carried on most of its investigations through its own committees, principally of the Senate.

In the meantime, the Supreme Court had rendered a series of decisions which affirmed the investigatory and contempt powers of Congress, but imposed limitations on the scope of their exercise. These went far to clarify the doubts raised by the *Kilbourn* case, and to strike an adjustment and balance between the legitimate requirements of Congress and the protection of individual rights. In chronological order and capsule form, these decisions are described below.

(1) In 1894, the Court upheld the constitutionality of the investigatory provisions of the Interstate Commerce Act, and approved the enforcement of Commission subpoenas by court order as provided in the Act.[61] Justice Harlan was careful to state, however, that the courts would review the Commission's authority in each case, and that its powers of inquiry were subject to the "constitutional limitations which, for the protection of personal rights, must necessarily attend all investigations conducted under the authority of Congress."

(2) In 1897, the Court declared constitutional the 1857 statute making failure to testify before a Congressional committee punishable as a misdemeanor.[62] Accusations of bribery against members of Congress, during the pendency of a tariff bill changing the duties on sugar, had caused the Senate to appoint a committee of inquiry. A sugar broker refused to tell the committee whether or not he had traded in sugar stocks for the account of any Senator, and was thereafter convicted under the 1857 statute. Affirming his conviction (the first since the passage of the statute), the Court made it clear that recalcitrant witnesses could be dealt with either by criminal prosecution under the statute, or by punishment under the inherent contempt powers of Congress.

(3) In 1906, the Interstate Commerce Commission commenced an inquiry into railroad consolidations, in the course of which the railroad magnate E. H. Harriman and the banker Otto Kahn were

called to testify concerning their stockholdings in various railroads. But the Court decided that the Commission's investigative powers could not be used to obtain general information, but only in connection with possible violations of law, and that Harriman and Kahn were therefore justified in declining to answer.[63] Justice Oliver Wendell Holmes declared that there was grave question whether Congress could constitutionally empower the Commission to conduct general inquiries by requiring witnesses "to disclose any facts, no matter how private, no matter what their tendency to disgrace the person whose attendance has been compelled."

(4) In 1916, the United States Attorney in New York published a defamatory and insulting letter to a House committee which was inquiring into his possible impeachment. By order of the House, the Sergeant-at-Arms arrested the attorney, who applied to the courts for release on *habeas corpus*. The Supreme Court ordered his release on the ground that his conduct, "unparliamentary and manifestly ill-tempered" as it was, nevertheless was not of such a nature as to obstruct Congress in the performance of its functions.[64] Chief Justice White observed that the object of the contempt power is not "punishment" but only "self-preservation," and that therefore Congress must exercise it in accordance with the principle "*the least possible power adequate to the end proposed.*" [65]

(5) In 1921, at the request of the Senate, the Federal Trade Commission embarked on an inquiry into tobacco marketing and prices, and called upon the American Tobacco Company to produce its books and records. But the Court adhered to its judgment sixteen years earlier in the *Harriman* case, and ruled that the Trade Commission had no authority to require testimony except in connection with possible violations of law.[66] Again speaking for the Court, Justice Holmes referred scathingly to "fishing expeditions into private papers," and declared that to grant the broad power asserted by the Commission would "sweep all our traditions into the fire."

Such was the state of the law in the spring of 1924, when the Senate launched its investigation of alleged maladministration of the Department of Justice under Attorney General Daugherty. The Senate Committee subpoenaed the Attorney General's brother Mally S. Daugherty, an Ohio banker, who disregarded the summons. Arrested by the Sergeant-at-Arms, banker Daugherty applied to an Ohio federal court for release. District Judge Andrew Cochran granted the writ and discharged Daugherty from custody, relying heavily on Justice Miller's opinion in the *Kilbourn* case, and drawing the conclusion that the Senate was not acting in a legislative capacity, but was usurping judicial functions by undertaking to try the Attorney General.[67] But Kilbourn had been questioned about a private real estate "pool" rather than a government department, and Judge Cochran's decision, had it stood, would have undermined the old and well-established power of Congressional inquiry into the conduct of the executive branch.

After long reflection,* the Supreme Court reversed Judge Cochran's decision, and declared that the Senate could require Mally Daugherty to testify.[68] Justice Van Devanter's opinion is perhaps the most important in the constitutional history of Congressional investigations, because he undertook to harmonize the conflicting strains of thought and adjust the competing pressures which had been in evidence in the Court's decisions ever since the *Kilbourn* case. The balance which Justice Van Devanter sought to achieve was embodied in the two generalizations which are the heart of his opinion: [69]

> One, that the two houses of Congress . . . possess not only such powers as are expressly granted to them by the Constitution, but such auxiliary powers as are necessary and appropriate to make the express powers effective; and the other, that neither house is invested with "general" power to inquire into private affairs and compel disclosures, but only with such limited power of inquiry as is shown to exist when the rule . . . just stated is rightly applied.

Expanding upon these propositions, Justice Van Devanter declared that, should the power be "abusively and oppressively exerted" by Congress, then the "limitations and restrictions" discussed in the *Kilbourn* and other cases pointed the way in which a witness might obtain relief from the courts. In the case of banker Daugherty, however, there was no such problem. Congress was not endeavoring to try the Attorney General, and its power to investigate official conduct was well recognized. "The only legitimate object the Senate

* Over two years passed between the argument and the decision of the case in the Supreme Court.

could have in ordering the investigation was to aid it in legislating; and we think the subject matter was such that the presumption should be indulged that this was the real object," as Senator Walter George had indicated on the floor when the resolution for an investigation was adopted. Banker Daugherty, therefore, must answer to the committee.

Two years later, the Court reaffirmed these principles in a criminal case. In 1924, the Senate had directed its standing Committee on Public Lands to investigate the disposition of the naval oil reserves at Teapot Dome by the Interior and Navy Departments. The Committee called the oil magnate Harry F. Sinclair to testify concerning various contracts and leases at Teapot Dome to which he was a party, but Sinclair refused to answer the questions of Senator Tom Walsh on the ground that the whole matter was of exclusively judicial concern, and therefore beyond the Senate's legitimate range of inquiry. Thereafter Sinclair was convicted and sentenced * under the 1857 statute. The Supreme Court affirmed the conviction.[70] Justice Butler in his opinion followed Justice Van Devanter's reasoning in the *Daugherty* case, and declared that Naval oil reserves and their disposition were clearly a proper matter for Congressional scrutiny. Justice Butler took care, however, to emphasize the duty of the courts to protect individuals against "all unauthorized, arbitrary or unreasonable inquiries and disclosures in respect of their personal and private affairs."

And so by the end of the twenties the Supreme Court had arrived at a well-balanced and dispassionate view of the powers of Congressional investigating committees. The heat generated by the tense background of the *Kilbourn* and *Harriman* cases had been largely dissipated. The practical necessity of the "informing function" had been judicially acknowledged, and Congressional committees were unlikely again to encounter the same sort of blanket denial and defiance of their powers as had been attempted by Daugherty and Sinclair.

At the same time, the Court had shown no patience with and had repeatedly rejected the notion that Congress' investigative power,

* He was sentenced to three months' imprisonment and to be fined $500. For a man in Sinclair's financial circumstances the fine was, of course, ridiculously ineffective as a penalty.

any more than its law-making power, is immune from legal limitations or judicial review. Investigation was shown to be not an end in itself, but rather an ancillary, though necessary, aspect of legislative power.

A court, for example, has no general authority to force witnesses to testify; it has the power to do so only when the witness' testimony is needed to help dispose of the controversy which the court is called upon to determine. Equally, the investigative power of Congress or any other legislature extends only to matters which bear an intelligible relation to the legislative function. Respect for privacy and the rights of individuals against oppressive inquisition are fundamental to our way of life; the inroads of investigations must be limited to what is necessary to give the legislature the information it needs in order to discharge its functions. "The least possible power adequate to the end proposed" is the touchstone in determining whether an individual may be compelled to reveal matters otherwise private and protected from public disclosure.

If the world had continued to follow what appears in retrospect as the even and sunny course of the twenties, very likely the whole question of Congressional investigations might have been laid to rest by the *Daugherty* and *Sinclair* decisions. But the nation was about to undergo pressures and convulsions of unprecedented severity. The Great Depression, the New Deal, the spread of Black, Red, and Brown totalitarianism, World War II, the responsibilities of world leadership, the Atomic Age, and the Soviet menace broke like so many huge waves upon the institutions which America had developed in simpler times. Among these institutions, the legislative investigation was destined, under these violent blows of circumstance, to be used in ways and for ends quite unforeseen in 1929.

CHAPTER IV

THE ILLUSION OF INVESTIGATIVE OMNIPOTENCE

> *"The procedure of Congressional investigations should remain as it is. No limitations should be imposed . . . The power of investigation should be left untrammeled . . ."*
>
> —Professor Felix Frankfurter (1924)

> *". . . there is wide concern, both in and out of Congress, over some aspects of the Congressional power of investigation."*
>
> —Mr. Justice Felix Frankfurter (1953)

DESPITE THE CARE and emphasis with which the Supreme Court and numerous state courts [1] expounded and applied constitutional limitations on the investigations of Congress and the state legislatures, after 1930 the opinion grew ever more general that the legislative power of inquiry is substantially unlimited and beyond the pale of judicial scrutiny. This opinion, nurtured during the between-war years, has gradually hardened into a preconception which grips even the well-informed official or publicist, and which may be fittingly described as "the illusion of investigative omnipotence."

Current controversies over the behavior of our more notorious Congressional inquisitors—even the open warfare between Senator McCarthy and the Department of the Army that broke out during the winter of 1953-54—have not served to dispel the illusion, even amongst those who profoundly distrust the aims and methods of the Senator and his collaborators. Commenting on the bitter controversy over Brigadier General Zwicker's cross-examination by Senator McCarthy, the distinguished journalist Theodore H. White wrote: [2]

> . . . under the American system, there can be no question of Congress' right to investigate or question the Army it has called into being. Yet equally, there exists no safeguard but Congressional restraint to prevent such investigations from becoming a process that bit by bit may rust the inner structure of the Army—or reorient it entirely—until one of the fundamental institutions of American life is hollowed out and filled with military politicians whose resemblance to the *juntas* of Latin America may ultimately become more fact than fancy.

Now, it is true enough that Congress' right to investigate the Army is unquestioned, but the rest of this extraordinary statement exemplifies the illusion of investigative omnipotence in its most virulent form. To begin with, Congress did not call the Army into being; the Constitution called both the Congress and the Army into being, and provides that the President, not Congress, is the Army's Commander-in-Chief. And there is indeed—as we shall hereafter observe in greater detail [3]—a safeguard other than "Congressional restraint" against the disintegration of the Army which Mr. White rightly fears. That safeguard is presidential comprehension of the constitutional powers and responsibilities of his office, coupled with the will and skill to exercise the powers so as to fulfill the responsibilities.

The illusion assumes even more extreme forms. The well-known Washington journalist, Sidney Hyman, recently wrote that the Senate and the House have [4]

> . . . the right to investigate everything below the earth, on top of it, and in the heavens beyond . . .
>
> The wide latitude to investigate follows from the Constitutional grant to the Congress of "all legislative power." Hence there can be no Constitutional limit on the exercise of this power, nor, by implication, on the exercise of any investigative activity incident to the use of that power.

How Mr. Hyman could have arrived at these views, unless he has totally overlooked what the courts have consistently said about the limitations of the investigative power or is unwilling to credit them with meaning what they say, passes all understanding. During the seventy-five years since the *Kilbourn* case, the constitutional and legal limits on investigative power have been stated and restated by the Supreme Court of the United States and the highest courts of New York and Illinois in opinions by Supreme Court Justices Field (1887),[5] Harlan (1894),[6] Holmes (1908 and 1924),[7] White (1917),[8] Van Devanter (1927),[9] Butler (1929),[10] Brandeis (1935),[11] and Sutherland (1936),[12] Judge Rapallo of the New York Court of Appeals (1885),[13] and Justice Duncan of the Supreme Court of Illinois (1920).[14]

As any lawyer knows, the social and political predilections of these ten jurists cover a very wide spectrum. What they have said has been categorical and emphatic enough, and it is certainly not judicial ambiguity that is to blame for the illusion of investigative omnipotence. How, then, did the illusion develop and gain currency?

Money Trust, Teapot Dome, and New Deal

In origin it was no illusion; it was indignation generated by the scandals of the Harding administration, and heightened by the obstacles thrown in the path of the committees most active in exposing the prevalent official corruption and maladministration.

When political stakes are high, words are hot. The investigational techniques of Senators Smith W. Brookhart, Burton K. Wheeler, and Tom Walsh were much criticized, especially by those whose political fortunes were jeopardized by the revelations. President Calvin Coolidge, in much less guarded language than that so far used by President Eisenhower, accused the investigators of breaking down the citizen's protection against "unwarranted search and seizure." The most patrician newspapers were the least restrained in their language: to *The New York Times* the probers were "assassins of character," while the *New York Post* called them "mud-gunners" and the *New York Tribune* dubbed Walsh and Wheeler "the Montana scandalmongers." All this was as nothing to the vituperation of the great jurist and foremost authority on the law of evidence, Dean J. H. Wigmore: [15]

> The senatorial debauch of investigations—poking into political garbage cans and dragging the sewers of political intrigue—filled the winter of 1923–24 with a stench which has not yet passed away. Instead of employing the constitutional, manly, fair procedure of impeachment, the

Senate flung self-respect and fairness to the winds. As a prosecutor, the Senate presented a spectacle which cannot even be dignified by a comparison with the persecutive scoldings of Coke and Scroggs and Jeffreys, but fell rather in popular estimate to the level of professional searchers of the municipal dunghills.

These diatribes—one critic of the probes described them as the product of "a gigantic international conspiracy . . . of the internationalists, or shall we call them socialists and communists"—stimulated vigorous responses in defense of the investigations. In a powerful topical article in the *New Republic*,[16] the then Professor Felix Frankfurter of the Harvard Law School declared that the purpose of the critics (including Judge Elbert H. Gary, Senator George Wharton Pepper, and the President himself) was "to divert attention and shackle the future by suggesting restrictions in the procedure of future investigations." On the contrary, in Professor Frankfurter's opinion: "Nothing in the experience of the Walsh and Wheeler investigations reveals the need of changing the process or confining the limits of congressional investigations," and he concluded that:

> The procedure of congressional investigations should remain as it is. No limitations should be imposed by congressional legislation or standing rules. The power of investigation should be left untrammeled . . . The safeguards against abuse and folly are to be looked for in the forces of responsibility which are operating from within Congress, and are generated from without.

Ten days after this essay appeared, Judge Cochran handed down his judgment discharging Mally Daugherty from the Senate's custody, and thereafter more than two and a half years elapsed before the Supreme Court reversed Judge Cochran and ruled that Daugherty could be compelled to answer. In the meantime, two formidable historical analyses of the investigative power, by Professors James M. Landis and Charles S. Potts, of the Harvard and University of Pennsylvania Law Schools respectively, appeared in leading legal periodicals.[17] Both of these roundly condemned Judge Cochran's decision, and strongly advocated a broad power of investigation. Small mention was made of the responsibility of the courts to determine and apply the constitutional limits on the power.

Of course, it would be absurd to imagine that these scholarly articles made much of a dent on general opinion, in the Indian-summer prosperity and complacency of the late twenties. By 1927, when the Supreme Court reversed Judge Cochran, the Harding scandals were well-nigh forgotten, and the Brookhart-Wheeler committee had ceased to function; Mally Daugherty never was made to testify.[18] But the cumulative and ultimate effect of the Frankfurter-Landis-Potts writings, caviar to the general as they were, was very substantial, especially among the younger lawyers who came to prominence in government and private practice during the thirties.

Historical scholarship and political science were thus mobilized in support of the investigative power. In the meantime, other factors of a much less rarefied nature were working in the same direction. These were the forces and interests—the combination of midwestern agrarian "radicalism," the industrial labor movement, and "liberal" intellectualism which, for want of a better expression, is often referred to as the "liberal movement"—that brought about the trend toward social and economic legislation, the beginnings of which we have already noted in connection with the Interstate Commerce Act of 1887. Investigation in order to expose economic and political abuses was a vitally important part of the movement, and although at first this was carried out principally by the Interstate Commerce Commission, it was obvious that Congressional investigating committees were far more powerful and flexible.

Iowa Grangers and New York textile workers have many but by no means all interests in common. The liberal interests were in conflict among themselves on a great many issues, and neither of the major political parties was their exclusive vehicle. In general, however, it was under Democratic administrations that liberal aspirations were converted into accomplishments. The Interstate Commerce Act was enacted during the first Cleveland administration and, while some regulatory measures date from the days of Teddy Roosevelt, the next major surge of social legislation came during Wilson's first term. The Federal Trade Commission, the Federal Reserve System, and—alas—the income tax, are all children of the Little New Deal that preceded the First World War. And it was during the dying months of the Taft administration, when the return to power of the Democrats appeared virtually certain, that the nation witnessed the first Congressional investigation conducted in the "grand manner" of modern times, and geared to the avowed purpose of proving and publicizing the need for major legislative enactments in new fields.

We have already referred to this inquiry by its popular title, the "Money Trust Investigation." [19] It was conducted by a subcommittee of the House Committee on Banking and Currency, under the chairmanship of Representative Arsène Pujo of Louisiana,* and the hearings it held are known today as the "Pujo Hearings," albeit Mr. Pujo was in fact a very minor character in the ensuing doings and dramatics. For the real director and principal actor was the distinguished and colorful New York lawyer Samuel Untermyer, one of the earliest in a long line of counsel to investigating committees which includes such forensic giants as Charles Evans Hughes, Owen J. Roberts and Ferdinand Pecora, and of which Roy Cohn is a recent if hardly the crowning example. Mr. Untermyer dominated his committee so completely that the members maintained silence throughout the hearings, leaving the questioning of the witnesses exclusively in their counsel's hands.

The resolution calling for the Money Trust investigation (introduced by Lindbergh's father, then a Representative) recited charges that control of the country's railroads and industries was "rapidly concentrating in the hands of a few groups of financiers in the city of New York." It referred to the need for "remedial legislation," and spelled out a great many matters for full investigation in order "to gather the facts bearing on the aforesaid conditions and charges." Practically all of the leading financiers of the time were summoned to face Mr. Untermyer's fire—George F. Baker of the First National Bank, Jacob Schiff of Kuhn, Loeb & Company, the railroad magnate James J. Hill, and, of course, J. P. Morgan the elder, acknowledged monarch of Wall Street, then seventy-five years old and within a few months of his death.

The encounter between Morgan and Untermyer had aroused much anticipation.[20] It was productive of no unpleasantness, but certainly revealed Morgan to the public as the *rocher de bronze* of

* Forty years ago is a long time, but it may seem less so to the reader if he will note that the other members of the subcommittee included the late Robert L. "Muley" Doughton of North Carolina, who only recently retired from Congress, and James F. Byrnes of South Carolina, leading figure of the Roosevelt era and presently the Governor of that state.

a private financial authoritarianism, not the less uncompromising for that it was already outmoded. The following exchange is characteristic of Morgan's terse repulses of Untermyer's efforts to endow the public with a legitimate concern for the way business is done in Wall Street: [21]

MR. UNTERMYER: [*sarcastically*] This consolidation and amalgamation of systems and industries and banks does not look to any concentration, does it?

MR. MORGAN: No, sir.

MR. UNTERMYER: It looks, I suppose, to a dispersal of interests rather than a concentration?

MR. MORGAN: Oh, no; it deals with things as they exist.

MR. UNTERMYER: It is for the purpose of concentrating the interests that you do amalgamate, is it not?

MR. MORGAN: If it is desirable, yes. . . .

MR. UNTERMYER: If it is good business?

MR. MORGAN: If it is good business for the interests of the country, I do it.

MR. UNTERMYER: But, Mr. Morgan, is not a man likely, quite subconsciously, to imagine that things are for the interests of the country when they are good business?

MR. MORGAN: No, sir.

MR. UNTERMYER: You think that you are able to justly and impartially differentiate, where your interests are concerned, just as clearly as though you had no interest at stake, do you?

MR. MORGAN: Exactly, sir.

But others among the moguls were less intransigent.* Notably Mr. George F. Baker, second only to Morgan in the financial hierarchy, admitted that the degree of concentration had reached a dangerous point, and other bankers were even more outspoken. The committee's report recapitulated this and much other evidence, and proposed a great many legislative measures—including regulation of stock exchanges, prohibition of interlocking bank directorates, separation of banking from underwriting, and compulsory competi-

* One witness—Mr. George Henry of Salomon Brothers—refused to answer questions relating to the participants in an underwriting syndicate, on the ground that his relationship to them was a confidential one. Mr. Henry was indicted under the 1857 statute, but died before the case came to trial.[22]

tive bidding for railroad securities—designed to remedy the worst abuses and check the trend toward concentration. Although twenty years were to elapse before the passage of legislation in line with these recommendations, the Pujo committee was the prototype of and set the pattern for the great legislative investigations of the New Deal years.

The New Deal was born of the Great Depression and, to the naked eye of the ruined investor and the unemployed apple-seller, the depression had been touched off by the stock market panic of October, 1929. Who was responsible for the crash? Were the Wall Street bankers to blame?

Clearly, a Senate investigation was the way to find out. In December, 1931 (by which time Congress was controlled by Democrats and "progressive" Republicans), the Senate Committee on Banking and Currency opened an inquiry into the circumstances surrounding the practices of the big investment houses in floating foreign bond issues, many of which were by then in default. Spurred by the revelations of this limited inquiry, the following spring (1932) the Senate gave the same Committee the comprehensive task of investigating "the buying and selling . . . of securities upon the various stock exchanges."

Early in 1933 the Committee appointed Ferdinand Pecora as its counsel. The ensuing bank failures and "holidays" aroused public indignation to fever pitch, and intensified popular interest in the Pecora disclosures. No investigation before or since matches the Stock Exchange Investigation for sustained and sensational publicity, for the economic significance of the disclosures, or for prompt results by way of important and far-reaching regulatory legislation.[23]

Just as during the Pujo hearings, the rulers of Wall Street beat a path to Washington and the witness stand. "Jack" (the younger J. P.) Morgan was small part of his father, but the name was still mighty; news promoters exploited his appearance by plopping a midget on his knee for snatch photographs that appeared on practically every front page the next day. For the House of Morgan, Thomas W. Lamont and George Whitney were now the chief spokesmen, while other "star" witnesses included Albert H. Wiggin and Charles Mitchell of the Chase National and National City Banks, the fabulous and ephemeral railroad promoter Oris P. Van Sweringen,

Otto Kahn of Kuhn, Loeb & Company, and Richard (George's brother) Whitney, President of the New York Stock Exchange.

With unemployment and destitution stalking the nation, the impact of the testimony was enormous. Country bankers and small investors were vastly intrigued by a series of lectures, under compulsion of subpoena, on the operations of security flotation "syndicates" and stock market "pools," in the course of which they learned how favorable publicity about a security could be bought and paid for and what was likely to happen when the managers "pulled the plug." Ruined customers of National City and Chase National brokers were not pleased to discover that Mr. Mitchell's salary as president of the former had been doubled ($100,000 to $200,000) amid the debris of the depression, or that Mr. Wiggin had sold short the stock of his own bank. Hollow laughter and sardonic cartoons greeted the news that J. P. Morgan had not for several years paid any income tax, and that other men of great wealth had escaped that unpleasant obligation by wash sales of securities in order to record a tax loss.

But certainly what bit deepest into the public mind was the famous Morgan preferred list of friends who had been cut in on the ground floor for a slice of the profits on security flotations—friends that included Cabinet officers, top officials of the Republican and Democratic party organizations, generals, a Supreme Court justice, and ex-President Calvin Coolidge. Under Pecora's cross-examination, Morgan partner George Whitney's knowledge of public men and affairs proved lamentably and miraculously scanty. Did not John J. Raskob (of the preferred list for Allegheny Corporation stock) have something to do with the Democratic National Committee? "I don't follow such things," said Mr. Whitney. Wasn't Silas Strawn the president of the United States Chamber of Commerce? "I really don't know," said Mr. Whitney. What had Mr. Whitney done with his own Alleghany shares? "I really don't know. I sold some, but I do not remember how many." Mr. Pecora thereupon showed from the records that Mr. Whitney had sold in 1929 at a profit of about $230,000.[24]

Preferred lists, pools, syndicates, plug pullings, "balloon ascensions," and poisoned financial news might at other times have been mere nine-day sensations. But in an atmosphere of bread-lines and closed banks, the demand for federal regulation of the Stock

Exchange grew overwhelming. The immediate fruits of the Stock Exchange Investigation were the Securities Act of 1933, the Securities Exchange Act of 1934, and the Public Utility Holding Company Act of 1935.

This legislative harvest was impressive enough, but the long-range effects, by way of the power of example, were profound indeed. The thirties were years of expanding federal power, exerted to counteract the blight of economic depression. Observing the immense success, both psychological and legislative, of the Pecora hearings, the leaders of the Roosevelt administration rightly concluded that investigations were unsurpassed as a means of formulating and awakening popular support for the governmental measures they had in mind.

Thus it came about that the political dynamism of the New Deal was reflected in the many and far-reaching investigations which were instituted and conducted, no less than in the laws that were enacted and the new agencies that were created. Under Senators "Young Bob" LaFollette and Elbert Thomas, the Senate Committee on Education and Labor studied unfair labor practices, while Senator Hugo Black was looking into lobbying, Senator Burton K. Wheeler into railroad reorganization and finance, and Senator Gerald Nye into the munitions industry and methods of preserving American neutrality in the event of foreign wars. At Congressional behest, the Federal Communications Commission conducted long investigations of the American Telephone & Telegraph Company and of radio network broadcasting, and the Securities and Exchange Commission scrutinized security-holders' protective committees and investment trusts.

From 1933 to 1938 Congress, working in close collaboration with the White House and the executive departments, continued to pour out regulatory statutes and to authorize the investigations which were the arsenal of the New Deal program. By no means was this social revolution accomplished without bitter opposition and recrimination, but the critics were overborne by the unusual conjunction of a strong and vigorous Congressional majority and an aggressive and politically expert President, working in harmony for positive objectives.

But what of the Constitution and the courts? Most of the federal judges had been appointed by Republican presidents, and over the past fifty years the Supreme Court had rendered many decisions invalidating federal and state laws, which boded ill for the constitutionality of such major New Deal statutes as the National Recovery and Agricultural Adjustment Acts. The first two years of the New Deal passed without any major legal test of its basic legislation, but apprehension of an unfavorable judicial reception was rife, and in the minds of many the courts loomed as a dangerous obstacle to the effectuation of the national will.

In 1935 and 1936 these fears were abundantly realized. During those two years the Supreme Court handed down no less than eleven judgments holding federal statutes unconstitutional.[25] In January, 1935, the "hot oil" provisions of the NRA were disapproved, and in May the entire act fell and the famed "Blue Eagle" was done to death. To the dismay of the liberals, the decision was unanimous; Justices Brandeis, Stone, and Cardozo denied the New Dealers even the consolation of a dissent. In another unanimous judgment that month the Frazier-Lemke Amendments to the Bankruptcy Act were knocked out, and the retirement provisions of the Railroad Retirement Act were invalidated by a five-to-four decision. At the next term of Court the following winter several minor statutes were set aside, and two more heavy blows were struck when the Agricultural Adjustment and Bituminous Coal Conservation Acts were declared unconstitutional, each by six-to-three decisions in which Justices Brandeis, Stone and Cardozo dissented.

Anger and dismay suffused the Administration. The NRA decision provoked President Roosevelt to sarcastic comparisons with "the horse-and-buggy days," and soon after his second inauguration he presented to Congress the famous court-packing plan, in order to obtain an "infusion of new blood in the courts." It aroused violent opposition, failed of Congressional approval, and caused a breach between the Capitol and the White House that never was completely healed. Nevertheless, the President achieved his immediate purpose in large part, for the Court proceeded to uphold, by five-to-four majorities, the Wagner Labor Relations Act, the Social Security Act, and the minimum wage law of the State of Washington. And then, within the next two years, three of the "conservative" justices (Van Devanter, Sutherland and Butler) resigned or died, and the new appointees (Black, Reed, and Murphy) gave the Court a "liberal" majority.

Such were the circumstances that created the climate in which the illusion of investigative omnipotence flowered. While the Supreme Court was invalidating the NRA, the AAA and other statutes, Senators Black, LaFollette, Wheeler, Nye, *et al.* were using the investigative process to pave the way for new and sweeping assertions of federal legislative power. The temper of the New Deal was favorable to the untrammeled use of Congressional inquiries to attain social ends thought desirable, and hostile to the intrusion of judicial power to check the Congress, whether on legislation or investigation bent.

Ironically enough, at the very time the Supreme Court began the series of eleven decisions invalidating the statutes, it handed down another opinion on the contempt power of Congress which, if sufficiently noted, would have gone far to dispel the illusion. A Senate committee investigating the Postmaster General's contracts for ocean and air mail carriage called a Washington lawyer, William P. MacCracken, Jr., who declined to produce the pertinent records without the consent of his clients. While he was communicating with them, some of the files were destroyed, and the Sergeant-at-Arms of the Senate arrested MacCracken for contempt.*

When the case reached the Supreme Court early in 1935, the only question was whether Congress could punish a past and completed contempt. The subpoenaed files that had been destroyed could not be restored, and therefore MacCracken's arrest could only be justified as punishment rather than compulsion.

The Court unanimously upheld the Senate's power under these circumstances to arrest MacCracken. However, Mr. Justice Brandeis' opinion took full account of the argument that Congress might abuse and oppressively exercise its contempt power. The revered Justice's reply was direct and categorical; any such fears had been [26]

> . . . effectively removed by the decisions of this Court which hold that assertions of congressional privilege are subject to judicial review.

In the hurly-burly of New Deal and World War this assurance

---

* This is almost if not quite the last occasion in which Congress has sought to enforce its investigative power by its own process for contempt, rather than by criminal prosecution under the 1857 statute.

passed almost unnoticed. But today, in the mounting constitutional crisis precipitated by current Congressional inquisitions, consequences of the utmost gravity turn upon whether the Court will pick up or will dishonor Mr. Justice Brandeis' promissory note.

The Wind Shifts: Loyalty and Subversion

The federal Wages and Hours law, enacted by Congress during the summer of 1938, was the last major piece of New Deal legislation. The wounds inflicted by the court-packing plan and by President Roosevelt's futile efforts to "purge" Democratic dissident Senators, together with Republican gains in the 1938 Congressional elections, shattered the powerful White House-Capitol majority combination that had rolled Roosevelt's bills through the three preceding Congresses. In 1939 the outbreak of the Second World War diverted the nation's attention from problems of domestic economy and, although the Roosevelt era was but half spent, the New Deal was at an end.

With the passing of the New Deal, its great sequence of legislative investigations likewise fizzled out. As America's involvement in the war deepened into outright belligerency, and the Administration confronted the gigantic problems of mobilization and the conduct of worldwide hostilities, Congress reverted to its traditional and congenial task of investigating the policies and performance of the executive branch.* Some committees jumped in with gleeful war whoops, others—notably the Senate's Special Committee to Investigate the National Defense Program, under Senator Truman's chairmanship—with the sober and responsible purpose of focusing criticism in such a way as to assist the executive branch in surmounting the staggering obstacles and solving the grave issues of the war years.

But in the meantime a quite different type of Congressional inquiry reappeared for almost the first time since the Know-Nothing investigative miscarriages. The decisive day was August 13, 1938, the second day of public hearings conducted by the Special Committee

* A few investigations of the executive branch did take place during the New Deal years, most notably those of the Tennessee Valley Authority, for airing the Morgan-Lilienthal disagreements, and of the National Labor Relations Board under the chairmanship of J. Warren Madden. These were conspicuous as exceptions to the general tenor of investigations at the time.

for the Investigation of Un-American Activities. The witness was John P. Frey, President of the Metal Trades Department of the American Federation of Labor, and the burden of his testimony was that the Congress of Industrial Organizations and many of its affiliated unions were Moscow-dominated, and that many of the CIO leaders were Communists. The press reaction was sensational, and the long-term effects enormous. As Kenneth Crawford put it: [27]

> It was probably the very success of the Frey testimony as an experiment in publicity that awakened Dies and his associates to a full realization of the potentialities of the political gold mine that they had struck. From Frey on it was catch as catch can with no holds barred.

To be sure, there had been a few previous investigations in the fields of loyalty and subversion.[28] During the First World War, the Senate had authorized an investigation of "the brewing industry and German propaganda," and in February, 1919, this was broadened to cover "any efforts being made to propagate in this country the principles of any party exercising . . . authority in Russia . . . and . . . to incite the overthrow of the government of this country or all governments, by force or by the destruction of life or property, or the general cessation of industry." * Public hearings were held at which such diverse personalities as John Reed, Catherine Breshkovskaya, and Ambassador David Francis testified about the nature of the Russian Revolution. The hearings and the Committee's report make interesting reading today, but attracted little Congressional attention and were soon forgotten.

There were no further investigative forays in this direction until 1930, and from that year until the late forties it was the House rather than the Senate that took the lead. Accusations by Grover Whalen (then Police Commissioner of New York City) that the Amtorg Trading Corporation was disseminating Communist propaganda stimulated the House to establish, in May, 1930, the Fish Committee "to investigate Communist propaganda in the United States and particularly in our educational institutions" and related matters. The witnesses included Whalen, Father Coughlin, Father Edmund Walsh, William Green, Roger Baldwin, William Z. Foster,

* This action was caused by two "pro-Bolsheviki" rallies at Poli's Theater and the old Masonic Temple in Washington, on February 2 and 3, 1919.

and numerous Amtorg officials. The caliber of the Committee's report may be gauged from its proposals that Treasury agents be dispatched to Russia (not then recognized by the United States) to study the use of forced labor, and that Russian manganese exports be embargoed. Representative Nelson of Maine submitted a dispassionate and well-documented minority report which, after the lapse of twenty-four years, is still worth reading. He concluded: [29]

> . . . The communist is a zealot, supremely self-confident, and as devoid of compassion as an executioner. Whether we like it or not, theirs is the old crusading spirit, modernized with the instruments and methods of today. All this gives them a strength and influence all out of proportion to their numbers, a kind of strength possessed, perhaps, by no other organization in this country. . . . we should proceed to put needed reforms into effect sanely and sensibly, without hate, or haste, or hysteria. Freedom should be the rule in America rather than restrictive legislation, and we should approach with reserve the consideration of any criminal statutes that seek to fetter the operation of the human mind or to encroach in the slightest degree on those rights guaranteed in our Constitution to the lowliest individual in the United States.

No action was taken on the Fish report, but from that time on the House received a flood of bills and resolutions dealing with subversion, sponsored by Fish, Martin Dies of Texas, Samuel Dickstein of New York, and others.* However, it was not Stalin but Adolf Hitler and the Nazis, who had seized power in Germany in January, 1933, that furnished the stimulus for the next investigation of this type. In March, 1934, the House adopted Dickstein's resolution for an investigation of [30]

> . . . (1) the extent, character, and objects of Nazi propaganda activities in the United States, (2) the diffusion within the United States of subversive propaganda that is instigated from foreign countries and attacks the principle of the form of government as guaranteed by our

* A curiosity of this period was the House Resolution of March 29, 1934, to investigate charges of Dr. William Wirt that New Deal officials were fomenting a "deliberately planned revolution." Speaking in support of the resolution, Congressman Hamilton Fish named in this group Jerome Frank and Fred Howe of the AAA, Henry T. Hart of PWA, Ambassador William S. Dodd, and such other figures as Rex Tugwell, Leo Wolman, Paul Douglas, James M. Landis, and Sidney Hillman. The House committee of inquiry rejected Wirt's charges as wholly unsubstantiated.

Constitution, and (3) all other questions in relation thereto that would aid Congress in any necessary remedial legislation.

Under the chairmanship of Congressman John McCormack of Massachusetts, the hearings were generally dignified; the Committee's report and recommendations, submitted in 1935, were modest and reasonable. The proposal that propaganda agents of foreign governments be required to register was later embodied in the McCormack Act of 1938.

But all of this was much less than enough to satisfy Fish, Dies and Dickstein, and in May, 1938, the House adopted a resolution sponsored by Dies, and patterned closely on the Dickstein resolution of 1934, quoted above. The only changes were the substitution of "un-American" for "Nazi" in the first clause, and the addition in the second clause of "un-American" and a provision covering propaganda "of a domestic origin." So amended, this language has been preserved unchanged ever since, as the House directive prescribing the work of its Un-American Activities Committee.

Martin Dies, sponsor of the resolution and chairman-to-be of the committee, spoke soberly and well in support of the investigation. "I believe all depends on the way the committee is handled," he declared, and went on to recognize "that a committee constituted or composed of men whose object is to gain publicity, or whose object it is to arouse hatred against some race or creed . . . might do more harm than good." However sincere these sentiments they did not, in the opinion of most observers, survive the opening hearings and the dazzling sunburst of publicity that followed Mr. Frey's assault on the CIO leaders. The next witness, a patrioteer named Walter Steele, charged 640 organizations and thousands of individuals with being "communistic," and impugned as dangerously "internationalist" such organizations as the Boy Scouts, the Campfire Girls, and the Catholic Association for International Peace. The cold civil war had begun.

In the fall of 1938 Dies demonstrated that his inquiry had sharp political teeth. A Republican member of the committee, J. Parnell Thomas of New Jersey, began to use the committee files in support of his charge that the New Deal was communistic. Investigating "sit-down strikes," the committee was made the vehicle for a violent attack on Frank Murphy, then running for re-election as Governor of Michigan. Murphy was defeated, as was Elmer Benson (another object of hostile testimony) in Minnesota.

Even before the anti-Murphy hearings, Dies had fallen afoul of Secretary of the Interior Harold Ickes, who had applied the sharp edge of his tongue when J. B. Matthews brought Shirley Temple's name into his testimony before the committee. But attacks on Democratic governors were no laughing matter, and President Roosevelt issued a long statement to the press denouncing the committee and defending Governor Murphy. It was the opening of bitter strife between the White House and Congressional loyalty inquisitions that has flickered and flared ever since, for sixteen years and under three presidents.

Throughout 1939 the Dies Committee continued at an intense level of activity, and public hearings continued to be held, though less frequently, during 1940 and the first half of 1941. Some of the hearings were well-conducted and produced useful information. The report published at the end of 1939, dealing especially with shifting organizational policies and individual views at the time of the Nazi-Soviet pact, was widely praised; *The New York Times* called it an "astonishingly able and balanced document." But its high quality would have been less "astonishing" if the mainstream of the committee's activities had been less turbulent, and free from the pollution of irresponsible accusations and headline hunting. Such at least was the verdict of most articulate observers and commentators. One of the committee members, Congressman Jerry Voorhis, later described the committee as "a political instrument of definite conservative bias," and the author of a thorough and reasoned analysis of its record and accomplishments, Father August R. Ogden, concluded: [31]

> This study of the Special House Committee for the Investigation of Un-American Activities indicates that the said Committee was neither an ideal nor a desired means of exposing subversive activities. It did not wholly fail in its endeavors, but, with different methods and better procedure, it could have performed far more efficient service. Hence, without disparaging the accomplishments of the Committee or impugning the motives of any person connected with it, it must be admitted that the history of the Committee reveals it to have failed in its essential

purpose. It stands in the history of the House of Representatives as an example of what an investigating committee should not be.

Pearl Harbor, and America's resultant preoccupation with foreign wars in which Russia was a major ally, brought about something of a lull in the cold civil war. The Un-American Activities Committee remained in existence, but few public hearings were held after August of 1941, and the committee's records and staff became increasingly the personal appurtenances of Mr. Dies. But this first of the Congressional Grand Inquisitors was on increasingly shaky political homeground; in 1944 it became apparent that he could not be renominated for Congress, and he withdrew from the race. His committee expired, and Dies himself vanished into political oblivion.*

When the Seventy-Ninth Congress assembled on January 3, 1945, not more than one member of the House would have given a plugged nickel for the chance that the investigation would be continued. The one member, however, was the resourceful and obdurate John Rankin of Mississippi, and he saluted his returning and unwary colleagues with an amendment to the routine opening-day resolution to carry over the rules of the preceding Congress, calling for the addition of the Un-American Activities Committee to the list of permanent committees of the House. Mr. Rankin correctly inferred that many members, despite their lack of enthusiasm for the inquiry, would be reluctant to commit themselves in opposition, and when he called for a record vote, his amendment carried, albeit the vote was close.[32]

Thus did the Un-American Activities Committee, by dint of Rankin's parliamentary dexterity, rise phoenix-like from the ashes of its late disregard, and attain the exalted status of a standing committee of the House, and the only such with permanent subpoena powers. The committee's record during the next two years, however, was unimpressive enough. Only a few days of public hearings were held, and none of major moment, although the calling in 1946 of officials of the Joint Anti-Fascist Refugee Committee resulted in the refusal of its chairman, Dr. Edward K. Barsky, to turn over

* The oblivion lasted eight years. In 1952 Dies was again elected to Congress as Representative-at-Large from Texas.

the organization's books and records, and thereby led to his prosecution under the 1857 statute, as we will soon examine more particularly.[33]

Following the Republican victory in the 1946 Congressional elections, Congressman Parnell Thomas, who had served on the committee from its inception, became chairman, while holdovers Mundt, Rankin, Wood and Peterson were joined by new members Richard Nixon, John McDonnell, and Richard Vail. Mr. Robert Stripling was appointed to head the staff, and the committee promptly announced a broad, eight-point program of activities:

1. To expose and ferret out the Communists and communist sympathizers in the Federal Government.
2. To spotlight the spectacle of having outright Communists controlling and dominating some of the most vital unions in American labor.
3. To institute a countereducational program against the subversive propaganda which has been hurled at the American people.
4. Investigation of those groups and movements which are trying to dissipate our atomic bomb knowledge for the benefit of a foreign power.
5. Investigation of Communist influences in Hollywood.
6. Investigation of Communist influences in education.
7. Organization of the research staff so as to furnish reference service to Members of Congress and to keep them currently informed on all subjects relating to subversive and un-American activities in the United States.
8. Continued accumulation of files and records to be placed at the disposal of the investigative units of the Government and armed services.

The 1947 hearings started off with avowed Communists such as Eugene Dennis and prominent suspects such as the Eisler brothers,* but the temper and targets of the inquisitors were soon revealed by their efforts to pin culpability for Hanns Eisler's admission to the United States in 1939 on Mrs. Eleanor Roosevelt, Sumner Welles, and George Messersmith. The lull in the cold civil war had come to an end.

Major operations began in October of 1947, and the *mise-en-scène,*

* As a by-product of the Eisler hearings, the committee subpoenaed Leon Josephson, accused of helping Gerhart Eisler to obtain a passport fraudulently. Josephson defied the committee's power and refused to be sworn, and like Barsky, thereafter became the subject of an important criminal proceeding.[34]

appropriately enough, was Hollywood, although the public hearings were held in Washington. "Friendly" witnesses such as Robert Taylor, Adolphe Menjou, and Mrs. Ginger Rogers *mère* endeavored to support the advance proclamations of Parnell Thomas and Rankin that Hollywood was ridden with Communists and its pictures suffused with Communism. Efforts to establish the latter point centered on such films as *Song of Russia* (Metro-Goldwyn-Mayer 1943), *Mission to Moscow* (Warner Brothers 1943), *North Star* (Sam Goldwyn 1943), and *None but the Lonely Heart* (RKO 1944).

The testimony was something less than convincing, and the committee's efforts to establish that the White House or "Roosevelt officials" had requested Hollywood to make pro-Soviet pictures came to nothing. But during the course of the investigation eight Hollywood screen writers (including John Howard Lawson, Dalton Trumbo, and Ring Lardner, Jr.), a director (Edward Dmytryk) and a producer (Adrian Scott)—the so-called "Hollywood Ten"—refused to answer questions concerning their membership in the Communist Party. Except that the witnesses did not invoke the privilege against self-incrimination under the Fifth Amendment, and relied instead on the free speech guarantee of the First Amendment and other legal challenges to the committee's power to conduct the inquiry, it was an episode destined to be paralleled many times from then to the present.*

In 1948 the Committee had another big year. Most of its hearings grew out of testimony given by Elizabeth Bentley and Whittaker Chambers, both self-confessed former Communists, each of whom named a number of individuals as having been Communist Party members while serving as government employees during the thirties and early forties. The aftermath of their testimony included the trial and conviction for perjury of Alger Hiss and William Remington, the Harry Dexter White accusations of recent political notoriety, and the denials, admissions, or refusals to testify of numerous individuals named by Chambers and Miss Bentley.

The election of 1948 returned the Democrats to control of the House; Parnell Thomas departed and John Wood of Georgia resumed the chairmanship. Nixon stayed on, but all the other members

---

* The "Hollywood Ten," like Josephson and Barsky, were prosecuted and convicted under the 1857 statute. These proceedings are discussed hereinafter.[35]

were new, among them Harold Velde of Illinois, chairman-to-be in 1952. The Committee held more hearings than before, but its great days were over. In a manner of speaking the Un-American Activities Committee fell victim to its own success in hitting the headlines. Such a powerful engine of publicity and political pressure could no longer remain the exclusive property of one House committee.

For the Senate was about to reassert itself as the investigating chamber *par excellence*. In 1946 it had established a permanent Senate Investigating Subcommittee,* chaired by Senator Homer Ferguson of Michigan, and it was to this group that Miss Bentley had told her story about Remington and others prior to her appearance before the Un-American Activities Committee. Then in 1950 the late Senator Patrick McCarran, Chairman of the Senate Judiciary Committee, established a Subcommittee on Internal Security, with himself as chairman. Soon the McCarran Committee embarked on a spectacular investigation initially focused on the Institute of Pacific Relations, but later embracing the whole range of American policy in the Orient.

By this time, of course, the cold civil war had spread far beyond the confines of Congressional committee rooms. In California, Washington and several other states the legislatures had established their own local versions of the Dies and McCarran committees. Universities and public school systems were in the throes of the loyalty oath issue, and the entertainment world was riven by "blacklists" and "red channels." Throughout American life the power of accusation grew by leaps and bounds. On February 9, 1950, Senator McCarthy delivered his now famous speech at Wheeling, accusing as Communists an uncertain number of unnamed State Department employees. Not until nearly three years later did McCarthy head an investigating committee, but during that time he made himself into a powerful and deeply-feared national figure by the sheer volume and boldness of his accusatory capacities.

And so this investigatory edifice, of which Fish, Dickstein and Dies laid the cornerstone, has grown to formidable proportions. The Un-

* This subcommittee of the Committee on Expenditures in the Executive Departments was established pursuant to the Legislative Reorganization Act of 1946. Subsequently the nomenclature was changed to the Permanent Subcommittee on Investigations of the Committee on Government Operations.

American Activities Committee carried on under Mr. Velde, apparently more than a little resentful at being thrown in the shade in spite of its seniority as first-comer. The Internal Security Subcommittee, since Senator McCarran gave way to Senator Jenner, and so far as the public hearings reveal, has concentrated on education and the United Nations, and is apparently the Eisenhower administration's preferred vehicle for political hearings, such as the Brownell-Hoover testimony on the Harry Dexter White case. Both Velde and Jenner have been outdistanced by the fast-moving and uninhibited McCarthy who, during the two years of his career as a duly authorized and fully armed Senatorial inquisitor, left his calling card at the Voice of America, the State Department, Fort Monmouth, the General Electric Company, Harvard University, the Columbia Broadcasting System, and the Pentagon Building, to mention only the more prominent recipients.

To be sure, there are and have been throughout these recent years numerous other Congressional inquiries dealing with a great variety of subjects other than loyalty. Indeed, the Senate "interstate crime" investigation, under the chairmanship of Senator Estes Kefauver, was probably the most widely publicized of all legislative inquiries to date. Others, such as the King Committee's investigation of internal revenue frauds and abuses, have been both intriguing and fruitful.

But it is not these other inquiries that people have primarily in mind today when they speak of the "problem of Congressional investigations." For it is the "loyalty-subversion" investigations, above all, that have helped to bring our domestic tensions and suspicions to fever pitch.

Illusion and Dilemma

The activities of the Dies Committee enraged the leaders of the Roosevelt administration and antagonized Democrats and liberals generally. However, and despite the deep political wounds inflicted as in the case of Governor Murphy, an aroma of burlesque, extravaganza, and sheer "corn" emanated persistently from the committee's proceedings, and many of its critics adopted disdainful rather than purposefully hostile attitudes. When Shirley Temple was accused by J. B. Matthews of endorsing a French communist newspaper (*ah*!

ces enfants terribles), and Congressman Joe Starnes sniffed suspiciously at the loyalty of Christopher Marlowe ("Put in the record that he was the greatest dramatist in the period . . . immediately preceding Shakespeare," replied Hallie Flanagan), it was easy to conclude that the entire affair was maddening, to be sure, but basically a farce. And soon everyone was much more worried about the Japanese fleet and the Wehrmacht than about Martin Dies.

Under these circumstances, New Deal hostility to judicial intervention, and faith in the legislature as a sufficient sole repository of freedom, were not noticeably shaken. In 1941, for example, the late Robert H. Jackson, then the Attorney General, wrote that: [36] "The vice of judicial supremacy, as exerted for ninety years in the field of policy, has been its progressive closing of the avenues to peaceful and democratic conciliation of our social and economic conflicts."

The illusion of investigative omnipotence thus survived the Dies hearings and the war, and now confronts us [37] at a time when the character and objectives of the principal investigations have shifted and, however they may be described or assayed, lie close to the roots of freedom. Many of those who supported investigations in support of social and economic legislation during the thirties are deeply disturbed by what they regard as totalitarian tendencies in the loyalty and subversion inquiries of the last few years. But if Senators Black, LaFollette, and Wheeler were entitled to press their investigations without interference by the courts, why should not the same apply to Senators McCarthy and Jenner, and to Representatives Dies and Velde?

No wonder there has been confusion and even schizophrenia among the liberals who find themselves impaled on these dilemmic horns. "By and large liberals have believed in giving wide scope to Congressional committees," wrote Mr. James Wechsler,[38] editor of the *New York Post*, soon after he had given a striking demonstration of how completely he believed this himself. Summoned to testify before Senator McCarthy's subcommittee (ostensibly because books that he had authored were in Information Service libraries overseas), Mr. Wechsler, when questioned about the personnel and policies of his newspaper, contended that the inquiry was "a clear invasion of what used to be considered the newspaper's right to act and function independently," and invoked the aid of "newspapers throughout the country" and of the American Society of Newspaper Editors in branding the inquiry a threat to freedom of the press. But Mr. Wechsler's insistence that his questioning on editorial matters was unconstitutional remained a moot issue, for he answered all questions put to him by Senator McCarthy, despite his belief that many of them were "far beyond the scope of the committee's authorized inquiry."

Why? Because, in Mr. Wechsler's judgment, his refusal to answer any question—no matter how irrelevant or outrageous and even if far outside the range of the committee's power—would be misunderstood and unfavorably regarded by the public: "I had resolved . . . that silence was suicidal in dealing with McCarthy."

Senator McCarthy also asked Mr. Wechsler to submit a list of all persons that he had known as Communists during his membership in the Young Communist League many years earlier. If the committee's inquiry was unauthorized, and, as Mr. Wechsler believed, a violation of the constitutional guarantee of freedom of the press, could the disclosure of other people's names be justified? Particularly when the period in question was so long ago that errors due to lapse of memory were quite possible, and many of the individuals had renounced communism so that the submission of their names "could do them irreparable harm and serve no conceivable national interest"?

Genuinely and deeply troubled by these considerations, Mr. Wechsler submitted the list of other people's names demanded by Senator McCarthy, telling the Senator that "I . . . submit the list because I do not propose to let you distort or obscure the clear-cut issue of freedom of the press involved in this proceeding." This decision was in no way due to timorousness, as the record of his testimony abundantly shows. Rather it reflects the adhesive and bitter quality of the dilemma, born of the illusion of legislative omnipotence, in which he felt himself gripped: [39]

> . . . The notion of placing any names in his hands was repugnant to me, yet to refuse to do so meant to abandon the argument or let him shift it to ground most favorable to him.
>
> I am an active anti-communist; McCarthy wanted to prove that I must be pro-communist because I am opposed to McCarthy. I did not see how I could persuade my perplexed countrymen that unwillingness to entrust such a list to McCarthy was different from the now stereo-

typed refusal of communists to answer questions before Congressional committees. . . .

. . . I found myself weighing rival expediencies. It was wrong to expose others to McCarthy's wickedness, but it was equally wrong, in my judgment, to embrace the principle that a former communist should tell nothing to anyone. Whatever I did was bound to be misconstrued.

But the irony of the shifting investigative winds is not limited to liberals like Mr. Wechsler. Many conservative Republicans are increasingly uneasy, among them the Chairman of the Chase National Bank, Mr. John Jay McCloy—formerly High Commissioner in Germany, President of the World Bank, Assistant Secretary of War, and before the war a prominent Wall Street lawyer—who recently declared that "Some of those televised hearings . . . take on an approach to the political spectacle that the totalitarians have followed in the public trials that have become a routine part of their governmental pattern." Who is to blame for this? According to Mr. McCloy: [40]

This tendency is not a new phenomenon. There exists a tendency among certain liberal elements in our population to view it as new merely because the shafts for the first time have been directed at them. It is the old matter of whose ox is gored. If the liberals had been more expressive when the so-called Congressional investigations of the thirties were studiously violating personal rights and when business was the target, there would have been less likelihood of excesses in this day and age. The conduct of the Munitions Investigations, for example, in those days was about as one-sided and biased an affair as anything anyone today can point to; yet liberal opinion in this country was then disposed to remain silent . . .

In other words, the current excesses of Congressional inquisitors are facilitated by the unqualified support given to the New Deal investigations by the liberals, whose chickens are now coming home to roost. In this charge there is enough substance to make it worth pondering. But however one assays it, the converse is equally to be reflected upon. The financial, industrial and other magnates who were the objects of Congressional scrutiny in the twenties and thirties did not lack for "conservative" lawyers to represent them before the committees or to denounce the investigations in print.[41] Today the witnesses before the several committees inquiring into subversive activities—whether because the issues are different, the fees smaller, or the likelihood of unfavorable publicity greater—find few "conservative" counsel available to defend them or to question publicly the tactics and purposes of the investigators. In short, no one lacks an ox for goring, and the roosting chickens are no more the exclusive property of liberals than of conservatives. Sharper tools than these shopworn labels must be used to lay bare the true issues.

Dispelling the Illusion: The General Nature and Limits of Investigative Power

And so it has come about that the illusion of investigative omnipotence, originally fostered by the New Dealers, is now propagated by those of a sharply contrary political outlook. Today it is the McCarthys, Jenners, and their supporters who proclaim the all-powerful beneficence of the Congressional investigation, and hail it as the most effective single weapon in our anti-Communist arsenal.

Now, if there is any one matter that this narrative should have made abundantly clear, it is that we must not allow general conclusions about Congressional investigations to be determined by our personal approval or disapproval of individual investigators, be they Senator McCarthys or Ferdinand Pecoras.* If such considerations are governing, then the whole problem does indeed become, as Mr. McCloy put it, "the old matter of whose ox is gored."

In a tense and dangerous world, America seeks to remain at peace, to grow and prosper, and to preserve its freedoms. Of these three the last is not the least, and by "freedoms" we mean a government which utilizes the intelligence and reflects the informed will of the citizenry, and a society in which the individual enjoys the safeguards of the Constitution, including the Bill of Rights. From time to time these

* In his excellent study of the Dies Committee, published in 1952,[42] Professor Carr has written: "A generation later the shoe was on the other foot. The Un-American Activities Committee and other Congressional committees had liberals sadly disturbed and inclined to look to the courts for help, whereas conservatives found it convenient to argue that it would be unfortunate were the courts to attempt to check these committees." In 1936, in a book critical of the Supreme Court's power of judicial review of Congressional action,[43] Professor Carr asked rhetorically, ". . . if the people want to preserve our fundamental constitutional principles . . . why suppose that an *elective* Congress would flout the wishes of the people?" And he answered, with magnificent simplicity, "It isn't logical."

freedoms—as well as peace and prosperity—are threatened or obstructed. Today all three are gravely endangered by the power of the Soviet bloc, exercised in conjunction with the totalitarian and repressive ideology of modern Communist doctrine.

In part the American citizen must meet the Communist menace by his own acts and thoughts and the power of example, and in part the peril can only be countered by governmental, including Congressional, action. Here, if anywhere, it is vital that Congress have the means of fully informing itself, so that its measures may be enlightened and effective. And this is equally true whether the particular facet of the menace is an external military or diplomatic threat, or is the internal danger of Communist espionage and conspiratorial infiltration into positions of power and influence.

Within the sphere of Congressional responsibility, therefore, the nature and activities of the Communist conspiracy are an appropriate subject for investigation, just as were the Indians, the "trusts," stock exchange manipulations, and the men who corrupted the Harding administration. If the investigative power is sometimes abused, it still does not follow that the function should be abolished, any more than the passage of stupid and harmful statutes justifies elimination of the law-making function. Neither is the circumstance that the loyalty investigations are injuring or embarrassing numerous individuals, in itself, a ground for condemning these inquiries. Of course, the injury should not be malicious, wanton, or careless, as it often is today. But it is idle to imagine that public investigations of controversial political and social problems can be carried on without harming anyone. Certainly Messrs. Albert Wiggin and Charles Mitchell [44] did not emerge unscathed from their encounters with Mr. Pecora. It is impossible to probe deep in the vital tissues of society without drawing blood and leaving scars.

But the first six words of the preceding paragraph—"within the sphere of Congressional responsibility"—are as important as the remainder. If the question be asked what are the limits of Congressional power to investigate the Communist conspiracy and other threats to constitutional government, the answer is that those limits are to be ascertained, as the Supreme Court has repeatedly declared, from the Constitution itself. Neither the New Deal nor the Soviet menace have altered the constitutional separation of powers or abolished the Bill of Rights. It behooves us, therefore, to dispel the illusion of investigative omnipotence without more ado, and see to it that the loyalty inquiries are carried on for the traditional purpose of all legislative inquiries—to inform the legislature—and not to aggrandize Congress, usurp the responsibilities of the executive and judicial branches, or maintain an inquisitional surveillance of the individual citizen which would fundamentally change the American way of life and make a mockery of the constitutional guarantees.

What are the limits imposed by the Constitution on the *power* of Congress, and thereby on the informing function? They are of three basic types, and they protect the other branches of the federal government, the states, and the individual citizen against unauthorized Congressional action. In constitutional parlance these are called (a) the separation of legislative, executive, and judicial powers, (b) the delegation of specified powers to the federal government and the reservation of all other powers to the states and the people, and (c) the Bill of Rights and other constitutional guarantees of individual liberty.

What all this comes to is that Congress, whether it is investigating or enacting laws, must confine itself to the legislative sphere; it cannot usurp the functions of the President or of the courts. Furthermore Congress, like the President and the federal judiciary, can exercise only those powers delegated to the federal government by the Constitution, and cannot invade the sphere reserved to the states. Finally, certain areas of individual liberty, which Congress must respect, are marked out in the Bill of Rights. And the same or comparable three limitations are applicable to the state legislatures.

Even if a particular inquiry is within the range of power of Congress, a refusal to reply may be justified by a claim of *privilege,* and this claim may likewise be advanced on behalf of another branch of the government, or of a state, or of an individual. The idea of privilege has grown up in the law in order to protect certain relationships or statuses from destruction by what might be termed "indecent exposure." Thus a party to a lawsuit may not be made to testify about what he and his own lawyer have said to each other; the privacy of medical consultations and the sanctity of the confessional are also frequently protected. If it were otherwise, the confidential and advisory relation between lawyer and client, doctor and patient, priest and communicant might be badly torn and ultimately destroyed. In general, it has been thought that the interests of society are better served by safeguarding these relationships than by extracting disclosures which would jeopardize them.

In this day and age, the best-known individual privilege is that a person cannot be required to give evidence against himself. This is known as the "privilege against self-incrimination," and is embodied in the Fifth Amendment to the Constitution, and nearly all of the state constitutions. The courts have ruled that this privilege may be claimed by witnesses before legislative investigating committees, in which event they may not be required to answer questions if the answers would tend to incriminate them. Many witnesses have "pleaded the privilege" when called before the Congressional loyalty inquiries and have thereby and involuntarily acquired from Senator McCarthy the sobriquet "Fifth Amendment Communist." To what extent this appellation is warranted, we will examine later in some detail.[45]

There are areas of privilege in the government as well as in private life. In the judicial sphere, the deliberations of judges in their chambers, and of grand juries, are good examples. Here, again, society places a high value on the security and secrecy of these consultations, so that there may be uninhibited exchange of ideas, and the participants may think aloud without fear of being called to account for the inevitable errors in a process of trial and error. The executive branch, too, may claim that it is not required to plan and conduct all of its operations in a goldfish bowl. The scope of executive privilege to withhold matters from Congressional scrutiny has been a troubled spot in relations between the legislative and executive branches ever since the time of George Washington. Today the issue is at least as important as it has ever been, and lies at the root of Senator McCarthy's explosive controversies with the Army and other executive departments.

Ordinarily, therefore, a Congressional investigating committee's authority to require a witness to give information will depend upon questions of *power* and *privilege.* There is a third problem that may arise, however, and that is *procedure*—the method by which the committee pursues its inquiry. May the witness be grilled in secret, or can he insist on a public hearing? If in public, how public? Is a witness not only under a duty to testify, but to lay bare his story before a television camera? Is he entitled to be accompanied by counsel? What recourse, if any, do government officials have when they are belabored by Congressional inquisitors, as when Senator McCarthy told General Zwicker that he was unfit to wear the uniform on which were sewn the General's decorations for heroism in the service of his country? To most of these questions the courts have as yet given answers which are inconclusive at best, and it is far from certain that they will regard such matters as within the realm of judicial review.*

These are the three p's—power, privilege, and procedure—of legislative investigatory authority. One other factor should be borne in mind as we examine them, and consider their contemporary political significance. That is the matter of the form in which these issues may be presented to the courts. At the present time, it is usually by way of prosecuting a recusant witness under the statute of 1857.[47] In other words, a witness who refuses to testify because he honestly believes that the committee has no legal power to make the inquiry must stake his judgment on the outcome of a criminal prosecution. If the courts decide that the witness was mistaken in his belief, be it ever so honest, he is likely to suffer a jail sentence. Needless to say, this does not encourage witnesses to test these complicated and doubtful questions of investigative authority. But other methods of court review of that authority have been used in the past, and it is well worth considering, as we will,[48] whether or not one or more of them might now be preferable to criminal prosecution.

I have been speaking in terms of judicial review of investigatory committee actions and practices, but of course it would be a serious mistake to look to the courts as the only or even the principal means of checking investigative abuses. In the interests of harmony, the courts have always—and rightly—been reluctant to interfere with the actions of a coordinate branch of the government. As Justice Frankfurter has recently pointed out,[49] "Self-discipline and the voters must be the ultimate reliance for discouraging or correcting such abuses."

---

* For certain purposes, discussed hereinafter, a distinction must be borne in mind between the usual type of legislative investigation, and certain special types conducted by the legislature which are nonetheless quasi-judicial in nature.[46] The latter include such proceedings as impeachment, and passing upon the election and qualifications of members of the legislature.

But the pillars of society are mutually self-supporting. When the judge firmly and dispassionately declares the law, it enables the private citizen, the legislator, and the government official better to combat lawlessness and develop sound public policies and practices. And it is to this end that the ensuing chapters are directed.

CHAPTER V

INVESTIGATIONS AND THE SEPARATION OF POWERS

> *"The legislative department is everywhere extending the field of its activity, and drawing all power into its impetuous vortex . . . it is against the enterprising ambition of this department that the people ought to indulge all their jealousy and exhaust all their precautions."*
>
> —James Madison in "The Federalist" No. 48 (1788).

> *"Boys, now you've had an education!"*
>
> —Brigadier General Ralph Zwicker (1954).

ADDRESSING HIS junior fellow-officers as he emerged from a session of Senator McCarthy's subcommittee in February, 1954, Brigadier General Ralph Zwicker gave vent to the sentiment quoted above. He had just felt the painful impact of Congressional power, wielded without respect or restraint, and he did not like it. He conveyed his feelings about the matter to the Secretary of the Army, and the result was that a long-simmering struggle for power between Congress and the executive branch erupted into a violent explosion.

General Zwicker was probably unaware that his unrehearsed and succinct observation was simply a modern-dress version of what James Madison had said, with elegant prolixity, 166 years earlier, during the discussions accompanying ratification of the Constitution. But we cannot fully grasp the meaning of the great constitutional crisis of 1954 unless we know what steps Madison and his contemporaries took, when they framed the Constitution, to curb the "enterprising ambition" of the legislature, against which he warned so forcefully.

The very first words of Article I of the Constitution are: "All legislative powers herein granted shall be vested in a Congress of the United States . . ." It is from this provision that the investigative power of Congress is implied, for nowhere does the Constitution mention it. Yet these are also limiting words, for Article II declares that "The executive power shall be vested in a President of the United States . . . ," and Article III that "The judicial power of the United States shall be vested in one Supreme Court, and in such inferior courts as the Congress may from time to time ordain and establish."

Far from being an unpremeditated design, this separation of federal power into legislative, executive, and judicial packages was deliberately intended by the Fathers of the Constitution to carry out, in line with Montesquieu's teaching, "the political maxim, that the legislative, executive, and judiciary departments ought to be separate and distinct" as "an essential precaution in favor of liberty." Indeed, Madison in supporting ratification was obliged to argue strongly against the criticism that the separation prescribed in the Constitution was not sharp enough.[1]

In determining the bearing of the separation of powers on Congressional investigations, two distinct concepts must be kept in mind. The one is *usurpation*, and the other *obstruction or destruction*. It is not the President's function, under the constitutional scheme, to enact statutes or appropriate public moneys; if he undertook to do these things, he would be *usurping* the legislative functions of Congress. It is certainly the President's constitutional duty and authority to command the army. But if he should exercise this authority by ordering the troops to prevent Congress from assembling or to coerce the Supreme Court so as to dictate its decisions, that would *obstruct or destroy* the legislative or judicial functions. And the same two concepts likewise apply, needless to say, to legislative and judicial action.

Congress vs. the Courts

It is clear that a legislative investigation cannot be condemned as a usurpation of the judicial sphere merely because it resembles a trial, in the sense that charges of misconduct against individuals or institutions are involved. This, in fact, was the very purpose of the Commons' investigation in 1742 of Sir Robert Walpole's administration of the Exchequer, and of the first Congressional investigation, involving General St. Clair. Granted that the efforts of legislative committees to fix individual responsibility for official malfeasance are often maladroit, nevertheless the power is there.

When it is plain that *official* conduct is the real subject of scrutiny, therefore, the inquiry will be treated as within the legislative sphere, even when the subject is so individual or specific that the resemblance to a trial is very marked. As long ago as 1885, for example, the New York courts upheld the power of the State Senate to investigate accusations of corruption leveled by the Union League Club against the head of the Department of Public Works in New York City.[2] Much more recently the Massachusetts Legislature's investigation of the granting of a pension to Boston policeman Oliver B. Garrett was likewise sustained.[3]

In the *Kilbourn* case, however, the Court did not treat the government's monetary claim against Jay Cooke as sufficient to make the subject of the inquiry "official" rather than "private." * Yet the claim arose out of the Secretary of the Navy's deposit in the London branch of the bankrupt bank. Suppose the House, instead of describing Jay Cooke and the "real estate pool" as the subject of its inquiry, had specified the Navy Department and its policies with respect to selecting depositaries of government funds? Would not such phrasing have given the inquiry the necessary "official" aspect, and could not the House investigating committee have then extracted full information about Jay Cooke's financial affairs, including Kilbourn's testimony about the "real estate pool" in which Cooke was a participant? Whether or not persuasive to Mr. Justice Miller in 1880, it is quite possible that today's courts would find sufficient legislative purpose

* A similar decision was rendered in New York in 1889.[4] Repairs to the Capitol at Albany, under a contract, aroused charges of exorbitant profits, and an investigating committee (chaired by Hamilton Fish, father of his current namesake) requested the Western Union office in Albany to turn over telegrams received by the contractor and subcontractor. The manager of the office refused, and was jailed for contempt. The court freed him, saying that no legislative object was in view, and that all further questions under the contract were judicial in nature.

in this more adroit wording, and that a modern Kilbourn might come off a jailbird instead of an innocent and aggrieved citizen.

But we may test the principle by a more extreme case which is still a real one. During the eighteen-nineties a Scottish-born religious enthusiast, John Alexander Dowie, arrived in Chicago and founded there an evangelical sect called the Christian Catholic Apostolic Church in Zion. A man of strongly patriarchal, not to say tyrannical, disposition, Dowie in 1900 established on the Lake Michigan shore north of Chicago a theocratic community known as Zion City. Several thousand of his followers built homes on land allotted to them under "leases" terminating in the year 3000, with stipulations ensuring observance of the sect's tenets: [5] "Zion City will tolerate no breweries, no saloons, no drug or tobacco stores, no physician's or surgeon's offices, no theaters, no gambling places, no dance halls, no secret lodge rooms, no keeping or selling of swine's flesh." Faith healing, literal and "infallible inspiration and sufficiency of the Scriptures" (from which was drawn the conclusion that the world is flat), and the Second Coming proved a combination of great magnetic power; money poured into Dowie's hands, industries developed in Zion City, and a veritable monotheocracy sprang up.

By 1905, Dowie's financial irresponsibility had brought the venture to the brink of failure. He suffered a stroke, was deposed as "General Overseer and First Apostle," and in 1906 Judge Kenesaw Mountain Landis appointed a receiver for the Zion industries and ordered the election of a new General Overseer. Dowie's successor, Wilbur Glenn Voliva, rehabilitated Zion City and ruled over it for the next thirty years.

But the *outré* and promotional aspects of the cult increasingly drew criticism. In 1919 a resolution was introduced in the Illinois legislature to investigate Zion City as a "blot upon the State of Illinois," on charges that Voliva "has been enticing . . . citizens of this and other states to invest large sums of money in leases of land in said city and in other Zion enterprises" under "leases pretending to extend over a period of a thousand years" and by means of a "pretense to secure and inveigle the moneys and property of innocent persons under the guise of a false and fictitious religion."

In the preachings of Dowie and Voliva there was a strong denunciatory strain. "ANARCHY-LAWLESSNESS—IN THE ILLINOIS

STATE LEGISLATURE" screamed the headlines of the Zion City *Theocrat* over a text of which the following is a fair sample: [6]

> The chief instigators and criminal conspirators of this proposed unconstitutional, illegal, anarchistic, and lawless investigation are the same bunch of porch-climbers, deep-dyed criminals, election thieves and tally sheet mutilators, whom we have fought for the last thirteen years, and whom, metaphysically speaking, we have pulverized to powder, so that today all they can do is to whine and writhe and lie . . . They have been defeated in the courts, and in their dying struggle they have turned to the State Legislature. . . . We have yet to find one man or woman in all of Zion's ranks who does not laugh heartily at this last foolish move of the Devil and his imps; and, like one hundred other moves made by the Devil and this same bunch to mar and to destroy Zion City, it will prove to be a veritable boomerange [sic] to those who started it.

Anarchists and porch-climbers the hapless legislators were probably not, but Voliva's accusation of lawlessness, in the sense of unconstitutionality, was fully upheld by the Supreme Court of Illinois.[7] Voliva's lawyers brought a taxpayer's suit against the State Treasurer to restrain him from disbursing state funds appropriated for the expenses of the investigating committee. The Illinois court sustained the suit, and held that the investigation was unconstitutional, under the doctrine of separation of powers. Speaking for the court, Justice Warren W. Duncan pointed out that all the charges against Voliva's church involved past conduct, and there was no apparent purpose bearing on future legislation. Therefore, the investigation was clearly an "invasion of the province of the judiciary," because the legislature had no power to investigate "for the purpose of instituting prosecutions, for the aid and benefit of a grand jury in finding indictments, or for the purpose of intentionally injuring or vindicating any institution or individual." In conclusion, Justice Duncan warned that:

> If the rights of private individuals and private institutions could be invaded by the legislature in that manner, their reputation and their character and their business would be greatly endangered if not entirely destroyed, and they would not have or enjoy in such public investigations their constitutional right of answering and making a defense to such charges, however false they might be.

Thus Mr. Voliva and his flock prevailed over the Devil and his imps, and there was rejoicing in Zion City. In this particular case, I believe, their cause was righteous and the court's decision a just one. If Voliva's solicitation of funds on the representation that the world is flat amounted to selling a man the Brooklyn Bridge, why, that was for the courts to decide. Many years earlier, Judge Rapallo of the New York Court of Appeals had made the same point in broader terms: [8]

> An investigation . . . merely intended to subject a party or body investigated to public animadversion, or to vindicate him or it from unjust aspersions, where the legislature had no power to put him or it on trial for the supposed offenses . . . would not, in our judgment, be a legislative proceeding, or give to either house jurisdiction to compel the attendance of witnesses or punish them for refusing to attend.

But the broader implications of all this are far from clear. Zion City was incorporated as a city under the laws of Illinois. Suppose there had been a legislative inquiry into the laws governing municipal corporations, and especially into the question whether experience with the "theocratic" regime in Zion City indicated any need for new legislation to prevent abuses? As in the case of our parallel suppositions in connection with the *Kilbourn* case, it would appear that, under a more broadly-phrased resolution of inquiry, the legislature could require the same information which the court held beyond its reach under the resolution as actually drawn.

Where private individuals are concerned, accordingly, the problem of legislative usurpation of the judicial function comes down to a question of *purpose*. In the case of the Volivites, the court was unable to detect any investigative purpose other than to subject them to "public animadversion" or to "vindicate" them. A Congressional investigation for the exclusive purpose of determining whether Harry Bridges should be deported, or whether Professor Furry is loyal or disloyal, or whether Louis Budenz has sincerely abandoned Communism, would probably be held unconstitutional for the same reason.

But if Congress announces a legitimate legislative purpose for the investigation—whether it be by way of information-gathering for law-making, or surveillance of the executive branch—then these and similar matters, so far as they are pertinent to that purpose, may be inquired into. Of course, Congress cannot adjudicate the deportability of Bridges, or determine the loyalty of Furry or Budenz. But as part of a general legislative inquiry it can elicit facts which bear closely on those issues, and there is no way to prevent investigating committees from publishing reports in which opinions and "conclusions" are set forth.

By the same token, alas, investigating committees may abuse their powers by using a general inquiry as a "cover" for proceedings which really have no purpose other than to broadcast accusations and otherwise subject individuals to "public animadversion." Nevertheless the courts will give the legislature the benefit of the doubt,[9] and the only sure cure for such abuses is by political action based upon the corrective pressure of enlightened public opinion.

Most Congressional investigations today are carried on under authorizing resolutions of great breadth, containing explicit assertions of legislative purpose. As long as these resolutions are drafted with reasonable skill, I think it unlikely that we shall again see an entire investigation—as in the Cooke-Kilbourn and Voliva inquiries—invalidated on the ground of usurping judicial functions.

The fate of the Cooke and Voliva investigations does, however, illustrate a principle which is of major importance today. That is that the doctrine of separation of powers is not only a basic element of our governmental structure, *but is also a protection to the individual citizen.** Accordingly, if Congress (or, for that matter, the executive branch) acts outside its allotted sphere in such a way as to damage an individual, the courts may give him relief.

In other words, Mr. Voliva was entitled to have any criminal charges against him determined by a court, and not by a legislative committee. A more recent illustration may be drawn from the recent Senate investigation of charges of subversion in the Army Signal Center at Fort Monmouth. Addressing a witness who had pleaded the privilege against self-incrimination Senator McCarthy "asked": [10] "Julius Rosenberg was convicted as a spy and executed. From your

* In this aspect, therefore, the separation of powers becomes part of the problem of individual liberties in relation to investigations, discussed in the next chapter.

refusal to answer you apparently engaged in the same type of espionage [sic]. Do you feel you should be walking the streets free—or have the same fate as the Rosenbergs?" In all probability the courts would hold that such an effort [11] to convert a legislative inquiry into a trial of criminal charges violates the doctrine of separation of powers, and that the witness (quite apart from the privilege against self-incrimination) could not be required to answer.

Turning from usurpation to obstruction or destruction of the judicial function, we are chiefly concerned with the privilege attaching to the deliberations of judges and juries. A few years ago the Grand Jury of Merrimack County in New Hampshire examined certain activities of the Public Service Company of New Hampshire, particularly with reference to possible perjury committal by its officers when testifying before the state Public Service Commission. A motion was then made in the Senate of New Hampshire, proposing a secret session to question members of the Grand Jury on why they had instituted their inquiry, and whether, in their opinion, there was any evidence of criminal conduct.

Now, it has long been the rule that the deliberations of grand juries are privileged against disclosure—every grand juror takes an oath of secrecy. Accordingly, the Senate called upon the Supreme Court of New Hampshire for an opinion on the question whether, despite the oath, the Senate could lawfully require the jurors to disclose their deliberations. The Supreme Court answered decisively in the negative,[12] observing that "The legislative power to investigate is not absolute," and concluding: "It is not considered necessary in aid of the investigatory power that grand jurors should violate their oath of secrecy . . . by voluntary or compulsory disclosure of their votes, deliberations or opinions expressed in the grand jury session."

In other words, exercise of the legislature's investigatory power in this instance would have destroyed a traditional and vital element of the judicial process. In all probability the same would be true of efforts to force disclosure of judges' deliberations.[13] This has never been decided by formal decision of a court, but in June, 1953, seven federal district judges in California declined to testify under subpoena before a subcommittee of the House of Representatives, on the ground that Congressional scrutiny of their handling of tax cases would violate the doctrine of separation of powers.[14]

Perhaps a different conclusion might be reached when Congress exercises its constitutional power to impeach and try federal court judges. But in its legislative sphere of action there is no reason for Congress to intrude into the jury room or the judge's chamber. The "informing function" can fulfill its purpose without being pressed so far that it threatens to break down these traditional and necessary judicial privileges. Fortunately, such efforts have so far been infrequent.

Congress vs. the Executive

As between the executive branch and Congress, however, friction and controversy have been the rule rather than the exception. Each has been powerfully armed by the Constitution against aggression by the other, but these arms can be used for offensive as well as defensive purposes. The executive branch could reduce Congress to a state of blind impotence by withholding all information about the state of the nation. The Constitution expressly requires the President to report to Congress on the state of the Union, and the investigative power is Congress' weapon with which to secure sufficient information for its legitimate legislative requirements. But that weapon, like the surgeon's knife, can be used to maim or kill instead of to expose and cure.

Over the years, the sharpest controversies have arisen in the sphere of executive privilege over military, diplomatic, and other matters of state. The courts have always recognized that the needs of private litigants for evidence to support their pleas and claims must give way before the requirements of official secrecy. In 1875, for example, the Supreme Court threw out a suit to recover money due under a secret contract for espionage between President Lincoln and a Northern spy,[15] on the ground that "the existence of a contract of that kind is itself a fact not to be disclosed." Two years later, the Governor of Pennsylvania was subpoenaed to appear before a grand jury and testify concerning deaths which had occurred during a Pennsylvania railroad strike. The Governor refused, and the grand jury asked the court to hold him in contempt. Declining to do so, the Supreme Court of Pennsylvania stated: [16]

> . . . We had better at the outstart recognize the fact, that the executive department is a co-ordinate branch of the government, with power to judge . . . what of its own doings and communications should or should not be kept secret, and that with it, in the exercise of these constitutional powers, the courts have no more right to interfere, than has the executive, under like conditions, to interfere with the courts . . .
>
> . . . the President of the United States, the governors of the several states and their cabinet officers, are not bound to produce papers or disclose information committed to them, in a judicial inquiry, when, *in their own judgment*, the disclosure would, on public grounds, be inexpedient . . . Thus, the question of the expediency or inexpediency of the production of the required evidence is referred, not to the judgment of the court before which the action is trying, but of the officer who has that evidence in his possession.

The administration of justice as between private litigants is important, and the public has an even greater stake in the just enforcement of the criminal law. Even so, governmental necessities may outweigh these considerations, so that official information may be withheld from the court, even if highly relevant. But does the same apply to a Congressional investigation? Here it is not merely the rights of individual litigants, or the fate of an individual accused, that is at stake. The legislative branch is asserting its need for information in behalf of the nation itself, so that the legislative power may be guided in its exercise by knowledge of what needs to be known. Can the executive pull down in the legislature's face the curtain of official secrecy?

This question, despite its transcendent political importance, has only once come before a court, and then but inconclusively. In 1951, an agency of the Massachusetts state government, the "development and industrial commission," retained a private firm to make an economic analysis of industrial conditions. Upon its completion, the Senate ordered a member of the commission (Mr. Del Monte) to appear at the bar and produce the report. Mr. Del Monte declined to give over the report, on the ground that the Senate's demand was an unconstitutional interference in executive affairs by the legislative branch. The Supreme Judicial Court of Massachusetts, however, upheld the Senate's power to enforce its demand for the report, if necessary by punishing the commissioner for contempt, saying: [17]

> If the legislative department were to be shut off in the manner proposed from access to the papers and records of executive and administrative departments, boards, and commissions, it could not properly perform its legislative functions. We are not dealing here with any question of diplomatic, military, or other secrets, involving the security of the State, or with any instance where for other sufficient reasons disclosure is forbidden by law.

The last sentence quoted reveals the limited nature of the decision. A survey of economic conditions in Massachusetts is a perfectly respectable document, but hardly to be classed with secret minutes of diplomatic conferences or military plans. Furthermore, Mr. Del Monte appears to have taken it upon himself to assert the executive prerogative. But if he had been acting under the Governor's express order to withhold the report, would the court have put him to the hard choice of disobedience or contempt?

Such questions have troubled our national government since its inception, as we have already observed in the story of General St. Clair.[18] When the House committee called upon Secretary of War Knox for the documents, Washington's immediate reaction was that "there might be papers of so secret a nature, as that they ought not to be given up," and after full consultation with his Cabinet the general rule was laid down that "the Executive ought to communicate such papers as the public good would permit, and ought to refuse those, the disclosure of which would endanger the public."

Broad and general as is that phrasing, it has stood ever since as the Executive's principle and policy when confronted with Congresisonal requests for official documents or testimony.[19] The St. Clair papers were delivered to the House committee, but four years later Washington refused a very insistent request by the House for the correspondence pertaining to a treaty with Great Britain.[20] In his reply to the House, Washington stressed the need for secrecy in discussions with foreign governments, and concluded: ". . . as it is essential to the due administration of the Government that the boundaries fixed by the Constitution between the different departments should be preserved, a just regard to the Constitution and to the duty of my office . . . forbids a compliance with your request."

In the years to come, Jefferson, Monroe, Jackson (thrice), Tyler (twice), Polk, Fillmore, Lincoln, Grant, Hayes, Cleveland, Theodore

Roosevelt, Coolidge, and Hoover (twice) encountered Congressional demands for information which they saw fit to reject. Secure and powerful in his relations with Congress during his first two terms, Franklin D. Roosevelt did not confront the problem until his third term, during which no less than six such requests were refused, and under Truman the issue was drawn to a still higher pitch of intensity. Although partisan politics have frequently generated these conflicts, it is apparent from the foregoing list that party affiliation has never affected the basic position of the Presidents, as expressed by William Howard Taft: [21]

> The President is required by the Constitution from time to time to give to Congress information on the state of the Union, and to recommend for its consideration such measures as he shall judge necessary and expedient, but this does not enable Congress or either House of Congress to elicit from him confidential information which he has acquired for the purpose of enabling him to discharge his constitutional duties, if he does not deem the disclosure of such information prudent or in the public interest.

How have the Presidents determined whether or not a disclosure would be "in the public interest"? Apparently on a case-by-case basis, and indeed in so delicate an area it is well-nigh impossible to lay down rules. On many occasions the request has pertained to confidential diplomatic or military matters,* while several have related to patronage or the removal of public officials. † Other Congressional demands were refused because they imputed misconduct to the President or his cabinet members. ‡ Most recently, the debate has centered on the availability for examination by Congressional committees of Civil Service Commission and Federal Bureau of Investigation dossiers on individuals.

---

* E.g., the Jay Treaty (Washington, 1796); conduct of naval officers (Monroe, 1825); Cherokee Indian negotiations (Tyler, 1843); acquisition of Sandwich Islands (Fillmore, 1852); despatches on defense of Fort Sumter (Lincoln, 1861); London Naval Treaty (Hoover, 1930); naval documents (Roosevelt, 1943); Pearl Harbor documents (Truman, 1945).

† E.g., removal of Surveyor-General Fitz (Jackson, 1835); list of federal employees appointed (Jackson, 1837); list of applicants for public office (Tyler, 1842); reasons for removal of 650 federal employees (Cleveland, 1886).

‡ E.g., list of executive acts performed at a distance from the Capitol District (Grant, 1876); list of companies in which Secretary of the Treasury Andrew Mellon was interested (Coolidge, 1924).

Clearly, the President cannot turn over documents to Congress so that Congress can then decide whether or not they should have been turned over. If there is an executive privilege to withhold information when disclosures would not be "in the public interest," then the President must be the one to determine in any particular case whether the public interest permits disclosure or requires nondisclosure. Just as clearly, this leaves open the possibility that the President may abuse his prerogative, especially in instances where the information would reflect unfavorably on him or his administration of the nation's affairs.

For these reasons, underlined by Congress' natural concern for its own prestige, the President's power to withhold information, in the face of Congressional insistence, has by no means gone unchallenged. The first serious conflict arose at the beginning of Grover Cleveland's first term, when the Democrats returned to power after twenty-five Republican years. Cleveland removed from office some 650 persons (*O tempora! O mores!*), and the Senate, still Republican-controlled, took a dim view of this when called upon to confirm Democratic successors to the Republican purgees. Things came to a head when Cleveland nominated a Democrat, Burnett, to succeed a Republican, Duskin, as federal Attorney in Alabama. The Senate Judiciary Committee requested the papers bearing on Duskin's removal, but the Attorney General refused, by Cleveland's direction, on the ground that "the public interest would not be promoted by compliance. . . ."

The majority report of the Judiciary Committee denounced the withholding of the documents, and took the flat position that either House could require the executive branch to submit any information it might request.[22] The Senate itself adopted a resolution condemning the Attorney General's action as "in violation of his official duty and subversive of the fundamental principles of the Government and of a good administration thereof." But Cleveland stood firm, and the long and bitter controversy ended in his victory when, despite the withholding, the Senate confirmed Burnett.

Sixty-two years later the same drama was enacted in modern dress. In March, 1948, the House Committee on un-American Activities released a report charging that Dr. Edward U. Condon, Director of the Bureau of Standards, was a "weak link" in national security, and called on his superior, the Secretary of Commerce, for Dr. Condon's personnel file, including FBI reports. Despite the issuance of a subpoena the demand was refused, and on March 13, 1948, President Truman issued his now-famous directive to all federal officials which, after calling attention to the Employee Loyalty Program, and "the long-established policy that reports rendered by the Federal Bureau of Investigation . . . are to be regarded as confidential," ordered that: [23]

> Any subpena or demand or request for information, reports, or files [relative to the loyalty of employees or prospective employees] received from sources other than those persons in the executive branch of the Government who are entitled thereto by reason of their official duties, shall be respectfully declined, on the basis of this directive, and the subpena or demand or other request shall be referred to the Office of the President for such response as the President may determine to be in the public interest in the particular case.* There shall be no relaxation of the provisions of this directive except with my express authority.

Simultaneously with the publication of the derogatory report on Dr. Condon, Representative Clare Hoffman of Michigan introduced a joint resolution: [25]

> Directing all executive departments and agencies of the Federal Government to make available to any and all standing, special, or select committees of the House of Representatives and the Senate, information which may be deemed necessary to enable them to properly perform the duties delegated to them by the Congress.

Any federal officer or employee who refused to furnish information so requested was to be liable to conviction for a misdemeanor and punishable by a fine not exceeding $1000 or imprisonment not exceeding one year, or both.

The Truman directive and the Hoffman resolution squarely raised the constitutional question. Had the resolution been adopted and enforcement attempted by punishment for contempt or criminal prosecution of federal officials who chose to obey the presidential directive rather than the Congressional resolution, the courts would

* Note the similarity to the conclusion of President Washington and his Cabinet in 1792 that [24] all executive documents, in whatever department, are "under the President alone."

have had to decide the issue of power between President and Congress.

As in Cleveland's time, it was the acrimony between a Republican-controlled legislative chamber and a Democratic presidential incumbent that drew the issue so sharply. The tense and bitter political feelings that lay behind the resolution are well exemplified by Hoffman's comment, in reply to the argument that such a measure had never been thought necessary through seventy-nine preceding Congresses, that: [26]

> Seventy-nine Congresses never found the Marshall plan to be necessary. Seventy-nine Congresses never found it necessary to give to other nations more than $80,000,000,000. . . .
>
> Never, during the existence of seventy-nine previous Congresses, has the Nation been confronted by a bureaucracy which was so egotistical, so arrogant, so defiant of the power of Congress as that which challenges the authority of the Eightieth Congress.

After vigorous debate, the House adopted the resolution by a vote of 219 to 152, with 70 members not voting. In the Senate it was referred to the Committee on Expenditures in the Executive Department, where it languished and died with the adjournment of Congress. Even if approved by the Senate, the resolution would have faced the certain prospect of presidential veto. It can hardly be said, therefore, that the resolution came close to enactment; nevertheless, its passage by the House amply demonstrated that the constitutional question was far from dead.

Support for what might be called the "Congressional" view is not confined to legislative halls. To be sure, no one contends that the President himself could be haled before a Congressional investigation, and few deny that presidential consultations and White House files are protected against disclosure. It may be recalled that during the hearings on General MacArthur's removal, General Bradley declined to describe his conversations on the matter with President Truman. Furthermore, if the presidential privilege is to be meaningful, it must certainly extend beyond the term of office, and protect ex-presidents so far as concerns the period of their incumbency.*

* In 1846, President Polk refused to comply with a request of the House of Representatives for vouchers and certificates for confidential expenditures through

Clearly, the privilege would afford no real protection to the President's confidential papers and discussions if it were washed out as soon as he ceased to hold office, and President Truman rightly asserted this position when the Velde Committee subpoenaed him in connection with the Harry Dexter White accusations by Attorney General Brownell.

But beyond the office of the President himself, there is much controversy. According to the "Congressional" view, the executive departments and agencies are mere creatures of the Congress, dependent on the legislative branch for their powers, for the appropriations that enable them to function, and indeed for their very existence.* The former Dean of the Harvard Law School, James M. Landis, wrote at the time of the Daugherty-Sinclair controversies: [27]

> Save for the few constitutionally organized departments of government, the administrative and executive agencies exist only by the will of Congress. Even the chief executive departments are all the work of the first and succeeding Congresses. No constitutional duty demanded their institution; no constitutional duty demands their continuance. Congress may abolish them at its pleasure, redistribute them, consolidate or divide them. . . . Congress does possess power to destroy the executive departments.

Such reasoning has led another legal scholar, Edward S. Corwin, to conclude that Congress could hold a Cabinet officer in contempt, should he defy a subpoena to produce official documents,[28] and was the basis of rhetorical questions asked by partisans of the Hoffman resolution in 1948: [29]

> Shall the Congress insist that departments created by it, dependent upon its will for existence, give to its committees the information necessary to enable it to act intelligently and wisely, or shall it permit its creatures to arbitrarily determine what information the Congress shall or shall not have? . . . If the executive departments . . . have authority to withhold some information from the Congress, do they not, by the same

the State Department which had been authorized by President Tyler in 1841, on the ground that it would be unwise if not unlawful for a president to "revise the acts of his predecessor and expose to view that which it had determined should not be 'made public.'"

* The Constitution mentions the Army and Navy and the "executive departments," but otherwise is silent on the structure of the executive branch.

> token, have power to withhold all information from Congress? . . . Should the departments be permitted to hide their errors and maladministration behind a cloak labeled "confidential" and thus defeat a needed remedy?

To these last two questions, the answer must clearly be "no." If the executive branch should attempt to "withhold all information" it would be abusing its privilege and threatening the very life of the legislative branch, and in such a constitutional crisis the Congress might well be justified in taking such corrective reprisals as lie within its very extensive powers. Nor is Congress without means of pulling the administration's dirty linen from underneath the "confidential cloak." But it does not follow from all this that Congress has absolute power, to which the President must bow, over all official documents, regardless of their character. If the shoe were on the other foot, surely Congress would vigorously resist any claim of power in either the President or the courts to require the revelation of its own secret consultations or records.*

Even if the problem is approached by formal constitutional logic, the argument drawn from Congress' admitted power over the funds and statutory authority of the departments appears superficial and unconvincing. Congress establishes and prescribes the jurisdiction of the lower federal courts, but it must set up the *kind* of courts contemplated by the Constitution—courts independent of Congressional dictation. It is the same with the executive branch.[30] Congress is not conferring a favor but discharging a constitutional duty when it creates and sustains the courts and executive agencies. Therefore it cannot set a price upon its acts by imposing conditions or restrictions which would destroy the constitutional scheme of things. The Constitution contemplates an independent executive branch and there-

---

* This very point was made in 1879 by Benjamin Butler, then Chairman of the House Judiciary Committee, and generally regarded as a vigorous partisan of Congressional power. George Seward, United States Consul General in China, had refused to turn over certain documents to a House committee, and Butler's report concluded (Rep. No. 141, 45th Cong. 3rd sess.) that: "The Executive is as independent of either house of Congress as either house of Congress is of him, and they cannot call for the records of his action or the action of his officers against his consent, any more than he can call for any of the journals and records of the House or Senate."

fore Congress, when establishing the departments and agencies, may not strip them of their constitutional endowment.*

The practical arguments against unlimited Congressional access to executive documents are even more compelling. So far as the current controversy centers on the personnel files of government employees, including investigative reports embodying miscellaneous accusations of varying reliability, the answer was given nearly 150 years ago by Thomas Jefferson. Requested by the House in 1807 to make available "any information in possession of the Executive, except such as he may deem the public welfare to require not to be disclosed" concerning Aaron Burr's conspiracy, Jefferson made a general report on the affair but withheld the documentary data, saying: [31]

> It is chiefly in the form of letters, often containing such a mixture of rumors, conjectures, and suspicions as renders it difficult to sift out the real facts and unadvisable to hazard more than general outlines. . . . In this state of the evidence, delivered sometimes, too, under the restriction of private confidence, neither safety nor justice will permit the exposing names. . . .

Equally, the administration of government, and especially the supervision of a large body of civil servants, requires constant investigation and leads inevitably to the accumulation of "rumors, conjectures, and suspicions" of the most diverse description. It is an inherent attribute of executive administration that it must retain a range of discretion over the publication of such information, as President John Tyler stated in 1843, perhaps better than anyone has since. Declining to turn over to the House of Representatives a confidential Army report on the Cherokee Indians, Tyler wrote: [32]

> . . . To be effective, these inquiries must often be confidential. They may result in the collection of truth or falsehood; or they may be incomplete, and may require further prosecution. To maintain that the President can exercise no discretion . . . would deprive him at once of the means of performing one of the most salutary duties of his office . . . and would render him dependent upon [a coordinate] branch in the performance of a duty purely executive.

Impertinence or malignity may seek to make the executive department the means of incalculable and irremediable injury to innocent parties

* All this was pointed out by President Grover Cleveland in 1886 in his message to the Senate during the Duskin-Burnett controversy.

by throwing into them libels most foul and atrocious. Shall there be no discretionary authority permitted to refuse to become the instruments of such malevolence?

What is true of personnel records and investigatory reports is doubly true of military and diplomatic secrets. Certainly Congress is entitled to be informed on these subjects as soon and as fully as is prudently possible. Certainly, too, a wise President will gladly join in arrangements for sharing secret information with Congressional leaders or committees of demonstrable discretion and trustworthiness. But there will always be matters that lie beyond these possibilities and must remain, for a long or short period of time, executive secrets.[33]

With the remarkable expansion of methods of warfare in recent years, this problem has grown in both complexity and significance. The critical importance of intelligence-gathering and scientific research, and the constant interplay of psychological and economic factors, have blurred the line between peace and war and between the civilian and the soldier. Many more soldiers than formerly are trained to understand and use secret implements of warfare. Hundreds of thousands of civilians are engaged in secret activities of the greatest military importance, whether at military laboratories such as Fort Monmouth or civilian agencies like the Atomic Energy Commission, the Central Intelligence Agency, and the Voice of America.

Congress is legitimately concerned with the efficiency of these agencies, including the trustworthiness of the men and women who staff them. Current preoccupation with the loyalty problem has heightened this concern. Nevertheless, Congressional scrutiny of these operations itself raises serious security problems. Last year a member of the House was excluded, because of questions raised concerning his background, from witnessing certain atomic tests to which other Congressmen were admitted. Yet it is a very delicate matter for any executive agency thus to discriminate among Congressmen, or even Congressional officials; witness the sultry and minatory displeasure voiced by Senator McCarthy's counsel, Roy Cohn, when refused admittance to a secret radar laboratory at Fort Monmouth.[34]

All of this calls to mind Juvenal's classic query, *Quis custodiet ipsos custodes*—who shall guard the guards themselves? Are the members and staffs of the Congressional loyalty investigating committees more or less trustworthy than the security agencies of the executive branch? It is well known that a number of ex-Communists have been employed by these committees, and that many others are in touch with their staffs, as sources and consultants. Is the discretion of the staffs, and the sincerity of conversion of these former Communists, beyond doubt? These questions must also be weighed in the light of our experience that the clashes between Congress and the executive branch are usually most violent when political passions are inflamed, and that those Congressmen who are most insistent to assert Congressional omnipotence are usually those who can least be relied on to rise above personal motives and ambitions in the use they might make of secret information.

In summary, I do not believe that the concept of unlimited Congressional access to executive information is either logical or practical. It may be that, within the literal wording of the Constitution, Congress, as Dean Landis said, "does possess power to destroy the executive departments." But this seems to me a highly conceptualistic and self-defeating interpretation. By the same token, each of the three branches can, by pressing its constitutional powers to the extreme, wreck the machinery of the other two. The system of checks and balances does not rest on philosophical absolutes so much as on common sense, and powers vested by the Constitution in the legislative, executive and judiciary alike are intended to be used to preserve and strengthen the Republic, and not as instruments of constitutional suicide.

We have so far examined the Congress-White House equation exclusively in terms of Congressional demands for secret information, because the conflict between investigative power and executive privilege has most frequently and significantly been focused on this issue. But of course it may arise in many other ways, and especially if an investigation is conducted in such a way as to threaten the President's ability to make his will felt and his orders obeyed through the vast federal bureaucracy. At times Congress has betrayed a penchant for usurping the President's administrative authority, as when the Legislative Reorganization Act of 1946 was under consideration in the Senate. Senator LaFollette proposed language contemplating Congressional "surveillance" of executive operations or, if this were thought too strong an expression, that the phrase "inspection and review" be adopted. But these proposals were forcefully challenged by Senator Donnell and others, who pointed out that words such as "surveillance" and "review" implied Congressional responsibility for and authority over the executive departments.* As a result of the discussion, the word "watchfulness" was substituted for "surveillance." [35]

In the course of these debates, Senator McClellan of Arkansas proposed to establish a joint committee of the two Houses to conduct a surveillance of the executive agencies, with power to summon by subpoena any federal employee and require him to give an account of his activities, and to examine any executive documents.[36] His proposal attracted little attention and was defeated. But that very year—1946—Senator LaFollette was defeated for re-election by Joseph R. McCarthy, soon to emerge as an implacable and ruthless foe of presidential power, and destined to launch so sharp an attack against the Executive that even Senator McClellan has had no stomach for it.

Senator vs. Commander-in-Chief

The effects of the constitutional crisis of 1954 are likely to be felt for some time to come, regardless of the political fate of the individual legislator who was its prime instigator. Its root causes long antedate Senator McCarthy's appearance on the national scene, and have aroused intense popular controversies and sharp governmental conflicts at several earlier stages of our national history.

To a degree, what we are going through is a repetition of the vigorous Congressional reaction which has followed each incumbency of a "strong" president. Especially was this true after the first six

* Discussing his wartime chairmanship of the Senate War Investigating Committee, ex-President Truman recently remarked: "One thing that added to my success as a committee chairman was that I made it my business to read the record of the Committee on the Conduct of the War Between the States. That way I found out what not to do. That committee tried to run the war for Lincoln and he wouldn't let them. If they had, they would have lost the war. Lee always figured that committee was worth three divisions to him." [37]

years of Franklin D. Roosevelt's presidency. Making all due allowance for the diversion of attention to war and foreign problems, the simultaneous cessation of "New Deal" legislation and growing Congressional support for the anti-Administration Dies Committee tells its own story of an anti-executive trend which was checked and obscured but not reversed during the war years.

Postwar disillusionments and fears awakened by the East-West split, the Communist envelopment of China, the cold war, Korea, and the brooding threat of atomic warfare gave new impetus to Congressional resurgence. In addition to major legislative issues (such as the Taft-Hartley law and civil rights) on which the Congress and President Truman were constantly at loggerheads, there developed a pronounced tendency in Congress toward cutting down the power of the presidential office itself.

The proposed "Bricker amendment" to the Constitution is a good illustration of this anti-presidential feeling. For all the lawyers' debate that surrounded it, the Bricker amendment appealed to Congressmen primarily because, at the expense of the president, it would increase their power in foreign affairs. Congress gets little credit for military and diplomatic victories, but is constantly obliged to grapple with problems and catastrophes of foreign origin—to levy taxes, authorize appropriations, and create new agencies made necessary by a Pearl Harbor or a Hiroshima, or by events in Greece, Czechoslovakia, Korea or Indochina. Not unnaturally, many Congressmen have come to feel that they are being torn and badgered by dilemmas for which they are not responsible, to distrust the strong presidents during whose terms these problems have multiplied, and to welcome anything which, like the Bricker amendment, would diminish the president's powers of initiative and commitment.*

The enormous expansion of the federal payroll during the last twenty years is another and powerful irritant. The executive branch in 1954 bears about the same relation to that of 1933 as does Macy's to the general store at the crossroads. In the meantime, Congress and the courts have remained comparatively unchanged. This enormous and complicated executive structure is a source of no joy to Con-

* The Twenty-Second Amendment to the Constitution (limiting the reelection of presidents) is a less controversial manifestation of the same desire to limit presidential power.

gressmen who are already finding it well-nigh impossible to stay abreast of even the most critical problems in a world that spins so fast as to snatch man's breath away and addle his brains. "Intellectuals" and "experts" permeate the departments and agencies, and often display little understanding of the facts of life at the Capitol.

It was under a strong president, Franklin D. Roosevelt, that the federal bureaucracy mushroomed. It was he who had a brain trust and brought the "hot dog boys" to Washington. And it was he who passed on an immense and constantly proliferating executive department to his successors, be they Democratic Trumans or Republican Eisenhowers. This has put an unprecedented abundance of resource at the disposal of the presidents which, according to their individual skill and will, is convertible into political power. Inevitably, Congress seeks to keep this new power in check.

These are the underlying elements in the continuing crisis of confidence between Congress and the White House. But more recently these have been overlaid with factors closely related to both the international cold war and the cold civil war. In particular the question of loyalty and disloyalty among the millions of federal government employees has become deeply involved in the conflict. Congressional concern with this matter is thoroughly justified and entirely in keeping with its traditional power to scrutinize the operations of the executive branch. But today this legitimate purpose is interlarded with a less admirable disposition to use the loyalty issue as a weapon with which to harass and discomfit the executive branch, undermine the president's control over his own agencies, and turn the bureaucracy into a political liability.

Whether or not Martin Dies was the first to sense the almost boundless possibilities opened up by this tactic, it was he who set the pattern. This is the real reason why all of the leading Congressional loyalty inquisitors—even though they have usually worn the same party label as the president—have been opponents of the Administration. It was true of Dies and Roosevelt, McCarran and Truman, and it is no less true of McCarthy and Eisenhower.

And so at a critical juncture of the cold war, the government's security system and standards have become the plaything of violent political currents and cross-currents. No security system, however wisely constructed, is going to be worth much unless government employees, civil and military, remain loyal to the President, to their superiors, and to the policies and purposes of the federal service.

The essence of the constitutional crisis of 1954, the chronology of which we will now trace, is *the effort of some legislators, notably Senator McCarthy, to destroy the President's effective control of the executive branch and bring it under their own domination.* By an ironic twist of fate, General Eisenhower's own Army furnished the principal field of this major battle of the cold civil war, which therefore became known as the "Battle of the Pentagon."

To anyone who has followed Senator McCarthy's accusatorial career this should have come as no surprise. The year before the Wheeling speech on subversion in the State Department which was his springboard to worldwide notoriety, the Senator had accused the Army[38] of "Hitlerian tactics, fascist interrogation, and the communistic brand of justice" in the postwar war-crimes trial of the Nazi perpetrators of the "Malmedy massacre" of American prisoners during the Battle of the Bulge in 1944. And Senator McCarthy had followed up his accusation by flouncing out of a Senate hearing where these charges were being investigated, and denouncing the Senate subcommittee for "attempting to whitewash a shameful episode in the history of our glorious armed forces."

A few months later the Senator jumped into the inter-service fracas over aircraft carriers and the B-36 bomber, demanding that Secretary of the Navy Matthews be impeached and charging that the security of the nation was impaired by "the current usurpation of Congressional prerogatives by the brass in the Pentagon." The focus of his allegations then shifted to the State Department as a result of his Wheeling speech on February 9, 1950, but in June, 1951, he returned to "the brass" with a 60,000-word vilification of General George Marshall, delivered on the Senate floor, in which he described the General as "steeped in blood" and accused him of complicity in "a conspiracy so black and an infamy so deep as to dwarf any such adventure in the history of man . . ." If the normal reaction to this performance was one of disgust, the Senator himself thought well enough of it to embody it in a book.[39]

Such was the record of Senator McCarthy's attitude towards the executive branch in general and the armed services in particular when, by dint of the Eisenhower sweep, the Senator became chairman of the Senate Committee on Government Operations and of its Permanent Subcommittee on Investigations. No longer a mere gadfly, and now for the first time an investigating Senator in his own right, he directed his opening major assault at the State Department, with dire consequences to the Voice of America. The Government Printing Office, the general question of commerce with communist countries, and a number of lesser matters likewise drew his fire. But it soon became plain that the Republican electoral victory had not dimmed the Senator's consuming passion for military matters, especially those of the most secret and sensitive description.

The first to feel the heat of this passion was Major General Richard C. Partridge, then the Chief Intelligence Officer (G-2) of the Army. At issue between him and the Senator was a document entitled *Psychological and Cultural Traits of Soviet Siberia*, prepared in 1951 for the benefit of intelligence and psychological warfare personnel who might be concerned with the Siberian population. The study was explicitly and emphatically anti-communist, but it was an effort to see things through the eyes of Soviet citizens; its purpose was analytical, not denunciatory. Furthermore, the compilers had been incautious enough to include in the bibliography works on the Soviet Union by Corliss Lamont and others regarded as extreme left-wingers or identified as Communists by Mr. Louis Budenz.

For these reasons, in September, 1953, General Partridge found himself before the Senator in a one-man executive session of the subcommittee. The general endeavored to explain the purposes for which the document had been prepared,[40] and to point out anti-communist sources and passages. But he was poorly prepared and was no match for the Senator at the kind of infighting that ensued. After Mr. Roy Cohn had quizzed the general like a schoolboy on books about communism,[41] Senator McCarthy declared:

> May I say, General, I realize you didn't select your job. Most likely you were assigned to that. I have been in the military long enough to see excellent truck drivers assigned to a job in the Signal Corps, for which they were completely unequipped, and I have seen outstanding Signal Corps men assigned to jobs as truck drivers. It is no reflection upon them to be assigned to the wrong job. He might be excellent in something else, but the thing I can't understand today, and I say I

assume you didn't apply for this job, I can't understand a man being head of G-2, when Communist Russia and international communism constitutes almost the sole threat to this nation, not having studied the Communist movement and the background of communism.

An interested spectator was Secretary of the Army Stevens, who observed at the end of the hearings that General Partridge's answers had not been "very satisfactory to the committee," but defended the general's willingness to cooperate with the committee to the best of his ability. However, the Senator was not to be mollified. He was "shocked beyond words," and roundly declared that General Partridge was "completely incompetent" for his job.[42] And a few weeks later, competent or incompetent, the general was transferred to a new assignment in Europe and ceased to be the G-2 of the Army.

In the meantime, Senator McCarthy's staff had been preparing for an inquiry of much larger proportions into the Army Signal Corps Engineering Laboratories at Fort Monmouth, New Jersey. At these laboratories the Army carries on its research and development work on radar, guided missile control, and other electronic and communications equipment of many types. Fort Monmouth is, in short, a major military research center, and much of its work is highly secret and vitally important to national defense.

Throughout October and most of November, 1953, the McCarthy subcommittee held executive sessions at which scientists and other Monmouth employees were called to testify about their political opinions and associations. Almost daily at the conclusion of these sessions Senator McCarthy gave out press statements of a sensational nature, purporting to describe what had taken place. On October 12 he announced that the situation at the laboratories "has all the earmarks of extremely dangerous espionage," and a few days later he declared that the Julius Rosenberg spy ring "may still be in operation" at the laboratories.

For the next several weeks, alarming and damning accusations such as these poured forth, one upon the heels of another. Finally, Secretary Stevens became alarmed at the picture of far-flung espionage, subversion and disloyalty in the Signal Corps which the Senator was presenting to the public. On November 13, the Secretary issued a statement that the Army had been "unable to find anything resembling espionage" at Fort Monmouth at the present time, and that none of the many scientists who had been suspended pending investigation was charged with espionage.

We will return later to the actualities of the Monmouth situation and the significance of the inquiry in terms of national security.[43] It concerns us here only as an important episode in the gathering storm, which did not, however, break into open hostilities for another three months. For, incredible as it may seem in the light of Senator McCarthy's unbroken record of truculence in the Malmedy, Matthews, Marshall, and Partridge affairs, Secretary Stevens was busily pursuing a policy of appeasement.

The Secretary solicited and bowed to the Senator's opinion on matters such as the proposed transfer of the commanding officer at Fort Monmouth (Major General Lawton), which were the Army's proper and sole responsibility. The Secretary allowed General Lawton and the McCarthy subcommittee to create an atmosphere of murky anxiety at the laboratories, especially inexcusable in a professional, scientific community such as Monmouth. He reduced himself to the level of the McCarthy subcommittee's staff, engaging in long telephone and luncheon consultations with Mr. Roy Cohn—that dour individual who appears never to have been really young, and therefore unable to grow up—in which the Secretary tolerated and responded without rebuke to Mr. Cohn's patronizing and contemptuous references to officers holding key positions on the Army's staff. And finally, in a desperate effort to cultivate the Senator's goodwill, Mr. Stevens allowed himself to become extensively involved in the military career of Mr. (later Private) G. David Schine, a consultant to the subcommittee and the object of special solicitude on the part of Messrs. McCarthy and Cohn. What with telephone calls, extraordinary dispensations, dinners with Schine's and Cohn's families, automobile lifts from Schine to Stevens, airplane lifts from Stevens to McCarthy and Cohn, and photographs of Stevens and Schine, the hapless and misguided Secretary allowed himself to be drawn into a morass in which he thrashed around desperately and ineptly.*

* In justice to Mr. Stevens, it should be remarked that it is now clear that he was not alone in the folly of his ways. Other high administration officials (including the heads of the International Information Administration) were equally culpable, apparently in accordance with a White House policy that sought, with

When Secretary Stevens announced that he knew of no evidence of current espionage at Monmouth, Senator McCarthy waxed mightily wroth. Alarmed at his displeasure the Secretary flew to New York to sue for peace, and issued a "clarifying" statement to the effect that he had intended to refer only to information in the possession of the Army, not of the subcommittee. He went on to praise the investigation as a good example of cooperation between the executive and legislative branches, and peace was restored for the time being.

But not for long, because Senator McCarthy soon shifted his attack and demanded that the Army make available for questioning the members of the loyalty boards that had previously reviewed accusations against the Monmouth scientists and restored many of them to duty. Compliance with this demand, however, would have violated the Truman directive of 1948,[45] which President Eisenhower had not withdrawn, and which prohibits the executive departments from giving Congress information about the loyalty of federal employees, without prior presidential approval. Therefore, Secretary Stevens was obliged to resist the Senator's efforts to pillory the loyalty board members. The Senator did not then press the issue to a showdown by issuing subpoenas, but relations between the Stevens and McCarthy official menages grew notably tense.

The storm was about to break, and it was precipitated by a theretofore monumentally obscure Queens dentist, Doctor Irving Peress, who had been called into the Army and commissioned under the doctors' and dentists' draft law. In January, 1954, while a major in the Army Dental Corps and stationed at Camp Kilmer, New Jersey, Major Peress was called before the McCarthy subcommittee in executive session, and pleaded the Fifth Amendment in response to questions about Communist membership and associations.

On February 18 he was called in public session, with the commanding officer of Camp Kilmer (Brigadier General Ralph Zwicker) and the legal counsel of the Army (Mr. John Adams) in the audience. It then developed that Major Peress had been honorably discharged from the Army a few days after the executive session at which he had pleaded the Fifth Amendment, and that he had previously been

---

utter futility, at all costs to avoid controversy between the executive agencies and Senator McCarthy.[44]

promoted from captain to major in accordance with standard seniority practice, but after he had declined to answer certain questions in an Army loyalty questionnaire, relying on the Fifth Amendment. At the public session Mr. Peress again pleaded the privilege, and was identified as having been a Communist by a New York City policewoman.

Major Peress' record as a military dentist was unexceptionable, and there was no suggestion that he had ever been close to matters of secrecy or security. His promotion and honorable discharge were in accordance with the applicable regulations. Furthermore, Secretary Stevens had written to the Senator confessing error in the Army's handling of Major Peress' case, and promising a review of the problem and correction of the procedures. Nothing would have been simpler than for the Senator to claim credit for plugging a loophole in the military security system, and adjourning the hearing on a note of victory.

But Senator McCarthy was not playing for such small stakes. He publicly called on Mr. Adams for the names of every Army employee who had had anything to do with the Peress promotion and honorable discharge. He accused the Army of "coddling and honorably discharging a known Communist," and declared that he had located "the key to the deliberate Communist infiltration of our Armed Forces, the most dangerous thing." And he ordered General Zwicker to appear before him that same afternoon in executive session.[46]

That afternoon things reached the breaking point. General Zwicker was forbidden by Presidential order to answer the Senator's questions about the Peress case. Furthermore, he was in no way responsible for the orders and regulations which governed the matter; it was his mission to command Camp Kilmer, not to formulate, explain, or defend Army policies on personnel and security problems.

Most unwisely, however, General Zwicker allowed the Senator to draw him into debate. He proved no more able than General Partridge to hold his own. Understandable as was his mistake under the pressure to which the Senator subjected him, the results were none the less unfortunate: [47]

THE CHAIRMAN: You know that somebody signed or authorized an honorable discharge for this man, knowing that he was a Fifth Amendment Communist, do you not?

GENERAL ZWICKER: I know that an honorable discharge was signed for the man.

THE CHAIRMAN: The day the honorable discharge was signed, were you aware of the fact that he had appeared before our committee?

GENERAL ZWICKER: I was. . . .

THE CHAIRMAN: Then, General, you knew, did you not, that he appeared before the committee and refused, on the grounds of the Fifth Amendment, to tell about all of his Communist activities? You knew that, did you not?

GENERAL ZWICKER: I knew everything that was in the press.

THE CHAIRMAN: Don't be coy with me, General.

GENERAL ZWICKER: I am not being coy, sir.

THE CHAIRMAN: Did you have that general picture?

GENERAL ZWICKER: I believe I remember reading in the paper that he had taken refuge in the Fifth Amendment to avoid answering questions before the committee.

THE CHAIRMAN: About communism?

GENERAL ZWICKER: I am not too certain about that.

THE CHAIRMAN: Do you mean that you did not have enough interest in the case, General, the case of this major who was in your command, to get some idea of what questions he had refused to answer? Is that correct?

GENERAL ZWICKER: I think that is not putting it quite right, Mr. Chairman.

THE CHAIRMAN: You put it right, then.

GENERAL ZWICKER: I have great interest in all of the officers of my command, with whatever they do. . . .

THE CHAIRMAN: Let me ask this question: If this man, . . . prior to his getting an honorable discharge, were guilty of some crime—let us say that he held up a bank or stole an automobile—and you heard of that the day before—let us say you heard of it the same day that you heard of my letter—could you then have taken steps to prevent his discharge, or would he have automatically been discharged?

GENERAL ZWICKER: I would have definitely taken steps to prevent discharge. . . .

THE CHAIRMAN: Let us say he went out and stole $50 the night before.

GENERAL ZWICKER: He wouldn't have been discharged.

THE CHAIRMAN: Do you think stealing $50 is more serious than being a traitor to the country as part of the Communist conspiracy?

GENERAL ZWICKER: That, sir, was not my decision. . . .

THE CHAIRMAN: Do you think you sound a bit ridiculous, General, when you say that for $50, you would prevent his being discharged, but for being a part of the conspiracy to destroy this country you could not prevent his discharge?

GENERAL ZWICKER: I did not say that, sir. . . .

THE CHAIRMAN: Would you tell us, General, why $50 is so much more important to you than being part of the conspiracy to destroy a nation which you are sworn to defend?

GENERAL ZWICKER: Mr. Chairman, it is not, and you know that as well as I do.

THE CHAIRMAN: I certainly do. That is why I cannot understand you sitting there, General, a general in the Army, and telling me that you could not, would not, hold up his discharge having received information—

GENERAL ZWICKER: I could not hold up his discharge.

THE CHAIRMAN: Why could you not do it in the case of an allegation of membership in a Communist conspiracy, where you could if you merely heard some private's word that he had stolen $50?

GENERAL ZWICKER: Because, Mr. Senator, any information that appeared in the press or any releases was well known to me and well known to plenty of other people long prior to the time that you ever called this man for investigation, and there were no facts or no allegations, nothing presented from the time that he appeared before your first investigation that was not apparent prior to that time.

While battering General Zwicker dialectically, Senator McCarthy could not resist the temptation to clobber him personally, and thereby the Senator made an even worse mistake than had the General: [48]

THE CHAIRMAN: Do you think, General, that anyone who is responsible for giving an honorable discharge to a man who has been named under oath as a member of the Communist conspiracy should himself be removed from the military?

GENERAL ZWICKER: You are speaking of generalities now, and not on specifics—is that right, sir, not mentioning about any one particular person?

THE CHAIRMAN: That is right. . . .

GENERAL ZWICKER: That is not a question for me to decide, Senator.

THE CHAIRMAN: You are ordered to answer it, General. You are an employee of the people.

GENERAL ZWICKER: Yes, sir.

THE CHAIRMAN: You have a rather important job. I want to know how you feel about getting rid of Communists.

GENERAL ZWICKER: I am all for it.

THE CHAIRMAN: All right. You will answer that question, unless you take the Fifth Amendment. I do not care how long we stay here, you are going to answer it.

GENERAL ZWICKER: Do you mean how I feel toward Communists?

THE CHAIRMAN: I mean exactly what I asked you, General; nothing else. And anyone with the brains of a five-year-old child can understand that question.

The reporter will read it to you as often as you need to hear it so that you can answer it, and then you will answer it.

GENERAL ZWICKER: Start it over, please.

(*The question was reread by the reporter.*)

GENERAL ZWICKER: I do not think he should be removed from the military.

THE CHAIRMAN: Then, General, you should be removed from any command. Any man who has been given the honor of being promoted to general and who says, "I will protect another general who protected Communists," is not fit to wear that uniform, General. I think it is a tremendous disgrace to the Army to have this sort of thing given to the public. I intend to give it to them. I have a duty to do that. I intend to repeat to the press exactly what you said. So you know that. You will be back here, General.

But General Zwicker did not come back. Soon after he finished his testimony, Senator McCarthy ejected both the General and Mr. Adams from the room. Emerging at the conclusion of the session, Senator McCarthy, in General Zwicker's presence, declared that, "We witnessed a disgraceful performance here today," which was true enough, though not in the sense intended by the Senator. General Zwicker replied that the Senator was giving the press "a colored and slanted" version of the testimony, and then turned to the officers accompanying him and remarked bitterly, "Boys, now you've had an education!"[49]

Senator McCarthy then ordered Mr. Adams to bring General Zwicker and the Adjutant General of the Army, Major General Bergin, to a public hearing to be held the following week. But this hearing never transpired. General Zwicker, who had had a distinguished combat record during World War II, reported the treatment he had received to Secretary Stevens. The public and official reaction to Senator McCarthy's statement that he was "unfit to wear that uniform" was widespread and indignant. Secretary Stevens ordered Generals Zwicker and Bergin not to appear before Senator McCarthy, saying: [50]

> I cannot permit the loyal officers of our armed forces to be subjected to such unwarranted treatment. The prestige and morale of our armed forces are too important to the security of the nation to have them weakened by unfair attacks on our officer corps.

Secretary Stevens communicated his decision to Senator McCarthy by telephone, and a stormy interchange resulted. Immediately the Senator publicly called the Secretary "an awful dupe" and announced that he would be called before the subcommittee to testify on the question: "Whether the Army is supreme over the Congress, other government agencies, and the American people, and can enjoy special dictatorial immunity in covering up its own wrongdoings." [51] Secretary Stevens replied that he would appear before the McCarthy subcommittee and present the Army's case, and stood firm in this posture—for three days.

Then, on February 24 occurred the now famous fried chicken luncheon at the Capitol. Invited by Senator Mundt to attend what was described as a peace conference but turned out to be a capitulation, Secretary Stevens found himself in the company of Senators Dirksen, Mundt and Potter, as well as McCarthy himself. As a newspaper writer described the occasion, it was like a goldfish in a tank of barracuda. After lunch the press was called in, and Senator Mundt read a "memorandum of understanding" by which Secretary Stevens agreed that every Army employee who had been involved in the promotion and honorable discharge of Major Peress would be made available to testify before the subcommittee, and that General Zwicker would be allowed to testify again as soon as Senator Symington (a Democratic member of the subcommittee) returned from Europe. In view of these arrangements, the hearing at which the Secretary himself was to have appeared was canceled.

Wonders never cease, and it appears to be the fact that Secretary Stevens really believed that he had successfully maintained the Army's position. "I do not consider I am a person that capitulates or retreats," he told reporters. But the nation's press headlined the episode as a total surrender by Secretary Stevens and the Army to Senator McCarthy, and in London *The Times* declared: "Senator McCarthy this afternoon achieved what General Burgoyne and General Cornwallis never achieved—the surrender of the American Army."

The conflict between the Senator and the Army had by now assumed the proportions of a major constitutional crisis, and still nothing had been heard from the man in whom was vested, under the Constitution, the executive power of the United States Government—President Eisenhower. Thoughtful writers such as Theodore H. White were gloomily predicting the complete collapse of Army morale and discipline, and lamenting what they wrongly imagined to be the constitutional impotence of the executive branch to defend itself.[52] Eisenhower was Commander-in-Chief as well as President and, as other commentators such as Walter Millis, Walter Lippman, and Hanson Baldwin emphasized, it was the President's constitutional duty to preserve the integrity and maintain the effective functioning of the Army, as of the entire executive branch. And if anyone should have been alert and qualified by experience and disposition to do this, it was Dwight D. Eisenhower, one-time General of the Army, USA.

Nevertheless, his reaction to the challenge was tentative and indecisive. He approved and allowed Secretary Stevens to read to the press a statement that the browbeating or humiliation of Army personnel would not be tolerated and that "members of the subcommittee" had given assurances "that they will not permit such conditions to develop in the future."[53] Senator McCarthy promptly declared this "a completely false statement," and said that witnesses would continue to "be examined vigorously to get the truth about Communist activities." A week later the President made a general statement at his press conference acknowledging errors in the handling of the Peress case, reaffirming his confidence in the military establishment in general and General Zwicker in particular, calling for fairness in investigations, and emphasizing his own responsibility as President for the conduct of the executive branch. Senator McCarthy struck back promptly and truculently:[54] "It is important to realize that this silly tempest in a teapot arose because we dared to bring to light the cold, unpleasant facts about a Fifth Amendment Communist officer

. . . If a stupid, arrogant or witless man in a position of power appears before our committee and is found aiding the Communist party, he will be exposed. The fact that he might be a general places him in no special class so far as I am concerned."

Clearly, Senator McCarthy had not yet lost his nerve or his tongue, but he had badly overplayed his hand, and the results began to show in a drawing-away from him in his own Republican Party. Vice-President Nixon and other Republican potentates administered public rebukes, and Secretary of Defense Wilson remarked that charges of Communist-coddling in the Army were "just damn tommyrot." Still, the situation was very confused, for on March 10 Messrs. Wilson and McCarthy were photographed for the press in genial and harmonious conference on how to handle Communists in the armed forces, at the very moment that President Eisenhower was endorsing an attack on Senator McCarthy's excesses by Senator Ralph Flanders of Vermont.

In the meantime, Senator McCarthy had endeavored to retain the initiative by accusations of Communist membership against a Department of Defense employee, Mrs. Annie Lee Moss, who, the Senator had publicly charged, was engaged in decoding top secret messages.[55] On March 11 she was called before the subcommittee, and categorically denied that she had ever been a Communist. Mrs. Moss was an unpretentious woman who appeared not even to recognize the name of Karl Marx, and had no access to the texts of official messages. Whatever the truth may have been, the hearing did not go well for Senator McCarthy, and it proved to be the last public hearing he was destined to preside over for several months.[56] For that very day this remarkable sequence of events took a new and sensational turn.

While Mrs. Moss was testifying, the Army was distributing to the press copies of a report on efforts of the Senator and his staff to get preferential treatment for their staff consultant, Mr. G. David Schine, in connection with his military service. Requests that he be commissioned instead of drafted, that he be given special duties in the vicinity of New York or Washington, and, after his induction, that he be given leaves of absence to complete his work for the subcommittee had been frequent, insistent, and backed by violent threats, according to the Army report. The subcommittee's counsel, Mr. Roy Cohn, appeared as the chief culprit, aided and abetted by the executive director, Mr. Francis P. Carr, and the Senator himself. It was flatly charged that the subcommittee's investigative power had been brandished in order to coerce the Army into favoring Schine.

To all this Senator McCarthy replied with the word "blackmail." Secretary Stevens and Army counsel John Adams had used Private Schine as a hostage, and threatened reprisals in an effort to stop the Monmouth investigation. They had even tried to divert the subcommittee from the Army as a target by urging it to "go after the Navy, Air Force, and Defense Department instead," and by promising to give leads to "plenty of dirt" in those quarters.

At once there arose a compelling demand, in and out of Congress, for an investigation of these charges and countercharges. But who should investigate the investigators and their quarry, the Army? Senator Kefauver argued with great force that the subcommittee was not the right body to investigate itself, and urged the Senate Armed Services Committee to take on the task. But that committee's chairman, Senator Leverett Saltonstall of Massachusetts, was facing reelection in a state where there was thought to be considerable pro-McCarthy voting strength, and he recoiled from the suggestion with visible horror.

And so it came about that the Permanent Subcommittee on Investigations, under the reluctant temporary chairmanship of Senator Mundt, voted to investigate "the controversy which has arisen with respect to the charges and countercharges of misconduct . . . with respect to the staff of the committee and the Department of the Army." [57] Five weeks elapsed while the subcommittee formulated its procedures, selected special counsel, and obtained formal written charges from each side of the controversy.

Dull, dramatic, farcical, enlightening, and frightening, the McCarthy-Army hearings were the nation's principal television, radio, and newspaper fare for nearly two months. Colorful as were many of the political and human tones and overtones, we are concerned here chiefly with the basic significance in terms of Congressional investigative power. Indeed, only if the underlying elements of the pitiless struggle for power are grasped, does the erratic course of the hearings become comprehensible and meaningful.

Daily and almost plaintively, as the hearings wended their dizzy way, *The New York Times* printed a little box entitled "Army-McCarthy Charges In Dispute Are Outlined," to remind its readers of the preferential treatment-hostage-blackmail-Schine issues that were supposed to constitute the controversy. But these were not what the hearings were really about at all, and through day after day of testimony and harangue they faded ever deeper into the background.

One reason for this was that the charges *on both sides* were plainly true in substance if not in every detail, and were known to be true before Senator Mundt ever lifted his gavel. Everyone close to the scene knew that Mr. Roy Cohn was aggressive, arrogant, and bent on making the Army show deference to his friendship for Schine, and to the latter's status as consultant to the subcommittee. After a few days of testimony, everyone who watched the television screen or read the newspapers also knew these things. It was equally plain that Secretary Stevens and Mr. John Adams, whether or not guided by higher orders, had first gone to the utmost lengths to placate the Senator, and then had tried vainly to divert and soften the blows that he was raining on the Army. Appeasement and lack of dignity and self-respect on one side, and on the other side arrogance, immaturity, and a wealthy young man with little stomach for basic training and an inflated notion of his own value to the government—these things told their own story, and it was essentially the story written in the charges and counter-charges.

This is one reason why the hearings were conducted and concluded without ever calling Private Schine himself as a witness,* even though the charges clustered around his person and he was, ostensibly, the *raison d'être* of the entire proceeding. But there were other and much more important reasons. What was really taking place in the Senate caucus room was a major battle of the cold civil war, as most of the participants and many of the spectators well knew. That is why the efforts of some politicians and commentators to brush aside the hearings as disgusting and trivial fell on deaf ears. Disgusting the hearings often were; trivial they were not, for much was at stake—much more than the fate of Messrs. Stevens, Cohn, Schine, and Adams.

* Except on the single and limited question of the famous "cropped photograph" of Secretary Stevens, Private Schine, and others.

More, to be sure, than the individual fate of Senator McCarthy, but he was nevertheless the symbol and focus of the proceedings. Utilizing the Senate's investigative power as sword, shield, and trumpet all in one, he was openly threatening to upset the constitutional balance of power—to destroy the President's effective control of the executive branch, and usurp his power at home and abroad.

This is why a discussion of the investigative power vis-à-vis the doctrine of separation of powers under the Constitution is no idle or academic exercise. Rather, these concepts are the very stuff of today's political strife.

And yet, for all that was at stake in the Army-McCarthy hearings, their upshot was murky and indecisive. One very good reason for this was that the Administration could not make up its mind what it wanted the outcome to be. Seemingly, the President and his advisers hoped to eat Senator McCarthy and have him too.

Secretary Stevens' zig-zag course can be explained in no other way. When he announced that he would appear, in place of Generals Zwicker and Bergin, to explain the Army's policies in the Peress and other loyalty cases, he did exactly the right thing. It was plainly out of order for Senator McCarthy to hold General Zwicker responsible on matters of security policy; the Secretary could rightly insist that he himself or some other authorized Departmental spokesman should testify.* To allow Congressional committees to determine who should appear in behalf of the executive branch, or to berate and insult federal officials at will, would soon break down the discipline and morale of the federal service.

The capitulation at the fried chicken luncheon, therefore, was as wrong as could be. After that, what federal employee might not feel that the favor of a powerful Congressman was a better path to security and promotion than loyalty to the service and his superiors? Perhaps Secretary Stevens' ineptness and inexperience were the principal reason for this debacle, but it was reliably reported that high Administration officials were worried about the Peress case and reluctant to support Stevens' stand. Even after the magnitude of the

* The Secretary would have been better advised, perhaps, to have simply announced that he himself would testify, and to have withheld his order to the two generals to ignore the subcommittee's demand that they appear.

defeat sustained by the executive branch became apparent, neither the President nor any top Administration spokesman acted decisively to restore the balance. But something had to be done, and presumably that is why the Army released the Schine report.

Unfortunately, the Army's battleground was poorly chosen. The conduct charged against Messrs. McCarthy, Cohn and Carr in the Schine affair was certainly unedifying. But pressure from Congressmen to obtain favors for constituents or persons to whom they are under obligation is a familiar political phenomenon, with which government officials must expect to be faced. All in all, this was not a very powerful attack, and it took the emphasis off the real vice of the McCarthy operations—the undermining of discipline and morale and corrosion of the entire executive fabric, exemplified in the case of General Zwicker and previously in the Voice of America inquiry.

Senator McCarthy's charges, on the contrary, were serious indeed. Utilizing the induction of Mr. Schine as a chip in a poker game, or as a means of easing the subcommittee's investigative pressure on the Army, was entirely improper administrative conduct.

And so, when the hearings opened, the Senator had much the stronger hand. The more that Secretary Stevens and the other Army witnesses complained of pressure and threats, the more they appeared as weaklings who could be made to yield, rather than as sternly bent on duty, as befits the military. The two senior Republican Senators, Acting Chairman Mundt and Senator Dirksen, were basically favorable to Senator McCarthy rather than the Administration. No one at the hearing knew what he wanted except Senator McCarthy; he alone was prepared to strike ruthlessly. Everyone else was tentative and indecisive until the later sessions, when Senator Stuart Symington dealt McCarthy several solid counter-punches that obviously hurt.

The Army "case" never was put in a clear, straightforward manner. Secretary Stevens might better have confessed error for his past truckling to McCarthy, denounced the subcommittee's conduct of the Monmouth investigation, and made a forceful statement of the executive branch's rightful insistence on preserving its dignity and integrity against Congressional encroachments. Instead, he unconvincingly denied the truckling and displayed abysmal ignorance of the facts at Monmouth. He was personable and good-tempered and impressed the television audience as an amiable man but, as was remarked by the sage Leo Durocher, late of the Gashouse Gang and now of Coogan's Bluff, "Nice guys come in last."

And so, by the contrivance of some and the clumsiness of others, the basic issue of the hearing—that is, the proper balance of Congressional investigative power and executive power *—was obscured for days on end. After all, the parties to the conflict were not pleading before a court, but were more like gladiators in the greatest arena of all time: the American television, radio, and newspaper communications system. The interplay and clash of personalities were more to the popular taste than discussion of constitutional and administrative questions. But once the hearings were well under way, the principle of separation of powers was suddenly projected at the center of the stage by a sensational development for which, as usual, Senator McCarthy was responsible.

Late in the afternoon of the ninth day of the hearings, and while Senator McCarthy was cross-examining Secretary Stevens, the Senator handed to the Secretary what purported to be a copy of a two-and-a-quarter-page letter, dated January 26, 1951, from J. Edgar Hoover to Major General Bolling, then the G-2 of the Army. The document was marked "personal and confidential," and contained the names, some of which were followed by the notation "derogatory information," of thirty-four individuals employed at Signal Corps laboratories.

The Senator's purpose in producing the document was to imply that the Army had been given ample warning that there were subversive and disloyal employees at Fort Monmouth, and nevertheless had done nothing about it. But the immediate effect was an electric shock of curiosity and apprehension among those present. Secretary Stevens declined even to look at the paper; everyone else to whom it was passed dropped it as if it burnt his fingers, and the document

* Interestingly enough, a perspicacious foreign observer put his finger on this crucial issue: [58] "The hearings . . . in Washington have not been dealing with the McCarthy-Army controversy; they have been dealing with the basic constitutional problems of the correct relationship between the two main branches of the American government."

practically took wings and flew back into Senator McCarthy's hands: [59]

SENATOR MC CARTHY: Now, I would like to, Mr. Secretary, give you a letter—one which was written, incidentally, before you took office, but which was in the file, I understand, during all the time you were in office. I understand that it's in the file as of today. . . . It is part of a series of letters from the FBI warning of the tremendous danger of Aaron Coleman and his associates' handling top secret radar material . . . Those repeated warnings were disregarded, ignored, until this committee opened its investigation. . . .

SENATOR JACKSON: Did the committee get this from the Army? Was it subpoenaed? Is it from the FBI? . . . How did it come into our possession? . . .

MR. WELCH: . . . I would like to have Mr. J. Edgar Hoover state that he wrote the letter and mailed it. Then we'd know what we were dealing with . . .

SENATOR MC CARTHY: Just, just a minute, now—Mr. Chairman, if Mr. Welch is going to say there's not a copy of this in the Army files he should be sworn, because that statement is untrue as far as I know.

MR. WELCH: I did not say that, Senator . . . I have an absorbing curiosity to know how the dickens you got it. . . .

MR. JENKINS: Mr. Chairman, apparently the contents of this letter are so inviolate, so important, so sacred, and carry with them so many implications, even of a violation of the law, that I respectfully decline . . . that I personally be the custodian of this letter and now in the presence of everybody I return it to Senator McCarthy.

The next day, after inquiry had been made of Mr. Hoover, it developed that what Senator McCarthy had offered was not a copy of any document ever signed by Mr. Hoover. Portions of it were, however, extracted from a much longer document of the same general description and bearing the same date. It became apparent that someone with access to the authentic document had "whomped up" the concoction produced by Senator McCarthy, and it soon became clear why this had been done.

Under questioning, Senator McCarthy stated that he had been given the paper by a young officer in the Army intelligence service, but flatly refused to reveal his name.* The Senator repeatedly de-

* The Senator was sustained in this refusal by Acting Chairman Mundt on the advice of Counsel Ray Jenkins, on the wholly irrelevant theory that [60] "law en-

clared that "the security information has been deleted," and tried again and again to have the document made part of the public record of the hearing. But Attorney General Brownell advised the subcommittee that it contained confidential information, and should not be made public. Senator McCarthy reacted violently and demanded that the Attorney General "should be called in executive session and made to answer why the parts of these letters not having to do with security but which might be awfully embarrassing . . . to some people . . . should not be made available . . . to the members of this committee, and . . . to the public. I think both." But the Attorney General stuck to his ruling, and added—and this explains many otherwise mystifying features of the episode—that the Department of Justice "has under consideration at the present time possible violations of the criminal law," and that publication of the document "might affect adversely or even defeat the proper prosecution of offenses involved in its preparation and dissemination."

Now, it had been plain from the outset that whoever in the executive branch had given this document or the information in it to Senator McCarthy, had done so in violation of the Truman executive order of 1948. Far from disputing this, the Senator boasted about it, and defiantly announced that federal employees should feel free to disregard the presidential directive, and bring him this type of information whenever they felt so inclined: [61]

> One of the reasons why I have been successful, I believe to some extent, in exposing communism is because the people who give me information from within the government know that their confidence will not be violated. It will not be violated today. . . . I want to make it very, very clear.
>
> I want to notify the people who give me information that there is no way on earth that any committee, any force can get me to violate the confidence of those people. . . .
>
> This came to me from someone within the Army . . . [who] felt that

forcement officers, investigators, any of those engaged in the investigative field who come in contact with confidential information are not required to disclose the source of their information." Of course Senator McCarthy was not a law enforcement officer. Furthermore, Senator McCarthy did not receive the document in his individual capacity but as chairman of the subcommittee, and therefore it was entirely within the power and responsibility of the subcommittee itself to decide whether the name of the person who gave the document to the subcommittee should be disclosed.

his duty to his country was above any duty to any Truman directive to the effect that he could not disclose this information.

But the conduct thus advocated by the Senator involved something far more serious than violation of a Presidential order. The federal espionage laws cover this situation very specifically. One section of those laws provides that anyone who is entrusted with any document or information relating to national defense, the disclosure of which might injure the United States, and who delivers the document or communicates the information to any person not rightfully entitled to it, shall be liable to imprisonment for up to ten years and a fine of $10,000.[62]

It is clear that Senator McCarthy was not "rightfully entitled" to receive the document in the manner in which he testified he did. To be sure, Mr. Hoover, or the Army G-2, or other officials of high and discretionary authority in the field of security may, for good reasons and with propriety, make confidential defense information available to a Congressional committee,* as for instance in the case of the Joint Committee on Atomic Energy. But Senator McCarthy was certainly not entitled to receive this information by clandestine means from a subordinate officer or employee acting without the sanction or knowledge of his superiors, and in direct violation of the orders of the Commander-in-Chief.

And so, when President Eisenhower at his press conference said that it was "reprehensible" and "insubordinate" conduct on the part of this subordinate official, he was making a stentorian understatement. What was actually involved was a felonious violation of the espionage laws. Yet Senator McCarthy openly boasted at the hearing that he would continue to encourage people to come to him with documents and information of this sort. This was nothing more nor less than an open invitation to everyone in the executive branch to violate the espionage laws by bringing him more documents like this one. It is hard to conceive of conduct which more clearly (in the language of the resolution establishing the Un-American Activities Committee) "attacks the principle of the form of government as guaranteed by our Constitution." As Chief Justice Stone once

* But in this particular case, even this could not have been done without Presidential approval, under the executive order relating to loyalty information.

observed,[63] these constitutional principles include at least "the principle that constitutional laws are not to be broken down by planned disobedience."

But there is another section of the espionage laws which applies to the unauthorized *receipt* of security documents and information. Anyone who comes into unauthorized possession of anything of this kind must put it into the hands of an official properly to be entrusted with it; if he fails to do this, he, too, is guilty of violating the espionage laws and liable to the same penalties.[64] In the light of this provision, it is easy to see why the document aroused so much excitement and alarm when Senator McCarthy produced it at the hearing, and why everyone who handled it was so eager to return it to Senator McCarthy.

Other circumstances of the mystery likewise are clarified. Almost certainly the original fifteen-page memorandum was shortened by the deletion of detailed accusations against the individuals listed therein, in a futile effort to conceal its high security nature—futile because the names of suspected government scientists remained in the shortened document and this was quite enough, as the Attorney General ruled, to bring it within the espionage laws. So, too, the reason is now apparent for Senator McCarthy's desperate efforts to have the document made part of the public record—because this would seem to establish its non-confidential character—and for his frantic reiteration of his own wishful thought, "security information has been deleted." As Queen Gertrude remarked to her son Hamlet, "The lady doth protest too much, methinks."

The episode of the bootlegged FBI report was not, of course, the only occasion during the hearings when the principle of separation of powers came to the fore. Secretary Stevens' departmental counsel, Mr. John Adams, refused on instructions from higher authority to testify about consultations among top Administration officials that had preceded release of the Army's report attacking Messrs. McCarthy, Cohn, and Carr for their conduct in the Schine affair. This irritated both Republican and Democratic members of the subcommittee, but President Eisenhower backed up Mr. Adams' silence on this matter, supported by a long memorandum from Attorney General Brownell, in which the precedents from Washington to Truman were rehearsed.[65] The gist of the President's decision was:

> Because it is essential to efficient and effective administration that employees of the Executive Branch be in a position to be completely candid in advising with each other on official matters, and because it is not in the public interest that any of their conversations or communications or any documents or reproductions concerning such advice be disclosed, you will instruct employees of your Department that in all of their appearances before the subcommittee of the Senate Committee on Government Operations regarding the inquiry now before it, they are not to testify to any such conversations or communications or to produce any such documents or reproductions.

This decision was abundantly justified in the particular case, but the general principle was, in my opinion, stated too broadly. A very large part of administrative work consists of advice and communication between and among government officials. If President Eisenhower's directive were applied generally in line with its literal and sweeping language, Congressional committees would frequently be shut off from access to documents to which they are clearly entitled by tradition, common sense, and good governmental practice. It is unlikely, therefore, that this ruling will endure beyond the particular controversy that precipitated it.

In any event, all this is of secondary importance compared to Senator McCarthy's frontal attack on the executive power, stemming from his production of the FBI document. For the Senator had openly exhorted the members of the executive branch to put their loyalty and duty of obedience to the President in second place, and render primary allegiance to him, Senator McCarthy. And the Senator displayed a bold contempt for the espionage laws enacted by Congress, equal to his disdain for executive authority. It was Mayor Hague who equated his own person with the law. It was Senator McCarthy who seemed seriously bent on turning that bravado into stark fact.

Still the executive branch seemed unable to shake off lethargy or take decisive action to protect its independence and integrity. At the Central Intelligence Agency, to be sure, the authorities sternly warned the staff against emulating the "young intelligence officer"[66] whom Senator McCarthy praised so highly. Elsewhere, however, the Administration contemplated the Senator with the helpless fascination of bird transfixed by reptile. When Senator Ralph Flanders introduced resolutions aimed to strip Senator McCarthy of his committee chairmanships, and censure him for misconduct, the Administration did nothing to aid him to bring to heel this man who was using the investigative power to wage ruthless war against the Army, the Presidency, the Constitution, and the law itself.

As matters developed, it was not the executive branch but rather Senator McCarthy's inability to temper his own blows that eventually checked his assault. This weakness, manifested in the episodes of General Zwicker and the FBI document no less than in his contemptuous treatment of all who crossed him, was seized upon by Senators Flanders, Morse, Fulbright, and other proponents of the censure resolution that led to the Watkins Committee hearings in September, and the Senate special session in November and December of 1954. By voting to condemn Senator McCarthy's conduct, the Senate officially registered the disgust which most of the legislators had long felt, and dealt a severe blow to his stature in the halls of government.

Nevertheless, the upshot was not an unqualified victory for the anti-McCarthy forces. The most serious charges, such as those arising out of the FBI documentary concoction, were not passed upon by the Senate; even the Zwicker affair was dropped from the resolution in the end. Among the some twenty-five Senators who opposed censure were the majority leader, Senator Knowland, and the influential and respected Senator Millikin. Both in and out of the Senate, there was a coalescence and hardening of support for McCarthy, who showed no signs of contrition or of having been chastised, and promptly announced the resumption of his subcommittee's hearings on subversion in defense plants.

It is especially noteworthy, as Senator Monroney pointed out on the closing day of debate,[67] that Senator McCarthy was not censured for his misuse of the Senate's investigatorial prerogatives, for his attack against the Executive branch, or for his treatment of anyone other than his fellow-senators. He was censured only for his sulphurous reaction to the Senate's undertaking to investigate and judge him —i.e. for *obstructing* rather than for *abusing* the Senate's power. In short, the Senate condemned Senator McCarthy as an individual, but it remains to be seen whether it checked McCarthyism.

It is perhaps a weakness in our governmental structure that the executive branch is largely dependent, for the preservation of its independence and effective strength, upon the skill and will of one man—the President. The judicial branch, composed as it is of hundreds of jurists with life tenure, is relatively impervious to sudden pressure—too impervious, in the eyes of the New Dealers of 1937. Congress may be swept by waves of courage and fear, wisdom and folly, but by its very nature strikes a common denominator. When it fails, it is the failure of many.

But the conduct of executive affairs is the ultimate responsibility of the President and no one else. He is elected for a fixed term, and cannot be pulled down, as can the first minister under the cabinet form of government. If the President does not comprehend or cannot or will not uphold the responsibilities and prerogatives of his office, the constitutional balance and distribution of powers is upset. If the President cannot or will not maintain his control of the civil and command of the military services, the entire executive establishment may fall to pieces.

Confronted with a lethal and revolutionary onslaught on the executive branch such as we have just witnessed, it is the President's constitutional responsibility to repel the assault and preserve the integrity of the branch of government entrusted to him. The legislative power of investigation was designed to scrutinize, not to destroy, the executive departments. These are the facts and duties which must, at all costs, be made as plain to President Eisenhower in 1955 as they were to President Washington in 1792.

CHAPTER VI

INVESTIGATIONS AND INDIVIDUAL LIBERTIES

"If there is any fixed star in our constitutional constellation, it is that no official, high or petty, can prescribe what shall be orthodox in politics, nationalism, religion, or other matters of opinion, or force citizens to confess by word or act their faith therein."

—Justice Robert H. Jackson (1943)

IN THE LAST CHAPTER we were concerned with the workings of the investigative power within the governmental framework, and the limits within which it must be held in order to avoid destructive or crippling effects on the other branches of the government. Now it is time to look beyond the legislative and executive halls, and to consider the impact of the investigative power on the individual citizen, and on the freedoms which are guaranteed to him by the Constitution.

Several of the most important of these freedoms are embodied in the early amendments to the Constitution, known as the Bill of Rights, which were formulated and approved by the First Congress in 1789 and finally ratified by the states in 1791. For our present purposes, the two most important are the First Amendment, which forbids Congress to enact any law "... abridging the freedom of speech, or of the press ..." and the Fourth, which provides that ... "The right of the people to be secure in their persons, houses, papers, and effects, against unreasonable searches and seizures, shall not be violated ..."

But the citizens' constitutional freedoms are not based entirely on the Bill of Rights. In our discussion of the separation of powers, we have already observed [1] that this principle not only governs the structure of the government, but also protects the individual against unauthorized governmental action. If the individual is injured by Congressional action which is not legislative and encroaches on the domain of, say, the judiciary, or which invades a field reserved to the states, he may ask the courts to put the matter right.

This, in fact, is the very reason why the Bill of Rights was not made a part of the original Constitution. In the Convention, a motion for its inclusion was decisively rejected. During the ratification process, Alexander Hamilton and others argued that the Bill of Rights was unnecessary, because Congress had been given no powers which could be used to restrict the basic freedoms. Why, they asked, was it necessary to write into the Constitution a guaranty of liberty of the press, when the Constitution gave Congress no power to legislate in that field? [2]

But these arguments proved insufficient during the ratification debates in the several states. The omission of the Bill of Rights was a chief object of attack upon the proposed Constitution, and several states ratified only upon the understanding that the personal guarantees would be immediately incorporated as amendments.

It is significant that popular demand for a Bill of Rights was coupled with the expectation that the courts would enforce its provisions, if necessary by declaring laws unconstitutional.[3] This thought was voiced again when the Bill of Rights Amendments were formulated during the First Congress in 1789. James Madison, the principal draftsman and patron saint of the Bill of Rights, pointed to the conjoint and cumulative force of the separation of powers and the Bill of Rights, declaring [4] that "independent tribunals of justice will consider themselves in a peculiar manner the guardians of those rights; they will be an impenetrable bulwark against every assumption of power in the Legislative or Executive."

But despite the high hopes entertained by Madison and many of his contemporaries, to this very day—163 years since the First Amendment was ratified—not one statute of Congress has ever been held unconstitutional on the ground that it abridged freedom of speech or of the press.* To be sure, no such cases reached the Court for over a century. Then, when political agitators were convicted under the federal espionage laws of the First World War, the Court upheld their constitutionality, on the basis of Justice Holmes' famous statement that the First Amendment does not protect speech which creates a "clear and present danger" to national security.[5] These guarantees, in other words, are not absolute, but are subject to the overriding national interest in order and security.

The heyday of legislative omnipotence during the thirties diffused a spirit of condescension toward the Bill of Rights. It was even regarded among some liberals as a bit quaint to worry about the possibility of oppressive Congressional action. But during the forties the changing temper of the times took legislative form, both nationally and in many states.

In 1940 Congress enacted the Smith Act, aimed primarily at Communists but broadly phrased so as to punish not only conspiring to overthrow the government, but *advocating* or *conspiring to advocate* its overthrow. Many liberals attacked the Smith Act as an infringement of free speech, but the Supreme Court, over the dissenting opinions of Justices Black and Douglas, upheld its constitutionality and sustained the convictions of the leaders of the Communist Party in the United States.[9] State and municipal laws such as New York State's Feinberg Law, forbidding the employment of public school teachers and other civil employees who fail to meet various tests of political orthodoxy, have also been sustained by the Court.[10]

There can be no gainsaying that these laws, wise or unwise, have perceptibly compressed the area of freedom to which many Americans had become habituated. Granting this does not, however, establish the futility of the constitutional guarantees. Concepts such as "freedom" and "security" are compounded of imponderables, and it

---

* The Bill of Rights limits the power of Congress, not of the states. However, the Supreme Court has held that the clause of the Fourteenth Amendment forbidding the states to "deprive any person of life, liberty, or property without due process of law" embraces some (but not all) of the guarantees in the Bill of Rights, including freedom of speech and press.[6] And several state statutes have been held unconstitutional under the Fourteenth Amendment on the ground that freedom of speech or the press was infringed.[7] A part of the federal Taft-Hartley Act labor leader loyalty oath requirements has so far been upheld as consonant with the First Amendment only by an evenly divided Supreme Court.[8]

cannot be expected that men—especially men who genuinely value both concepts and fully understand their mutual interdependence—will always agree on how to strike the balance and where to draw the lines.

This disagreement has been as sharp and frequent in connection with Congressional investigations as with statutes. No such inquiry has yet been invalidated by the Supreme Court as an abridgment of free speech. Nevertheless, the spirit of the First Amendment has been immanent throughout the history of legislative investigations in the United States. As long ago as 1832 it was voiced by ex-President John Quincy Adams, then newly elected to the House of Representatives. A resolution had been introduced "to examine into the affairs of the United States Bank," which Adams criticized on the ground that it would encompass inquiry into all sorts of private matters beyond the constitutional authority of the House. He argued successfully for a more restricted wording, and the Bill of Rights was plainly in the forefront of his mind: [11]

> . . . the authority of the committee and of the House itself did not extend, under color of examining into the books and proceedings of the bank, to scrutinize, for animadversion or censure, the religious or political opinions even of the president and directors of the bank, nor their domestic or family concerns, nor their private lives or characters, nor their moral, or political, or pecuniary standing in society; . . .

Twenty-four years later James T. Brady denounced the efforts of the "Know-Nothing" investigators to stigmatize New York City's Irish Catholic policemen, and Judge Daly disallowed as irrelevant the questions about their national origin. When Justice Holmes ruled that Congress had given the Interstate Commerce and Federal Trade Commissions only limited investigatory powers, he dwelt emphatically on the constitutional guarantees of freedom, especially the Fourth Amendment. Indeed, nearly all of the decisions of the Supreme Court dealing with the investigatory power have been infused with awareness of the burden and close bearing of the Bill of Rights.

Now, this line of decisions [12] demonstrates a very important and potent quality of the Bill of Rights, and that is *its capacity for indirectly pervading, coloring, and affecting decisions of the courts which are ostensibly based on other grounds.* It is especially important to bear in mind this latent strength as we examine its impact on Congressional investigations of loyalty and security matters. For the illusion of investigative omnipotence is still widespread. Two years ago, it was written in a leading legal periodical [13] that "The prevailing opinion in Congress has been that the first ten Amendments do not protect parties before committees since these proceedings are only inquiries and bear no relation to court procedure." As recently as March, 1953, Mr. Alan Barth of the *Washington Post,* speaking before the American Association of University Professors, declared that he did not "question the authority of Congress to investigate the church or the press" because "Congress has plenary power—and must have such power—to look into any area of American life." [14]

That same month, however, the Supreme Court handed down a decision reversing a witness' criminal conviction for declining to furnish information to a Congressional committee, with an opinion which should serve as a timely reminder that the investigative power is indeed subject to the Bill of Rights. We will now examine this decision and its implications in some detail, for in the long run the issues which it touches are as important as any with which this book is concerned, and may profoundly affect our political and social standards of conduct.

Mr. Rumely, the Lady from Toledo, and the Supreme Court

Whatever may be the faults and flaws of Mr. Edward A. Rumely, he is not indifferent to the welfare and betterment, as he conceives them, of his fellowmen, nor does he hide his opinions under a bushel. Born in Indiana and educated at Notre Dame, Oxford, Heidelberg, and the University of Freiburg (where he received a medical doctorate in 1906), he has been an educator (founder of the Interlachen School and author of *How to Teach Boys to Live*), businessman and pioneer in the distribution of vitamin foods, publisher of the *New York Evening Mail,* and public relations consultant.

But today Mr. Rumely is best known as the executive secretary (since 1937) of an organization called the Committee for Constitutional Government (CCG). The principal activity of the CCG has been the distribution of very large quantities of books and pamphlets dealing with questions of political and social opinion. For example, when the Taft-Hartley law was under discussion in Congress, the CCG distributed 250,000 copies of a pamphlet by John W. Scoville entitled *Labor Monopolies or Freedom.* Mr. Frank Gannett financed this controversial broadside, and copies went to every member of Congress. Also distributed by the CCG was John T. Flynn's *The Road Ahead,* described by Mr. Rumely as calling for a halt to "the march of socialism and the destruction of our form of government," and urging the repeal of New Deal-Fair Deal legislation. Undeniably, in contemporary parlance the CCG is near the extreme right end of the political spectrum.

In 1950 Mr. Rumely and the CCG fell afoul of a House investigating committee—not, however, the Un-American Activities Committee, but a special committee set up under a 1949 resolution calling for an investigation of: [15]

> (1) all lobbying activities intended to influence, encourage, promote, or retard legislation; and (2) all activities of agencies of the Federal Government intended to influence, encourage, promote, or retard legislation.

The "Buchanan Committee," as it came to be known from its chairman, became interested in the CCG partly as a result of reports made to Congress by CCG under the Regulation of Lobbying Act of 1946, showing that it had spent some $2,000,000 from 1946 to 1950. Substantial as was this figure, there was a question whether it was not evasively understated. The Act required the disclosure of contributions of $500 or more received or spent to influence legislation "directly or indirectly." After its passage, CCG adopted a policy of accepting payments of more than $490 only if it was specified that the funds were to be used for the distribution of CCG's books and pamphlets. These payments were then treated as purchases of the literature rather than as contributions, and were not reported to Congress under the Lobbying Act. But didn't the distribution of a pamphlet such as *Labor Monopolies or Freedom,* at the very time Congress was debating the Taft-Hartley law, constitute "lobbying" which might influence legislation, at least indirectly? So thought the Buchanan Committee, and it reported to Congress that: [16]

> Our study of this organization indicates very clearly that its most important function is the distribution of books and pamphlets in order to influence legislation directly and indirectly. It attempts to influence legislation directly by sending copies of books, pamphlets, and other printed materials to Members of Congress. It attempts to influence legislation indirectly by distributing hundreds of thousands of copies of these printed materials to people throughout the United States.
>
> Of particular significance is the fact that Edward A. Rumely and the Committee for Constitutional Government, Inc., in recent years have devised a scheme for raising enormous funds without filing true reports pursuant to the provisions of the Federal Regulation of Lobbying Act. This scheme has the color of legality but in fact is a method of circumventing the law. It utilizes the system outlined above whereby contributions to the Committee for Constitutional Government are designated as payments for the purchase of books, which are transmitted to others at the direction of the purchaser . . .

In order to probe the issues so raised and to determine whether these were legitimate sales or concealed contributions, the Buchanan Committee issued a subpoena to CCG calling for the name and address of each person from whom it had received $500 or more for any purpose—i.e., whether as contribution or purchase payment—from 1947 to 1950. Mr. Rumely responded that he was willing to reveal the total receipts of CCG, but not the identity of his purchasers (or distributees), on the ground that "*under the Bill of Rights, that is beyond the power of your committee to investigate.*"

The Committee therefore requested the House to direct the Speaker to certify Mr. Rumely's defiance to the United States Attorney for prosecution under the 1857 criminal statute. A vigorous debate ensued. Congressman Halleck of the Republican minority argued that "lobbying" meant only direct pressure on Congressmen; Chairman Buchanan contended that it included attempts "to saturate the thinking of the community." [17] Finally the certification to the United States Attorney was directed by a very close vote—183 to 175.

Mr. Rumely was then indicted and tried for his willful failure to produce the CCG records covered by the Committee's subpoena, including specifically the name and address of a lady from Toledo who had paid the CCG two thousand dollars for distributing copies of John T. Flynn's *The Road Ahead.* At the end of the trial, Mr. Rumely was convicted and sentenced to imprisonment for six months and a fine of one thousand dollars, but the Court of Appeals for the District of Columbia reversed his conviction, ruling that the House direction to investigate "lobbying" did not cover the mere distribution of political literature, and that a broader construction would raise serious problems under the First Amendment.[18]

Before the courts, Mr. Rumely got precious little aid from liberals in his defense of the Bill of Rights, for which he was risking a jail sentence. The American Civil Liberties Union did not support his position. Many liberals declared that it was old-fashioned not to recognize that lobbying could be conducted by indirect propaganda as well as direct pressure and, still gripped by the illusion of investigative omnipotence, scoffed at Mr. Rumely's reliance on the First Amendment.

The Supreme Court showed itself considerably wiser and more alert to the trend of the times than many of its liberal critics. Two of the justices did not participate in the decision; [19] the remaining seven unanimously upheld the Court of Appeals and set aside Mr. Rumely's conviction.[20] Nothing better illustrates the flexibility of the judicial process and temper than the circumstance that the Court's opinion was written by Justice Frankfurter, whose article twenty-nine years earlier in the *New Republic* was one of the springs from which flowed the broadening stream of investigative power.[21]

The grounds of the decision, however, were not unanimous. Justices Black and Douglas thought the House resolution authorizing the investigation could not be so narrowly construed as to rule out the demand for the names of CCG distributees, and that therefore the question had to be squarely faced whether compelling Mr. Rumely to disclose them would abridge the freedom guaranteed by the First Amendment. These two justices thought that it would, and we will examine their reasons shortly. But the other five justices, for whom Justice Frankfurter spoke, took a more cautious and traditional tack, following the pattern set by Justice Holmes years earlier in the *Harriman* and *American Tobacco* cases.[22]

Clearly, Justice Frankfurter's views on Congressional investigations were no longer as unqualifiedly favorable in 1953 as they had been in 1924. Preliminarily, he quoted Woodrow Wilson's opinion, expressed in 1901, that [23] "The informing function of Congress should be preferred even to its legislative function," only to observe that

"President Wilson did not write in light of the history of events since he wrote"—a dictum with which, to be sure, it is impossible to disagree—and that "more particularly he did not write of the investigative power of Congress in the context of the First Amendment." But the First Amendment had been in effect for over a century before Wilson wrote, and Justice Frankfurter's next sentence made plain his real meaning—that recent investigative abuses had brought home the force of the First Amendment in a way that Wilson could not have foreseen:

> . . . we would have to be that "blind" Court, against which Mr. Chief Justice Taft admonished . . . that does not see what "all others can see and understand" not to know that there is wide concern, both in and out of Congress, over some aspects of the exercise of the congressional power of investigation.

Nevertheless, Justice Frankfurter and his four colleagues did not say that the demand made on Mr. Rumely was beyond the power of Congress. Just as had Justice Holmes in similar circumstances twice before, the Court in 1953 fell back on the principle that, if a broad construction of a statute or resolution raises doubt of its constitutionality, a narrow construction will be given in order to avoid the constitutional question. And so here Congress had authorized the Buchanan Committee to investigate "lobbying activities," which could readily be construed as limited to "representations made directly to the Congress, its members, or its committees," and as excluding the public dissemination of literature which might indirectly influence the Congress. Defensively, Justice Frankfurter insisted that this "meaning is not barred by intellectual honesty." But the House itself, albeit by a close vote, had approved the broader construction, and Justice Frankfurter plainly felt himself on shaky ground. As on previous occasions, it was the burning proximity of the First Amendment that forced the Court to a narrow construction of dubious Congressional intendment:

> Surely it cannot be denied that giving the scope to the resolution for which the Government contends, that is, deriving from it the power to inquire into all efforts of private individuals to influence public opinion through books and periodicals, however remote the radiations of influence which they may exert upon the ultimate legislative process, raises

doubts of constitutionality in view of the prohibition of the First Amendment . . . it would not be seemly to maintain that these doubts are fanciful or factitious.

What were these "doubts" then? Justice Douglas, writing for himself and Justice Black, thought they had to be stated and resolved. Influences and pressures on the process of law-making, direct or indirect, were surely matters of legitimate concern to Congress, and both the Buchanan Committee and the House had declared unequivocally that it was necessary to learn the identity of the customers of or contributors to CCG in order to arrive at conclusions about the effective scope and possible need for amendment of the 1946 Lobbying Act. Therefore, wrote Justice Douglas:

> Of necessity I come then to the constitutional questions. Respondent represents a segment of the American press. Some may like what his group publishes; others may disapprove. These tracts may be the essence of wisdom to some; to others their point of view and philosophy may be anathema. To some ears their words may be harsh and repulsive; to others they may carry the hope of the future. We have here a publisher who through books and pamphlets seeks to reach the minds and hearts of the American people. He is different in some respects from other publishers. But the differences are minor. Like the publishers of newspapers, magazines, or books, this publisher bids for the minds of men in the marketplace of ideas. . . . The command that "Congress shall make no law . . . abridging the freedom of speech, or of the press" has behind it a long history. It expresses the confidence that the safety of society depends on the tolerance of government for hostile as well as friendly criticism, that in a community where men's minds are free, there must be room for the unorthodox as well as the orthodox views.

So far so good, but in what way would freedom of speech or the press be impaired if Mr. Rumely were obliged to disclose his *clientèle*? After all, his own freedom to publish or distribute literature was not denied by the Buchanan Committee's subpoena. But at this point, the anonymous Lady from Toledo—who had sent in $2000 for the distribution of John T. Flynn's words of wisdom—emerged as the central figure in this drama of the Bill of Rights.

Speech and press are meaningless in desert solitude; spoken and written words are addressed to listeners and readers. Speech and press are a form of communication, and it takes at least two to communicate. The Lady from Toledo was the recipient of communicated thought, and if she were to be put in fear of exposure of her listening or reading habits, the process of communication might be fatally impaired. In other words, the "freedom" guaranteed by the First Amendment is not that of the speaker or publisher alone. It is freedom "of speech," not of the speaker, and "of the press," not of the publisher. It is, in short, *freedom for the process of communication within the nation*, and the dangerous pressure of exposure on the Lady from Toledo was therefore an abridgment of Mr. Rumely's constitutional rights:

> . . . A requirement that a publisher disclose the identity of those who buy his books, pamphlets, or papers is indeed the beginning of surveillance of the press . . . Once the government can demand of a publisher the names of the purchasers of his publications, the free press as we know it disappears. Then the spectre of a government agent will look over the shoulder of everyone who reads. The purchase of a book or pamphlet today may result in a subpoena tomorrow. Fear of criticism goes with every person into the bookstall. The subtle, imponderable pressures of the orthodox lay hold. Some will fear to read what is unpopular, what the powers-that-be dislike. When the light of publicity may reach any student, any teacher, inquiry will be discouraged. The books and pamphlets that are critical of the administration, that preach an unpopular policy in domestic or foreign affairs, that are in disrepute in the orthodox school of thought will be suspect and subject to investigation. The press and its readers will pay a heavy price in harassment. But that will be minor in comparison with the menace of the shadow which government will cast over literature that does not follow the dominant party line. If the lady from Toledo can be required to disclose what she read yesterday and what she will read tomorrow, fear will take the place of freedom in the libraries, bookstores, and homes of the land. Through the harassment of hearings, investigations, reports, and subpoenas government will hold a club over speech and over the press.

These expressions are of great interest, but represent the announced views of only two members of the Court. The collective wisdom of nine—or even seven—highly individualistic justices is bound sometimes to recall the Delphic oracle rather than Mr. Dooley. Did the Congress, as *per* Justice Douglas, authorize an unconstitutional investigation, or did it, as *per* Justice Frankfurter, *not* authorize a broad investigation because, had it done so, the result might have been unconstitutional? No one will ever know, and it is idle to speculate. What is important is that in 1953, in the midst of the cold civil war, all seven justices agreed, and reminded the nation, that the First Amendment is still a vital reality, and that the investigative process must be tempered to its governance.

Thus was the Bill of Rights reinvigorated by the intransigence of Mr. Edward A. Rumely, a man whose political views are so far to the "right" that many liberals would question the genuineness of his adherence to democratic-constitutionalism. To seize on a phrase often mouthed by Senator McCarthy, few liberal hearts bled for Mr. Rumely when the chips were down.

But if it be so that hard cases sometimes make bad law, it is equally true that unpopular causes enable law to rise above sentiment. It is the Nazis and Communists who debase law by equating it to the "healthy feeling of the people." All of which deserves prayerful recollection as we examine the impact of the investigative process when concentrated on the "left" end of the spectrum.

"Are You or Have You Ever Been a Communist?"

How many times since 1938 has this question been asked by investigating committees and government security officers? Most of those asked have answered, but many have declined, pleading their Fifth Amendment privilege against self-incrimination—a response we will scrutinize in the next chapter. Only a few have anticipated or emulated Mr. Rumely's tactic of squarely challenging an investigating committee's authority to require that the question be answered.

Of those few, at least a dozen have paid for their boldness by serving a jail sentence. Nevertheless, the bearing of the Constitution on this now famous question is still a matter of inference, speculation, and uncertainty. The Supreme Court has not yet spoken on the issue, although it has had the opportunity. Three decisions by two lower federal courts, each of which the Supreme Court declined to review, carry no conclusive legal authority,* but the opinions may

* It is definitively settled, and frequently reiterated by the Supreme Court, that its denial of a petition to review the decision of a lower federal court carries

well serve as the starting point of our analysis. All three grew out of 1946 and 1947 hearings, previously mentioned,[24] of the Un-American Activities Committee.

(1) In the course of the Eisler hearings, the Committee subpoenaed Mr. Leon Josephson of New York City, who appeared but refused to be sworn or answer any questions whatsoever, on the ground that the entire inquiry and the Committee itself were unconstitutional. Therefore, the Committee's right to require Mr. Josephson to answer as to his Communist membership or non-membership was not specifically decided, but the court's judgment sustaining Mr. Josephson's conviction under the 1857 statute covered the issue at least by implication.[25]

Two of the three federal circuit judges, sitting in New York, upheld the Committee's authority to inquire into matters of thought and opinion, in furtherance of its task of investigating "un-American propaganda." Judge Charles E. Clark, dissenting, thought that an investigation of un-American propaganda was so broad and vague as to be unconstitutional under both the First and Fifth Amendments. If, however, the inquiry had been confined by Congress to "propaganda for the overthrow of the government by force and violence," Judge Clark indicated that the Committee could rightfully "inquire whether or not the person investigated was a member of any organization that advocated such principles"—including, presumably, the Communist Party, although Judge Clark did not say so. In other words, for him it was the unwarranted breadth of the whole inquiry, rather than the personal nature of the membership question, that was the unconstitutional feature of the case.

(2) The Un-American Activities Committee subpoenaed the records of the Joint Anti-Fascist Refugee Committee, to discover whether or not funds raised by the Anti-Fascist Committee avowedly for postwar foreign relief were in fact being spent for political propaganda. Dr. Edward Barsky and other officers of the Anti-Fascist Committee refused to produce the records, and were indicted and convicted in the District of Columbia under the 1857 statute. On appeal, the conviction was affirmed by two of the three circuit judges,

---

no implication that the decision below is either correct or incorrect. The Court rarely gives its reasons for declining to review decisions, and none was given in these three cases.

despite Dr. Barsky's contention that the records were desired in order to establish his Communist membership or sympathies.[26] Judge Prettyman's opinion upholding the Un-American Activities Committee's power to require individuals to disclose their Communist affiliations, and Judge Edgerton's dissent, are the most comprehensive and articulate so far rendered on this issue.

(3) The "Hollywood Ten" case grew out of the Un-American Activities Committee's 1947 investigation of subversive propaganda in motion pictures.[27] John Howard Lawson and Dalton Trumbo, both prominent Hollywood writers, were subpoenaed to testify before the Committee, and declined to answer the question whether or not they were or had ever been members of the Communist Party. Their refusal was based squarely on the contention that the Bill of Rights, and especially the First Amendment's guarantee of free speech, protects the individual against being compelled to disclose his beliefs and associations. The federal Court of Appeals for the District of Columbia, relying on its earlier decision in the *Barsky* case, rejected this argument and ruled: [28]

> . . . we expressly hold herein that the House Committee on Un-American Activities, or a properly appointed subcommittee thereof, has the *power* to inquire whether a witness subpoenaed by it is or is not a member of the Communist Party or a believer in Communism and that this power carries with it necessarily the power to effect criminal punishment for failure or refusal to answer that question . . . This is equally true of the inquiry whether appellants were members of the Screen Writers' Guild, a question which only Trumbo refused to answer. To hold otherwise would indeed be holding that the power to inquire is a "powerless power."

Whether or not this ruling is valid is a question that the Supreme Court has carefully left unsettled, both by its refusal to review these three decisions and by the narrow basis and guarded language of Justice Frankfurter's opinion in the *Rumely* case. The majority judges of the two lower courts—six in number [29]—supported a sweeping range of Congressional power and construed the First Amendment narrowly. Justices Douglas and Black, Judge Edgerton and, less decisively, Judge Charles Clark conceived narrower limits on Congressional power in the fields of speech, opinion, and association, and favored a broad application of the First Amendment's guarantee of free speech.

In analyzing these two conflicting judicial approaches, we must keep in mind this distinction between *range of Congressional power* on the one hand, and the *scope of the free speech guarantee* on the other. For example, under the Constitution, Congress is expressly given power to levy taxes, but it must not exercise this power in such a way as to abridge freedom of speech or the press, as by imposing prohibitive and discriminatory taxes on newspapers. But Congress has no powers other than those delegated to it by the Constitution—no power to regulate purely intrastate commerce, punish ordinary crimes such as private robberies or murders, issue orders to the armed forces or to do countless other things which remain under the authority of the states or the other branches of the federal government,—and Congressional efforts to exert authority not so delegated are invalid irrespective of whether or not they also contravene the First Amendment.*

In the situation with which we are now concerned the Constitution, Supreme Court decisions, and common sense all support the conclusion that Congress has power to enact laws to protect the government from violent overthrow. The investigative power may therefore be used to obtain information necessary as a basis for legislation of this type.† In testing the validity of Congressional action—whether statutory or investigative—in the field of communism or other subversion, *the decisive questions are whether the action bears some reasonable relation to the purpose of protecting the government, and whether the action violates any prohibitory provisions of the Constitution, including the First Amendment.*[31]

---

* It will be recalled that Alexander Hamilton argued that there was no need for a constitutional Bill of Rights for just this reason—i.e., that Congress had no delegated power to legislate in the field of speech or press, and therefore the specific prohibitions later embodied in the First Amendment would be unnecessary.

† There is an interesting foreshadowing of this purpose in one of the earliest (1858) state court decisions on legislative investigations: [30] "The very tranquillity and existence of the state might require the utmost latitude as to form and subject matter of the questions . . . in order to expose . . . some widespread conspiracy to overthrow the government, or some combination to paralyze its powers by corrupting the high officials under the government."

Of course, these two questions are closely related. The guarantees of free speech and press are not absolute, and the apparent reasonableness or unreasonableness of the statutory or investigative abridgment is very likely to affect the courts' conclusion on the applicability or non-applicability of the First Amendment. Until recent years, Justice Holmes' "clear and present danger" phrase was authoritatively invoked to describe the scope of permissible abridgments of freedom. But when in 1951 the constitutionality of the Smith Act came before the Court, the majority justices found the classic language of 1920 ill-adapted to the issues raised by the world-wide, highly-organized Communist conspiracy. Chief Justice Vinson's opinion approved and adopted a new verbal test, as written in the opinion of the lower federal court by Judge Learned Hand,[32] under which the validity of governmental action restricting freedom of speech depends upon the courts' answer to the question

> . . . whether the gravity of the "evil," discounted by its improbability, justifies such invasion of free speech as is necessary to avoid the danger.

This is, indeed, an equation of imponderables * to which different minds and tempers will find different solutions, as did the individual judges in the *Josephson, Barsky,* and *Hollywood Ten* cases. The three key values are *gravity, probability,* and *necessity,* and Judge Hand's test may be paraphrased as the principle that the graver and more imminent the danger, the deeper is the justifiable incursion on freedom of speech, as long as it is no deeper than is necessary to meet the danger.

But who is going to fill in these quantities in actual cases—Congress, or the courts, or both? The policy judgments, clearly, must be those of Congress, and the disposition of Justices Holmes and Frankfurter has been to shun judicial overturn of Congress' judgment; hence their decisions avoiding difficult constitutional questions, as in the *Harriman, American Tobacco,* and *Rumely* cases. Justices Douglas and Black, on the other hand, sense a more immediate and dynamic judicial obligation to preserve and stimulate the vitality of the guarantees, in line with Madison's prediction [33] that "independent tri-

* It might be mathematically diagramed thus:

$$\text{gravity} \times \frac{\text{probability}}{\text{improbability}} = \begin{array}{c}\text{necessary scope of}\\ \text{abridgment}\end{array}$$

bunals of justice will consider themselves in a peculiar manner the guardians of those rights."

All these quantities were the subjects of disagreement in the *Josephson, Barsky,* and *Hollywood Ten* cases. In terms of the seriousness and imminence of the danger—"gravity of the evil, discounted by its improbability," in Judge Hand's words—there was a fundamental divergence of views about the menace of internal Communism. The majority of the justices thought that it was such as to justify a very broad range of investigative action. Judge Prettyman, for example, declared that the decision in the *Barsky* case turned upon "the present nature of communism and the Communist Party . . . as respectably indicated to the Congress," and for these respectable indications he cited authorities ranging from President Truman (in his Message to Congress of March 12, 1947), General George Marshall, Secretary of State Dean Acheson, J. Edgar Hoover, and Cardinal Spellman to Eugene Lyons, Max Eastman, and Father Edmund Walsh.

When Congress has been advised of a grave potential menace to our government, Judge Prettyman declared, it may use the investigative power, not merely in its traditional role as the "informing function" to enlighten the law-makers, but as an independent weapon of governmental self-preservation. The minority judges did not find communism so grave or imminent a peril as to warrant this extraordinary expansion of investigative power.[34]

In terms of the *necessity* for such sweeping investigative power, the cleavage of opinion was even sharper. Judge Charles Clark thought that the Un-American Activities Committee had been given an unnecessarily broad area in which to roam, covering fields in which Congress has no legislative authority. The minority judges, on the other hand, declared that the appropriate bounds of inquiry are far broader than those of law-making. As Judge Prettyman put it in a later case: [35]

> . . . there is a vast difference between the necessities for congressional inquiry into a subject or situation and the necessities for legislative action . . . Inquiry may be justified when danger is merely potential; danger must be factually real to justify action.

Otherwise, Judge Prettyman pointed out, the danger might grow overwhelmingly grave and proximate before Congress learned of it. And once the power to investigate communism was recognized, so also must be recognized the power *"to identify the individuals who believe in communism and those who belong to the party"* (and the acceptance or rejection of this clause is the key to the entire problem), for the nature of communism and the scope of its program and activities "depend in large measure upon the character and number of their adherents." In short, "Personnel is part of the subject."

To Justices Douglas and Black and Judges Edgerton and Charles Clark, all of this was anathema. If the investigative power is in no way limited to the reach of the law-making power, asked Judge Clark, would not the investigative be left virtually unlimited? "A doctrine that the lesser legislative power always justifies the exercise of the greater investigative power, including control over opinion, will lead to strange analogies indeed!" In fact, "the practical consequences of such a theory" would make "the power to investigate limitless," and for this there was no necessity; a much narrower range of investigation would accomplish the desired purpose.

Judge Edgerton's objections were much more fundamental and rested upon a broad interpretation of the First Amendment. "Freedom of speech is freedom in respect to speech and includes freedom not to speak," he declared, pointing to the injury, both psychological and financial, that may be inflicted on an individual who is required to express unpopular views: "The privilege of choosing between speech that means ostracism and speech that means perjury is not freedom of speech." Apart from the injury to the witness himself, Judge Edgerton, like Justices Douglas and Black, envisaged serious inroads on freedom in the community as a whole: "People have grown wary of expressing any unorthodox opinions." These consequences were quite unnecessary; Congress could obtain the necessary information about communism from the Department of Justice or the intelligence services. Congress could also institute its own investigations, but there was neither need nor power to "compel men to disclose their personal opinions, to a committee and also to the world, on topics varying from communism, however remotely and peaceably achieved, to the 'American system of checks and balances,' the British Empire and the Franco government of Spain."

And so the ten jurists were divided in opinion in a ratio of six to four, but all ten of the Hollywood writers, as well as Messrs. Josephson and Barsky, learned about the true inwardness of jails. Other witnesses, who choose to challenge the authority of the committees to inquire into political affiliations, face the same hazard. Nevertheless, the tone and implications of the *Rumely* case have recently encouraged a number of individuals—Corliss Lamont, Harvey O'Connor, the economist Paul Sweezy (in an investigation conducted by the Attorney General of New Hampshire), and others—to start down that same road of uncertain destination. We will now try to descry a few landmarks, which may serve as a poor substitute for a compass.

We have studied the language in which the judges talk about these issues, and we should keep the judicial approach in mind as we continue their examination. In the last analysis, the courts determine the legality of the conduct of committee members and witnesses when controversies arise.

The courts, however, are not the first but the last determinants of investigative behavior. That an inquiry is constitutional and legally valid does not make it necessary, wise, or impartial. Investigations are authorized and conducted by legislators, and legislators are elected by voters. Legislators and voters alike are responsive to prevailing, changing and conflicting public beliefs and sentiments about investigations. "Congressional capering is going to be stopped, not by the courts, not by the disapproval of lawyers, but by the adverse votes of the voters," a shrewd critic of investigative behavior has written,[36] adding that: "We want the Court to help us, but this is our fight, and the Court had better keep out of the front line. We'd do well to stand up for our civil liberties ourselves instead of running cry baby to the Supreme Court, when we ought to be wringing the political neck of the Committee and of those Congressmen who allow it to continue capering." This is, in short, a political question long before it is a legal problem.

It is also a very practical problem of individual behavior under the stress of investigative pressure. A witness may be governed by any one or combination of the most diverse and inconsistent emotions and purposes. A feeling of obligation as a citizen to assist the committee in its search for information should be the basic and customary point of departure, but the times are too turbulent for this admirable attitude to be all-sufficient. Nor is every witness so happily situated or strong-minded as to govern himself solely by civic rather than personal standards. An individual may testify for praiseworthy motives of frankness and courage, or selfish motives of fear, hate, revenge, or simply out of a lazy desire to take the easy way out. He may refuse to testify for equally good or bad reasons. We must not lose sight of the human problem in a welter of legal precedents and judicial apothegms. Apart from the pressure of the investigating committee's official status and authority, the witness is buffeted by violent currents and counter-currents of public feeling,—the currents of which Mr. Wechsler found himself the sport,[37] when he bewailed the difficulty of explaining to his "perplexed countrymen" the reasons for his choice among "rival expediencies."

Back of this bewilderment and division of public opinion about investigations of communism is disagreement and misunderstanding about what is being investigated. For Whittaker Chambers, regarded by many as an expert on the subject, the American Communist Party is not "an organization like other political parties"; [38] it is "an instrument of conspiracy" and its purposes "are utterly different from those of other political parties." These purposes are to overthrow our present government and establish in America a Communist government and society, and to this end the Party "wages constant war." Congress has explicitly adopted much of this thinking in the Internal Security Act of 1950 and, more recently, the Communist Control Act of 1954.*

If the Communist Party is, then, not a political party but a criminal conspiracy to overthrow the government, are not all Communists criminal conspirators? Here is the root of much confusion. Congress has declined so far to declare Communist membership a crime, and has only recently, and in a confused political *mise en scène*, "outlawed" the Communist Party as an organization and a political party. The Smith Act punishes conspiracy to advocate violent overthrow of the government and many Communists have been convicted of

* Section 2 of the Internal Security Act sets forth findings based upon "evidence adduced before various committees" of the Senate and House, and concludes that the American Communist organization, although a self-designated political party, is in fact a constituent element of the world-wide Communist conspiracy. Comparable findings are embodied in the so-called "stump speech" section of the Communist Control Act, which expressly "outlaws" the Communist Party.

this crime, but some (including self-confessed Communists) have been acquitted. The Internal Security Act declares that Communists "in effect repudiate their allegiance to the United States, and in effect transfer their allegiance to the country in which is vested the direction and control of the world Communist movement"—presumably, Soviet Russia. One might readily assume that such conduct is criminal under the Smith Act, but the Internal Security Act carefully and explicitly provides [39] that neither membership nor even office-holding in "any Communist organization" shall in itself constitute criminal conduct.

But no such ambivalence characterizes Mr. Chambers' attitude. Asked "what is a Communist," he replied: "Most simply, a Communist is the soldier, in uniform or business suit, whom you or your children have faced, or will face, in one form or another in military or civil combat." * This is indeed a "simple" definition, and if every Communist is in effect an enemy soldier, every effort to expose and render him harmless is fully justified. But is this not *too* "simple" an analysis?

No doubt it is closer to the full truth today than it was during the thirties and forties, when depression and war produced a parallelism between certain announced communist policies and liberal-democratic-internationalist thinking.† Communist economic totalitarianism still has drawing power in poverty-stricken southern Europe and Asia, but has had little or none in the United States since the depressed thirties. The "united front" against the Axis lost its *raison d'être* in the fulfillment of military victory in 1945. The hope for a stable and enduring peace based on Soviet-American friendship, which underlay the Wallaceite-Progressive-American Labor Party coalescences of the forties, has frozen in the cold realization that a

---

* Other publicists have been even more categorical. According to one Hamilton Long, whose views have been embodied in an official House document,[40] every Communist is "pledged to treason," and there are "no innocents" in the conspiracy.

† These parallelisms are still traps for the unwary. During the recent "Reece" Committee hearings on tax-exempt foundations, the Committee's associate research director testified, before their authorship had been disclosed to him, that certain excerpts from the papal encyclicals of Leo XIII (1891) and Pius XI (1931) "paralleled very closely Communistic ideals." [40a]

sunny, friendly world of Communist-capitalist cooperation is not what the Kremlin wants.

These were the great "pulls" that Communism once exerted on the American mind, and they are all nearly if not quite dead. In the meantime, the ugliness of Soviet totalitarianism and imperialism has been more widely perceived. The Party's psychological and numerical strength in the United States has dwindled correspondingly. Likewise, the Party has been penetrated by government agents, and no doubt its leaders are now much more circumspect about new recruits. For all these reasons, joining the Party or continuing a membership today carries much sharper implications than formerly, and in all probability the present membership is more homogeneous and intransigent.

It is fair to conclude, then, not only that the Communist Party embodies a conspiracy to overthrow the government, but also that the conspiracy bulks large in the sum total of the Party's current aspects and activities. But from this it does not follow that the Party is only and nothing more than a conspiracy, or that every member or adherent is a conspirator. Communism also embodies, and the Party espouses, a system of thought—the Marxist dialectic—which is intended to be applied to the solution of historical, economic, and political problems.

This doctrine is controversial, and parts of it are widely regarded as obsolete and discredited, but it is not criminal. Communism likewise includes a bundle of attitudes on current political issues, which the Party has promoted much in the manner of political parties generally, by nominating candidates for public office, or publishing newspapers and magazines.* These attitudes shift as the "line" of ex-

* This was recognized by Chief Justice Hughes when, in 1937, he wrote the Court's opinion declaring unconstitutional an Oregon statute making it a crime to participate in a meeting held under the auspices of an organization that advocates violent overthrow: [41]

"Thus if the Communist Party had called a public meeting in Portland to discuss the tariff, or the foreign policy of the Government, or taxation, or relief, or candidacies for the offices of President, members of Congress, Governor, or state legislators, every speaker who assisted in the conduct of the meeting would be equally guilty with the defendant in this case, upon the charge as here defined and sustained. The list of illustrations might be indefinitely extended to every variety of meetings under the auspices of the Communist Party although held for the discussion of political issues or to adopt protests and pass resolutions of an entirely innocent and proper character."

pediency dictates, but some are relatively stable, and parallelisms with powerful currents of non-Communist thinking often occur even today, such as opposition to racial discrimination or to German rearmament.

Even though the Party is dominated by conspiratorial leaders, therefore, it is apparent that individuals may seek to join it for much less sinister reasons. Indeed, they may be impelled toward the Party not so much by rational processes as by psychological and circumstantial causes. Many are soon disillusioned and endeavor, more or less successfully, to retrace their steps. Are all these ex-Communists to be regarded as ex-criminal conspirators?

The complications are infinitely greater when we spread the problem back over the thirties and forties, and over "front" organizations as well as the Party proper. There was a conspiracy then, too, but it may well be doubted that many of those who joined the Party in those years were aware of its existence, much less its activities. In government circles, where espionage might be profitably conducted, the conspiratorial aspect would more often become apparent. But in journalism, the stage, Hollywood, science, law, labor organizations, and the academic world, many of those who joined the Party and most of those who joined what were or later became "fronts" did not want to conspire, or to overthrow the government. They wanted political and economic reforms, aid for the Spanish Loyalists, and a strongly anti-Axis foreign policy.* After the war they wanted peace.

Now the iron curtain and the cold war have overlaid those years with a blanket of recrimination and fear. Yesterday's stock market quotations are worthless, but yesterday's membership lists are still the stock in trade of the loyalty investigators. It is into a past which is not dead, but tense and quivering, that the question "Are you *or have you ever been* a Communist" is plunged like a hot knife.

Even if the question can be truthfully answered in the negative in

---

* The statement of Dr. V. Jerauld McGill, one of three members recently dismissed from the faculty of Hunter College for refusal to name other former members of the Communist Party, is characteristic: "I became a Communist in the Nineteen Thirties together with hundreds of thousands of my generation because, like them, I feared that Hitler might dominate Europe and the world, and that a new world depression was on its way, entailing unemployment, intolerance and oppression. I turned away from Communist ideas when I realized that in practice they were incompatible with my conception of human values."[41a]

both its tenses, it usually leads to other inquiries involving a dense and tangled web of associations, meetings, speeches, memberships, and contributions—a weird *pasticcio* of sharecroppers, poll-taxes, Scottsboro boys, labor organizers and labor spies, munitions merchants and bankers, Spanish loyalists, refugees, boycotts, Russian war relief, Chiang Kai-shek, agrarian reform, the Stockholm "peace appeal" and what not else.

This is the major subject matter of the Congressional loyalty investigations; it is idle to imagine that they are principally occupied in identifying present members of the Communist Party, eager as some of the investigators are to give that impression, as by mouthing the phrase "Fifth Amendment Communist." Therefore the wisdom and validity of current Congressional methods of inquiry into these things cannot be determined simply by declaring that the Communist Party is a conspiracy, for this is but one of many facets of a highly complicated historical, political and moral situation.

Who is properly entitled and legally authorized to expose individual strands of this taut and touchy pattern of our past decades of depression and of war? Who should be expected and who can be compelled to disclose his own record, or those of his friends, throughout those years?

Investigation, Identification, and Inquisition

Relating his experiences with the McCarthy committee,[42] Mr. James Wechsler observed that "there is in the American tradition a very real belief that the man who has nothing to conceal will speak up when spoken to; muteness has not often been equated with valor." He went on to quote from an article he had written in 1947:

> It would be nice if the world were prettier, but it isn't; espionage and sabotage are facts of modern life. I have no brief for anybody who refuses to testify before a congressional committee; no matter how foolish or fierce the committee, an American ought to be prepared to state his case in any public place at any time.

There is indeed an American tradition of outspokenness, but it is by no means the only one. In frontier days questions were not asked or answered without good reason, and in more sophisticated circles it has never been considered bad form to mind one's own business and keep one's own counsel. Furthermore, there is a missing link in Mr. Wechsler's reasoning; to be sure, espionage and sabotage are no imaginary perils, and any citizen who has information helpful to their detection and prevention ought to disclose what he knows to the proper authorities pronto. But it is to be doubted that "any public place" is likely to be the right one for such revelations, and it is impossible to establish a logical nexus between espionage and sabotage on the one hand and stating one's case on the other.

In any event, I question whether reluctance to recount one's life and expound one's opinions "in any public place at any time"—whether from reticence, reserve, modesty, timidity or other quality—is rightly to be put down as intrinsically un-American. We have observed that free speech in the empty desert is an empty liberty; so is it also if everyone is so busy talking that none can hear. If they do not serve, they also live and breathe who only sit and listen. Mr. Wechsler's viewpoint is that of a highly articulate and forthright editor and publicist. It is his business to state his case in public places at all times. His admirable qualities are exercised in an honored occupation, but it takes all sorts and conditions of men to make a world.

The very word "inquisition," by its pejorative quality, testifies to the high value men have placed on privacy and security. In past centuries, however, when they were called upon to "state their case," it was usually in connection with a prosecution or punitive proceeding to establish their guilt of some crime, frequently heresy or treason. And it was as rules of criminal procedure, to protect the accused against oppressive tactics, that two great principles developed: that a man cannot be made to testify against himself, and that his premises and possessions shall not be subjected to unreasonable searches and seizures. The first became part of the Fifth Amendment and is discussed in the next chapter; the second is embodied in the Fourth Amendment and is closely tied up with the idea of privacy.

Outside the criminal courts, however, is privacy anything more than a desirable condition? Is it a legal right, like one's physical person or property, which can be protected by civil suit if it is trespassed against? Strangely enough, the question has seldom arisen, and the answer is still far from clear. A few cases have involved the unauthorized publication of letters, photographs and other *per-*

sonalia. In this context, an English judge wrote, as long ago as 1769, that [43] "every man has a right to keep his own sentiments, if he pleases; he has certainly a right to judge whether he will make them public, or commit them only to the sight of his friends." Perhaps this was so generally assumed in nineteenth-century England and America that there was no further occasion for judges to say so; at all events, the problem attracted little or no attention until 1890, when Samuel Warren and Louis D. Brandeis published a pioneer legal study entitled *The Right to Privacy.*[44] Since then, privacy has been explicitly recognized as a legally enforceable right in a few court decisions,[45] but its substance and scope are still unsettled and elusive.

As between the individual and the government, however, the concept of privacy is much less amorphous. In the colonies, James Otis thundered against the writs of assistance, under which British revenue officers were breaking into homes and places of business, and declared that the writs placed "the liberty of every man in the hands of every petty officer." In England during the early 1760's, John Wilkes denounced the practice of issuing general warrants to search private houses for books and papers that might be used to convict the owners of seditious libel, and in 1765 the warrants were declared illegal and void in a famous decision by Lord Camden.[46]

These events were fresh in the minds of the members of the First Congress and the contemporaneous state legislators when the Fourth Amendment was drafted and adopted. Security of persons, houses, papers and effects against unreasonable searches and seizures is a *desideratum* primarily based on the idea of privacy, and in the first great Supreme Court decision interpreting the Fourth Amendment, Justice Bradley wrote that its underlying principles [47] "apply to all invasions, on the part of the government and its employees, of the sanctity of a man's home and the privacies of life."

If government officers cannot ransack a man's private papers for evidence against him, should they be allowed to "search" his oral speech for this purpose? Before the days of recorded sound the question did not arise, but today it is the nub of the debate about wiretapping. In 1928 the Supreme Court, in an opinion by Chief Justice Taft, ruled that the Fourth Amendment applies only to the "material things"—person, house, papers and effects—expressly mentioned, and the Court allowed transcripts of wire-tapped conversations to be used in evidence against a bootlegger.[48] Justice Brandeis dissenting, in language redolent of his article written thirty-eight years earlier, delivered the classic statement of the Constitution's protection of privacy: [49]

> The makers of our Constitution undertook to secure conditions favorable to the pursuit of happiness. They recognized the significance of man's spiritual nature, of his feelings and of his intellect. They knew that only a part of the pain, pleasure and satisfactions of life are to be found in material things. They sought to protect Americans in their beliefs, their thoughts, their emotions and their sensations. They conferred, as against the Government, the right to be let alone—the most comprehensive of rights and the right most valued by civilized men. To protect that right, every unjustifiable intrusion by the Government upon the privacy of the individual, whatever the means employed, must be deemed a violation of the Fourth Amendment.

Is the First Amendment's guarantee of free speech also impregnated with this philosophy? Like the Fourth Amendment, the First has its roots in the eighteenth-century prosecutions for seditious utterances and publications, such as that of the New York printer, John Peter Zenger, in 1735.[50] Its historical purpose, however, was not so much to prevent inquisition as to liberate public discussion, and especially criticism of the government and its officials, from the inhibiting restrictions of the sedition prosecutions. And it has, therefore, been both doubted [51] and denied [52] that the First Amendment confers any right of silence, of refusal to speak, or of privacy in speaking.

But, so far as concerns Congressional and other legislative investigations, there seems no longer to be any doubt that witnesses do have rights of refusal to speak or to produce documents, derived from the First and Fourth Amendments.* The Supreme Court's progress toward this conclusion, which has been instinctive rather than precisely reasoned, reveals a high degree of concern for "privacy." Justice Miller spoke somewhat artlessly of "private affairs" in his opin-

* Of course, even if this were not so, Congress' right of inquiry would nevertheless be limited to its constitutionally delegated powers. On the Hamiltonian theory that these include *no* powers in the field of speech and press,[53] the upshot would be even more restrictive of Congress.

ion in the *Kilbourn* case,[54] and in nearly every subsequent opinion of the Court dealing with Congressional investigative power the phrases "private affairs," "private papers," or "right of privacy" have been used to denote an area in which the power is constitutionally limited.[55] Then in 1936, in an opinion discussing constitutional limitations on an administrative agency's regulatory power, Justice Sutherland described—[56]

> . . . the three protective rights of the individual—that against compulsory self-accusation, that against unlawful searches and seizures, and *that against unlawful inquisitorial investigations.*

On what article or amendment is this third right based? Justice Sutherland did not say, nor did Justice Jackson when he wrote in 1943 that: [57]

> If there is any fixed star in our constitutional constellation, it is that no official, high or petty, can prescribe what shall be orthodox in politics, nationalism, religion, or other matters of opinion, *or force citizens to confess by word or act their faith therein.*

The *Rumely* decision, reaffirming the bearing of the First Amendment on the investigative power,[58] followed logically from these declarations. One may look at the matter as did Judge Edgerton, primarily from the standpoint of the individual, and interpret "freedom of speech" as conferring freedom of choice to speak or not to speak, on the theory that inquisition is as hateful and as destructive of free speech as is censorship. Or one may, as did Justice Douglas and Judge Prettyman,[59] treat freedom of speech not so much as an individual right as a desirable condition in the community, and conclude that inquisitorial abuses choke off public discussion of controversial issues by spreading fear. On one footing or the other or both, "unlawful inquisitorial investigations" by legislative committees are forbidden by the Bill of Rights.

But the Supreme Court has not told us, in the *Rumely* case or elsewhere, how the line is to be drawn between lawful investigation and unlawful inquisition. Judge Prettyman, who participated in both the *Barsky* and *Rumely* cases, sought to draw a distinction between investigations into matters such as communism, which had been "respectably represented" to Congress as a danger to national security, and other subjects, such as lobbying, which could not be regarded as sufficiently threatening to warrant incursions into the Bill of Rights. When Communists are the quarry, the First Amendment must bend if not break under the investigative power, and "If Congress has the power to inquire into the subjects of Communism and the Communist Party, it has the power to *identify* the individuals who believe in Communism and those who belong to the party." [60]

This is what may be called the "identification" theory of investigative power in the field of subversive activities, and it is the theory upon which the leading Congressional red-hunters have usually based their authority. Senator Jenner's Internal Security Subcommittee, for example, has recently specialized in quizzing teachers in public schools and private colleges and universities about their past political affiliations. When challenged on the ground that municipal or private education is no concern of the federal government, Senator Jenner and his spokesmen have replied that they are not investigating education, but only seeking to identify and expose individual Communist or fellow-traveling educators. Less fastidious, Senator McCarthy is fond of describing his own activities as "hunting skunks."

Now, the major flaw in this "identification" theory of investigative power is that it has no terminal facilities—it leads anywhere and everywhere.* Let us limit our consideration for the moment to the standard opening question—"Are you or have you ever been a Communist?" Few would deny that government employees may rightfully be required to answer, as well as members of the armed services, scientists or others having access to official secrets or classified documents, or workers in areas readily susceptible to sabotage. Beyond this we run into the more controversial field of teachers, scriptwriters, entertainers, labor union officers, factory employees, and passport-seekers.

All this some of us may be prepared to swallow, but the identifica-

* There is another difficulty with the theory, in that it takes no account of the separation of powers. Assuming that every individual's political affiliations, past and present, should be subject to investigation and disclosure, it would seem that this should be done by the executive or judicial branches under statutory authority, rather than by a legislative committee acting under a resolution.

tion theory has sped ahead while we paused for reflection. Judge Prettyman rightly observed that the size and composition of the Communist Party are facts which Congress needs to know. Coupling this object with the identification method, we must be prepared to accept the conclusion that an investigating committee can "pop the question" to the housewife on the Grand Concourse, the dirt farmer in Iowa, the elderly retired couple in their trailer in Florida or cottage in California, the corner druggist, the country doctor on his rounds, the lady sewing upstairs and the man mowing his lawn next door—in short, to anyone.

And the next step is everyone. Lecturing recently before a women's club in Forest Hills, Mr. Louis Budenz was asked by an eager member whether "there are more Communists in Astoria than there are in Forest Hills?" [61] If the numerical strength of the Party is the question, can not the investigating committee, like the Ancient Mariner, stop "one of three," or every tenth passerby at selected vantage points, and conduct a confessional poll on the question? In New York City there is a particular Congressional election district with a concentration of American Labor Party strength; may Congress interrogate every resident to determine whether there is a corresponding concentration of Communists or ex-Communists? In 1853 the New York police force was under attack as overloaded with Irishmen; in 1953 the press reported accusations that the force was infiltrated by Communists. Is Senator Jenner's committee empowered to call every member of the "Finest" for questioning? Perhaps the accomplishment of these tasks would exhaust Congress' investigatorial manpower, in which event there is always the census. On the identification theory, would it not be legitimate as well as economical to turn the matter over to the Bureau of Census, and require *everyone* to tell the census-taker under oath whether or not he or she is or has ever been a Communist?

But we have only scratched the surface with this single question of past or present Communist membership. Mr. Dalton Trumbo was jailed for his additional refusal to say whether or not he belonged to the Screen-Writers' Guild. Today, every man drafted into the armed forces is supposed to be shown a copy of the Attorney General's list of hundreds of organizations that he has determined to be Communist-dominated—the so-called "front" organizations—and the new recruit must state under oath which, if any, he has been connected with.[62] I share the doubts of many about the suitability of this list for the uses to which it is often put, but certainly no seriously-intended investigation of communism can rest upon the single question of Communist Party membership as the all-sufficient test of loyalty. And from this it follows, if we adopt the identification theory, that anyone and everyone can be required to disclose all organizational affiliations that might be deemed significant in terms of communism.

Still this is not all. An investigating committee worth its salt is not necessarily satisfied with the answers given to direct questions. It is part of our tradition that public bodies—whether judicial or administrative tribunals or legislative committees—dealing with disputed factual questions, rely heavily on cross-examination to detect accidental or deliberate errors in testimony. And so a witness who may rightfully be asked whether or not he is or ever has been a member of the Communist Party or any of numerous suspected organizations, and answers in the negative, is subject to cross-examination to test the truth of his denial.

What is the permissible scope of the cross-questioning? The Communist Party is officially atheistic, and it has been argued that the lack of an explicit and overt faith in the Deity may reveal a Communistic propensity.* What does the witness think about Tito, Mikhailovitch and Archbishop Stepinac? About General Franco and Aneurin Bevan, or Chiang Kai-shek and Dean Acheson? About outlawing the Communist Party, or cutting off American aid to countries that trade with Red China? About German rearmament and the Nuremburg trials? Most particularly, about the activities of Messrs. McCarthy, Jenner, Velde, *et alii*?

As tests of loyalty, these questions will seem absurd if not alarming to some, and wholly appropriate to others. Be that as it may, these are entirely characteristic of the sort of questions put to witnesses by investigating committees and loyalty boards almost every day of the year. Senator McCarthy's suspicions of Mr. Wechsler, for example,

---

* Whittaker Chambers defines the Communist faith [63] as "an aggressive faith that rejects God and calls upon man to stand alone, to use the resources of his own mind, especially technology and science, to create his own heaven on earth and to give meaning to his history and his destiny."

seemed to stem chiefly from the latter's critical opinion of the Senator and his ways, and the cross-examinations of such reluctant notables as Owen Lattimore, Theodore Kaghan, Reed Harris, as well as many others examined in executive session, are full of similar illustrations.

Those who view such goings-on with a jaundiced eye will do well to remember that it is no easy matter to draw the line of wisdom and propriety to govern questioning on matters of opinion, once we are launched on the search for political unreliability. In some foreign countries, the accusation that the United States Air Force resorted to germ warfare in Korea raised a debatable issue; nevertheless, invidious inferences may justifiably be drawn about the loyalty of Americans who support the truth of the charge. If we are seeking to perceive the true color of an individual's thinking, it may be relevant to discover his opinion of Max Lerner's writings, or those of any other outspoken publicist. What is truly worrisome is that our loyalty sleuths never seem to be interested in uncovering a weakness for such lucubrations as those of Westbrook Pegler.

But we are not now concerned with how far a government employee—or other individuals in "sensitive" positions—may be required to travel down the road of introspection and self-revelation, presumably stopping somewhere short of the psychoanalyst's couch. We are concerned with the constitutional limits of legislative investigative power in the field of loyalty and subversion. This is where the identification theory has led us, and we now find ourselves deep in what can accurately be described only as *inquisition.*

We will return shortly to the political and social implications of this analysis. So far as concerns the law and the courts, we may immediately conclude that the identification theory will not suffice. Our courts will never, short of a revolutionary re-evaluation of the Constitution and its meaning, support an exercise of the investigative power that puts every man's past record of association and opinion to the test of either public or secret inquisition under oath.

It has been said since long ago that criticism is easier than craftsmanship. We shall be little the better for this excursion if we do not attempt to work out a guide that is less vulnerable to analysis than the identification theory. We have been discussing freedom and privacy, but security, too, has its claims. Mr. Wechsler's assertion of the duty of Americans to be outspoken is perhaps an overstatement, but it is not devoid of substance. In the *Josephson* case, Judge Charles Clark put the same thought in perspective when he noted "The general feeling that one should stand up and show his true colors" and declared that: [64]

> This quite normal reaction that a Communist, as well as anyone else, should say what he is when the fact is of importance to the public good could be allowed its natural scope if, first, however, the investigating authority is properly limited to constitutional objectives.

The constitutional limitations should correspond to the public good, and Judge Learned Hand has identified the materials with which we have to work—*gravity* and *proximity* of the danger, to be balanced against the *necessity* and *extent* of the abridgment of freedom. There is no single formula to solve such an equation. No more is it possible to call in the Bureau of Standards to give us an absolute measure of "negligence" in automobile accidents, or "reasonable doubt" in criminal trials.

This is a tense area where the law, to sustain its growth, must feed upon finger-tip judgment rather than formal logic. I believe, therefore, that the Supreme Court will avoid the straitjacket of sweeping decisions and categorical determinants. It is, for example, highly unlikely that the Court will hold either that *anyone* or that *no one* can be required to disclose his political associations. Considerations such as the following are likely to carry weight in decision-making.

(1) A world-wide revolutionary movement such as communism, based on a doctrinaire and intransigent dialectic, comprising millions of disciplined and devoted adherents, dominating most of the geopolitical heartland of Eurasia, and led by the only other nation that can presently hope to match our military strength, is by definition an extremely grave threat to the security and tranquillity of the United States. If the gravity of the ultimate peril were the sole criterion, in order to ward it off we should be prepared to accept the most unpleasant restrictions and radical readjustments, short of destroying the very core of the values we seek to defend, of which freedom is probably the one most treasured. But the ultimate gravity of the danger is not the only element; its nature, direction and proximity are equally important dimensions.

(2) Many facets of the Communist danger from abroad, particularly its military and diplomatic manifestations, are not directly relevant to any necessary abridgment of our civil liberties. To be sure, growing Soviet power, or serious American setbacks in the cold war, will tend to increase our tolerance of domestic restrictions of all kinds. But the Russians and Chinese would give us plenty to worry about today—in Korea, Indochina, Central Europe and elsewhere—even if there were no question of the loyalty and militant anti-communism of every single American citizen.

There is, however, one aspect of the Communist peril which is very proximate and very relevant in terms of investigation and disclosure of individual backgrounds. I refer to espionage by agents of Soviet Communism.* In areas susceptible to espionage, it would appear that the most searching investigation of an individual's political background is both justifiable and desirable.

(3) There remains what might be called "domestic and psychological warfare," by which I mean Communist efforts to influence American opinion on public issues, by means of open political activity, front organizations, and so forth. We have already noted that, lacking the depression and nazism to exploit, communism finds it much more difficult than formerly to attract followers and fellow-travelers in America. In this respect the danger seems to be receding. Let it also be noted that there is nothing intrinsically criminal about this type of activity. We ourselves endeavor to influence opinion behind the iron curtain; this is the very purpose of agencies such as the Voice of America and Radio Free Europe.

Nevertheless, it is in the opinion- and attitude-forming occupations—education, entertainment, journalism, and science especially—that the loyalty issue is contested most furiously. But if there is a serious present danger from Communist infiltration in these fields, it is surely unfortunate that attention is so rarely focused on current or even recent circumstances, and that instead there is such intense preoccupation with events of five to twenty-five years ago. Even more disturbing is it that our investigators seem so much more concerned about individual political backgrounds than about concrete

* In general discussion, sabotage is customarily coupled with espionage, though there is much less publicly available evidence that the Russians are seriously attempting sabotage in the United States at the present time.

manifestations of Communist machination. These are superficial and short-sighted—or worse, politically vengeful—attitudes that serve chiefly to obscure the present extent of Communist penetration.

If investigating committees and courts are to make wise decisions on the circumstances, if any, under which individuals engaged in professional and cultural pursuits may be compelled to disclose their political records, the committees and courts must know whether they are dealing with substantially possible or chimerical dangers. For example, Hollywood script-writers might more reasonably be required to reveal their political pasts, if the investigating committee had first produced credible evidence that motion pictures are actually infused with subversive propaganda, than if such a showing is wholly lacking.* There are so many real perils to national security that we can ill afford to waste time and energy, much less jeopardize our liberties, in the angry revival of old misunderstandings and recriminations.

(4) Furthermore, if we turn to the second magnitude of Judge Hand's test equation—the extent of the invasion of free speech—it is by now abundantly clear that the actual encroachment is very considerable, and the potential truly alarming. The world of ideas congeals when governmental power is used to degrade and ostracize dissenters. The public policy underlying free speech is not only to secure the benefits of individual freedom, but to profit by free and open discussion.

This we cannot do if ideas are to be tested by personal accusation rather than on the merits. Oscar Wilde replied to the *ad hominem* by declaring that the fact that a man is a poisoner is nothing against his prose. This is, of course, an epigrammatic overstatement. We certainly do want to know that a man is a poisoner if his prose consists of a pharmaceutical prescription. But President Eisenhower himself opined that Dashiell Hammett's detective stories should not be judged by the author's political eccentricities and, to come closer to the point at issue, should not the same principle hold good for Howard Fast's *Citizen Tom Paine*?

There is no need for multiple illustrations. If the First Amendment is to retain any effective force, it must at least be held to mean that

* It is a familiar principle in courts of law that questions cannot be put unless a "foundation" has been laid to show their relevance to the matter in hand.[65]

freedom of speech and press shall not be abridged, in the interests of national security, one jot or tittle more than may reasonably be regarded as *necessary* to preserve the governmental and constitutional framework which itself creates those freedoms. If the abridgment bears no substantial relation to the peril or is needlessly drastic, or if adequate protection can be obtained by other means, then the incursion must be repelled. In terms of Congressional investigations into matters of opinion and association, this means that the power must be restricted in accordance with the rule repeatedly stated by the Supreme Court: [66] "the least possible power adequate to the end proposed."

(5) In the first instance, the necessity of a legislative inquiry into any particular subject must be determined by the legislature itself. In the past, when dealing with issues such as corruption in public office, the courts have given the legislatures very wide latitude in making this determination, and have declared that every reasonable presumption must be indulged that the inquiry has a legitimate legislative purpose.

The necessity for investigating a potential threat to national security must likewise be determined in the first instance by Congress. But if the investigation is then carried out in such a way as to impinge upon the constitutional guarantees by forcing individuals to disclose their opinions and associations, then the necessity for such a course of action must be substantially supported. The investigation is itself endangering constitutionally protected values, and this cannot be justified by loose or casual presumptions; these may not be indulged when a deep issue of personal freedom is at stake. When personal inquisition and political aggrandizement masquerade as legislative investigation, and when the legislative benefits are trivial as compared to the incursion on the Bill of Rights, the courts should not lend their aid to force witnesses to answer.

(6) The more closely an investigation is directed to governmental operations or to matters commonly regarded as of a semi-governmental and public nature, the greater is the possible justification for compelling the disclosure of personal backgrounds. The courts will, for example, more willingly require government officials or the employees of a company manufacturing secret military equipment to

reveal their political affiliations, than they would in the case of a farmer, a country doctor, or a playwright.[67]

Since Congress appropriates the funds and specifies the powers and general structure of government agencies, it may reasonably assert an interest in the loyalty of individual employees, even though the final authority to decide particular cases must remain in the executive branch. Outside the field of government operations, however, where Congress' only legitimate concern is with obtaining information for use in general law-making, the necessity or justification for extensive scrutiny of individual cases is not equally apparent. The unending exposure of individuals ceases to be investigation and becomes, basically, a police or judicial action having no reasonable relation to the legislative function.

An illustration from quite another field may make the point clearer. The state governments have the power to pass laws regulating marriage and divorce, and criminal laws governing crimes such as adultery and other sexual-social offenses. Obviously, a very wide range of information about human behavior may be useful in framing these laws, and a state legislature may properly decide to obtain it by means of a committee investigation.

Does this mean that the committee could, in effect, run a Dr. Kinsey survey, with individual questioning backed by the subpoena power? Certainly the legislature does not really need to procure the information by any such method or in specific and individual detail. If it were attempted, surely the courts would hold that the legislative interest in personal peregrinations, predilections and peccadillos is far too slight to justify the humiliation and pervasive fear which would be caused. And this is also true in other fields of inquiry, including the one with which we are now chiefly concerned.

(7) In fixing the limits of investigative power in the field of loyalty and subversion, should it make any difference whether the witness is asked about his own political background, or is called upon to testify about the opinions and associations of other persons? Almost certainly, the courts will *not* hold that a witness has any special right to refuse to give information, derogatory or otherwise, about other persons. The witness' personal feelings about informing have nothing to do with the question of the investigating committee's authority to obtain the information.

In passing upon particular cases, however, the circumstance that the witness is asked to furnish derogatory information about others may well affect the courts' attitude, particularly if the inquiry is far removed from governmental affairs. It is not so much any notion of sportsmanship that is likely to carry weight. Rather it may be felt that government compulsion, exercised outside a court of law and for merely informational purposes, to force an individual to discuss the political views and affiliations, and even the private conversations, of others, might well be a greater hazard to freedom of discussion and relaxed social intercourse than compulsion limited to the individual's own opinions and associations. This problem of "other people's names" also involves the Fifth Amendment privilege against self-incrimination, and we will return to it in the next chapter.[68]

Certainly many other circumstantial factors, in addition to those we have now reviewed, will come into play in the process of judicial adjustment of this vexed and delicate equation between security and freedom. Furthermore, the courts are most unlikely to grasp these nettles with alacrity, and this reluctance is not solely due to fear of the sting. In the *Rumely* case, Justice Frankfurter and a majority of the Court thought it wise to dispose of the case without facing up to the huge constitutional issues that loomed, because questions of such gravity "are matters properly to be decided by this Court only when they inescapably come before us for adjudication."

It may well be a long time before the Court is confronted with a case in which it can find no avenue of escape from the constitutional issues. In the meantime, these problems must be considered and dealt with by voters, witnesses, and, above all, by Congressmen. As a political matter, how did we get started on this slow march toward inquisition, and what measure of investigative activity in the field of political opinion and association should we now support, not as lawyers but as citizens and voters?

The Interdependence of Freedom and Security

Our cold civil war has many roots and antecedents, some of which were discussed in earlier chapters.[69] Congressional investigations of "un-Americanism," by whatever committee, are a major part and projection of this background, and they have generally been under the domination of extremist politicians of the Dies-McCarran-McCarthy stamp.

But to say this merely denotes, without analyzing, this remarkable and controversial phenomenon—perhaps the most revolutionary development in recent American political history. Only too clearly, many Americans are not much concerned about whatever damage the inquiries may be doing to the separation of powers and the Bill of Rights. This can only be because the investigations are giving them something that they think they want, and that they do not think they are getting anywhere else.

Now, in my opinion, that "something" is an *extra-legal means of inflicting punishment on individuals* who are distrusted by these many Americans. Extra-legal obloquy and mistreatment are nothing new in the world; religious and racial minorities have long been subjected to them in many forms. Nor is this the first time that investigations have been made to serve such purposes. A century ago many New Yorkers disliked and distrusted the newly-arrived Irish immigrants; the Board of Aldermen's investigation of the police, instigated by the Know-Nothings, was undertaken to degrade and discredit the Irish Catholic minority,[70] a purpose which could not have been accomplished by regular legal processes because, although it was unpopular to be Irish, it was not criminal.

No more do the issues with which the loyalty investigations are primarily concerned lend themselves readily to statutory formulation. Fourteen years ago a vast radio audience heard the perennial presidential aspirants Thomas E. Dewey and Harold Stassen debate the question whether or not membership in the Communist Party should be declared a crime. Today that argument is still with us, and despite the Smith Act of 1940, the Internal Security (McCarran) Act of 1950, and the Communist Control Act of 1954, Communist membership, without more, is still not criminal under the laws of the United States.*

But present or even past membership in the Party is only a small part of the picture. The Attorney General has "listed" hundreds of

* Some states have enacted statutes outlawing Party membership, notably Texas, where membership is punishable by up to twenty years in prison and a fine of $20,000. The constitutionality of such statutes is still an open question.

organizations as Communist-dominated, but this does not make them illegal. The McCarran Act has established a new federal agency —the Subversive Activities Control Board—to make legally binding determinations that accused organizations are or are not "Communist-action" or "Communist-front" organizations. It also requires all members of the first category to submit their names to a public register maintained by the Attorney General. However, the Board's procedures, based upon hearings and findings subject to judicial review, are necessarily time-consuming.

None of these statutory provisions meets the needs of those who put their principal faith in the investigations. Statutes cannot make it criminal to *have been* a member of the Young Communist League at college, or of the American League for Peace and Democracy in the late thirties, or to have supported the Spanish Loyalists because they were fighting Franco, or to have spoken favorably of the Chinese Communists because they were fighting the Japanese. Yet past associations and opinions such as these have become hateful to millions of Americans who, since the criminal law is useless for the purpose, have come to rely on Congressional and state legislative investigations to expose, discredit, and, so far as possible, to render unemployable individuals who held and acted upon those or similar opinions during the thirties and forties, or who now oppose this use of the investigatory process.

These feelings, and the ambitions of those who exploit them, are what the cold civil war is all about. And this is why the loyalty investigations have been led by men such as Dies, Tenney, McCarran, Jenner and McCarthy. If these investigations had been conducted by moderate politicians—by Paul Douglases, Richard Russells, Leverett Saltonstalls, or even Robert Tafts—*the investigations would not have produced the results that their most powerful supporters wanted.* It is noteworthy that two moderate Senators who actually undertook inquiries of this type—Millard Tydings and Raymond E. Baldwin—promptly became the objects of the most vicious and ruthless political attack, and neither remained long in the Senate.*

* Senator Tydings of Maryland was chairman of the Senate committee that investigated Senator McCarthy's initial and spectacular charges against the State Department. He was defeated for re-election shortly thereafter. Senator Baldwin of Connecticut was chairman of the Senate committee that investigated Senator

This is what lies behind the statement, often made today, that Congressional loyalty probes are "the only way to handle" the internal Communist menace. Here, for example, are the views of the columnist David Lawrence: [71]

> There is only one effective way to combat the Communist conspiracy, and that is by exposure. There is only one instrument by which that can be done without encountering technical barriers—the congressional investigating committee.

Why is this so? Mr. Lawrence cited as his principal proof the case of Alger Hiss, and declared that if Whittaker Chambers had accused Hiss anywhere "outside a committee hearing," the libel laws would have prevented any publication and thereby shielded Hiss from exposure. Furthermore, it was the House Committee's questioning of Hiss that "subjected him to a perjury charge, on which he was later put in jail"; the Department of Justice was helpless to prosecute him on any other charge because the limitations period had expired. Then, moving to a different illustration in conclusion, Mr. Lawrence writes:

> If the congressional committee powers are restricted, however, or made to conform to the so-called "due process of law" procedures used in courts . . . then a repetition of the frustrating tactics of the courtroom such as occurred in the lengthy trial of the eleven Communists in New York will prevent the complete exposure of the tactics of the Communist agents in America.

Unfortunately for Mr. Lawrence's thesis, every item of his "proof" refutes it. Whittaker Chambers did repeat his accusations outside the privileged committee hearing, Hiss did sue him for libel, and it was in the libel proceeding, *not* the Committee hearing, that the crucial evidence against Hiss—the State Department documents—was first disclosed. Nor was Hiss's testimony before the House committee the basis of the perjury charge; rather it was his testimony before a grand jury, investigating the accusations in accordance with regular criminal procedure. Finally, and irrespective of the wisdom or unwisdom of the Smith Act, the "lengthy trial" of the Communist

---

McCarthy's accusations against the Army in connection with the "Malmedy massacre" war crimes trial. He shortly resigned from the Senate to become a judge of the Connecticut Supreme Court.

leaders in New York ended in their conviction and imprisonment, a consummation quite beyond the powers of any investigating committee.

This is not to say that the disclosures of the loyalty investigations have been entirely valueless. They have certainly revealed that membership in the Communist Party, and in front organizations, has been considerably more extensive than was previously realized by the general public. Some individuals in official or semi-public positions, whose records or lack of candor strongly suggested their unsuitability for public trust, have been discredited.

But the truth of the matter is that Congressional investigations have been notably ineffective in exposing present members of the Communist Party. In terms of the existing conspiracy and the menace that currently confronts us, it is the regularly responsible executive agencies that do the job. The small part played by investigating committees is not altogether due to incompetence for such a task. The principal reason is that they are pursuing other objectives; they are combatants not in the international cold war but in the cold civil war.

For this internecine strife, the Congressional investigation is certainly a potent and irreplaceable weapon. An executive agency must function in accordance with the laws under which it is established. An indictment must be supported by credible evidence or the courts will throw it out. But a legislative investigation can operate just as irresponsibly and loosely as its members desire.[72] It can accuse and denounce with complete abandon under the shield of legislative privilege. No statute of limitations limits its memory, and witnesses may therefore be taxed with murky charges dredged from twenty years past.

If what the nation wants and needs is a powerful and flexible governmental mechanism for political inquisition and denunciation, there is truly no substitute for a Congressional investigation operated by a Dies or a McCarthy. But it is certain that Woodrow Wilson would never recognize, in these angry and fearful doings, the "informing function" of which he wrote so glowingly in the dawn of the twentieth century.

That observant French traveler in nineteenth-century America, Alexis de Tocqueville, declared [73] that "the doctrine of private rights" is "a doctrine always unpopular in a democracy." His observation is, I believe, a valuable corrective to the common and erroneous assumption that democracy and individual liberty are, like the Gold Dust Twins, inseparable.

De Tocqueville was not, of course, addressing himself to the question of Congressional investigations, but the attitude he describes has been put in that context in an article by one of our ablest federal judges, Charles E. Wyzanski, Jr. of Massachusetts. Commenting on the objections voiced by Walter Lippman, John T. Flynn and others to the remarkable expansion of investigative activity, Judge Wyzanski writes: [74]

> Some of these persons temperamentally have a strong sense of privacy or have a feeling that dignity and decorum are among the highest values. But to them the fundamental answer is that the democratic process is an open process in which we have deliberately chosen to sacrifice a large measure of the privacy, dignity and decorum which characterizes other types of society in order to have in Pericles' words, "discussion and the knowledge that is gained from discussion" (Thuc. II, 40).

Would Pericles agree that knowledge can be gained from discussion only by sacrificing privacy, dignity and decorum? I surmise that he—or, for that matter, Hamilton, Jefferson, or Lincoln—might reply that useful knowledge is seldom gained from needlessly intrusive, undignified, and indecorous discussion.* As for other forms of government, if Judge Wyzanski is referring to old-fashioned regimes in the aristocratic tradition, perhaps there was more privacy and dignity for those at the top of the heap, but hardly for those who were urged to eat cake. As for modern totalitarianism, red, brown, or black, surely democracy compares favorably in terms of these qualities.

But it is Judge Wyzanski's description of democracy as an "open process" that raises more fundamental questions. This theme he develops as follows:

---

* This point of view is, admittedly, not universally shared. Mr. Roy Cohn's idea of "discussing" his exclusion from a secret military laboratory at Fort Monmouth was to threaten to use the investigative power to wreak vengeance on the Army. Senator Dirksen of Illinois remarked that Mr. Cohn's discussion was "in the great American manner and in the great American tradition" because, as Americans, "we go in for those expressions that deal with the superlative." [75]

> Congressional investigations are only one, if an extreme example of our belief that exposure is the surest guard not only against official corruption and bureaucratic waste, inefficiency and rigidity but against private malpractices, divisive movements and anti-social tendencies in the body politic. That this confidence in legislative investigations as a prophylactic is not absurd is demonstrated to some extent by the difference in the strength and survival quality of democracy in English-speaking countries where such investigations are encouraged and Continental countries where they have been held within close bounds. . . . Perhaps France would have been better off if the Stavisky scandal had been investigated rather than hushed up.

Insofar as Judge Wyzanski speaks of official corruption and other governmental abuses, of which the Stavisky scandal is certainly a prime example, there can be little disagreement today—much as there would have been in the Harding-Coolidge era—with his praise of investigation as a corrective scourge. But when we come to "private malpractices, divisive movements and anti-social tendencies" there is cause to pause. These are vague expressions, but they appear intended at least to encompass individual political affiliation, if not opinion.

Do we really believe that massive and unlimited doses of compulsory "exposure" of such matters are good for the body politic? Certainly the idea finds no support in the development of Anglo-American politico-legal thought since the middle of the eighteenth century, nor in the decisions and opinions of our courts and judges—quite the contrary, as we have seen.

But perhaps the old order changeth. Judge Wyzanski's article is not the only indication that Justice Brandeis' treasured "right to be let alone" is losing ground, even in circles of high responsibility and great intelligence. Mr. Wechsler's conception of a duty to be ever ready to state one's case publicly is of a piece with Judge Wyzanski's faith in exposure. Indeed, I have recently heard a distinguished professor of law declare that, in the area of political opinion, there is an absolute duty of full disclosure to the government not only of one's own views, but of those of others; thus college students' themes and essays on political subjects, and casual political conversations at dinner parties, are as fit material for dossiers and Congressional hearings as anything else.

Justifying this faith in exposure, Judge Wyzanski points to the "strength and survival quality of democracy in English-speaking countries" where legislative investigative power is recognized, in contrast to the Continental countries. It is true, as we have earlier observed,[76] that legislative investigations have never caught on in, for example, France and Germany. So too, Judge Wyzanski's suggestion that this factor may account for the comparative instability of Continental democracy had been anticipated by a legal scholar who, in 1943, advised us that: [77] "The European experience shows conclusively that where facts can be ascertained only by a curtailment of the citizen's individual freedom there should be no hesitation in paying that price, lest the freedom of all be endangered."

Now, with all respect to these distinguished judges, journalists, and professors, it seems to me that there could be no more accurate description of the totalitarian attitude toward the individual than the sentence just quoted. What, indeed, is left of the "freedom of all" if "individual freedom" is destroyed? For the Communists as for the Nazis, individual freedom is a meaningless concept, and the "freedom of all" is not freedom at all; rather it is total and devoted adherence to official doctrine. Therefore, in Soviet Russia as nowhere else, great faith is placed in exposure of what are there regarded as "private malpractices, divisive movements, and anti-social tendencies," and there as nowhere else every individual is under a constant and absolute duty to disclose to the government his political and social attitudes and those of everyone else with whom he comes in contact.

Similarly, the Soviet government relies heavily on investigation and exposure to keep the body politic in a good state of repair. These are not carried out by legislative committees, but inquiry and exposure alike are efficiently accomplished by NKVD interrogations and Party "cleansings." Every Soviet citizen is expected to be a part of the "informing function," to the extent that children are encouraged to inform the authorities of any "divisive" or "anti-social" tendencies manifested by their parents.

Another and even more compelling illustration is to be found in the Western Hemisphere. Argentina enjoys a form of government modeled on our own; it has also enjoyed a Committee on Anti-Argentine Activities. This committee initially embarked on an investigation of police tortures and abuses, but soon interested itself in newspapers critical of the Peron regime. During 1950 it was directly responsible for the closing or forced sale of some fifty opposition newspapers. Then, in 1951, a joint resolution of the Argentine Congress established a "Joint Congressional Committee to intervene and investigate the business organization which owns the newspaper *La Prensa* and the firms commercially linked to it with the purpose of determining a definite program to be adopted as a result of the activities and proceedings of the same newspaper." Acting to all intents and purposes as an executive arm of the government, this committee immediately took over control of the eighty-one year old, independent *La Prensa*, closed up its branch offices, and decorated its main office in Buenos Aires with photographs of President and Señora Perón.[78]

If it be suggested that these examples are far from American shores and traditions, let the reader contemplate the situation of four employees of the Pacific Gas & Electric Company, recently discharged as "poor security risks" at the request of the California State Senate Fact-Finding Committee on Un-American Activities.[79] One cannot escape the conclusion that it is more than a little naïve to ascribe the misadventures of democracy in Continental Europe to restrictions on investigative power, in the face of such compelling examples of its capacity for the suppression of liberty. The notion that Anglo-American democracy has drawn strength from inquisitorial exposure of individual beliefs and associations is equally superficial. Neither in Great Britain nor the dominions have legislative investigations been utilized in the manner of the Dies-McCarran-McCarthy operations. As Sir Hartley Shawcross told the New York City bar association,[80] British opinion "would never tolerate . . . a roving commission to inquire into peoples' political or other beliefs." And so far as concerns our own country, there is certainly abundant evidence that the current passion for Congressional exposure and denunciation is one of the most dangerously divisive forces that our democratic form of government and traditional way of life have ever faced.

I have endeavored to analyze the relation between the investigations and the Constitution in terms of general principles, and the inferences that may reasonably be drawn from matters of common knowledge. This is a study of the powers and purposes of legislative investigations, not of the merits and demerits of particular inquiries. Any systematic and comprehensive evaluation of the accomplishments and effects of the principal loyalty-security investigating committees, federal and state, would be far beyond the compass of this book, although I have ventured some general observations in the concluding chapter.

So far as concerns the legal power of Congressional or state investigating committees to inquire into matters of political opinion, it is my belief that obsession with either free speech or national security, at the expense of the other, leads to impossible results. At bottom, the two concepts are mutually complementary rather than conflicting. Lawless subversion is as much a menace to freedom as to security, and irresponsible disregard of the Constitution undermines security as well as freedom.

The temptation is strong to take a more categorical positive or negative view of the investigative power. On the one side or the other, several powerful minds have, in my humble opinion, succumbed too readily to that impulse, as when Dr. Albert Einstein completely rejects the authority of Congress under any circumstances to inquire into matters of political belief, or when Judge Wyzanski sees in such inquiries the cement that holds together our democracy. These absolutist conceptions of individual liberty and legislative power overlook, I believe, the tempering wisdom of Justice Holmes: [81]

> All rights tend to declare themselves absolute to their logical extreme. Yet all in fact are limited by the neighborhood of principles of policy which are other than those on which the particular right is founded, and which become strong enough to hold their own when a certain point is reached.

To determine when that "certain point is reached" as between the investigative power and individual freedom—whether of speech or silence—I know of no better general test than Judge Learned Hand's. I have tried to add to it some color and texture in order to make the formula less abstract and more meaningful in terms of contemporary issues and circumstances.

To those readers who may be disappointed at my failure to state any single and all-sufficient standard, I can say only that the ingredients of freedom and security can not be stacked and compared like children's blocks. We will never strike a final and definitive balance as between the claims of the individual and those of the body politic, and must strive rather for greater wisdom and skill in their constant adjustment and readjustment.

CHAPTER VII

THE PRIVILEGE AGAINST SELF-ACCUSATION

"*. . . an inherent natural right, recognized in this country by a constitutional guaranty which protects every citizen, the President as well as the humblest in the land, from being made a witness against himself.*"

—President Ulysses S. Grant (1876)

DASHIELL HAMMETT, widely acclaimed as author of *The Maltese Falcon*, *The Thin Man*, and other remarkably gripping tales of adventurous mystery, declined to tell Senator McCarthy's subcommittee whether or not he was or ever had been a Communist. To answer, he declared, might tend to incriminate him.

The Senator had evinced little or no interest in Mr. Hammett's literary works, nor in the significance to be attached to their inclusion in State Department "information centers" overseas—the ostensible reason for Mr. Hammett's enforced appearance before the McCarthy subcommittee. But there was no apparent doubt in the Senator's mind of the inferences justifiably to be drawn from the famous writer's refusal to testify: [1]

THE CHAIRMAN: Well, now, you have told us that you will not tell us whether you are a member of the Communist Party today or not, on the ground that if you told us the answer might incriminate you. That is normally taken by this committee and the country as a whole to mean that you are a member of the Party, because if you were not you would simply say, "No," and it would not incriminate you. You see, the only reason

> that you have the right to refuse to answer is if you feel a truthful answer would incriminate you. An answer that you were not a Communist, if you were not a Communist, could not incriminate you. Therefore, you should know considerable about the Communist movement, I assume.

Thus, for Senator McCarthy, it is all very simple: if a man truthfully denies that he is a Communist, the answer does not incriminate him; therefore the only possible reason for refusing to answer is that a truthful answer would be an incriminating admission of membership. *Q.E.D.*

This is the foundation upon which Senator McCarthy bases his now famous descriptive phrase, "Fifth Amendment Communist," the application of which to Professor Furry in particular and Harvard in general we observed in the opening chapter.[2] The Annual Report of his subcommittee lists seventy-one individuals who invoked the Fifth Amendment during the subcommittee's public hearings held during 1953, and advances the claim that by virtue of these hearings, the subcommittee has exposed and removed "Fifth Amendment Communists" from government service and defense plants.[3] Some of these persons, furthermore, the Senator has publicly accused of being Soviet spies, because they declined on the same ground to answer questions about espionage.

In thus equating use of the Fifth Amendment with proven guilt, Senator McCarthy enjoys widespread public support. Nor is agreement in principle, if not in degree, by any means confined to his devotees. President John Dickey of Dartmouth College, for example, has declared that any teacher who pleads the Fifth Amendment "has compromised his fitness to perform the responsibilities of higher education." [4] An avalanche of magazine articles and letters to newspaper editors reveals a prevalent and pervasive attitude that, whatever the legal technicalities of the privilege against self-accusation (more commonly described as the privilege against self-incrimination), no one is likely to invoke it unless he has "something to hide." Elmer Davis has written [5] that the privilege was orginally intended "for the benefit of the innocent rather than the guilty," but that "it seems highly probable that in this country it is much more often the guilty who have got the benefit."

It is, I think, fair to say that invocation of the Fifth Amendment before investigating committees has brought about an almost hopeless confusion in the public mind with respect to the merits and meaning of the privilege. In large part, the situation has grown out of the recent and extensive use of investigations as a means of exposing individuals to public disapproval and mistrust. This, in turn, has raised novel and touchy problems for the employers, associates, neighbors, and friends of those who have "taken the Fifth."

Justice Holmes's famous phrase, "a page of history is worth a volume of logic," has been much overworked, but here it is singularly apt. For this bitter, turgid argument about the nature of the privilege—whether it is a shield for the innocent or a cloak for the guilty—reflects a fundamental misunderstanding of its historical purpose. Here as elsewhere history will not solve our problems, but without its aid we cannot even identify and define the true issues, much less bring informed reason and judgment to bear on their solution.

The Origins of the Privilege

Crime and punishment in the Middle Ages were greatly concerned with treasons, oaths, and heresies. Cruelties and superstitions abounded in the methods of determining guilt or innocence; in England trial by battle or by ordeal of fire or water was common practice, and in the powerful ecclesiastical courts throughout western Europe torture was used as a routine method of testing those who were accused of heresy or other offenses against the canon law.

Accordingly, in those times it was no light or laughing matter to be accused of crime, even if the charge was malicious and highly improbable. What was to prevent vengeful or pliant bailiffs or clerics from putting the most blameless to the ordeal of strolling barefoot over red-hot plowshares, or to the twist of screw and turn of rack? Nothing very systematic or certain by modern standards, but by the early thirteenth century the custom had attained general observance that a man could not be accused and sent to torture or ordeal unless there was evidence which warranted his trial.

What this amounted to was a rule that a man should not be forced to be his own *first* accuser. In this general form it appears as the thirty-eighth clause of Magna Carta (1215)—"No bailiff upon his own bare word without credible witnesses is to send a man to trial"—

and a few years later in the canon law Decretals of Gregory IX (Pope, 1227–41), in the coldly comforting declaration [6] that "torture ought not to be resorted to until some evidence has been forthcoming." In canon law and English common law alike, however, if the charge was supported by witnesses or by general "rumor" (*fama*), the accused was required to clear his reputation by testifying and standing trial, or otherwise have his guilt taken as confessed. Indeed, until the middle of the seventeenth century, the principal feature of English criminal trials was the questioning and testimony of the defendant, and both in the ordinary courts and the dreaded Star-Chamber, torture might be applied.

Throughout the sixteenth and seventeenth centuries, the England of the Tudors, Stuarts, and Roundheads was in a state of religious and political ferment. King and Commons, Church and State, and Roman Catholics, Anglicans, and Puritans wrestled for power interminably. Matters of theological faith and of private morals were closely intertwined with law and politics. The bifurcated judicial system of ecclesiastical and common-law courts was a reflection of these deep cleavages; the ecclesiastical courts asserted a very broad authority not only over the clergy and church matters, but also to punish heresies, "enormities," and other offenses among the laity. In the trial of these charges, the ecclesiastical authorities asserted the right to administer the "oath *ex officio*," * by which the accused swore not only that he was innocent, but also that he would answer fully and truthfully whatever questions might be put to him.

The King's common-law judges vigorously opposed this intrusion of the clergy into the field of criminal law, and from the fourteenth century on efforts were made, without lasting success, to confine the authority of ecclesiastical courts to matters of church discipline and matrimonial and testamentary questions. This conflict came to a head toward the end of Queen Elizabeth's reign, when the ecclesiastical Court of High Commission, under the militant and intolerant Archbishop of Canterbury John Whitgift, launched what amounted to a general inquisition, in the course of which many laymen as well as non-conformist Puritan clergymen were put to the oath *ex officio*

* So-called because originally it was taken only by holders of clerical office. The oath *ex officio* originated with Pope Innocent III at the end of the twelfth century, and was the foundation of the Inquisition procedure.

on penal charges, even without any evidence or general rumor against them. Public indignation at these abuses now was joined with the jealousy of the common-law judges, and soon after the turn of the century and the accession of James I, the Court of High Commission's jurisdiction was finally restricted to clerical matters.*

But the Court of Star-Chamber was still busily grilling political suspects, and putting them to their oath. After the accession of Charles I, the pressures rapidly approached the pitch of revolution. In 1637, the Star-Chamber caught a Tartar, by name Freeborn John Lilburne, accused of importing seditious and heretical books. He denied the charge, but refused to take the oath to answer all questions, declaring that he would not be "ensnared by answering things concerning other men." However, it is plain that his principal objection was against the inquisitorial Star-Chamber procedure, for he declared that he would have answered questions had he been proceeded against by indictment and trial for a specific offense in the regular courts.

For his contumacy, the Star-Chamber sentenced Lilburne to be whipped and pilloried. But Freeborn John, like Mr. Rumely, was stiff-necked and determined to stand on his rights, and the tide of events was on his side. In 1641 when the Long Parliament assembled, this stubborn foe of the Stuarts was on hand with a petition and considerable public backing. Promptly Parliament obliged by declaring his sentence illegal,† and shortly thereafter it entirely abolished

---

* The campaign to cut down the authority of the ecclesiastical courts was led by the great common-law jurist Sir Edward Coke, and it was Coke who in 1589, while representing a client accused of incontinency before the ecclesiastical authorities, successfully argued that the oath *ex officio* could not be administered, because *nemo tenetur prodere seipsum*. This is the first known use of the Latin phrase commonly regarded as the progenitor of the privilege against self-accusation. But more accurately it signifies that no one is bound to *come forward in the first place* with evidence against himself. This, as we have seen, was a rule dating back to Magna Carta and Gregory IX's decretals in the early thirteenth century. Coke's phrase, therefore, cannot rightly be equated with the modern principle that a man already accused by others is not bound to testify in his own defense.

† In 1648, Parliament voted Lilburne £3000 reparation, declaring that his punishment had been "illegal and most unjust, against the liberty of the subject, and law of the land, and Magna Carta." But the following year this tempestuous character was again in the toils of the law, on trial for treason before the courts of Cromwell's Commonwealth, a charge of which he was acquitted. Of

both the Court of High Commission and the Star-Chamber. The oath *ex officio* was a thing of the past, and the common-law judges' long struggle for full authority in the field of penal law was crowned with success.

And now occurred a sudden, spontaneous and remarkable transmigration of legal doctrine. Up to 1641, while the tide of battle swirled about the Courts of High Commission and Star-Chamber and the inquisitorial oath *ex officio,* the common-law courts, enforcing the ordinary criminal laws, had continued to require the accused to answer to the charges by his own testimony. Lilburne himself had acknowledged in 1637 the right of the common-law courts to question him upon proper charges. But the wave of revolutionary reform that ended the extraordinary courts and oaths spilled over into the common-law courts, with the result that the old rule that a man could not be required to provide the *first* evidence against himself, speedily became a rule that he could not be required to testify against himself *at all.**

This was, in fact, the privilege against self-accusation in the general form that we have it today. Nothing better illustrates the rapidity and firmness with which it became imbedded in English criminal practice than the fact that, although the Puritans were its original protagonists, they gave it full effect at the trial of King Charles II in 1649, and that after the Restoration in 1660 the royal judges were willing to extend its benefits to the regicide Scroop. In 1679, it was held that witnesses as well as accused could decline to give self-accusatory testimony.[7]

By that time, the privilege had also taken root in the criminal practice of the American colonies. Theocratic Massachusetts Bay was hardly a cradle of individual liberties, but its Puritan leaders were mindful of their persecutions in England, and the Massachusetts "Body of Liberties" of 1641 already contains the germ of the privilege. In 1677 it was agreed by the Virginia Burgesses that "noe law can compell a man to sweare against himself in any matter

---

him it was said that "if the world was emptied of all but John Lilburne, Lilburne would quarrel with John, and John with Lilburne."

* Thus Coke's maxim *nemo tenetur prodere seipsum* became *nemo tenetur accusare seipsum,* and was quoted to the court in this form in the trial of William Penn and William Mead in 1670.

wherein he is liable to corporal punishment." Connecticut, Pennsylvania and the other colonies soon followed suit,[8] and by the early part of the eighteenth century it was firm common-law doctrine on both sides of the Atlantic that neither defendants in criminal trials nor witnesses called to testify in judicial proceedings could be required to give evidence that might tend to incriminate them.

At this time, however, another radical shift in criminal practice caused the privilege to lose much of its importance. The rule had been developed in civil suits that the parties themselves were not competent witnesses, because their testimony was too likely to be affected by their stake in the outcome. Early in the eighteenth century this viewpoint was extended to criminal law, and soon it became—and remained until the middle of the nineteenth century—the rule that the accused could not testify at all; his mouth, and his wife's as well, were closed whether for or against himself.* So far as a criminal defendant's testimony was concerned, the privilege against self-incrimination became meaningless, although it continued to have substance with respect to witnesses.[9]

After this decline in the practical significance of the privilege, it might be wondered that it was thought important enough to be included, as it was, in most of the early American constitutions. But in the colonies, recollections of the Star-Chamber and other inquisitorial abuses were refreshed by the oppressive conduct of the royal governors. In Pennsylvania, for example, the behavior of Governor Blackwell aroused such resentment that in 1689 copies of the colonial charter were clandestinely printed and circulated to remind the citizenry of their lawful privileges. The only printer in all Pennsylvania, William Bradford, was called for public questioning, and the Governor sought to extract his confession that he had printed the charter copies, but Bradford refused to answer, as have so many since, on the ground that he was not bound to accuse himself.[10]

As friction between the colonists and the crown grew toward revolution, an atmosphere developed reminiscent of Freeborn John Lilburne's days, and it was in this atmosphere that the early state

* In Continental criminal trials to this day, the accused cannot testify under oath, although he is examined extensively before the trial, and may make unsworn statements to the court.

constitutions were drafted. Accordingly, it is hardly surprising that we find the privilege against self-accusation, as an express provision, variously phrased, in seven of the state constitutions adopted prior to 1789, beginning with the Virginia Declaration of Rights of June, 1776,[11] which provided that a man could not "be compelled to give evidence against himself." And in the fullness of time, the privilege found specific constitutional expression in every state of the Union except New Jersey and Iowa.[12]

In that contemporary setting,* it would have been more than extraordinary if the framers of the Constitutional Bill of Rights had omitted to make express reference to a principle which had had so long a period of historical evolution and had figured so prominently in the struggle for freedom from inquisition and the oppressions of extraordinary tribunals established to compel religious and political conformity. And it is for these reasons that the Fifth Amendment was made to include the guaranty that: "No person . . . shall be compelled in any criminal case to be a witness against himself . . ." Controversial as these words have become in recent years, nothing seemed more fitting and natural to the citizens of the infant Republic when the Bill of Rights was ratified.

The Privilege in Investigations

It may be remarked that the language of the Constitutional guaranty is considerably narrower than the common-law rule on which it is based, both because of its explicit restriction to "any criminal case" (whereas persons testifying in civil suits may also decline to give self-incriminating testimony), and its implicit restriction to defendants (whereas witnesses as well as accused are entitled to the privilege). The second of these features is easily explained by the surrounding context, for this clause is but one of a package of provisions for the protection of accused persons; most of the Fifth and all of the Sixth and Eighth Amendments comprise this package.[14]

But despite the words "in any criminal case," it is clear that the

* In 1780 Major General Nathanael Greene, presiding over the board of general officers (including St. Clair, Lafayette, Steuben and Clinton) that interrogated Major André, extended to André the benefits of the privilege.[13]

constitutional guaranty against compulsory self-accusation was not intended to apply only during the course of a regular criminal proceeding. To begin with, the defendant did not then need this protection, for once on trial he could not testify at all. More important, it was on vague or secret charges before extraordinary political and religious tribunals and commissions, rather than after indictment by a regular court, that the worst abuses had been perpetrated—the very abuses that brought the privilege into being. The first clause of the Fifth Amendment sought to guard against trial and punishment outside the regular course of criminal justice,[15] and it is unthinkable that the privilege against self-accusation was not likewise intended to give protection against this danger.

For all these reasons, the constitutional provision in question fulfills its plain intent and purpose only if construed as if it read "no person shall be compelled to be a witness against himself *with respect to any criminal charge.*" And this, indeed, is the meaning the courts have given it and comparable clauses in the state constitutions, as we shall soon see. So interpreted, the protection of the privilege may be invoked by the parties and witnesses in any proceeding in which there is power to compel the giving of testimony or the production of documents.

For nearly a century, the constitutional privilege led a very uneventful existence in the courts. This was true of many other provisions of the Constitution, but in this case there was the special reason that criminal defendants were not allowed to testify at all until after the Civil War.[16] From time to time witnesses in court proceedings invoked the privilege, either on constitutional or common-law grounds, as did Aaron Burr's secretary during Burr's trial for treason before Chief Justice Marshall in 1807. In Pennsylvania, New York, Connecticut, Arkansas, Georgia, and Indiana, in both criminal and civil cases arising from 1803 to 1861, court witnesses were allowed its benefits without much controversy.

But did the privilege apply to witnesses before Congressional or state legislative investigations? In 1742, Nicholas Paxton had asserted it before the Parliamentary committee investigating the Walpole regime, but for his pains had been adjudged in contempt and committed to Newgate jail, where he was "debarred the use of paper, pen, and ink." [17] Since then it has been universally accepted that the privilege is of no avail before Parliamentary committees of inquiry.*

But whereas Parliament's power rises above the common law, the Constitution limits the power of Congress, and from the time of Andrew Jackson, testimony before American legislative committees has been generally regarded as within the protection of the Fifth Amendment privilege. The point seems to have first arisen in 1834, during the second House investigation of the Bank of the United States, when Nicholas Biddle and his fellow directors declined to produce the bank's records in response to a committee subpoena, giving as their reason that "as corporators and directors, we are parties to the proceeding, [and] we do not consider ourselves bound to testify, and therefore respectfully decline to do so." The members of the committee were divided on the question whether the particular circumstances justified resort to the privilege, but none of them suggested that there was any doubt of its general applicability to testimony sought under the compulsion of a Congressional subpoena.[19]

Three years later the shoe was on the other foot. President Jackson's sweeping extensions of the spoils system aroused intense criticism, and the House appointed a committee to review the integrity and efficiency of the executive departments. The committee promptly demanded from Jackson and his Cabinet members lists of all civil servants appointed without the consent of the Senate. Jackson's fiery reply did not mention the Constitution, but otherwise amounted to an explicit invocation of the privilege against self-incrimination: [20]

> You request myself and the heads of the Departments to become our own accusers, and to furnish the evidence to convict ourselves . . . If you either will not make specific accusation, or if, when made, you attempt to establish them by making free men their own accusers, you will not expect me to countenance your proceedings.

But the plainest proof that legislators treated the privilege as applicable to testimony sought in investigations, is found in the numerous statutes enacted shortly before and after the Civil War to overcome the privilege by granting immunity from prosecution. Witnesses who were granted this immunity could no longer decline to

* Parliamentary committees to determine contested elections, which often had to inquire into charges of indictable bribery, did allow witnesses to decline to incriminate themselves.[18]

answer on the ground of self-incrimination, for they could not thereby incriminate themselves. The 1857 statute of Congress providing for the prosecution of witnesses for failure to appear and testify in response to committee subpoenas, contained another section declaring that no witness "shall be held to answer criminally in any court of justice . . . for any fact or act touching which he shall be required to testify before either House of Congress . . ." * Comparable laws were enacted in Wisconsin (1858), Massachusetts (1871), and other states.

Accordingly, it was entirely in line with contemporary thinking when Judge Daly, in the first American judicial decision (1855) dealing with investigations,[21] declared (although the point was not directly involved) that a witness before a legislative committee need not "answer any question that would tend to incriminate him." [22] And then in 1871 the question was squarely raised in Massachusetts during an investigation of bribery and corruption in the state police. One Henry Emery, upon being asked whether he had ever paid money "to any state constable," declined to answer on the ground that "the answer thereto will furnish evidence against me." Committed to jail for contempt of the Massachusetts Senate, Emery sought his release by *habeas corpus,* in answer to which the state Attorney General argued, relying on British Parliamentary practice, that the privilege against self-incrimination had no application to legislative investigations, which are "not for the purpose of punishing any specific crime, but of purifying the public service." But the Supreme Judicial Court of Massachusetts held unanimously [23] that Emery was entitled to claim his privilege, saying that it applies equally "to investigations conducted by the legislature itself, or by one of its branches, or by a committee of its own members, as when conducted before the courts, or by commissioners, or other tribunals established by law." [24]

Only once thereafter was this conclusion seriously challenged. In 1879 a House committee investigating the State Department called upon George F. Seward, who had until shortly theretofore been Consul General in Shanghai, to produce the books and records from that office. Seward refused to do so or to answer questions, and his

* This provision was repealed in 1862, for reasons discussed later in this chapter.

counsel claimed his protection under the Fifth Amendment. A majority of the investigating committee, pointing to the words "in any criminal case," argued that the privilege was not available before a committee. The House took the argument seriously enough to refer the whole matter to the Judiciary Committee, which unanimously reported that Seward was entitled to claim his privilege, and this conclusion was thereupon adopted by the House itself.[25]

The United States Supreme Court has not yet passed upon the Fifth Amendment in relation to Congressional investigations.* But unquestionably the Court will hold that testimony before investigating committees is within the scope of the privilege, as has been uniformly decided many times by the lower federal courts.[27]

Furthermore, the Supreme Court has unanimously ruled that affirmative answers to questions about Communist Party membership, office-holding, and employment are answers which tend to incriminate. Individuals who refused, on this ground, to answer such questions before a federal grand jury in Colorado, were entitled to remain silent because of the risk of prosecution inherent in the Smith Act, as described in Mr. Justice Black's opinion: [28]

> These provisions [of the Smith Act] made future prosecution [of the witness] far more than a mere "imaginary possibility" . . . she reasonably could fear that criminal charges might be brought against her if she admitted employment by the Communist Party or intimate knowledge of its workings. . . . Answers to the questions asked by the grand jury would have furnished a link in the chain of evidence needed in a prosecution of petitioner for violation of (or conspiracy to violate) the Smith Act.

It is clear, therefore, that testimony concerning membership in the Party, or close association with Communists, is testimony within the scope of the privilege. If a witness before an investigating committee is asked questions of this general description, and if a truthful answer would tend to incriminate him, he is entitled to decline to

---

* At the time this book went to press, however, the question was involved in the case of Julius Emspak, General Secretary of the United Electrical, Radio & Machine Workers of America, who declined to answer questions put to him by the House Un-American Activities Committee, and was thereafter convicted under the 1857 statute. The Supreme Court is reviewing this case, which raises numerous questions under both the First and Fifth Amendments, and it is to be reargued during the current term of the Court.[26]

respond, and cannot be held in contempt or prosecuted for his silence. But those two words "tend to" are often overlooked, both by opponents and supporters of the privilege, and thereby arise the angry confusions which Senator McCarthy has shrewdly exploited in his well-known coined expression.

"Fifth Amendment Communists"

We have noted the early episodes wherein those two arch-antagonists, Andrew Jackson and Nicholas Biddle, each on a different occasion, referred to the privilege against self-accusation as a reason for not complying with a Congressional demand for information. So far as I have been able to determine, however, the first person to invoke by express mention the constitutional guaranty of the Fifth Amendment in such a situation was President Ulysses S. Grant.

The circumstances have an amusingly contemporaneous flavor. President Grant was prone to repeated absences from Washington for recreational purposes. During his last year of office, the Democratic House of Representatives sought to make political capital of this trait, which had led him to take a long vacation at Long Branch, New Jersey. The House then passed a resolution calling upon Grant for a list of all executive acts, since his election as President, which had been "performed at a distance from the seat of government established by law," together with an explanation of the necessity "for such performance." [29]

Much annoyed, Grant replied that he could find no necessary legislative purpose in the request. Was the information, then, sought in aid of the power of impeachment? If so, declared Grant

> . . . it is asked in derogation of an inherent natural right, recognized in this country by a constitutional guarantee which protects every citizen, the President as well as the humblest in the land, from being made a witness against himself.

When Grant's reply was read in the House, according to contemporary accounts,[30] the Democratic members tittered, and "derisive laughter" greeted Grant's appeal to the constitutional guaranty. But soon "all traces of merriment among the Democrats were dissipated, and they sat grim and silent beneath the well merited rebuke contained in every line of the message."

Senator McCarthy, I presume, would call President Grant a Fifth Amendment loafer. Yet it is plain from the history of the privilege, as we have traced it, that no notion of actual or even probable guilt was intended to attach to those who claimed its protection. On the contrary, an automatic equation of the claim with actual guilt would rob the privilege of its purpose and its value to the accused. More than that, it would strip the privilege of all logic and intelligibility, for if the claimant is in fact guilty, why should he not then be made to say so, and convicted and sentenced without more ado?

Here is the prime source of the general confusion and misunderstanding. "The rule was intended for the protection of the innocent, and not for that of the guilty," wrote a British judge in 1862.[31] The privilege was originally intended for the innocent, but today the guilty are getting the benefit, complains Elmer Davis in 1954. But the prominent Washington lawyer Abe Fortas concludes [32] that "in large measure, though not entirely, it is a protection to the lawbreaker," while Professor Sidney Hook, speaking of the teacher who invokes the Fifth Amendment on questions of Party membership, declares that [33] "even if we do not contest his constitutional right to refuse an answer, no one can reasonably protest our constitutional right to say there is a good presumption that he is a member of the Communist Party." But the question is not whether we have a "constitutional right" to make such a presumption, but whether it is factually and logically warranted.

Now, all of this, from whichever viewpoint, overlooks that *the privilege against self-accusation operates before it is known whether the witness is innocent or guilty*. It is, in fact, one of the principles that is utilized in determining innocence or guilt. In a broad sense, every such principle of criminal evidence or procedure is for the protection of the innocent and the detection of the guilty. But it does not follow that these rules should be operative only where it is known that the accused is innocent, for if the answer were known in advance, there would be no reason to have a trial at all.

Therefore, there is no more sense in describing the privilege against self-accusation as for the benefit of the innocent on the one hand or the guilty on the other, than there would be in so describing the constitutional requirement that the accused be given a speedy and public jury trial. These are rules for the benefit of the *accused*, before it is known whether or not he is guilty. And the reason for these rules is that they are thought, rightly or wrongly, to be useful in determining accurately the question of guilt or innocence. The privilege accorded to the accused's own testimony, like the exclusion of hearsay testimony, is what is known as a *prophylactic* rule, and is a part of the judicial process itself.

The wisdom of the privilege against self-accusation, when the accused is on trial on specific charges, is not universally acclaimed. Its abolition or modification may be a good question for bar associations and legislatures to discuss. Be that as it may, the privilege is still firmly imbedded in legal practice and in the federal and nearly all the state constitutions, and so long as that state of affairs endures, the privilege ought to be respected and observed.

Furthermore, whatever may be the ultimate judgment on its usefulness in court, the privilege has special value in non-judicial proceedings, such as investigations, where there are no specific charges, or where the bounds of inquiry and accusation are nebulous. As we have seen, it was abusive inquisitions of precisely this type that originally gave rise to the privilege. For it is in such proceedings that the witness is most completely at the mercy of political ambition, malice, and blackmail, and that despotically-inclined politicians find opportunity to advance their ends by tearing down the basic framework of democracy and freedom.[34]

In short, the expression "Fifth Amendment Communist" is a monstrous perversion of history, logic, law, and fact. By the same token, every defendant in a criminal trial who chooses (often on the insistent advice of counsel) not to take the witness stand, is already guilty, even though the jury may (as often happens) return a verdict of acquittal.*

It is easy, however, to see why the phrase has won such popularity

* Examples are legion. It might be that an innocent defendant's own testimony would be the only source of strong circumstantial evidence against himself which, once given, would require him to prove self-defense or some other exculpating circumstance that, true in fact, a jury might nevertheless regard with skepticism. Likewise, an innocent defendant may have a personal record or characteristics which would fatally prejudice him in the eyes of the jury were he subjected to cross-examination.

among the leaders and supporters of Congressional loyalty investigations. If it were not for the inclusion of Fifth Amendment pleaders, the exposures and accomplishments of these investigations would look very slim indeed. The Annual Report of the McCarthy Subcommittee, for example, mentions no witness who admitted present Communist membership and only a very few—such as Professor Furry—who admitted past membership or associations; it deals almost exclusively with witnesses who invoked the Fifth Amendment.[35] The same is generally true, although not so markedly, of the reports of Senator Jenner's Internal Security Subcommittee.[36]

No doubt many of these persons had been Communists, and perhaps some of them still were. Some were identified by other witnesses as Communists in past years. But the actual facts and circumstances, whatever they may be, are not established by the claim of privilege.

In practice, the privilege seems to have contributed to a mischievous distortion of the informing function, in that the leading investigators are more anxious to find witnesses who will plead the Fifth Amendment at a public session, than they are to obtain the information which is thus withheld from the legislative body. Regardless of the truth, the plea is usually good for a newspaper headline, and always good for another tally on the score-sheet for entry in the committee's report of its accomplishments.

Use and Abuse of the Privilege

The unwarranted assumption that everyone who invokes the privilege before an investigating committee is guilty of whatever charges are projected in the unanswered questions, is a most serious abuse for which the committees are largely responsible. The immediate result, in my opinion, has been a superficial, inflated, and generally unreliable public representation of the extent and duration of Communist infiltration, both in and outside of government.

This abuse is greatly aggravated by a technical feature of the privilege, generally known as the "waiver" doctrine. For the privilege does not come into play automatically; it must be specifically *claimed* by the witness, on the basis that the answer would tend to incriminate him. There then arises the question, may the witness voluntarily answer some incriminating questions, but claim the privilege as to other questions relating to the same subject? May he pick and choose in this manner?

Obviously an implicated witness at a criminal trial might be able to aid (or harm) the defendant by answering only questions helpful (or harmful) to the defendant, and claiming the privilege as to all others. Furthermore, if a witness "waives" his privilege by voluntarily answering questions in such a way as to admit his own guilt, there is then no reason why he should not be required to answer further questions about the details, since the additional revelations will not increase the danger of prosecution to which he has voluntarily exposed himself. As the Supreme Court has recently put it,[37] "Disclosure of a fact waives the privilege as to details," and the Court went on to quote with approval from a decision by the Supreme Court of Michigan, where it was stated: [38]

> Where a witness has voluntarily answered as to materially criminating facts, it is held with uniformity that he cannot then stop short and refuse further explanation, but must disclose fully what he has attempted to relate.

Such a rule may be all very well when the witness is concerned about his own implication in a theft or embezzlement or other well-defined crime. But it is quite another matter when the questions are asked, not by a court operating under rules of evidence but by a committee conducting a broad inquest, and when the possible crime is advocating or conspiring to advocate the violent overthrow of government—a charge which might be supported by evidence of opinions and associations of the most diverse nature. For a witness before a Congressional loyalty investigation who has had some associations which he fears might be used against him, the "waiver" rule presents a treacherous riddle. How much can he admit or deny without running the risk of entirely losing his privilege under the waiver doctrine? In a dissenting opinion, Justice Black has described this dilemma as follows: [39]

> . . . On the one hand, they [witnesses] risk imprisonment for contempt by asserting the privilege prematurely; on the other, they might lose the privilege if they answer a single question. The Court's view makes the

protection depend on timing so refined that lawyers, let alone laymen, will have difficulty in knowing when to claim it.

But for the investigating committees, the waiver doctrine is a lethal weapon, which they have not scrupled to employ ruthlessly. Senator McCarthy's favorite trick, for example, is to ask a witness whether or not he has ever engaged in Communist espionage. If the witness denies that he has, the Senator then takes the position that "you have waived the Fifth Amendment insofar as the field of espionage is concerned," and puts a series of questions having to do with Communist association, threatening the witness with prosecution if he fails to answer.[40] However, if the witness, perhaps to forestall the waiver doctrine, declines to state whether or not he is engaged in espionage, then the Senator promptly and loudly castigates him as a spy, as ripe for the electric chair as the Rosenbergs! [41]

The other committees sometimes use a different technique. If a witness claims the privilege, a long series of related questions is put, to each of which the witness also pleads the privilege, to protect himself against waiver. A careful tally is kept of the number of times this occurs—a number limited only by the physical endurance of the participants—and at the end of the hearing it is solemnly reported that witness X invoked the privilege against self-incrimination thirty-two or seventy-eight or umpteen times. In the newspapers this looks very insidious, but rarely do these numbers have any real significance whatsoever.

I have said that the investigating committees are "largely" responsible for these confusions and abuses about the Fifth Amendment, but by no means are they solely at fault. Witnesses also, and their counsel especially, are likewise to blame. For there is little doubt that the privilege has been invoked by many witnesses who were probably not entitled to its benefits, and by many others who would have been better advised to forego them.

Foremost among these are the misguided individuals who have invoked the privilege before loyalty investigating committees under the illusion that they are thereby challenging the authority of the committee to conduct the inquiry and ask the questions.[42] By a strangely distorted conception, it is imagined that an issue of principle as to the committee's authority is raised by invoking a personal privilege extended by the criminal law. No more than for Senator McCarthy's Fifth Amendment Communist contraption is there the slightest basis for this notion in the history, logic, or purpose of the privilege. In the very first decision on the question, by the Supreme Judicial Court of Massachusetts in 1871, it was clearly stated: [43]

> It is to be observed that the provision relates to the privileges of the subject, and not to the authority of any tribunal or body before which inquisition may be made. It places a limit upon all inquiry to which he may be subjected, not by defining the extent of the authority by which it is made, but by surrounding him with a privilege of exemption, which cannot be set aside by any authority without his own consent.

So this idea of challenge by silence is bad law, but that is not its only defect. By every practical test, it has been totally ineffective and worse, extremely harmful. Nothing has strengthened the hands of McCarthy, Jenner and Velde so much as have repeated invocations of the privilege by teachers, former government employees, and others who are expected to maintain a standard of conduct higher than what is necessary to stay out of jail. Assuredly pleading the Fifth Amendment does not establish one's guilt; neither should its use [44] "be considered as affording the witness a certificate of good character."

Then there are others who invoke the privilege for a reason that can be described by the single word *fear*. Paul Shipman Andrews, Dean Emeritus of the Syracuse University Law School, has told the story [45] of a mathematics professor who was erroneously identified by others as having been a member of a Communist group while a graduate student many years earlier. The professor was called before the Velde Committee, and pleaded the Fifth Amendment, despite an unblemished and affirmative anti-Communist background. Why? Because—

> . . . he knew that if he stated under oath that he never had been a Communist he would thereby be contradicting the sworn testimony of the other professors, and that there might be an investigation and perhaps a prosecution for perjury, either of himself or of the others.
>
> By the time he and his attorney reached Washington for the hearing, X was in a state of mental agony. He was quite literally at the end of his rope. His attorney urged him earnestly not to use the Fifth Amendment.

But X felt that he could endure no more; could just not face the uncertainty of a possible investigation and prosecution for perjury if under oath he denied ever having been a Communist.

From this, Dean Andrews drew the conclusion that "using the amendment is by no means always an indication that the person has anything to hide or is a Communist." Agreed, but it does not follow that its use in the instance he describes was justifiable, let alone commendable. The excesses of Congressional investigations are unlikely to be corrected by witnesses who themselves abuse the privilege against self-accusation by invoking it when they are not entitled to it. In this particular case, so far as appears from Dean Andrews' account, truthful answers would not in any way have tended to incriminate the distraught professor.

But what about the professor's fear of prosecution for perjury because of the conflict of testimony between the others' erroneous identifications of himself as a Communist, and his own truthful denials? This affords no valid ground for pleading the privilege, and a moment's reflection will make the reasons clear. It is the purpose of any trial or formal hearing to elicit truthful testimony, and the law *must* proceed on the assumption that the truthful witness will not be wrongfully convicted of perjury, even though that possibility in fact exists. But if that chance were to be recognized as a sufficient basis for the claim of privilege, then *every* witness would be entitled to decline to answer whenever there was an actual or probable conflict of testimony. Such a result, as can readily be seen, would soon break down the entire system of trial and judgment based on evidence. Therefore, it has always been the rule that a witness cannot decline to answer merely because a truthful answer might conflict with other evidence, and thus raise the possibility of a perjury prosecution.[46]

By no means do I wish to convey the impression that there are nc situations in which a witness before an investigation committee may be well advised to invoke the Fifth Amendment. As Dean Griswold of the Harvard Law School has pointed out in an excellent analysis,[47] there are circumstances in which an individual, although innocent of any personal culpability of a subversive nature, is legally justified in pleading the privilege because of associations which, if revealed, might furnish part of the basis for prosecution under the Smith Act or the McCarran Internal Security Act. This latter statute has greatly broadened the possible basis of criminal liability under such circumstances, for it provides: [48]

> It shall be unlawful for any person knowingly to combine, conspire or agree with any other person to perform any act which would substantially contribute to the establishment within the United States of a totalitarian dictatorship . . . under the domination or control of any foreign government . . .

Depending upon one's point of view, a very wide variety of acts might be deemed criminal under this language. The Communist Control Act of 1954 has enlarged even more the basis for claim of privilege, for it prescribes fourteen indicia of Communist membership.[48a] Some of them are entirely innocent in themselves, yet each is now declared by law to be evidence of membership, and in conjunction they seem to provide a virtually unlimited basis for invoking the Fifth Amendment.

If legally warranted, pleading the privilege may be wise or unwise, worthy or unworthy, depending upon the resolution of practical and ethical issues which may be very difficult. Of course, the theoretical possibility of prosecution under the Smith or McCarran or Communist Control Acts does not necessarily mean that the actual possibility is more than remote. As a practical matter, the individual who finds himself in such a dilemma must weigh the extra-legal consequences—in terms of employment and personal standing in the community—of revealing the ambiguous features of his political history, or of claiming his constitutional privilege. In making the decision, he cannot overlook the ammunition which misuse of the privilege has put at the disposal of the Congressional inquisitors.

In concluding this analysis of use and abuse, two factors, extraneous to the particular circumstances of the witness, should not be overlooked. The first is the mounting evidence that the Communist line is to encourage pleading the Fifth Amendment on the slightest excuse. Of course, this alone is not a sufficient reason to reject recourse to the privilege; here as elsewhere, we must avoid the automatic and invariable negativism which all too often leads us into awkward and illogical postures, to the delight of the Communists. But awareness of this Communist tactic underlines the conclusion that, although resort to the privilege may upon occasion be necessary, it is nevertheless an unfortunate necessity. It is always *faute de mieux,* and never *le meilleur des mondes.*

The second and related factor is the sorry record of the legal profession in counseling witnesses who find themselves in these miserable dilemmas. It is curious but apparent that most lawyers today will more willingly represent an accused gangster or murderer than a college professor in trouble because of an allegedly left-wing past. The result has been that the representation of witnesses before Congressional committees has only infrequently been handled by leading lawyers of "conservative" outlook. This reluctance on their part is in no true sense "conservative," and can only be described as an abdication of traditional professional responsibilities. And one unfortunate result has been that persons who fall into this kind of trouble sometimes end up as clients of attorneys for whom pleading the privilege is the standard prescription.

Other People's Names

Freeborn John Lilburne told the Star-Chamber that he would not answer "as to things concerning other men," and surely he was not the first to take this stand. Ever since their inception, official inquisitions have precipitated the political and moral issues raised by demands for other people's names, and for information about their doings. In 1876 Hallett Kilbourn declined to disclose the membership of the Jay Cooke "real estate pool," and forty years later Mr. George Henry refused to tell Mr. Samuel Untermyer the names of the participants in a Salomon Brothers underwriting syndicate.[49] The feeling which dominates many persons in such a situation was succinctly expressed in 1676 by one Francis Jenks, called before Charles II for criticizing royal policies. When directed to name those who had been advising him, Jenks answered: [50]

> To name any particular person (if there were such) would be a mean and unworthy thing, therefore I desire to be excused from all further answer to such questions.

Today this problem of other people's names is with us in more diverse and controversial guises than ever before in the history of the nation. Within the last few years it has confronted such contrasting individuals as Messrs. Edward Rumely, Elia Kazan, James Wechsler, and Corliss Lamont, Professor Wendell Furry, Miss Lillian Hellman, and Senator McCarthy himself. The legal and practical implications of these situations are, of course, by no means limited to the privilege against self-accusation. Indeed, to my way of thinking they have comparatively little relation to the privilege. Nevertheless, there is such a relation in the minds of many persons, and it is often said that pleading the Fifth Amendment is the only sure and the best way to avoid becoming an "informer."[51]

Now, in fact, nothing is clearer than that the Fifth Amendment has no such purpose. Neither in its history nor its modern development does it relate to a right to avoid accusing *other people*. Indeed, if any such right were to be recognized, the entire process of trial by testimonial evidence would break down. In a court of law, we do not think the less of a witness who truthfully accuses another of criminal conduct. On the contrary, we regard it as the duty of every citizen to uphold law and order, and the efficient administration of justice, by reporting to the police and testifying in court when he has information useful to the detection, prevention, or punishment of crime.

And the same considerations must apply to an authorized legislative inquiry. Congress (or a state legislative body) is entitled to whatever information it reasonably needs to discharge its functions, and that may well include—whether the subject of inquiry be stock exchanges or subversion—testimony from a witness which is derogatory of others, or even which implicates them criminally. And neither before a committee nor in court do considerations of personal friendship or of reluctance to injure other individuals, justify the witness in defying the power of inquiry for the public good. The privilege against self-accusation does not protect a witness against the pain of discharging the duty of responding to the inquiry by naming other people to their injury. As the Supreme Court has put it in a recent decision involving grand jury proceedings,[52] "a refusal to answer cannot be justified by a desire to protect others from punishment, much less to protect another from interrogation."

In the light of the foregoing, let us glance at the case of the famous playwright Lillian Hellman. Summoned before the Un-American

Activities Committee in 1952, she wrote to the committee in advance of her appearance: [53]

> I am not willing, now or in the future, to bring bad trouble to people who, in my past association with them, were completely innocent of any talk or any action that was disloyal or subversive. I do not like subversion or disloyalty in any form, and if I had ever seen any I would have considered it my duty to have reported it to the proper authorities. But to hurt innocent people whom I knew many years ago in order to save myself is, to me, inhuman and indecent and dishonorable. . . .
>
> I am prepared to waive the privilege against self-incrimination and to tell you anything you wish to know about my views or actions, if your committee will agree to refrain from asking me to name other people. If the committee is unwilling to give me this assurance, I will be forced to plead the privilege of the Fifth Amendment at the hearing.

The committee refused to give any such assurance, and Miss Hellman pleaded the privilege. Was she legally justified in so doing, or was her refusal "to bring bad trouble" to others precisely what the Supreme Court declared to constitute no basis for claiming the privilege?

At this point it became necessary to distinguish between *basis* and *motive*, for in this distinction lies the key to the answer. Miss Hellman herself had been identified to the committee as a former member of the Communist Party, and the committee had publicly accused her of membership in a large number of "front" organizations. It may well be, therefore, that there was a sufficient legal basis for Miss Hellman to claim the privilege for herself, irrespective of other persons. That being so, does it make any difference that her motive in making the claim was to protect others rather than herself? Clearly not, as the courts have repeatedly declared. This precise question came before William Howard Taft in 1896, when he was a federal circuit judge, and Judge Taft ruled that the question of motive is irrelevant if the basis for the claim is present.[54]

A witness who is entitled to refuse to answer questions on the basis of self-accusation has the choice of whether or not to avail himself of the privilege. The reasons which he considers in exercising that choice are legally of no importance; they may be wise or unwise, creditable or discreditable. Accordingly, concern for the reputation of other persons does not affect a person's right to claim the privilege, one way or the other. If the basis for the claim is not otherwise present, the possibility of injury to others will not furnish it; if the basis is present, concern for others will not remove it. Miss Hellman was, therefore, legally entitled to claim the privilege. Whether or not her course of action was commendable in a civic sense is a much more complicated matter, but it is essentially no different from the questions presented by other individuals who have invoked the privilege, and which we will shortly discuss.[55]

So far as concerns the problem of other people's names, Miss Hellman's example is of no assistance to those who are not entitled or are unwilling to claim the privilege. For them, the issue must be resolved, not in terms of the privilege, but of the principles discussed in the preceding chapter. And since those issues, pertaining to the scope of legislative authority and of the Bill of Rights, are very controversial, it is not surprising that highly intelligent witnesses have differed sharply in their handling of questions pertaining to other people. We have already observed Mr. Wechsler, tortured by the dilemma, give over the names with a plea that the McCarthy subcommittee keep them secret, while Mr. Rumely obstinately refused a similar demand which he regarded as unauthorized. In the opening pages, we saw Professor Furry abandon the Fifth Amendment and admit his own former Communist membership, but decline Senator McCarthy's demand that he name his fellow members.[56] Before the McCarthy subcommittee, Mr. Corliss Lamont denied that he had ever been a Communist, but refused to answer any other questions pertaining to his opinions or associations with other persons, on the ground that they were beyond the constitutional power of Congress.

Apart from the Fifth Amendment, accordingly, a witness' duty to give information about others depends upon whether, in his best judgment, the information lies within the committee's lawful scope of inquiry. If he believes that the committee is acting within its powers, then he should respond, whether the questions concern himself or others, just as he would if he were a witness in a trial for arson or murder. Personal compunctions do not, under these circumstances, justify silence, however understandable in human terms.

Accordingly, I would find it difficult to justify Professor Furry's refusal to disclose, to the authorized government authorities, the identity of his five fellow-members in the Party while he was working for the Army Signal Corps. What was the actual degree of hazard to national defense secrets I can only surmise; it may have been slight, and all five may now be thoroughly reliable and patriotic citizens. But this affair lies so close to the security of the state that I believe a citizen with knowledge of its details should put that information in the government's hands. Whether Senator McCarthy's subcommittee was an authorized channel for such information or, in view of its irresponsible record and the preposterous pronouncements of certain of its members on security matters, a safe channel, is a much more doubtful question.

However that may be, the revelation of other people's names presents a very different question where the investigation, in the witness' best judgment, has far outrun the bounds of its legitimate authority, or the information sought is far removed from the range of governmental concern. In this connection it should also be borne in mind that Congressional investigating committees are not law enforcement agencies, and that all too frequently their interest in derogatory information about individuals has no reasonable legislative basis. Such were the conclusions reached by Messrs. Rumely, Wechsler, and Lamont about the questions which were put to them. For that reason, it seems to me that there was an intrinsic inconsistency in Mr. Wechsler's decision, in that he gave over the names to a committee which he believed and stated was not authorized to demand them. Personal compunctions cannot be permitted to obstruct valid official inquiries, but they are entitled to weigh in the scales when legal authority is lacking.[57]

To summarize my thinking in this vexed and controversial field: generally speaking, a witness before a Congressional committee has the same duty to answer questions about other persons as about himself. But if the committee has no legal authority to ask the questions, then the witness may be under a moral if not a legal duty to protect others from injurious and unauthorized exposure.[58] So far as concerns the privilege against self-accusation, the desire to protect others affords no basis for its invocation. If, however, the basis for claiming the privilege is already present, the motives which influence the witness to make the claim—whether to protect others, or whatever else—are legally irrelevant. The civic implications of claiming the privilege raise other questions, to which we now turn.

Inferences and Consequences

In September, 1953, the Special Committee on Communist Tactics and Strategy of the American Bar Association adopted a unanimous report which stated:

> Perhaps better than laymen, an attorney can weigh his past acts and more accurately determine whether or not his testimony concerning them might be incriminatory. Therefore, when a citizen, who is an attorney, refuses to testify on the ground that his testimony might tend to incriminate him of undisclosed crimes, then upon his own sworn statement, which we must assume is honestly and sincerely asserted, his personal constitutional right must be honored, but in asserting this right he himself has thereby disclosed disqualification for the practice of the law.

The view that any lawyer who invokes the privilege against self-accusation should be disbarred has gained considerable currency in legal circles since the emergence of loyalty and security as major issues of the times. It is most unfortunate that members of the legal profession, who of all people ought to understand the true nature and meaning of the privilege, should lend themselves to perverse and distorted maunderings such as those just quoted. For these sentences betray the same basic misconception—that the privilege can be rightfully claimed only by the guilty—which is embodied in the epithet "Fifth Amendment Communist."

It is beyond belief that at least some of the Bar Association committee members should not have been aware of how grossly this report traduces elementary legal principles, familiar to every law clerk. There is a well-merited rebuke for this betrayal of professional responsibilities in the words of a distinguished former federal judge, Simon Rifkind. Calling attention to the conflict between the growing popular assumption that pleading the privilege is an admission of guilt, and the fact that judges daily instruct juries that it is no such thing, Judge Rifkind declared: [59]

> Either the courts are all hypocrites or the public does not understand the significance of the Fifth Amendment. One thing is sure, we cannot play it both ways. A society which practices one set of ideals and preaches another is in the process of dissolution, or at least is suffering from a disease that may lead to its dissolution.

The Bar Association committee's wretched funking is the more inexcusable in that the New York courts have repeatedly held that a lawyer's reliance on the privilege establishes no basis for his disbarment. Around the turn of the century, the New York City law firm of Howe & Hummel attained great notoriety [60] for the conduct of a spectacular and piratical practice which ultimately led to the trial and conviction of Mr. Hummel for conspiracy to obstruct justice. A clerk in the office, one Abraham Kaffenburgh, was called to testify at Hummel's trial, whereupon he refused to answer various questions, on the ground that the answers might tend to incriminate him. Disbarment proceedings were instituted against Kaffenburgh, one of the charges being that "in so refusing he was intentionally deceiving the court or else his connection with these matters was criminal"—the very argument currently advanced by the Bar Association committee. But the Court of Appeals of New York State categorically rejected this contention, saying: [61]

> The defendant . . . had the right to refrain from answering any question which might form the basis of or lead to the prosecution of himself for a forfeiture of his office of attorney and counselor at law. To now hold that by availing himself of such privilege it amounted to a confession of his guilt upon which a forfeiture could be adjudged would, in effect, nullify both the provisions of the Constitution and the statute.

And the same result was reached by the Court of Appeals in 1940 in the case of attorneys who refused to sign waivers of immunity before testifying in a judicial investigation of ambulance chasing.[62] The court declared that the privilege is a fundamental constitutional right for an attorney as for anyone else; therefore "its exercise cannot be a breach of duty to the court."

When lawyers can display such wrongheadedness on matters within their special province,* it is small wonder that laymen are in

* A panel of jurists appointed to advise the Secretary General of the United Nations likewise concluded that the privilege could not be honestly pleaded unless the witness was guilty, and the student editors of the Harvard Law Review declined to elect to membership two law students, otherwise eligible, because they had refused to answer questions put to them by the Jenner Committee. The virus is spreading; on September 3, 1954, a lawyer was disbarred, for use of the Fifth Amendment on loyalty questions, in Florida; the judge stated: "I do not think the American legal profession desires to have as members lawyers who shield themselves behind the Fifth Amendment." [62a]

an equal state of confusion. A number of universities and colleges have discharged faculty members on the sole ground that they resorted to the Fifth Amendment, and the General Electric Company and, no doubt, other industrial concerns have adopted the same policy. By executive order, federal government employees are subject to automatic dismissal if they invoke the privilege, and the same is now true for public school teachers in New York City. In all or most of these cases, the policy of automatic dismissal seems to rest upon the assumption that anyone who pleads the privilege in response to a question about Communist associations is either a member of the Party or misusing the privilege. As we have seen, there is no basis in law or fact for such an assumption.

Now, it by no means follows that invoking the privilege under such circumstances should be wholly disregarded by employers and associates of the claimant. If resort to the privilege does not establish guilt, neither is it, as we have already observed, a certificate of good character. Invoking the privilege means that there is *some* evidence of Communist associations which, alone or in conjunction with other evidence, might establish the criminality of those associations, or which, in the absence of or if controverted by other evidence, might establish nothing whatsoever of a criminal or even mildly derogatory nature. In other words, invoking the privilege means that there is *an unresolved question.*

Any individual is legally entitled to leave the question unresolved unless and until the state undertakes to resolve it by bringing him to trial. And the fact that he so chooses does not give the state any ground for visiting upon him penalties or forfeitures such as disbarment, which could be justified only by his actual guilt. But there are many situations in which such an unresolved question should disqualify a person from public trust or responsibility. A frequent and apt illustration is that of a policeman who pleads the privilege rather than answer questions concerning bribery or other corruption. We do not want policemen who choose to leave unresolved questions of their guilt or innocence in such matters. No more do we want national defense secrets entrusted to those who plead the privilege rather than answer questions relating to their Communist associations. And this is so not because the privilege-pleaders are thereby proven or even presumptively guilty, for they are not, but because in such positions we must have public servants whose records are open to inspection.

Well, are there *any* positions in which we want people who plead the privilege when questioned about Communism? Especially, do we want such people practicing law, or teaching in school or college, or working in big factories, or appearing on the stage or screen? It is easy to answer in the negative, and that is why the expression "Fifth Amendment Communist" has proved a catchy one. And yet a moment's reflection must reveal the fallacious and dangerous nature of such a conclusion.

It is fallacious because, as Judge Rifkind put it, "we cannot play it both ways." If pleading the privilege does not imply actual guilt, as indeed it does not, then we cannot make it the basis for rendering individuals unemployable—in effect, outlawing them. It is dangerous because it would aggravate the tensions and strengthen the divisive forces that are already rending the country.

In an absolute sense, everyone is in a "sensitive" position with respect to national security. Bums and derelicts, even, might be successfully used for sabotage. But lines must be drawn somewhere if life is to go on in this country with anything like the degree of liberty to which the Constitution is dedicated. And it seems to me that in private enterprises, apart from those which the government for special reasons hedges about with secrecy, the Fifth Amendment pleaders should not be automatically excluded from participation. Ordinarily, the employer has sufficient leverage to obtain a full explanation from an employee who has pleaded the privilege, and can thereby satisfy himself whether or not there are any sinister or disgraceful implications or hazards. Dean Andrews' nervous professor may have acted unwisely, but I do not see why he should not be allowed to continue to teach mathematics and remain a member of the faculty club.

Recently the Un-American Activities Committee held hearings in Detroit on Communist infiltration in labor unions. Just before the hearings opened, the president (Walter P. Reuther) and other officers of the United Automobile Workers issued a public statement of the union's policy and attitude with respect to the testimony of union members before the Committee, which included the following: [63]

Each witness appearing before these committees must, of course, make his own individual decision as to the course of action which he will follow in his testimony. This is a matter of individual conscience and judgment.

However, we in the UAW-CIO sincerely urge any witness called before the House Un-American Activities Committee, if it is at all possible to do so, to avoid using the privilege of the Fifth Amendment.

Unfortunately, a long string of known hoodlums and a certain per cent of known Communists, who have repeatedly invoked the Fifth Amendment, have created the emotional public climate wherein anyone, for whatever purpose, who may use the Fifth Amendment, is prejudged as guilty. Every time an innocent person uses the Fifth Amendment, the Communists are provided with a bigger and more protective umbrella under which to hide and the reckless and irresponsible political headline hunters are afforded another field day. The price of freedom requires that people who are called upon to appear before this type of Congressional committee summon the courage to meet this challenge without the use of the Fifth Amendment, in order to avoid giving the Communists a protective umbrella and to deprive the reckless headline hunters of an opportunity to make personal political capital of such action. . . .

The UAW-CIO, while urging the above approach, clearly recognizes that there may be situations in which people appearing before such Congressional investigating committees may feel compelled, in good conscience, to resort to the Fifth Amendment for the very reasons for which the founding fathers of our country wrote it into the Bill of Rights.

For these sound and democratic reasons, it is the declared policy of the UAW-CIO that no member or employe will be prejudiced in any degree in his relationship to the union merely and solely because he claims the privilege of the Fifth Amendment. We will resist through the procedures of our collective bargaining agreements any discharge or other discipline of any member of the union by his employer on the sole ground of his having claimed the privilege. The UAW-CIO is determined not to become a party to the erosion of any of our basic liberties or democratic safeguards assured by the Bill of Rights.

Such a person who in good conscience does resort to the privilege of the Fifth Amendment because of compelling personal reasons will not be judged by the UAW-CIO on that fact alone. Rather, that person will be judged in our Union by his actions, past and present, and by the positions that he has taken on the basic issues which sharply divide members of the Communist Party and fellow travelers from the great and overwhelming masses of loyal workers in the American labor movement.

I know of no better expression of the legal and civic significance of invoking the constitutional privilege against self-accusation, and of the inferences and consequences that are rightly to be drawn therefrom.

Immunity Grants and Baths

Ever since the privilege against self-accusation became established as a basic principle of criminal law, there have arisen circumstances in which it has seemed so important to obtain information which a witness was withholding under claim of the privilege, that he should be granted immunity from subsequent prosecution and required to answer. In other words, the state's access to the information is deemed of greater social value than prosecution of the witness for whatever breach of the law he might be accused of. To bring this about, legislatures pass statutes providing that certain witnesses or categories of witnesses shall be granted immunity from prosecution, thus removing the basis for claiming the privilege.

In England, as we have already seen,[64] it was proposed to grant immunity to Nicholas Paxton during the great Commons inquest of 1742, following Sir Robert Walpole's fall from power. On that occasion the Commons voted to grant immunity to Paxton and other witnesses before the Secret Committee, but the Lords did not concur. Since that time, however, it has become standard practice in Parliament not to compel a witness to answer an incriminating question without a grant of immunity.

In the United States, the need for immunity statutes for witnesses before investigating committees and grand juries was first felt about the middle of the nineteenth century. In 1857, as we have seen,[65] the contumacy of *The New York Times'* Washington correspondent led to the passage of the federal statute punishing recalcitrant witnesses before Congressional committees, and the second section of that statute contained an automatic and sweeping grant of immunity to witnesses testifying under the compulsion of Congressional power:

> That no person examined and testifying before either House of Congress or any committee of either House, shall be held to answer criminally in any court of justice, or subject to any penalty or forfeiture, for any fact or act touching which he shall be required to testify before either House

of Congress, or any committee of either House, as to which he shall have testified, whether before or after this act; . . . . Provided, That nothing in this act shall be construed to exempt any witness from prosecution and punishment for perjury committed by him in testifying as aforesaid.

At the time of its enactment, this provision was defended as necessary in order to force witnesses to disclose evidence of bribery or corruption among members of Congress. But it was sharply criticized, especially by the able Senator Pugh of Ohio, who predicted [66] that the automatic grant of immunity would "operate in practice as an advantage to those who are most guilty and least scrupulous, enabling them to escape the just consequences of their own crime by the betrayal of their less culpable associates."

Things worked out precisely as Senator Pugh had foretold. Witnesses before investigating committees did not even have to invoke the privilege to get the benefit of the immunity; they were, in effect, pardoned in advance of all criminal responsibility for any matters they might testify about. Corrupt rascals flocked to the committees to say the few words that ensured their undeserved exemption from the penalties of the law, and soon the situation became intolerable. In 1862 a bill was introduced in the House to repeal the immunity provision, and in the debates it was revealed that the embezzlers of millions of dollars in Indian trust bonds from the Interior Department had escaped prosecution by appearing before an investigating committee, and that "almost every day persons are offering to testify . . . in order to bring themselves within the pardoning power of the Act of 1857 . . ." In the Senate, it was stated that committees had become reluctant to investigate anything for fear of exculpating "great rascals" from criminal liability.[67]

Thus Congress learned the hard way about the dangers of "immunity baths," and the statute which had been enacted with near unanimity in 1857 was repealed by a unanimous vote in 1862. It was replaced by a provision that "No testimony given by a witness before either House, or before any committee of either House . . . shall be used as evidence in any criminal proceeding against him in any court, except in a prosecution for perjury committed in giving such testimony." [68]

But did the 1862 law furnish witnesses with enough protection to remove the basis for claiming the privilege? To be sure, their own testimony could not be used as evidence to convict them, but there was nothing in the new provision to prevent its being used as a lead in discovering other evidence of crime, and no assurance against prosecution and punishment. In 1887, Congress inserted a similar provision in the act creating the Interstate Commerce Commission, authorizing the Commission to require witnesses before it to testify despite any claim of privilege against self-incrimination, but providing that testimony so given "shall not be used against such person on the trial of any criminal proceeding." And five years later the Supreme Court held that this did not afford witnesses sufficient protection against subsequent prosecution to remove the basis for the claim of privilege,[69] saying "no statute which leaves the party or witness subject to prosecution after he answers the incriminating question put to him, can have the effect of supplanting the privilege conferred by the Constitution of the United States."

Reacting to this ruling, Congress amended the Interstate Commerce Act by inserting language granting every witness before the Commission full immunity from prosecution "on account of any transaction, matter or thing concerning which he may testify." And in 1896 the Supreme Court held that this provision was sufficient to accomplish its purpose of removing all basis for claiming the privilege.[70] This sort of language has subsequently been inserted in some twenty federal statutes creating administrative agencies, such as the Federal Communications Commission and the Securities and Exchange Commission.[71] Many state statutes of this description, applying to committees, grand juries, and other investigative agencies, have also been enacted. Witnesses before these bodies cannot rest on the privilege and must testify even though they thereby reveal their own criminal conduct; they cannot, however, thereafter be prosecuted.

But, so far as concerns Congressional investigating committees, Congress left unchanged until this year the narrow language adopted in 1862 which, under the principle of the Supreme Court's 1892 decision, does not remove the basis for claiming the privilege. Nor, indeed, had there been until recently any noteworthy agitation for legislation which would accomplish this purpose.[72]

Then at the inception of the Eighty-third Congress in January, 1953, the late Senator Pat McCarran introduced a bill under which, by a two-thirds vote, Congressional investigating committees would be authorized to grant full immunity from subsequent prosecution (except for perjury) to a witness who had claimed the privilege, so that the witness would thereafter be obligated to testify.[73] After considerable debate, this bill was amended on the floor of the Senate, on the principal initiative of Senators Estes Kefauver and Wayne Morse, so as to require either that the Attorney General concur in the particular grant of immunity or, failing his agreement, that the House or Senate, as the case might be, by a majority yea-and-nay vote approve its committee's action granting immunity.[74]

Senator McCarran's bill was avowedly stimulated chiefly by the large number of witnesses before the Internal Security and Un-American Activities committees who had invoked the privilege rather than answer questions and accusations relating to communism. His major thesis was that valuable information about subversion was being concealed from the government under cover of the privilege. In its original form, his bill would have opened wide the door to immunity baths, just as had the soon-repealed statute of 1857. It was to meet this danger that Senators Kefauver and Morse pressed their argument that the Attorney General's assent should be required, on the theory that the chief law enforcement officer would not agree if important prosecutions would thereby be wiped out. The additional provision that the House or Senate might grant the immunity despite the Attorney General's objections was adopted on the floor as a compromise solution.[75]

So amended, the bill passed the Senate in July, 1953,[76] and the following year it and comparable substitute bills were considered by the House Judiciary Committee. The Attorney General supported immunity legislation as part of the Administration's "package" security program, and in the closing days of the session the Judiciary Committee reported out a drastically amended immunity bill which was passed by both Houses of Congress without much further consideration. President Eisenhower signed the bill and it became law on August 20, 1954.[77]

The new immunity statute is confined to investigations [78] involving threats to "national security or defense of the United States by treason, sabotage, espionage, sedition, seditious conspiracy or the overthrow of its Government by force or violence"—in short, to investigations such as those of the Un-American Activities and Internal Security committees. The Attorney General's role is purely advisory, and therefore the provision added by the Senate, for a grant over his objection by vote of the House or Senate, was eliminated as unnecessary. The important new feature is that the proposed immunity grant must be approved by the federal district court for the locality where the investigation takes place. The Attorney General is given an opportunity to be heard in the district court before the judge passes on the investigating committee's application for approval of the contemplated grant.

This addition to the statute books bears the scars of the haste and lack of consideration that marked its passage. It is exceedingly badly drafted from a technical standpoint, and is of doubtful constitutionality.* Nevertheless, its purpose is worthy of serious consideration. If it proves unconstitutional or unworkable in its present form, no doubt, rather than abandoning the project, efforts will be made to amend the law so as to overcome the difficulties. It is the basic theory of the law, rather than its technical details, that calls for careful public scrutiny.

It is urged with much force in favor of immunity-granting powers for Congressional committees that Congress has conferred the power on numerous administrative agencies, and its own investigating committees are no less deserving. Yet the parallel between a legislative investigating committee and an administrative agency is far from perfect. Each administrative agency operates within a relatively narrow area as compared to the major Congressional committees. Furthermore, the agencies are usually as desirous of enforcing the laws they are concerned with as the Attorney General or the courts, whereas elected legislators are prone to deal with these matters on a less judicial and more political basis. The danger cannot be overlooked that irresponsible, publicity-seeking investigating committees will be more interested in claiming credit for public exposure than in furthering the processes of justice,[79] or may even induce mendacious, ne'er-do-well informers, by promise of immunity, to concoct smears and accusations against individuals that the committee desires to discredit.

---

* See Appendix II: A Note for Lawyers on the New Federal "Immunity" Statute, *infra*, pp. 296-300.

Nevertheless, it is certain that Congress has the power to grant immunity to witnesses before its committees, and occasions may well arise when the power should be exercised, in order to obtain information which Congress needs and which otherwise would be withheld under the claim of privilege. Both Houses of Parliament and numerous state legislatures have asserted and utilized this authority for many years. Accordingly, the question is not so much whether, as by what methods and procedures, Congress should exercise its similar power.

It is my opinion that, under present circumstances, Congress should not delegate the power to grant immunity to all or any committees, but should delegate the power to each of its two Houses, acting by a majority yea-and-nay vote.* Granting immunity is a serious and weighty act of dispensation, which should be approved in every instance by the House or Senate, as the case may be. There is no reason that this requirement should unduly delay or hamper the investigative work of the committees. Furthermore, in recent years the behavior of some investigating committees has been so reckless and irresponsible that it would be extremely dangerous to put the immunity-granting power into their hands.[80]

I cannot see the slightest reason for interjecting the courts into the immunity-granting process, as the new statute does. In the case of witnesses before legislative committees, it is for the legislature to weigh the value of the information to be gained against the policy of uniform law enforcement. The courts are not qualified to do this, and the federal courts are probably barred by the constitutional separation of powers from undertaking this non-judicial function.

The role of the Attorney General, I believe, should be purely advisory, as it is generally with respect to legislative matters.[81] Therefore, any immunity statute should provide for adequate notice to him of a proposed grant of immunity, and require that he submit his recommendations to the House or Senate within a reasonable period

---

* It is arguable that no delegation whatever is necessary. In England, immunity for witnesses before Parliamentary committees has always been granted by statutes, enacted by both Lords and Commons. But the relation between the two Houses of Congress is different, and the investigative power is employed much more frequently and extensively by Congress than by Parliament. Accordingly, I believe it is appropriate that either House or Senate, acting alone, should be empowered to grant immunity in aid of the informing function.

of time, so that his views will be taken into account when the proposed grant is voted upon.

With safeguards such as are described above, an immunity statute would be, I believe, unobjectionable and possibly beneficial. But I do not share the view, expressed by the late Senator McCarran, that its enactment will open up a vast new field of vital security information.* On the contrary, its immediate consequences are likely to be far from earth-shaking. This in itself may be a good thing, in that it will help to explode the notion that Congressional committees are effective police or security agencies, by removing the basis for the excuse, frequently offered,[83] that their best efforts are constantly blocked by the Fifth Amendment.

* Attorney General Brownell has publicly invited Communists who want to "rejoin decent society" to tell their stories to the authorities under protection of the new law.[82]

CHAPTER VIII

OTHER LIMITATIONS AND PRIVILEGES

"If the union you're attacking doesn't fear the whip you're cracking,
Call it un-American!
If you rouse to indignation all the decent population,
Call it un-American!
When the gravy that you're getting keeps the taxes mounting higher,
When you thunder 'I'm the law' and people answer 'you're a liar!'
Simply throw a few red herrings and with patriotic fire
Call it un-American!"

—*Pins and Needles*, 1937

IN THE PRECEDING three chapters we have examined those constitutional limitations and privileges, relating to legislative investigations, which are most significant at the present time. Within the governmental framework, federal or state, the doctrine of separation of powers stops the legislature short of destroying the other branches. That doctrine and the Bill of Rights likewise impose barriers to investigative suppression of personal rights and liberties. And when the power of inquiry is pushed close to questions of criminal liability, individual witnesses may decline to assist in building up charges and accusations against themselves.

But there are other limitations and privileges affecting the investigative power. We have observed and analyzed the division of the federal government's power among the three branches of government; equally basic to the constitutional design is the division of sovereign power between the federal government and the states, the essence of the "federal system." Then, too, there is another basic guaranty in the Bill of Rights that we have not yet considered in its application to investigations—the due process clause. There are other privileges, in addition to that against self-accusation, which witnesses may endeavor to invoke as a matter of self-protection. And finally, there is often a question whether the legislature has in fact authorized an investigating committee to demand the particular information which it is seeking to obtain.

Delegated Powers and States' Rights

Even the most acrimonious conflicts over the separation of powers have been settled without bloodshed. Not so the ebb and flow of the federal system, which engulfed the country in the War Between the States and which, throughout our history as a nation, has been the fulcrum of painful, grinding, and often violent pressures and encounters. Regional customs, attitudes, loyalties, and ambitions are often centripetally manifested in a repulsion of federal power under the banner of states' rights. But they may also furnish the motive force for efforts to capture the federal citadel, and exert the federal authority for the promotion of regional objectives. In either case and on either side, the legislative power of inquiry may be used as a weapon in the fray, or its exercise may jar the federal framework in unforeseen ways.

Such was the case very recently when Congressman Velde made his ill-starred effort to preëmpt for the Un-American Activities Committee the leading role in exploiting the Harry Dexter White affair. Subpoenas were issued to ex-President Truman, and to Supreme Court Justice Tom Clark and Governor James Byrnes of South Carolina, who had been respectively the Attorney General and the Secretary of State at the time of Mr. White's appointment to the International Monetary Fund. Messrs. Truman and Clark, as we have seen, rejected the subpoenas, invoking the doctrine of separation of powers.[1] Governor Byrnes was by no means loath to give the Velde Committee his version of the business, but the command that he betake himself to Washington to appear before the committee struck a stubborn vein of Southern states'-rightism. He replied: [2]

> I cannot, by appearing in response to this summons, admit your right to command a Governor to leave his state and remain in the city of Washington until granted leave by your committee to return.
>
> If your committee has the power thus asserted it could summon to Washington the Governors of the forty-eight states and paralyze the administration of the affairs of the sovereign states. . . .
>
> While I doubt your authority to require me to testify, I shall answer, under oath if you desire, any questions you may propound, relevant to the inquiry authorized by the House of Representatives, . . .
>
> A Governor must be the sole judge of when he can leave his state and he must be free to return to it without permission of a committee of the Congress.

Mr. Velde was not disposed to challenge so proud a response. A subcommittee was sent off to South Carolina to interview Governor Byrnes, and the episode passed off without friction.[3] Yet it is suggestive of explosive and by no means far-fetched possibilities.

Up to the present time, however, the legislative power of inquiry has very rarely come into conflict with the federal system. Viewed historically, this is somewhat surprising. Ever since the *Dred Scott* case in 1857, the most frequent hazard to the constitutionality of federal and state statutes has been that they transcended the constitutionally delegated powers of the federal government or the reserved powers of the states, as the case might be. From the early federal child labor laws to the National Industrial Recovery and Agricultural Adjustment Acts, Congressional efforts to enact laws to deal with economic and social problems have most frequently foundered in the Supreme Court on the rocks of the federal system: [4] "There is no power vested in Congress to require . . ." whatever reform the statute was designed to effectuate. *A priori*, it might have been expected that the courts would likewise have found occasion to invalidate Congressional investigations for invading the preserves of state power, or state legislative investigations for intruding in the federal sphere.

Now, precisely this has in fact happened in Australia, which has a constitution similar to our own in that the federal government has only those powers delegated to it by the Australian constitution, and all other powers are reserved to the individual states. Early in this century, the Australian Parliament enacted the Royal Commissions

Act, under which the Governor General was authorized to appoint commissions of inquiry, with subpoena powers, to look into any matters affecting the "peace, order, and good government of the Commonwealth."

In 1912, such an inquiry was directed into the economic problems of the sugar industry in Australia, and a subpoena was issued to a sugar refining company calling for extensive information about its organization and operations. The company challenged the federal commission's authority, saying that the subject was beyond the scope of federal power. The High Court of Australia by a close vote [5] upheld the company's position, and then the dispute was appealed to the Judicial Committee of the Privy Council, the highest judicial body of the British Empire. In an opinion by the Lord Chancellor, Viscount Haldane, the Privy Council not only sustained the company's challenge to the subpoena, but declared the Royal Commissions Act invalid as *ultra vires* under the Australian Constitution, because it undertook to authorize federal inquiries into matters which were not within the federal government's delegated powers.[6]

But nothing quite like this has so far happened in the United States. No Congressional investigation has been held invalid as an encroachment on state sovereignty, and it seems unlikely that the bounds of federal investigative power will be so rigorously defined here as they have been in Australia. Rather, our constitutional tradition is one of liberal interpretation to meet changing conditions, and the result has been an enormous expansion of federal authority, far beyond the literal wording of the Constitution itself. Today the pattern of federal power is so extensive, flexible, and interlaced that it is easy to devise plausible arguments that almost any subject of inquiry bears a relation to some recognized federal power.

Judge Wyzanski, for example, has suggested that even a Congressional investigation of the divorce laws and practices in the various states might be justified as relevant to a study of federal personal income tax exemptions and deductions.[7] Senator McCarthy was quick to grasp the general idea; Professor Furry's appearance before his committee moved the Senator, as we observed in the opening pages,[8] to suggest that federal tax exemptions be withdrawn from educational institutions such as Harvard (where Judge Wyzanski sits on the Board of Overseers), that retain "Fifth Amendment Communists" on the faculty. Thus the federal government's constitutionally delegated power to levy taxes is seized on as the legal basis for the investigation of private educational institutions, which normally would be regarded as outside the bounds of federal authority.

Of course, the trouble with this sort of argument is that it proves too much.[9] The federal government, as a matter of tax policy, has determined that not only educational institutions, but also all married couples are entitled to certain income tax exemptions. Does it follow that every married man can therefore be forced to state to a Congressional committee whether or not he believes in the privilege against self-accusation, and whether he employs in his factory or store or office any "Fifth Amendment Communists," on the theory that the Committee is studying the desirability of amending the tax laws [10] so as to deny the exemption to those whose attitude toward the Fifth Amendment is "unsound"? If so, the taxing power can be used to justify almost any inquiry into individual opinions and associations.

The implications of this question were forcefully portrayed by Dr. Arthur S. Adams, President of the American Council on Education, in his testimony before the House (Reece) Committee to Investigate Tax-Exempt Foundations. Commenting on the contention of the committee's director of research that the granting of federal tax exemption carries along with it the right of federal supervision or control, Dr. Adams stated:

> This doctrine is itself one of the most revolutionary concepts in the history of American government. It could lead to federal control, either by direct regulation or by threat of removal of the tax-exempt status, not merely of foundations but of health services, education, religion, and the operations of state and local government.

Carried to this extent, the whole federal idea breaks down and becomes meaningless. Somewhere short of these extremes, lines must be drawn so as to confine Congressional investigative power within the federal scheme of things. Nevertheless, the courts will be cautious, and rightly so, to declare a subject of inquiry wholly outside of the federal province.

Such issues may well arise in the future, and the converse case—i.e., state encroachment on federal authority—has actually arisen.

The Works Progress Administration, better known as the WPA, has long since faded from the national scene, but in the depressed mid-thirties it loomed large in the public mind. In 1936, the Republican-controlled Senate of Pennsylvania denounced the activities of WPA in that state, charging that it was "functioning as an arm of the Guffey-Earle-Lawrence Democratic State Administration and being used for the purpose of building up a political machine rather than for the alleviation of unemployment." There were 170,000 persons on the state relief rolls who, it was charged, could be absorbed into WPA operations, thereby relieving Pennsylvania taxpayers. To investigate these accusations, the state Senate authorized a full investigation, backed by the power of subpoena, into the administration of WPA in Pennsylvania. The committee was duly appointed, and promptly issued subpoenas to various officials of WPA in Pennsylvania—who were, of course, federal government employees—commanding them to produce WPA records and to appear and testify before the committee.

But Mr. Harry Hopkins, then the administrator of WPA, would have none of this, and instructed his Pennsylvania subordinates to disregard the subpoenas. Furthermore, at his request the Department of Justice stepped into the picture, and filed suit in the federal district court to enjoin the Pennsylvania committee from investigating federal matters. The district judge granted the injunction,[11] observing that "The attempt . . . to investigate a purely federal agency is an invasion of the sovereign powers of the United States of America." To approve such an exercise of state investigative power might seriously obstruct federal government functions. Furthermore, the subject matter was distinctly federal, and wholly outside the state's reserved powers: "The investigatory power of a legislative body is limited to obtaining information on matters which fall within its proper field of legislative action."

This decision was never taken to a higher court, but it seems clearly correct, and the same principle must logically apply to federal investigative actions which intrude in the domain of state power.[12] Especially would this be true if a Congressional investigating committee should endeavor to enforce its power in such a way as to obstruct the state governmental machinery.

Recently, for example, the Senate Internal Security Committee has been investigating the loyalty of individual teachers in the municipal school systems in New York City, Philadelphia, and elsewhere. Senator Jenner has sought to justify federal intrusion on the ground that it is not the city schools but the individuals that are under scrutiny. But by the same token the Pennsylvania Senate committee might have argued that they were not investigating the WPA, but merely the individuals who administered its affairs in Pennsylvania. The attempted distinction is a worthless one; it is because they were municipal school teachers that the Jenner committee was interested in these individuals.

The New York City Superintendent of Schools, Dr. William Jansen, made a different defense of the Jenner investigations: [13]

> I would say that legislative committees and Congressional committees have been very definitely of assistance to us because the committee through its facilities for investigation has made it possible for us to get information which we would not be able to get in any other way.

Perhaps this was true in fact, but I do not believe it is a sound argument. It is the State of New York, not the federal government, that specifies the standards and qualifications for teachers in the New York public schools. So far as those standards are constitutionally valid—and the existing statutory standards have been upheld by the Supreme Court [14]—the state has ample power to enforce compliance with them, by investigation or other appropriate means.

It is, in my opinion, difficult to find any legitimate Congressional interest in this field. Toleration of the Jenner committee's intrusion may in the long run lead to the very frictions and disturbances which it is the purpose of the federal design to prevent.

Suppose, for example, the Jenner committee were to subpoena teachers who have been investigated and cleared of disloyalty charges by the state authorities, and to interrogate them with the object or effect of discrediting the state's standards and procedures, and demoralizing the educational system? One may well ponder the result if the state should then instruct its teachers not to testify before the Congressional committee, on the ground that the state's own loyalty program for teachers was being interfered with, or that the morale and efficient functioning of the state's educational system were being undermined by unwarranted federal interference.

That would be the Pennsylvania WPA case with reverse English. And however the Supreme Court might decide the question, it is pretty clear how Governor James Byrnes would answer it.

Vagueness: "Call It Un-American!"

During the First World War, Congress enacted the Food Control Act, by which it was declared a criminal offense to make "any unjust or unreasonable rate or charge in handling or dealing in or with any necessaries." The purpose of the law—to prevent war profiteering—was laudable enough. But what did the statute mean? How could any merchant know what prices the courts might consider "unreasonable"? Indeed he could only guess, and the Supreme Court described the statute as one "the scope of which no one can foresee, and the result of which no one can foreshadow or adequately guard against."

And so the Court declared the Food Control Act unconstitutional [15] under the familiar principle that a criminal statute which is so vaguely drawn that it is difficult to determine what acts are prohibited, violates the due process clause of the Fifth or Fourteenth Amendments.[16] Under this rule the Court has also set aside state statutes prohibiting being a "gangster," [17] and acts "injurious to public morals." [18] As Justice Butler expressed it,[19] "No one may be required at peril of life, liberty or property to speculate as to the meaning of penal statutes."

Now, the federal statute dating from 1857 which makes it a criminal offense to refuse to testify before Congressional investigating committees, punishes the refusal to answer "any question *pertinent to the question under inquiry.*" How is a witness to determine what questions are "pertinent"? Obviously, he must look to the committee's authorizing resolution to determine what is the matter under inquiry. But suppose that resolution, in turn, is so vague and loosely worded that it is next to impossible to learn what that matter is. Could not a recalcitrant witness then defend himself, if subsequently indicted, by invoking the due process clause and the rulings of the Supreme Court that we have just noted?

This defense is entirely sound in theory, but as yet no court has held that a resolution authorizing a Congressional investigation was so vague that no one could be prosecuted for declining to testify. The argument was vigorously pressed in behalf of both Mr. Josephson and Mr. Barsky, the recalcitrant witnesses before the Un-American Activities Committee whose other contentions based on the First Amendment have already been studied.[20] In each of those cases the dissenting judge alone was persuaded that the House resolution establishing the Un-American Activities Committee is so vague as to furnish "no ascertainable standard of guilt" under the 1857 statute.

That resolution, it will be recalled,[21] authorized an investigation of "un-American propaganda activities in the United States" and of "subversive and un-American propaganda that . . . attacks the principle of the form of government as guaranteed by our Constitution." The key word is "un-American," and none of the judges seemed to think it sufficiently precise for penal purposes.[22] Judge Charles Clark pointed out that the committee had applied the term so broadly as to imply that motion pictures that "placed bankers in an unfavorable light" were un-American.[23] Judge Edgerton observed that "The term un-American is completely indefinite. Government counsel do not attempt to define it and concede that they cannot define it. . . . In a literal sense whatever occurs in America is American." He called attention to the fact that, when proposed after the outbreak of the Second World War, universal military training had been condemned by its opponents as "un-American"; to this the President's Advisory Commission on Universal Training had replied: [24] "An epithet is not an argument. 'Un-American' means simply that it has not been done before in America."

But the two judges whose votes decided the *Barsky* case ruled that the resolution was saved by the phrase "principle of the form of government as guaranteed by the Constitution." There are, Judge Prettyman declared, certain basic constitutional principles which are universally recognized. Judge Edgerton was not impresssed; is it un-American to favor amendments to the Constitution? But the majority views prevailed, and the Supreme Court declined to review the decision, since when the Un-American Activities Committee has gone its merry way, undisturbed by further worries about vagueness and due process.

Now, it is important to note that we are not here concerned—as we were when considering separation of powers, the federal system, or the First and Fourth Amendments—with limits on the breadth of Congress' investigative *power*, but rather with the *precision* with which investigative missions are delegated to its committees. And for this reason a distinction is properly to be drawn between punishing a witness in the old-fashioned manner by committing him for contempt until he purges himself by testifying, or in the modern manner by criminal prosecution under the 1857 statute. Because in the former circumstance the witness is haled before the bar of the House or Senate itself and ordered to respond to specific questions. There is then no longer any question of the precision of the resolution empowering the committee to investigate, for the House or Senate itself has taken over the inquisitorial role. Furthermore—and here is the even more crucial point—once the witness discovers at the bar of the House or Senate that the question is indeed deemed pertinent, he has an opportunity to answer it and thus avoid punishment. But if his case is sent to the courts for criminal trial, his fate hangs on the accuracy of his original judgment of the question's pertinency to the authorizing resolution. It is too late for him to stand corrected and mend his ways. If wrong, he goes to jail.

For these reasons, the precision of a legislative resolution authorizing a committee to investigate a matter is of no great importance when testimony is to be compelled only by the legislature's own power to punish uncooperative witnesses for contempt. That is why this issue never arose in early times, and why the broadest and most general authorizations to committees aroused no criticism. In 1781, for example, the Virginia House of Delegates authorized several of its standing committees—e.g., on religion, courts of justice, and trade —to send for persons and papers, without further specification.[25] This amounted to no more than a division of general categories of legislative business among several committees, but no one worried about this generality because no one was going to be criminally liable for refusing to answer questions.

But under the 1857 or any other criminal statute punishing failure to testify before a committee or other agency to which the legislature's power of investigation is delegated for a specific purpose, the situation is altogether different. And therefore it may be strongly argued that the *Josephson* and *Barsky* and other lower federal court cases, holding witnesses who have declined to testify before the Un-

American Activities Committee criminally responsible, are wrong. If Congress chooses to punish as criminal the failure to answer "pertinent" questions, it should be held to accepted constitutional standards of precision, so that witnesses are not obliged to take wild gambles in deciding whether questions put to them are or are not pertinent.*

The importance of this question has been heightened by the enactment of the Legislative Reorganization Act of 1946.[26] Until the passage of that act, none of the regular or "standing" committees of the House or Senate had the power of subpoena. Investigations supported by the subpoena power were always authorized by special resolutions particularizing the subject of inquiry, and committing its execution to either a select or a standing committee. But the Legislative Reorganization Act for the first time gave permanent statutory subpoena power to each and every standing committee of the Senate, available for use in connection with "any matter within its jurisdiction."

The jurisdiction of each Senate committee is described in another part of the Act specifying the categories of bills which are to be referred to each committee for study and report. Since this part was not drafted with investigations and subpoenas in mind, but merely the routing of bills, the wording is extremely general: the Committee on Labor and Public Welfare is given jurisdiction over "public welfare generally," the Committee on Armed Services over "common defense generally," the Committee on Interstate and Foreign Commerce over "interstate and foreign commerce generally," and the Committee on the Judiciary over "civil liberties."

The result is that any regular Senate committee can at any time

---

* Some state investigatory resolutions are even broader and less precise than the Un-American Activities authorization. The Washington legislature, for example, has established a Joint Legislative Fact-Finding Committee on Un-American Activities in the State of Washington, which is authorized to "investigate, ascertain, collate and appraise all facts concerning individuals, groups or organizations whose activities are such as to indicate a purpose to foment internal strife, discord and dissension; infiltrate and undermine the stability of our American institutions; confuse and mislead the people, and impede the normal progress of our state and nation either in a war time or a peace time economy." The Supreme Court of Washington has upheld the criminal conviction of witnesses who declined to answer "material and proper" questions before this committee.[27]

subpoena a witness to answer any question "pertinent" to these very broad categories of subjects. The only effective limitation is the amount of money at the committee's disposal to finance investigations. What questions are pertinent to "public welfare generally"? It is quite impossible to draw lines with any degree of certainty, and therefore it is at least doubtful that, if an inquiry were carried out under this general authorization, a recalcitrant witness could be successfully prosecuted under the 1857 statute. Surely it could be argued with great force that these sweeping provisions of the Legislative Reorganization Act afford no reasonable basis for determining pertinence, and therefore no adequate standard of guilt or innocence, any more than did the Food Control Act of 1917 with its prohibition of "unreasonable" rates and charges.

It is noteworthy that the Legislative Reorganization Act did *not* confer the power of subpoena on the standing committees of the House of Representatives.* The reason for this difference was not officially explained at the time, but it is now known that neither the Republican nor Democratic leaders in the House (Messrs. Martin and Rayburn) thought it wise to give the House committees permanent and general subpoena power. It was feared that such power might make the committees uncontrollable, and lead to sensational "fishing expeditions" motivated by publicity-seeking and political ambitions. Subsequent events have certainly confirmed the wisdom and foresight of the House leaders,[28] for at least the House itself still determines what investigations shall be undertaken by its committees, while in the Senate the McCarthy and Jenner committees charted their own courses, with little effective supervision by the parent legislative chamber.

Safety Valve: Pertinence and Impertinence

Assuming that there is no problem of legislative power, and that the subject matter of the investigation to be conducted by the committee is described with reasonable precision, there remains the issue whether the questions put to or documents demanded from the wit-

* The single exception is the Un-American Activities Committee itself, which had been made a standing committee in 1945, and was given statutory subpoena power, like the Senate committees, in 1946.

ness are pertinent to the inquiry. As we have seen, this question will not arise if the legislative body enforces its demands only by contempt. However, the penal statutes, both Congressional and state, punish failure to furnish information which is "pertinent"—or "relevant" or "material" depending on the language of the law—to the subject matter. Accordingly, "pertinency" is simply another way of expressing the issue of whether a particular question is within the investigatory mission authorized by the legislature.

The purpose of this rule of pertinency is to keep investigating committees on the track, and prevent them from harassing witnesses with frivolous or malicious questions which are unnecessary to the inquiry. This is a very salutary checkrein to maintain, especially in these times of free-wheeling and publicity-hungry Congressional sleuths. And the courts have uniformly held that, when an individual is indicted for refusing to answer questions, it is up to the government prosecutor to prove that the questions were in fact pertinent to the purpose of the inquiry, and if the prosecutor is unable to do this, there must be a verdict of acquittal.[29]

Recently, for example, a witness before a Congressional committee was indicted for refusing to say whether or not he knew certain named individuals. The prosecutor was unable to show that these questions had any bearing on the inquiry, and the federal court acquitted the witness, saying: [30] "We seriously doubt whether the 'Do-you-know-a-certain-person' question, without more, can ever be said to be pertinent for the purposes of a criminal prosecution." Such decisions may well have a desirable effect on investigative proceedings, by tightening up the questioning and discouraging irrelevancies.

But the requirement of pertinency has fulfilled another and quite different function, and that is as a sort of safety valve to relieve the pressure of highly controversial issues. The questions of power and privilege which we have studied are not easily answered. Some of them involve the decision of very fundamental constitutional questions; nearly all of them cut deep into our governmental structure, and affect the interplay of major political forces.

And so, although pertinency is not a constitutional question, the Constitution lurks nearby. Three times the Supreme Court has resorted to a narrow construction of resolutions or statutes authorizing investigations—in the *Harriman* (1908), *American Tobacco* (1924), and *Rumely* (1953) cases[31]—in order to avoid the constitutional issues which a broader interpretation would have raised. This is the sense in which the concept of pertinency and materiality may be regarded as a safety valve, and there is no reason to believe that it has outlived its usefulness for this purpose.

Doctor, Lawyer

The Un-American Activities Committee, deep in its investigation of the Hiss-Chambers case, was concentrating on the fate of Mr. Alger Hiss's old automobile. Mr. Hiss testified that he "threw it into" the deal for Chambers' lease of the Hiss residence in Georgetown; Chambers swore that Hiss gave the car to a member of the Communist Party. Eventually the District of Columbia motor vehicle records disclosed that the car had passed from Hiss to the Cherner Motor Company, and immediately from the company to one William Rosen.

And who was he? Mr. Rosen and his wife were called as witnesses before the committee, accompanied by their attorney, Mr. Maurice Braverman. But not much information was forthcoming, for both Mr. and Mrs. Rosen invoked the Fifth Amendment privilege against self-accusation, apparently on the slightest pretext. Soon the Chairman, J. Parnell Thomas, grew impatient: "I am getting pretty sick of this refusing to answer questions on the ground that it might incriminate you, . . ." he admonished Mrs. Rosen. "Mr. Chairman, perhaps counsel can explain to the committee why the witness is answering in this manner," interjected Mr. Robert Stripling of the committee's staff. But Mr. Braverman was not disposed to be enlightening. He was simply advising his clients of their constitutional rights.

Never noted for patience or judicial restraint, Chairman Thomas ordered Mr. Braverman to abandon his role as counsel, and stand and be sworn as a witness. Mr. Braverman declared that he would stand, but would not be sworn. He was present as counsel to the Rosens; if the committee wanted his testimony as a witness they would have to subpoena him, and in that event he would want counsel himself. Furthermore, it was apparent that the committee was trying to intimidate him, and to extract information about his clients the Rosens. On that score, declared Mr. Braverman:[32]

I think the committee has no right to ask questions regarding relations between me and my client.

The committee backed away from the issue,[33] as investigating committees often have. But it is a question of great practical importance. If not satisfied with the testimony given by a witness, can the committee turn upon his lawyer, and demand the revelation of confidential discussions between attorney and client, in the course of which the client may have made unguarded statements or admissions? Or are such professional consultations privileged against disclosure? If not, many people may think twice before making a clean breast of the damaging as well as the helpful facts to their lawyers.

This presents the general problem, familiar to courts and lawyers for several centuries, of *privileged communications*. There are various confidential relationships which, as a matter of social policy, deserve protection, to the extent that the courts will not require divulgence of communications within the protected relationship, even to obtain evidence which might be of great or determinative weight in a civil or criminal trial. Safeguarding the confidential relationship is deemed more important than the information which is thus withheld, and the suppression of which may on occasion even work injustice.

The privilege covering confidential discussions between attorney and client is the oldest of these, dating from Elizabethan times. The common law extended this protection also to communications between husband and wife, and among the members of juries. Several distinguished British judges have declared that the confessional relationship between priest and penitent should be similarly safeguarded. But, perhaps because of England's turbulent religious history, perhaps because the issue was generally avoided by tacit agreement, the British courts have never given a conclusive answer. However, in a majority of our states, the priest-penitent privilege has been established by statute.

Surprising as it may seem, no similar protection for consultations between physician and patient has ever won any observance in the British courts. It was first recognized in a New York State statute of 1828, and since that time about half the states have followed suit. This privilege has been strongly criticized on the ground that medical consultations are rarely confidential, in that people are generally more prone to dilate upon than to conceal their ailments. But to this there are some notable exceptions, and with the growth of modern psychiatry there is perhaps more basis now than formerly for recognizing a medical privilege, at least in some circumstances.

Any of these privileges recognized by the courts might, as happened with the Rosens, come into question before legislative investigating committees. But it is uncertain whether they would be regarded as available to witnesses before a committee.* The attorney-client privilege, for example, is firmly imbedded in British trial procedure, but Parliamentary committees of inquiry do not treat it as binding upon them, and in 1828 a solicitor was actually required to disclose information given him confidentially by a client.[34] This is in line with Parliament's non-recognition of the privilege against self-incrimination, on the theory that common-law limitations do not govern the prerogatives of a Parliament which is omnipotent and above the common law, which it can change at will.

Very different concepts and circumstances must be reckoned with in the United States. Nonetheless, it cannot be said with any certainty that the attorney-client privilege is applicable to proceedings before Congressional or state investigating committees. Indeed, the prevailing opinion in Congress has been to the contrary. In 1934, many years before the Un-American Activities Committee tried to make Mr. Braverman testify, the Special Senate Committee Investigating Ocean and Air Mail Contracts subpoenaed all the relevant documents in the possession of Mr. William P. MacCracken, a Washington attorney representing many of the carriers whose affairs were under investigation. On this occasion Mr. MacCracken's clients all waived the privilege and consented to the production of the documents, and so the issue was no longer in the case by the time it reached the Supreme Court.[35] But it is clear that the Senate did not feel bound to respect the privilege, and it may be added that in 1873 the House had taken the same position,[36] and that there are several old decisions of state courts in which it is stated (but not decided,

* In 1913, Mr. George Henry of Salomon Brothers asserted a privilege for bankers' clients, and during the recent Watkins Committee hearings Mr. Walter Winchell, like many news reporters before him, said that he would decline to reveal his sources. But there was no legal basis for either of these claims.

since the point was not at issue) that the attorney-client privilege is not available to witnesses before investigating committees.[37]

But all of this is highly inconclusive, and it is my belief that, under present circumstances, the courts should and probably would rule that this privilege can be invoked before the committees. As for the legal aspect of the problem, it should be borne in mind that the Sixth Amendment to the Constitution provides that: "In all criminal prosecutions the accused shall . . . have the assistance of Counsel for his defense." Unlike certain other provisions of the Bill of Rights (including the privilege against self-accusation) which have remained binding only on the federal government, the Supreme Court has held that the right to counsel is an essential element of fairness, and consequently that the Fourteenth Amendment's due process clause, which is binding on the states, includes the right to counsel.[38] Likewise, although the Sixth Amendment accords that right only in "criminal prosecutions," the courts have been quick to extend it, as an elementary ingredient of fair procedure, to civil and administrative proceedings.[39]

Does the constitutional right to counsel include the right to have discussions with counsel protected against disclosure? It is always said that the right is not a mere formality, but embodies the *effective assistance* of counsel.[40] Would not that be jeopardized or even destroyed if counsel or client could be compelled to reveal their private consultations? In the trial of Judith Coplon in the District of Columbia, it was charged (and not denied) that agents of the Federal Bureau of Investigation by wire-tapping had intercepted telephone communications between Miss Coplon and her counsel. On this ground the federal appellate court in the District of Columbia set aside her conviction, saying: [41] "It is well established that an accused does not enjoy the effective aid of counsel if he is denied the right of private consultation with him." On this basis, it would seem to follow that observance of the attorney-client privilege is part of the "effective assistance" of counsel guaranteed by the Constitution.

But the Supreme Court has not yet said so, nor has it said that either the right to counsel or the attorney-client privilege is binding on Congressional investigating committees. However, the Court has come close to saying this. Many years ago Congress authorized the Interstate Commerce Commission to inspect the books and records of railroad companies. The Court held that this did not include correspondence, and especially did not cover confidential correspondence between a railroad and its counsel: [42]

> The desirability of protecting confidential communications between attorney and client as a matter of public policy is too well known and has been too often recognized by textbooks and courts to need extended comment now. If such communications were required to be made the subject of examination and publication, such enactment would be a practical prohibition upon professional advice and assistance.

As the sentence last quoted states, this is a very practical problem—far more significant today than in 1915, when Justice Day wrote it. Witnesses before Congressional loyalty investigating committees are constantly subjected to pressures and confronted with problems far more acute and critical than generally arise in court proceedings. We have just reviewed the thorny thicket of issues that surrounds the Fifth Amendment. Obviously, a lawyer cannot intelligently advise a witness with respect to its use or non-use unless he knows the circumstances that might tend to incriminate. If the lawyer can then be required to divulge what the client has told him, the client might be better off to rely on his own untutored impulses, and shun the lawyer's office, thus transmuted into an echo-chamber.

Millions of citizens have recently watched the doings at the Army-McCarthy hearings. Would anyone seriously contend that Mr. Joseph Welch could have been required by the committee to take the stand and relate what he had been told by Messrs. Stevens, Adams and Hensel while preparing for the hearings? Or that Senator McCarthy and Mr. Roy Cohn, even though it was never clear which was client and which counsel, could have been required to disclose what each privately told the other?

Such proceedings, in which not only are personal and political reputations at stake, but which may also result in criminal prosecutions, bear no resemblance to the decorous if thorough inquiries into public issues conducted by Parliamentary committees of inquiry. And that is why the British practice of disregarding the attorney-client relationship is ill-suited to the torrid climate of a Congressional investigation.

CHAPTER IX

INVESTIGATING COMMITTEE PROCEDURES

"The rights you have are the rights given you by this committee. We will determine what rights you have and what rights you have not got before the committee."

—Representative J. Parnell Thomas, 1948

MEMORIES ARE SHORT, and in this year of the graceless Army-McCarthy hearings it is an effort to recall that these were by no means the first Congressional investigative sessions to be viewed through the medium of television by millions of citizens. Nor were they the most widely viewed; in 1951 and 1952 several hearings of the Senate crime investigation—in which Senator Kefauver, the late Senator Tobey, counsel Rudolph Halley, and an extraordinary assortment of underworld characters such as Mr. Frank Costello played stellar roles—enjoyed much the largest television audience that this type of program has ever reached. Even before that, the Un-American Activities Committee hearings in 1948 on the Hiss-Chambers accusations were televised and watched by millions.

Now, while there are no statutory rules or standards governing the procedures to be followed by investigating committees, it is fair to say that the Hiss-Chambers and Kefauver hearings were typical, in that they observed methods and customs which are generally characteristic of present-day Congressional investigative hearings. The television audiences of 1948 and 1951–52 were thus given a glimpse of investigations in action which were reasonably representative of investigations in general.

Not so the thirty-six days of televised Army-McCarthy hearings. Political events so fell out that these proceedings resembled nothing that had ever seen the light of day before or, so it please the Lord, will ever be seen again.

In part, this atypical and eerie quality was due to the fundamental incongruity of a committee investigation of itself and its own staff, and of charges and counter-charges between its own chairman and highly-placed government officials. In order to camouflage this basic anomaly and create the semblance of impartiality, the committee resorted to various pseudo-judicial devices, such as the designation of six individuals as "parties" to the controversy and the allotment of time for cross-examination of the witnesses. The courtroom atmosphere was initially heightened by the circumstance that counsel for the committee and for the Army who figured prominently in the proceedings, Messrs. Ray Jenkins and Joseph Welch, were both much more at home before a jury than in the Senate chamber.

But all this procedural paraphernalia was, to borrow Al Capp's apt expression, strictly "whomped up." The judicial overlay was spurious and soon wore thin, revealing the political and emotional underpinnings. In any event, I think it most unlikely that this 36-day wonder will have progeny. As the vacuous and ineffably good-humored Senator Mundt explained at the outset,[1] "It is not our intention that these rules should establish a precedent which should necessarily be followed by other Congressional committees or in other investigations where the circumstances differ markedly from the conditions which we have here in the current controversy." Amen!

In part, the Mundt Committee's difficulties arose because it sought unsuccessfully to combine the characteristics of two quite different types of Congressional investigative proceedings, the one legislative and the other quasi-judicial. Of course, all Congressional proceedings are and must be legislative in the ultimate sense, but there are some that partake, much more than others, of the judicial quality and which can be effectively discharged only by restraining partisan and political motives and acting in a judicial spirit. Impeachment, wherein the House accuses and the Senate tries, is one such function; the judicial element is underlined by the Constitutional requirement that, when the President is impeached, the Chief Justice shall preside at his trial by the Senate. Another quasi-judicial responsibility is that each House is the judge of the election and qualification of its own members, and may punish or expel them.[2]

When either House is acting under these special powers, it is fitting that its procedures and standards should be assimilated, as far as practicable, to those of tribunals charged with the trial of issues of fact and law. That is why the Watkins Committee, with considerable success, followed judicial practices and attitudes while considering the McCarthy censure resolution. And that is also why the Mundt Committee, seeking at one and the same time to investigate the conduct of one of its own members (Senator McCarthy) and its own staff (Messrs. Cohn and Carr), and to investigate the Department of the Army, fell into such a hopeless procedural tangle.

It is, to be sure, difficult enough for a legislative body to act like a judicial tribunal under the best of circumstances. In Britain the process of impeachment has been obsolete since 1806, and the judging of contested elections to Parliament has been committed to the courts since 1868.[3] When President Andrew Johnson was impeached, Chief Justice Chase thought that the Senate was actually transmuted into a court for purposes of the trial, but the Senate majority disagreed.[4] Whatever labels are applied, however, impeachments, election contests, and proceedings for the punishment (including censure) and expulsion of members are rightly subject to much more rigorous procedural requirements than are legislative investigations of the usual type.

Lo! The Poor Witness

Unlike the leading participants in the Army-McCarthy hearings, most witnesses before Congressional loyalty investigations do not take the stand clothed in the majesty of the Senate or of the United States Army. No special rules or procedures are contrived for their benefit, and more often than not there are no rules whatever, or none that the committee is bound to observe. As a matter of general principle, the chilly and comfortless observation of Congressman Thomas, quoted above as the theme song of this chapter, is quite correct as applied to questions of procedure.

Accordingly, the witness summoned before an investigating committee has no guide to these questions other than what he can find out about the committee's current attitudes and practices. Is he entitled to be accompanied by counsel during the hearings? Usually this is allowed. May his counsel volunteer advice, or comment upon or ask questions about the proceedings? The practice varies widely; when Senator McCarran was chairman of the Internal Security Committee during the Lattimore and Institute of Pacific Relations hearings, counsel were severely admonished and threatened with expulsion if they broke silence. Is the witness entitled to reasonable advance notice of a hearing, and to be informed of the subjects about which he will be questioned? May he make a statement of his own in addition to answering questions? May he call other witnesses to confirm his own testimony? What about cross-examination of other witnesses who make derogatory statements about him? Is the witness entitled to a transcript of the proceedings upon their conclusion? And what if any protection does he have against public denunciation of himself by members or employees of the committee?

To none of these questions is there any precise or generally recognized answer. Nor have the courts shown any disposition to review committee procedures and check abusive practices. In historical perspective, it is easy to see why this is so. In earlier times, legislative investigations were regarded and conducted as informal, fact-finding inquiries for legislative ends. Of course, even in hearings of this type, reputations were often at stake on disputed questions of fact, as we saw to be the case in the investigation of General St. Clair's defeat. Nevertheless, it seems to have been the feeling that lawyers had no necessary place in the investigative picture. Committee counsel were unknown. Witnesses rarely if ever were accompanied by counsel, and there are several old cases holding—in line with British practice to this day—that witnesses before legislative committees have no right to counsel.[5]

But by no means does it follow that witnesses, and persons under investigation, were then dealt with more harshly or arbitrarily than they are today. On the contrary, the atmosphere was, on the whole, far more courtly than what now prevails. Furthermore, persons under inquiry were often given the right to call their own and cross-examine hostile witnesses—a privilege almost unheard of today. In the St.

Clair hearings, for example, General St. Clair, Secretary of War Knox and Quartermaster Hodgdon were all permitted to call witnesses, and to participate in the questioning.[6] As late as 1924, witnesses before the Brookhart-Wheeler Committee investigating the Department of Justice were cross-examined by counsel representing Attorney General Harry Daugherty.[7] And Professor Felix Frankfurter, in his contemporaneous article opposing restrictions on investigating committees, declared: [8]

> Of course, the essential decencies must be observed, namely opportunity for cross-examination must be afforded to those who are investigated or to those representing issues under investigation. Despite Daugherty's statement to the contrary, that opportunity has been scrupulously given by the Brookhart committee.

If cross-examination is no longer regarded as an "essential decency," still these circumstances of past years explain why little attention was paid to committee procedures until recently. And for the same reasons it is natural that, over the course of years, the courts have come to assume that committees are entitled to determine their own procedures. Now that criticism of their procedural practices is widespread, the courts are still reluctant to prejudice harmonious relations between the legislative and judicial branches by interjecting themselves into the situation. As expressed in a recent decision by a federal court of appeals: [9]

> In general a witness before a congressional committee must abide by the committee's procedures and has no right to vary them or to impose conditions upon his willingness to testify.

This is gentler language than Congressman Thomas employed, but it comes down to much the same thing. The witness has no procedural rights that the committee is bound to respect.

Secret and Not-So-Secret Hearings

Throughout the history of legislative investigations, hearings have on occasion been conducted in secret when the committees have thought that circumstances so required. These are now referred to as "executive sessions" (as distinguished from public hearings), and there is no doubt that they have their *bona fide* uses.

For example, the testimony may involve military or diplomatic secrets, or otherwise endanger national security, as was the case during the hearings on General Douglas MacArthur's relief as Far Eastern commander-in-chief.[10] Or it may be that serious accusations against individuals should first be heard and scrutinized in secret, in order to weed out frivolous, malicious, and obviously erroneous charges and suppress them in advance of public hearing, so as to avoid unnecessary injury to individuals. For such purposes, secret sessions are not only entirely appropriate but also highly desirable, and there should be no question of an investigating committee's authority to exercise its discretion in this regard.[11]

But whereas until recent years secret sessions were the exception rather than the rule, the Congressional loyalty investigations now conduct more executive than public sessions. During 1953 the McCarthy committee took far more testimony *in camera* than in public.[12] For the past few years the Jenner and Velde committees have examined a great many witnesses in executive session.

It is highly probable that many of these secret proceedings have no normal legislative purpose. Rather it seems apparent that they are part of the extensive process of "identification" which we discussed in an earlier chapter. Essentially, these committees are functioning as a sort of special loyalty police, and are amassing records and dossiers on individuals in permanent or semi-permanent fashion. But legislative committees are not supposed to be a police force, and in a heated and cutthroat political atmosphere it is inevitable that the contents of these secret records will be distorted and misused. Certainly it is apparent that the existence of these extensive dossiers puts enormous power of injury into the hands of their possessors.

But there is a much more immediate and flagrant abuse of the executive session which has been repeatedly committed by Senator McCarthy's investigating subcommittee. In effect, Senator McCarthy has devised and exploited a new type of hearing which is neither secret nor public. It is secret in the sense that the press and the general public are excluded, but public in the sense that specially-invited guests having no proper official connection with the proceedings are present, and at the end of the hearing the chairman, or members of the committee or its staff, give the press their version of what has occurred.

This sort of mongrel proceeding is thoroughly outrageous. Obviously, the only purpose of a secret session is that it shall be secret from everyone except those officially entitled to participate. It is a shocking perversion of legislative power for a committee to stage what amount to private circuses for the delectation of the friends, relatives, and personal guests of the committee and staff. During the recent hearings concerning the Signal Corps Engineering Laboratories at Fort Monmouth, Senator McCarthy constantly invited or permitted the presence of relatives and friends of staff members, of Army officers and their wives, and of others who had no business to be present at an official executive session. When witnesses were bold enough to ask who was present, Senator McCarthy refused to identify them. The practice reached the extreme of absurdity when, at a closed hearing in Albany on alleged Communist infiltration of workers at the General Electric plant in Schenectady, Senator McCarthy admitted thirteen girls from a nearby seminary.[14] Whatever the nature of the educational benefits to the young ladies, this was an inexcusable and vulgar affront to the integrity and dignity of the Senate.

Of course, this practice has a more practical and sinister purpose than that of display. Paradoxically, this is the use of secret sessions for publicity purposes. By excluding the press, the McCarthy committee gained control of what was reported about the hearings, and exploited that control to make sensational headlines having no basis in fact. Thus the early reports of the Fort Monmouth secret hearings were carried by *The New York Times* under headlines such as: [15] RADAR WITNESS BREAKS DOWN, WILL TELL ALL ABOUT SPY RING; ESPIONAGE IN SIGNAL CORPS FOR TEN YEARS; REDS JOKE ABOUT HOW EASY IT IS TO OBTAIN RADAR DATA.

The testimony actually given at these executive sessions gave little or no support to the frightening messages carried by these headlines. The whole thing was a shameless case of synthetic publicity-seeking, carried out with no regard for the facts or the national welfare. Eventually, of course, the press was able to penetrate closer to the shabby truth, but in the meantime great harm had been done both to the Signal Corps and to individuals. Effective prohibitions against this dangerous and disgusting perversion of the investigative process should certainly be included in any reforms of investigative procedure which may be adopted.

With Gun and Camera

There is a lovely French song, often sung by Edith Piaf and the Compagnons de la Chanson, called *Les mains de ma mère, les mains de ma mie*. But in our present context, when we think of hands we think of one pair only: *les mains de* Frank Costello. More than any other episode, the televising of his twisting, nervous hands during the Kefauver hearings symbolized the revolution worked by the conjunction of television and public proceedings.

But it is just this highly dramatic quality of televised hearings which involve sensational charges against prominent or intrinsically colorful personages, that has aroused the sharpest criticism. It is bad enough, we are told, to collar a man by subpoena, seat him in the witness chair before a committee of determined and politically-minded inquisitors, and shoot him full of questions, without at the same time putting him on involuntary display before millions of watchers. The citizen is not a wild beast of the African veldt, to be hunted with gun and camera.

Still other and weighty objections are urged by eminent and well-informed observers.[16] Public attention is diverted from more important but less spectacular issues, and is concentrated on matters which are essentially trivial. The enormous publicity accorded by television has a deleterious effect on the legislators who conduct the hearings, by stimulating them to play to the gallery and thus vulgarize and needlessly prolong the hearings. No one suggests that court proceedings—even the most sensational—be televised or even photographed. What then is the justification in the case of legislative hearings?

Such were the adverse arguments vigorously pressed three years ago, at the conclusion of the Kefauver crime hearings. Serious as they are, they did not prevail. Since then many other hearings have been televised, with diminishing opposition. Perhaps it may be urged that this growing acceptance of television in the committee room is chiefly a sign of declining standards of propriety in such matters. But I am inclined to think otherwise.[17]

For as I see it, the televising of legislative investigations presents no new basic issue. If a witness can be required to appear and testify on the record before a public sitting of the investigative body, if the record of his testimony may be printed and distributed in official reports and quoted in the press, and if—as has long been the practice—the press and movie newsreels may publicize his appearance visually as well as verbally, there is little logic in drawing the line this side of radio and television.

For the public character of legislative inquiries (in the absence of security or other special considerations which require secrecy) is no superficial appendage, but highly functional. In judicial proceedings, the public is admitted in order to minimize the risk of secretly corrupted "star chamber" proceedings. But the public is not expected to participate in or influence the actions of judge or jury; on the contrary, the utmost precautions are taken to insulate them from outside pressures.* The legislative process in a democracy, in contrast, should be responsive, though not necessarily submissive, to the expressions of the electorate.

The public, in short, is entitled not only to receive the information uncovered in legislative investigations, but also to comment on it and supplement it to the legislature, by petitions and letters or through other appropriate channels. Public participation is an organic part of the legislative process, and it is a necessary part of the lawmakers' function that the lightning of the public's anger should beat about their heads and the sunshine of its smile warm their hearts. This is why maximum publicity, within the limits of decorum and fairness, is desirable.

But publicity is far less important than fairness. And there are, I believe, three principal respects in which television may tend to undermine the fairness and decorum of Congressional investigations, unless preventive measures are adopted.

Excessive noise, light, heat or other disruptive circumstances. Much has been made, and rightly, of the glare of lights and general disturb-

* For this reason, the Watkins Committee was, in my opinion, quite right in excluding television and newsreel cameras from those proceedings, which were of a quasi-judicial nature. The heads of the two major networks, Messrs. David Sarnoff and Frank Stanton, both objected to the exclusion of television from the Watkins hearings.[18] Much as I agree with their position that legislative hearings generally should be available to radio and television, it seems to me that they chose the wrong instance for their protests.

ance which now accompany an important Congressional investigation. It is unfair to a witness to subject him to the interminable popping of flash bulbs, the heat and dazzle of klieg lights, and the jumping about of innumerable photographers seeking "new angles." Furthermore, it makes a Roman holiday of the occasion and degrades the legislative process.

Does a witness have any legal basis for objecting to any or all of these paraphernalia? In a recent case in which two witnesses were prosecuted for refusing to answer questions at a hearing of the Kefauver investigating committee, justifying their refusal by disturbances such as these, District Judge Schweinhaut dismissed the indictments. He ruled that no constitutional question was involved, but that the entire atmosphere of the hearing was so chaotic as to destroy the witnesses' concentration, and to justify their declining to answer. He wrote: [19]

> The only reason for having a witness on the stand, either before a committee of Congress or before a court, is to get a thoughtful, calm, considered and, it is to be hoped, truthful disclosure of facts. That is not always accomplished, even under the best of circumstances. But at least the atmosphere of the forum should lend itself to that end.
>
> In the cases now to be decided . . . there were, in close proximity to the witness, television cameras, newsreel cameras, news photographers with their concomitant flash bulbs, radio microphones, a large and crowded hearing room with spectators standing along the walls, etc. . . . The concentration of all of these elements seems to me necessarily so to disturb and distract any witness to the point that he might say today something that next week he will realize was erroneous.

This decision seems to me correct, and to foreshadow a healthy development in judicial review of investigations. It is important to note, however, that Judge Schweinhaut did *not* rely on the presence of television cameras alone, but on the entire concatenation of microphones, flash bulbs and cameras. And in fact television is not the sole or even the principal offender. At the Kefauver crime hearings in New York, the television cameras were placed in the corners of the room and were relatively unobtrusive. In large part, the glare and heat of lights and the flash bulbs and almost incessant motion were due to the newsreel and press photographers.

Nearly, if not quite all, of this disturbance is wholly unnecessary in a chamber which is properly equipped. At the United Nations, television cameras are located in glass booths, the room is brightly but not oppressively illuminated, and the camera work proceeds practically unnoticed. At the Nuremberg trials, newsreel and other cameras were likewise confined to corner booths and other inconspicuous vantage points, and their operation in no way detracted from the solemnity and quiet of the proceedings.

There is no reason why similar restrictions cannot be enforced in Congressional hearings, and every reason why they should be. Neither flash bulbs nor the clicking of cameras nor any moving about of press representatives within the "operational area" of the hearings should be permitted while the committee is in session. Installing the necessary booths will run up the costs. But if Congressional hearings are important enough to be photographed and televised, they are important enough to justify the expense of preserving the proper atmosphere, in fairness both to the witnesses and to the legislative process itself.

If these precautions are observed, I do not think that "mike fright" or "stage fright" will discomfit many witnesses. It is, in any event, the inherent tension of public controversy that is the primary cause of nervousness. The microphone has become a standard item of furniture in large public rooms, and witnesses may legitimately be required to accommodate themselves to it. No doubt the witness who is poised and articulate, or who conveys an impression of simplicity and sincerity, will appear to best advantage with the public. But this is characteristic of all human intercourse, and these qualities are just as valuable before a jury as before the microphone or camera.

Incomplete presentation. One of the most serious hazards is that television may carry only the most sensational parts of a hearing, or that the portions selected may distort or "slant" the presentation. This may occur by design, by accident, or by the pressure of commitments to broadcast other programs during the course of the hearings. Of course, this risk is not peculiar to television; it is also inherent in newspaper coverage. But variety in reporting techniques and editorial points of view is at least a mitigating factor in the case of the press. Furthermore, the public has become accustomed to expect an editorial slant in news reporting; it does not expect this from a radio or television station. Scurrilous and one-sided journalism is tolerated in our society, but these qualities cannot be allowed to pervade the radio waves.

It is highly necessary, therefore, that television broadcasts of Congressional investigative hearings be complete, or if unavoidable circumstances necessitate selection, that the most scrupulous fairness be exercised so that the nature of the selection does not work to the damage of any individual or to the prejudice of a fair presentation of the issues. Congressional committees should not permit broadcasts of their hearings without advance plans and assurances that satisfy these standards.

Commercial sponsorship. During the Kefauver crime hearings, one of the New York television networks obtained a commercial sponsor—*Time Magazine*—for these programs. The propriety of allowing a private concern to exploit for commercial advertising a governmental proceeding has since been much debated. For the defense, it has been argued that sponsorship helps the networks meet the costs and thus encourages them to carry more of such events than would be the case if sponsorship were prohibited.

However, it may be doubted whether this would be the effect in the long run. Private concerns sponsor programs for advertising or good will advantages. In the nature of things, they will seek to capitalize on the most colorful hearings or portions of a protracted hearing. If commercial sponsorship is permitted, the networks will come to depend on it, and the inevitable result will be selective coverage based on advertising considerations—the very outcome which it is vital to avoid.

Furthermore, one cannot overlook the possibility that a venal committee and an uninhibited advertiser might prostitute the investigative process and concoct a "show" to the political advantage of the one and the financial benefit of the other. And in any case, it would be most unfortunate if the determination whether or not to broadcast a governmental proceeding or a part of it should hang upon the advertising judgment of a commercial concern. Rather we should continue to enforce the public interest responsibilities of the networks, perhaps assisted by grants from non-profit foundations, and eventually supplemented by the operations of non-commercial radio and television stations.

Nor is the question of taste a trivial one. It has been argued that advertising sponsorship of the Kefauver telecasts was no more to be condemned than advertising in newspapers the circulation of which was raised by coverage of the hearings. This overlooks the basic difference between use of the same general medium and direct sponsorship of the coverage itself, as if an advertiser bought and paid for the newspaper space in which the press accounts were carried.

It simply is not seemly that Presidential addresses, proceedings of Congress and its constituent committees, or other official events should come to us "by courtesy of" soap, beer, or bubblegum, or even any less personal and more dignified commodity. All considerations lead to the conclusion that commercial sponsorship should not be permitted. To this end, at the conclusion of the Army-McCarthy hearings, Senator Bennett of Utah introduced a resolution, approved by thirty-six other Senators, to ban commercial sponsorship of any future televised Senate hearings.[20]

No doubt there are problems to be worked out in addition to those discussed above. Now that millions of people can be given a window through which to watch Congressional investigations, it is high time that the general standards of procedure should be overhauled and raised, in the interests both of good legislation and fair play for individuals. Under proper safeguards, the televising of public hearings should be a highly beneficial thing, both in principle and in fact. The citizen's opportunity for direct contact with governmental proceedings has been greatly enhanced. If the opportunity is intelligently exploited, our democracy may be strongly reinforced.

Codes of Fair Practices

The issues and abuses that we have discussed in this chapter, underlined by the tensions and emotions awakened by controversial investigations and investigators, have now led to a veritable flood of proposals for "codes of fair practices" to govern Congressional investigative procedures. During the last (Eighty-third) Congress, bills and resolutions embodying such codes were introduced by Senator Estes Kefauver of Tennessee (for himself and eighteen other Democratic Senators), Senators Paul Douglas of Illinois and Prescott Bush of Connecticut, and by Representatives Javits, Keating, and Celler of New York, Scott of Pennsylvania, and Frelinghuysen of New Jersey. Numerous private organizations and individuals have also engaged in code-drafting, and in New York State the Legislature during its 1954 session enacted a statutory code to govern the procedures of its investigative committees and commissions.

Some of these proposed codes are more extensive and drastic than others, but there is a high degree of similarity among them. Nearly all provide that witnesses shall have the right of counsel, and some go on to specify that the attorney may raise procedural or substantive objections, ask his client questions to bring out favorable evidence, and generally conduct himself more or less like a lawyer in a courtroom.

Very commonly, too, these codes provide for notice to the witness in advance of his appearance, specifying with reasonable precision the matters about which he is to be questioned. The witness is authorized to make a statement of his own in addition to answering questions, and is to be furnished with, or given access to, a copy of his testimony at its conclusion.

Beyond these provisions, however, the differences among the proposals are much greater. Some of them give individuals who have been unfavorably mentioned the right to appear and reply, to call witnesses in their own behalf, and to cross-examine hostile witnesses. Usually, however, the extent to which these rights may be availed of is limited in some way, so that investigations will not become uncontrollable or so protracted as to destroy their usefulness. The proposals with respect to visual publicity show little agreement, but it is most commonly prescribed that during the testimony the witness cannot be photographed or put on television if he objects.

In addition to protections for witnesses, the codes usually contain rules governing the initiation of investigations, issuance of subpoenas, executive sessions, and reports. "One-man committees" are frequently prohibited, with the requirement that members representing both major political parties must be present at hearings. The main purpose of all of these is to guard against an irresponsible monopoly of the committee's powers by the chairman, and they are plainly stimulated by the uninhibited methods of Senator McCarthy, Congressman Velde, and other chairmen who have treated their committees as their private property.

But the respect in which the proposed codes vary most widely is that of how they are to be enforced. This question is of primary importance, particularly from the standpoint of witnesses, who will be chiefly interested in knowing what they can do and what relief they can obtain if the rules are broken.

Some of the codes make no provision for enforcement whatsoever, apparently on the basis that the mere adoption of the rules will assure their observance by virtue of their own weight and dignity. It may be doubted that this assumption is warranted, especially as applied to committee chairmen such as Senator McCarthy. Senator Kefauver has proposed a supervisory committee of Senators to investigate complaints of violations, "advise committee chairmen of their conclusions and their suggestions," and recommend appropriate "remedial and disciplinary action" by the Senate itself. But Senators are chronically and notoriously reluctant to yield to admonition from their fellows or to discipline each other. With all respect to the distinguished sponsors of this proposal, I question that it would result in effective enforcement.

None of the codes provides for direct judicial intervention, but a few are based on indirect enforcement by the courts, in that a witness cannot be punished for refusing to testify, either by contempt or criminal prosecution, if the governing rules have been broken in such a way as to prejudice the witness. Without question this is the method best calculated to ensure that the rules will be obeyed. However, it raises other issues which point up certain fundamental difficulties and complexities that must be taken into account.

For the fact is that these proposals cannot all be tied in a single bundle. Some of them are simple and easily enforceable, such as the witness' right to the effective assistance of counsel, to reasonable notice of the time and subjects of his appearance, to make a statement, and to have access to the record of his testimony. Judge Wyzanski, indeed, has argued that codes of fair practice should be limited to a few basic reforms such as these,[21] and there is much to be said for his viewpoint. There is, it seems to me, no reason why these should not be enacted into statutory law as absolute requirements of investigative procedure, so that Congress' power to punish recalcitrant witnesses would be conditioned on its observance of these elemental rules of fairness.

But when we turn to propositions for giving persons under investigation the right to call witnesses in their own behalf and to cross-examine hostile witnesses, we must guard against encumbering the investigative power and destroying its flexibility and efficacy. Courts are concerned with individual rights and liabilities, and their procedures are governed accordingly. Legislative committees have broader functions which require looser procedural standards; the informing function will wither if unduly circumscribed. A committee investigating social, economic or political problems cannot be required to weigh every disputed question of fact as if it were a judicial tribunal. I do not believe that it is feasible or practical to lay down rigid requirements with respect to the summoning and cross-examination of witnesses without undermining the investigative process itself.

There is another and equally serious objection. The only method of law enforcement that is consonant with our constitutional democracy is judicial enforcement. The more investigating committees are hedged about with legal restrictions on their procedures, therefore, the more the courts would be called upon to perform a supervisory function. Increasingly, the committees would appear to be inferior tribunals, subject to appellate review by the courts.

But this is not the relationship envisaged by the Constitution, or embodied in our governmental traditions. It is, therefore, most unlikely that Congress will ever bind its committees by an elaborate procedural code, to be enforced by the courts. And it would be most unwise, because such a relationship would be a fertile field of friction and jealousy between the courts and Congress.

These difficulties would be even more acute as applied to the far-reaching restrictions on loyalty investigations that have been proposed by the able Washington attorney and former Under Secretary of the Interior, Mr. Abe Fortas. Having been exposed for many days, as counsel for Mr. Owen Lattimore, to the heat of the McCarran committee, Mr. Fortas wrote a magazine article entitled "Outside the Law," [22] the thesis of which is that, since investigating committees and loyalty boards have become a much more frequented arena for the scrutiny of loyalty than the courts, and since their adverse conclusions do greatly injure those on trial, the committees and boards should not be outside of or above specific legal principles. In addition to procedural reforms he proposed standards for the evaluation or rejection of evidence. Accusations of disloyalty should be disregarded unless based on evidence of "activities inimical to the United States" within three to five years prior to the hearing. Evidence relating to membership in Communist-front organizations prior to their official listing as such should be excluded, unless the accused was in the controlling group of members.

Much as I agree with Mr. Fortas' diagnosis, I have little faith in his cure. His proposals, like many of the more elaborate and restrictive proposed codes of procedure, are based on the assumption, which I believe to be erroneous, that a legislative investigating committee can be made to resemble and operate like a court.[23] But all the statutes, rules, and regulations in the world can never accomplish any such transmigration of the judicial to the legislative soul, and it is a mistake to try.

The elected members of legislative bodies are politicians, whose duty it is to take into account the most varied and often conflicting views and pressures in the processes of election and legislation. Judges, in contrast, are under a solemn obligation to be non-political, and to exclude extraneous pressures from the field of decision. It is a total incompatibility, not of person but of function, that renders futile and unwise any effort to assimilate an investigative committee to a court. Of course, committees should function as fairly as legislative necessities permit. But they should not be expected to weigh factual issues or determine individual rights and liabilities in the way that courts do. Rather, they should be expected not to.

In fact, one of the dangers of these far-reaching proposals for reform of investigative procedures is that, in the event of their adoption, the public would conclude that committee hearings had been turned into real trials, in the course of which guilt or innocence might be determined. It would, I believe, be far more useful for Congress to reaffirm that investigations are *not* trials, and to adopt as legally mandatory a few simple and basic reforms such as those suggested by Judge Wyzanski. Some others—such as the right of an individual accused before a committee to call and cross-examine witnesses—might be tried out as voluntary, non-mandatory committee practices. The rule proposed by Congressman Kenneth Keating for opportunity to call witnesses in behalf of an accused,[24] for example, leaves "the extent to which this privilege may be availed of . . . to the discretion of the committee."

Of course, there would be less need and less pressure for restrictive rules and procedures if investigating committees would confine themselves to their traditional purposes of scrutinizing the operations of the executive branch and gathering information for legislation. But when educators, teachers, movie actors, writers, publishers, and union members are daily put to an inquisition of their political connections and opinions, past and present, naturally there is outcry and richly-deserved criticism of investigative methods as well as objectives.

The true remedy is not to try to adapt investigative committees to functions that they were never intended to and never can properly perform, but to repulse their incursions into the domains of the executive and judicial branches and their trespasses on the Bill of Rights, and confine them to their proper functions. Codes of fair practices will not accomplish this. And that is why the proposed codes and the procedural reforms which they are intended to bring about, laudable and desirable as they are, do not strike at the root of the problems we have been considering.

Two Suggestions: Starting and Stopping Investigations

Fundamentally, the problem of Congressional investigations is a political rather than a legal problem, and must be dealt with by political means. It is a reflection of the cold civil war, and so long as Congressmen and Senators so gauge the temper of the country that they are unwilling to put a curb on the inquisitions, there is little enough that can be accomplished by new regulations and statutes. But there are, I believe, two things that Congress might do—both simple and neither experimental—that would bring worthwhile improvements over the present situation.

These two propositions relate to starting investigations in the first instance, and to stopping them when they overleap their authority and assert powers of inquiry which they do not rightfully possess. They relate, in short, to *initiation* and to *challenge*. For it is clear that it has become far too easy—especially in the Senate—to set in motion an investigation backed by the power of subpoena. And it is equally plain that present procedures make it far too risky a business to test the power of a Congressional committee to make an inquiry, because the probable penalty for an unfounded challenge, even if based on honest mistake, is a jail sentence. In each case, something can and should be done about it.

In 1792, the House investigation of General St. Clair's defeat was prompted by pervasive and vociferous public demand. Nevertheless, the entire House of Representatives considered and debated the matter before authorizing the inquiry. In 1935, widespread railroad bankruptcies and receiverships led investors and public officials to advocate a Senate investigation of railroad finance. Senator Burton K. Wheeler introduced a resolution for this purpose, which was referred to the Senate Interstate Commerce Committee. That committee held public hearings for several days on the question whether an investigation was necessary or desirable. The record of these hearings and the committee's report were available to the Senate when it considered and authorized the inquiry,[25] and conferred the subpoena power on the committee that was to carry it out.

But by whom and how was Senator McCarthy's recent investigation of the Army Signal Corps laboratories at Fort Monmouth initiated and authorized? The Senate itself never considered the matter, nor so far as has been learned, did the other members of the Government Operations Committee or its Subcommittee on Investigations. There was no responsible opinion among government officials, civil or military, that a Congressional investigation at Fort Monmouth was necessary or desirable. The entire affair was the brainchild of Senator McCarthy and one or two members of his staff.

That, however, was all that was required to launch the inquiry, because: (1) Congress, in the Legislative Reorganization Act of 1946, had given the Government Operations Committee, like all standing Senate committees, permanent and general power of subpoena, which can be used in support of the very broad range of subjects within the purview of each committee; and (2) the members of the Government Operations Committee, like many of our legislators, displayed small sense of responsibility in the use of Congress' investigative power, and allowed Senator McCarthy to take off on a frolic of his own without paying sufficient attention to the matter. As Senator

Wayne Morse has put it, the Senate has "written a series of blank checks" to its committees.

Now, there was no sufficient reason for this revolutionary change in 1946. As we have seen,[26] no such change was made in the House of Representatives, where each and every new investigation must be authorized by vote of the House itself. It is anomalous that there should be so radical a difference between House and Senate in this respect. Historical tradition and practical experience both argue the greater wisdom of the House practice, as Messrs. Sam Rayburn and Joe Martin foresaw when the 1946 Act was passed.

An investigation backed by compulsory process of subpoena is no minor venture to be undertaken frivolously or lightly. Its prospective advantages and disadvantages should be carefully weighed in advance by the legislative body whose authority is to be exercised. Until 1946 this was taken for granted in both House and Senate, and the Senate's departure from this conservative practice clearly appears in retrospect as ill-considered and productive of disastrous consequences.*

I believe, accordingly, that a first, simple, and highly desirable step in the rehabilitation of Congressional investigations would be to repeal the provision of the Legislative Reorganization Act which gives permanent subpoena power to all the standing committees of the Senate, and return to the requirements that had proved their value for over 150 years before 1946. Of course, this is no sure preventive of unnecessary or misdirected investigations, for the House and Senate are themselves quite capable of error in this regard. Only last year the House launched the second investigation of tax-exempt foundations in as many sessions, which proved not only shockingly duplicative and wasteful, but so incredibly misconducted as to disgrace a debating society at a reformatory for wayward and backward children. In both Houses of Congress a rebirth of restraint,

* One of the worst consequences is the duplication and rivalry among the Velde, Jenner and McCarthy investigations, all of which have been primarily concerned with accusations of disloyalty and subversion against individuals. This unedifying and wasteful spectacle has prompted proposals (advanced by Senator Hendrickson and Representative Frelinghuysen, among others) to establish a single, non-partisan Joint Committee on Internal Security (modeled on the existing Joint Committee on Atomic Energy), with exclusive authority to conduct investigations in this field.

common sense, and courage is necessary to check investigative excesses. Repeal of the Senate committees' permanent subpoena power might be hoped to trigger a renaissance of legislative decorum.

My second suggestion concerns the method by which the investigative power is to be enforced and, when unlawfully exercised, how it is to be checked. Once again, our very first case of the Know-Nothings, the Irish policemen, and Judge Daly [27] furnishes what I believe to be a fruitful suggestion.

For it may be remembered that, when the members of Chief Matsell's force refused to answer the questions of the Know-Nothing Aldermen, they were not locked up for contempt like Hallett Kilbourn, nor prosecuted criminally, as is now the standard Congressional practice. Rather, and in accordance with the statute of the New York State Legislature, the investigating committee applied to Judge Daly for an order directing the police officers to answer the questions. After hearing argument, the learned judge ordered the witnesses to answer certain of the questions, but not those relating to their nationality, which he held to be beyond the committee's rightful powers.

Under that New York statute, the witnesses were thereby enabled to challenge and obtain an adjudication of the committee's powers without risking a jail sentence. After a court order to answer particular questions, the witnesses were liable to punishment only if they persisted in their refusal despite the court's ruling.

This method of judicial review, I believe, has decisively superior characteristics to criminal processes, despite the present popularity of the latter. The purpose of a legislative inquiry is to obtain information; prosecution does not achieve this end directly or efficiently but, if at all, slowly and uncertainly *in terrorem*. Thus the committee's objectives are not well served. Furthermore, a witness who is genuinely doubtful whether the committee has authority to require him to reply, must stake his judgment against the risk of conviction and imprisonment. As the Supreme Court has bluntly warned, the witness "was either right or wrong in his refusal to answer, and if wrong he took the risk of becoming liable to the prescribed penalty." [28]

In view of the numerous, complex, and doubtful questions of power, privilege, and procedure, this seems an unconscionable hazard, particularly since the legislature's ends are not thereby furthered.[29] Where the constitutionality of state statutes or the validity of executive action can only be tested at the risk of criminal liability or other irreparable injury, the federal courts have invoked their equity powers to make possible a safe test by injunctive proceedings.[30]

Logically, the same considerations should apply to legislative action when, as in investigations, it operates directly on individuals. And in fact there is considerable authority for the issuance of injunctions to enjoin unauthorized proceedings by investigating committees.[31] Conceivably this view might win more authoritative endorsement where a governmental body is the petitioner, and there is a very strong basis for equitable jurisdiction, perhaps to prevent multiplicity of suits.[32] But the federal courts are not habituated to checking legislative proceedings, and it seems most improbable that injunctive process will be held available to review investigative process.[33]

For the benefit of both committees and witnesses, therefore, there should be a better method—speedier and more effective for the committee and less hazardous for the witness—to test and enforce investigative power. And such a method can be successfully developed along the lines of the New York statute that Judge Daly applied in 1855—that is, enforcement of the committee's process by court order. It is a procedure well-suited to obtain for the committee the information to which it is entitled, and it permits the witness to resist queries that he believes to be unauthorized and test the committee's power without incurring the risk of prosecution.

This means of enforcement is widely and successfully used in many comparable situations. Congress early resorted to it for the benefit of administrative agencies (which generally have no contempt power), to enable them to compel testimony by applying for a court order, disobedience to which is punished by the court as a contempt. This is now a standard form of judicial proceeding in connection with administrative agencies, which has been upheld and applied by the courts in many cases.[34] It is entirely adaptable to legislative committee investigations,[35] and in fact has twice been authorized for joint investigating committees of the two Houses of Congress.[36]

Utilization of this procedure today,* in place of criminal prosecution, would give investigating committees speedy and direct compulsory process, and would relieve witnesses of the grave and unnecessary hazards which now attend the testing of legal questions. The over-all result, in Representative Kenneth Keating's words, would be "salutary for everyone concerned." [37]

---

* Representative Keating's bill to authorize this method of enforcement (H.R. 4975, and H. Report No. 2612, 83d Cong. 2d Sess.) was passed by the House on August 3, 1954, but died in the Senate. However, this bill would have made this procedure available in addition to, not in substitution for, criminal prosecution under the 1857 statute. It seems to me that, with both the traditional power to commit for contempt and the proposed new procedure available, the 1857 criminal procedure would be unnecessary and should be repealed, or else that it should come into play only if the witness disobeys the court's order that he give evidence.

CHAPTER X

THE COLD CIVIL WAR

"Fear is never a wise counsellor."

—General Hans Von Seeckt

THE CONSTITUTIONAL and procedural issues reviewed here have been manifest since long before Martin Dies started down the sawdust trail in 1938. The excesses and abuses of investigating committees have drawn the fire of lawyers, publicists, and some very powerful politicians—even presidents—but still no compelling public demand for investigative limits and reforms has been evoked.

The reason is clear enough. In times of tension and fear, people are less interested in method or character than in aims and results. When the public views the Congressional loyalty inquiries seriously rather than as spectacles, it sees them in the light of the perils, real and imaginary, on which the public's attention is concentrated. These are the dangers that are associated with communism: the cold war abroad, espionage and subversion at home. Are the investigations giving substantial protection against communism? At present, the average citizen's attitude toward them is very likely to be determined by the answer to this question.

Any war, hot or cold, consists of two elements: preservation of things that are treasured—life, land, symbols and traditions—and obstruction or, better, elimination of the forces that threaten what is treasured. Communism is such a force. But the first element is no less important than the second, nor is communism the only threat to the values to which our nation is dedicated.

It is, in fact, our greatest peril that the United States is now caught in a turbulent and treacherous rip between the tides of the international cold war and of the cold civil war. While our national power and security are assailed by the forces of international communism, our internal unity and free traditions are under challenge by what I have called the nationalist alignment. As a result, not only are we in violent disagreement about how to meet the Communist menace, but we are likewise sadly divided in our conception of what is to be preserved and safeguarded against that menace.

This national schizophrenia is manifest in the Congressional loyalty inquiries which have been the citadel of the nationalist alignment, and which are tearing at the fabric of our constitutional system. Scrutinizing their role in these troublous times, we must take into account not only their own actions, but also their influence and indirect effects. By so doing, we may more accurately gauge their value, both in fending off the menace of communism and in preserving the American way of life.

How to Hunt a Skunk

Popular support for our Tenneys, Jenners, and McCarthys is by no means limited to the adherents of the nationalist alignment. These men do, of course, enjoy the backing of many extremists who are seeking revolutionary changes in our government and society. So, too, the investigations which they head are a magnet for bigots and adventurers eager to exploit political and social antagonisms.

But the mass support for the loyalty probes and probers comes from those who believe, or who do not question, that the investigations are providing a valuable and irreplaceable protection against communism. This belief is the keystone of Senator McCarthy's power, and those who hold it are not impressed with arguments about the separation of powers or stories of Lustron fees. For these believers, the Senator is like the little Dutch boy with his finger in the dike. Whoever really believes that tonight the boy is fending off the torrent will not much care whether or not he was raiding the orchard or breaking windows the night before.

Of all this, Senator McCarthy is well aware. When criticized for making exaggerated or unsupported accusations, he has been fond of comparing his own activities to a "skunk hunt," which cannot be carried on "with a top hat and silk handkerchief."

To this it may be answered that there is no point to a skunk hunt in which the hunter permanently absorbs the odor of the animal. Furthermore, when this happens the hunter's olfactory apparatus becomes desensitized and indiscriminate, so that he can no longer distinguish between skunks and other more useful and attractive creatures. And, to abandon his favorite figure of speech, the plain fact is that Senator McCarthy has never shown the slightest talent for hunting communists. Nor, for all the investment of money and manpower that they represent, have the Congressional loyalty investigations come up with more than a very few communists that had not already been identified and earmarked by the executive branch's regular investigative agencies.

A prime example of this "warmed-over spy" technique was the public hearing held by Senator McCarthy in July, 1954, to substantiate his oft-repeated claim that his subcommittee had discovered 134 communists in defense plants.[1] The witness was one James W. Glatis, an undercover agent of the FBI, so presumably everything he told the McCarthy subcommittee was already known to Mr. Hoover's men. Furthermore, Mr. Glatis had recently testified publicly before the Subversive Activities Control Board, and secretly before the Un-American Activities Committee, so that what Senator McCarthy was parading as his contribution to national security was a fourth warming-over of accusations already well known to the authorities. The hearing did not help to establish whether or not the accusations were well-founded; whether it was harmful to the FBI to expose one of their agents can only be surmised.

Now, of course it is true that not all Congressional hearings on loyalty questions have been as futile and redundant as this one. The committees, over the many years that they have been in operation, have uncovered and followed up some leads on their own and, as we have already noted,[2] can point to various accomplishments.

But this is the time for striking balances. Even the duffer makes a few good shots at tennis; even Lefty Gomez hit an occasional home run. By and large, the loyalty committees have failed, as instruments of effective anti-communism, in at least four basic respects:

(1) In general, the evidence they have accumulated and pub-

licized has been already known to the regular investigative and law-enforcement authorities;

(2) They have been concerned chiefly with the past rather than with current dangers;

(3) They have completely failed—indeed, they have hardly attempted—to assess dispassionately the actual harm done by or danger inherent in the persons and circumstances questioned and exposed; and

(4) They have been woefully sloppy and undiscriminating in the task of defining and developing guides and standards for security and loyalty, and thereby have blunted and befogged both official and public ability to distinguish between mere controversy and real danger.

As we observed earlier,[3] the underlying reason for these shortcomings is that the Congressional loyalty investigations have been conducted mainly for political rather than legislative or truly investigative objectives. There is no better example of this than one of Senator McCarthy's recent skunk-hunts, otherwise known as the Senate investigation of the Signal Corps Engineering Laboratories at Fort Monmouth.

We have already noted in another context the sensational charges, clearly implying that Monmouth was riddled with spies and subversives, with which Senator McCarthy launched his subcommittee's hearings on Fort Monmouth.[4] In fact, however, not one of the Monmouth scientists was charged with espionage, past or present. Only one was charged with an actual violation of security regulations of any consequence. Without exception, the accused scientists denied the charges or the implications sought to be drawn. Not one invoked the Fifth Amendment. Furthermore, most of the charges had been considered and rejected by the Army loyalty review boards several years earlier. The McCarthy Subcommittee contributed substantially nothing new by way of information; all it did was grill the employees about accusations already well known to both the FBI and the Army.

Well, but perhaps the Army had treated the charges too lightly? Certainly that was the implication of Senator McCarthy's threat to call the members of the Army loyalty boards. But upon examination, a number of the charges proved to be such utter and empty froth that it was plain they should never have been brought in the first place. Of one scientist it was charged that his father had been a registrant of the American Labor Party during the La Guardia period; another was accused of an affinity for the writings of Max Lerner; still another was blamed for delivering classified documents to a man who in fact was a fellow-employee at the laboratories, and entitled to have the information.[5]

For this mess to make the angels weep, the Army was responsible in the first instance. The security section at Monmouth appears to have been neither perceptive nor efficient, and the commandant, Major General Lawton, did not improve matters by making speeches to the staff in which he extolled Senator McCarthy, and is said to have held out as a shining example his aunt who "gave her last five dollars to Gerald L. K. Smith." The principal effect of the McCarthy operations was to bring out the worst features of the Army security system, and to prod and browbeat the Army into suspensions and accusations which, under sober and reflective conditions, would never have been made.

Failing to find any "Fifth Amendment Communists" at Monmouth, and confronted with an ever more critical public reaction to these irresponsible escapades, Senator McCarthy cast his investigative net far and wide among former Monmouth workers, and the employees, past and present, of neighboring private electronics concerns handling government contracts. Relatives of the employees, regardless of their occupations, were likewise subpoenaed in considerable numbers. Fishing in the ocean instead of the lake the Senator had better luck, and came up with several witnesses who pleaded the Fifth Amendment when asked about Communist associations. Among these was one Harry Hyman, formerly an employee of one of the electronics companies, but since 1951 an insurance salesman.

Giving the Senator the benefit of the doubt by assuming that Mr. Hyman's political proclivities were previously unknown to the FBI or the state investigative agencies, so that his invocation of the Fifth Amendment might be regarded as a new lead, the McCarthy subcommittee proceeded to mangle and botch the lead in a way that would have disgraced a correspondence-course detective. At the public hearing Senator McCarthy produced with great flourish a list of several hundred telephone calls made by Mr. Hyman to various government installations and private laboratories during 1952 and 1953.[6] On the basis of this "evidence," Senator McCarthy denounced Mr. Hyman as "one of the most active espionage agents that we have run down."

I know nothing about Mr. Hyman or why he pleaded the Fifth Amendment or what he was talking about on the telephone. But I do know that the list of phone calls should have been regarded as the beginning, not the end, of an investigation to determine the facts. Spies do not ordinarily solicit secret information by telephone, least of all at wholesale, and without something more conclusive the horrible suspicion lingers that Mr. Hyman was using the telephone to sell insurance in places where he had acquaintances. In any event, if there were more sinister inferences, the surest way to explode the possibility of proving espionage was to give wide publicity to Mr. Hyman's telephonic activities before the proof was in hand. Unfortunately, Senator McCarthy was interested not so much in proof as in publicity, and one does not catch skunks by shouting that there may perhaps be one in the woods on the other side of the river.

Inexpert skunk-hunting is likely to have no worse effect than that skunks are not caught. But the consequences of amateurish and irresponsible Communist-hunting, and of exploiting the Communist issue for personal publicity and aggrandizement, are far graver. Not only are Communists not caught, but all kinds of damage is bound to be caused to the institutions and individuals involved in the bungled process.

At Fort Monmouth, this damage appears to have been especially serious, on account of both the unnecessary loss of skilled scientific workers and the inevitable harm to the spirit and capacity of the technical staff generally. These factors cannot be measured with mathematical precision, but a careful assessment of the consequences was made under the auspices of the Federation of American Scientists, which abundantly confirmed the alarming conclusions previously arrived at by several able and respected journalists.[7] The scientists' survey revealed that a large proportion of the accused employees were key personnel; fifteen were section chiefs, and altogether they supervised some six hundred workers. The results of their suspension or, in some cases, denial of access to classified information, were expressed as follows: [8]

> It is clear, especially to scientists, that the removal of a key engineer or a senior scientist who carries the main responsibility for a project will almost invariably cripple that project . . . The reports to us indicate that the shifts of personnel did in fact hurt at least 20 projects. Several of those removed were acknowledged to be the "spark plugs" of their projects, and it was generally agreed that their projects were seriously crippled. Some men were not allowed to complete reports on work already finished. . . . One employee held the responsibility for a large segment of an air-defense project on which some $32 million had been spent.

But the immediate loss of highly skilled men was probably not the most injurious result of this sorry affair. Scientists generally prefer private employment or an academic environment; it is difficult enough to induce them to work for the government under the best of circumstances. What happened at Monmouth will inevitably make it more difficult than ever for the government to attract and hold first-rate scientific talent. If Scientist A can be suspended, put to financial hardship, and perhaps discredited on the basis of flimsy and ill-considered charges, the same can happen to Scientist B. The result, as the scientists' survey concluded, is to weaken the technical resources of the government: [9]

> The Monmouth affair has had wide consequences. Already our Committee has had from students and scientists anxious requests for advice as to whether they should apply for work in government laboratories. It is difficult to advise them with any confidence, for there is no assurance that similar interference may not occur at other defense laboratories and perhaps in industries working on military projects. . . . The events at Monmouth accentuated a security trend which is dangerous to the nation. In the words of John Stuart Mill: ". . . a State which dwarfs its men, in order that they be more docile instruments in its hands even for beneficial purposes, will find that with small men no great thing can really be accomplished."

The Monmouth story is but one of a number of examples of the mischief that can be worked by clumsily or unscrupulously handled loyalty investigations. For instance, Senator McCarthy's earlier probe of the Voice of America has been described by a leading news analyst, Frederick Woltman, as "the most disgraceful, scatter-brained, inept, misleading, and unfair investigation in Congressional annals . . . It was a mighty victory for the Kremlin." The disastrous effects of the Senator's influence on the entire information and propaganda service has been pungently described by the "Eisenhower Democrat" who served as deputy to Dr. Robert L. Johnson, President Eisenhower's first appointee as Director of the International Information Administration. Employment at this agency became so unattractive a prospect that, in November, 1954, the entire staff was obliged to drop all other work for a day of emergency recruiting, in a desperate effort to meet a critical shortage of skilled specialists.[10]

But apart from the direct consequences of such blunderings, the impact of these methods and attitudes on the public mind has been disastrous. The Congressional loyalty inquiries have given rise to wholly false conceptions of what constitutes security and loyalty, and the public service is being rent asunder by frightened and unrealistic security standards.

An illustration drawn from the German experience during World War II may be enlightening. The enormous long-range rockets known as V-2's, that came crashing down on London and Antwerp toward the end of the war, were developed by a special branch of the German Army Ordnance. Most of the critical developmental work was done in a group of installations and laboratories at Peenemuende on the Baltic Coast near Stettin, under the command of General Walter Dornberger. Peenemuende, in other words, was a vital military scientific research institution, in many ways comparable to Fort Monmouth or the "Manhattan District" atom bomb project.[11]

In October, 1942, Peenemuende achieved successful firing of the V-2. Nevertheless, General Dornberger found it impossible to persuade the High Command of the rocket's value as a weapon, and Hitler would not interest himself because he had dreamed that no V-2 would ever reach England. By dint of a striking motion picture demonstration, Hitler's enthusiasm was finally aroused, and a major program for the manufacture and operational use of the V-2 against England was commenced in 1943. Instead of suffering from neglect and indifference, Peenemuende found itself the object of unwelcome and avaricious interest on the part of Heinrich Himmler and others, who now wanted a "piece" of the sensational new weapon.

Himmler's primary method of ousting the Army and seizing control of Peenemuende for himself was to concoct spurious charges of disloyalty and insecurity against Dornberger's staff. In March, 1944, Dornberger was suddenly summoned to Wehrmacht headquarters and informed that his principal rocket scientist, Dr. Werner Von Braun, and two other key engineers had been arrested and locked up by the SS on charges of sabotaging military rocket development. Dornberger's interview with Field Marshall Keitel was a depressing one: [12]

KEITEL: The sabotage is seen in the fact that these men have been giving all their innermost thoughts to space travel and consequently have not applied their whole energy and ability to production of the V-2 as a weapon of war.

DORNBERGER: Who was the informer, sir? There can be nothing but malice behind this. Or does it come from someone without the first idea of what's involved?

KEITEL: I don't know. I know only what I have told you.

DORNBERGER: These arrests will be ruinous for the whole project—especially as the rocket is soon due to come into service and we haven't even tracked down the latest trouble. There must be some incomprehensible misunderstanding or mistake.

KEITEL: I can't do anything about it. Himmler has taken over himself. . . .

DORNBERGER: Sir, I wish to put on record that if these arrests stand, completion of development will be problematical and employment of the rocket in the field will have to be postponed indefinitely. . . . It is my duty to demand immediate release of these men in the interests of the program.

KEITEL: Be reasonable! I can't release them without Himmler's agreement. I must also avoid the least suspicion of being less zealous than the Gestapo and Himmler in these things. . . .

After a futile effort to appeal directly to Himmler, Dornberger was allowed to see the head of the Gestapo, SS General Heinrich Mueller. By way of reaction to Dornberger's defense of his subordinates, Mueller challenged the loyalty of the Peenemuende chief himself, in a manner which makes gloomy reading indeed in the aftermath of the Oppenheimer and Monmouth episodes: [13]

MUELLER: You are a very interesting case, General. Do you know what a fat file of evidence we have against you here?

DORNBERGER: Why don't you arrest me, then?

MUELLER: Because it would be pointless as yet. You are still regarded as our greatest rocket expert and we can't very well ask you to give expert evidence against yourself.

DORNBERGER: Very good of you. But I really should like to know what all these things are that you have against me.

MUELLER: Well, first of all there's the delay in the development of the V-2 missile. That's a question that will certainly have to be tackled one day.

DORNBERGER: I entirely agree. But a lot of people are going to get a surprise when they see who's to blame. Anything else?

MUELLER: Yes. Your entire activities with rockets in the Army Weapons Department will have to be gone into.

DORNBERGER: Ah, yes! Putting the brake on development, eh? Is that all? If so, it's damned little!

MUELLER: No. Those were only a few general points. Perhaps you would like to hear about a specific case at Peenemuende? The charge there is one of deliberate or culpably negligent incitement to sabotage.

DORNBERGER: That's a rather serious charge. What was the occasion?

MUELLER: At the end of March last year you said at a meeting of your directors that the Fuehrer had dreamed that the V-2 would never get to England. You said you were powerless against the Fuehrer's dreams. By that expression you exercised a harmful, pessimistic, almost defeatist influence on the zeal and enthusiasm of your senior staff and so sabotaged rapid progress.

Dornberger defended himself vigorously, and succeeded in obtaining the release of Von Braun and the two engineers, who were put back at work. But it was a Pyrrhic victory, for soon an SS general was put in charge of V-weapons, and Peenemuende was added to Heinrich Himmler's empire.

Such were the bitter fruits of "ideological security" in the scientific community of the Third Reich, and it is an object lesson which we would do well to heed. Dornberger and his staff were patriotic Germans, whose fault perhaps it was that they did not concern themselves sufficiently with the objectives for which their new weapons might be put to use by Hitler. But they were not part of the Nazi gang, and showed little interest in the myths and manners of the new regime. Consequently, as Germany's legal and moral traditions rotted away, they were increasingly helpless against ruthless opportunists such as Himmler, who were only too happy to portray the scientists' workmanlike detachment as lack of zeal, and the equivalent of sabotage.

Something approaching this dislike for detachment and individuality is creeping into American life, fed chiefly by the effluvium of the Congressional loyalty investigations. I seriously doubt that any of those who brought or tried the charges against the Monmouth scientists, or against Dr. Robert Oppenheimer, were really concerned that these men might play fast and loose with secret information. But discretion and loyalty are no longer the approved test of security. To be scientifically reliable today it is prudent to disapprove of "liberal" commentators and desirable to espouse such as Fulton Lewis or George Sokolsky; it is not as safe to belong to the American Veterans' Committee as it is to be a member of the American Legion; above all it is necessary to approve—heartily and enthusiastically—the new attitudes and security standards which are being cultivated and formulated in this atmosphere.

Inevitably, under these circumstances, the security system becomes a device which can be exploited by ambitious, unscrupulous, or jealous men, or even by those who simply are in violent disagreement with each other. Dr. Oppenheimer, as well as being a remarkably able scientist whose services to his country appear to dwarf those of many of his critics, is an opinionated man who has made powerful enemies, and has at times been out of sympathy with official policy. Perhaps for these reasons the government would have been warranted in dispensing with his services as a consultant. But to have accomplished this by means of the security system, and thus to have exiled him under stigma from the atomic world which he had done so much to shape, was an unforgivable and shameful blunder, of which the Kremlin is likely to be the ultimate beneficiary.

Of course, scientific security is a complex and delicate problem which in large part lies outside the scope of this book. But the strongest forces and pressures which are currently being exerted in this sphere emanate from the Congressional loyalty investigations, and the results to date have been alarming in the extreme. Dr. Vannevar Bush has recently warned that government scientists "are discouraged and downhearted" and are working "without enthusiasm and without fruitful inspiration," and Dr. James Killian, President of the Massachusetts Institute of Technology, testifying before a House committee which has recently studied the entire question of relations between the government and the scientific profession, observed that: [14]

> There has been, unhappily, a deterioration in recent months in the relationships between Government and science. The reasons for this deterioration are much more fundamental than the more simple problem of the relationship between members of the military services and scientists. . . . The problem has now come to be one of various trends, movements, and policies in this country having created a condition where members of the scientific community are clearly discouraged and apprehensive about the lack of understanding of scientific methods and an undue regard to what sometimes seems to be a preoccupation with security procedures and policies at the expense of scientific progress.
>
> I believe that the whole problem of security procedures and policies at the present time may be one of the things that is most hazardous to our future research and development activity in this country in relation to military problems.

There is, of course, one sure way to prevent Communist espionage at our atomic installations and other military scientific research centers like Fort Monmouth. That is to close them down and cease to engage in research. If we have no science worth infiltrating and no secrets worth stealing, Soviet espionage will cease; if we had never invented the A-bomb, Communist spies would never be able to betray any of its secrets.

This method is infallible and foolproof, but I doubt that it will commend itself to any thinking American. Our great reservoir of scientific talent, and the inventions and developments that flow from it, are among America's most valuable resources. We must reckon with the probability that the Communists will try to penetrate the laboratories, and must, therefore, have an efficient security system to protect them from espionage.

But if our scientific resources are to remain strong, we must not only keep the spies outside the laboratory; we must also keep the scientists inside. Furthermore, we must keep them there under conditions which will stimulate them to their best efforts. We may still hope that these conditions prevail, despite the Monmouth and Oppenheimer episodes. We may be equally sure that they will not survive many more such inroads.

Is there a discernible common denominator of the several governmental agencies that have been Senator McCarthy's principal objects of attack? The State Department has been, of course, his favorite target. Next, Harold Stassen and the Foreign Operations Administration, handling economic assistance to other countries. Then the Voice of America. Then, *via* the unfortunate General Partridge, the intelligence branch of the Army. Finally, the major assault on the military scientific laboratories at Fort Monmouth. In the ensuing fracas, the Senator disclosed as his next intended victim the Central Intelligence Agency, and clawed at the vitals of the security system by encouraging federal employees to disobey security regulations and violate the espionage laws.

As we scan this list, it is apparent that there are two things common to all items. First, these are the weapons with which the international cold war is being and must be fought. Intelligence, security, science, propaganda, diplomacy, economics—these things are the very stuff of the cold war.

Second, these agencies comprise those parts of our national defense structure which are concerned not with the conventional wartime skills such as aiming a gun or navigating a vessel, but with ideas and ideals. This is the intellectual side of that scholar-athlete Mars, the god of war. Success in war, diplomacy and politics, as in civilization itself, rests on man's ability to reason and, having reasoned, to choose—to distinguish shadow from substance and see beyond his own nose.

A good intelligence officer must be able to analyze and report objectively, and to do this he must creep into the enemy's mind and see with his eyes. A good diplomat knows that unyielding opposition and constant denunciation do not constitute a fruitful foreign policy or method of negotiation. It is just these faculties and viewpoints that the investigators seize on to distort and condemn, when in truth these things are the stuff of civilization, as well as the bedrock of our way of life and our best means of defense in a turbulent world. If they are destroyed, we will perish with them.

In short, the Senator has wreaked his havoc in the very areas where it was bound to have the most damaging effect on our conduct of the cold war. The State Department intimidated and shackled to the point where veteran, conservative diplomats publicly express their fear of its total ruination; [15] the Voice of America reduced to whispered platitudes; the intelligence services threatened with the loss of that detachment and anonymity that are so vital to their functioning; the security system contemptuously kicked aside; the scientists alarmed and alienated—how could anything more helpful to communism be done? The victim of this kind of hunting will not be the skunk, but the American eagle.

Freedom and Security Under Law

Twenty years ago in Germany a military, civil and cultural élite of remarkable ability and prestige was smashed and discredited by political hoodlums, because it did not dare to remain true to its own best traditions. America is not a land of élites, but the German lesson must not be lost on us. America is a land of traditions, albeit very different from those of the German officers' corps or civil bureaucracy. It is not only our plains and mountains and rivers and lakes, beautiful as they are, that we arm ourselves to defend; even more it is the traditions by which we live in and among them. The spirit of free inquiry and free enterprise; tolerance for differing beliefs within the framework of ordered government; enforcement of the law without fear or favor—these things may not be sacrificed even in the face of great national peril, because without them our national existence loses its meaning.

If there is any one purpose above all others to which the investigation of un-American activities and the other Congressional loyalty inquiries should have been directed, it is the preservation of these values. Nevertheless, in earlier chapters we have observed the destructive effect of the powers asserted and procedures followed by several of these committees. Now in conclusion it may be useful to take an over-all look at the chosen areas of the Dies, McCarran and like committees since their inception in 1938.

Some of their inquiries into political action associations have undoubtedly been motivated by sincere and at times effective anti-communism. Others, such as the Michigan labor union hearings of 1938,[16] have been crassly partisan in their immediate purpose, and have also reflected a deep-rooted hostility toward organized labor which seems to be characteristic of this group of men. But, especially in recent years, these committees have concentrated increasingly in the realm of ideas and ideals and their work, all too often, has reflected anti-rationalism and frightened emotionalism.

The great media of mass communications—motion pictures, radio and television—are of primary importance, but journalism, publishing, and the stage have not escaped investigatorial attention. The entire field of education is under constant and frequently hostile legislative scrutiny, and occasional threatening glances are directed at the other learned professions, notably the clergy. Endowed research has been the object of special attack, culminating in what is generally regarded as one of the most preposterous and benighted legislative inquiries on record, the Reece Committee's "hearings" on the Ford, Rockefeller, Carnegie and other leading foundations.

During the past year or two, a great deal of sport has been made with the expression "egg-head." Ridicule is a legitimate political weapon, and it is certainly true that academic learning does not automatically provide the key to true wisdom. No one can object to a desirable emphasis on hard-headed practicality rather than absent-minded scholarship. Egg-heads or no egg-heads, however, this is no time to be ruled by blockheads.

It takes no graduate degree to observe that Communist tactics in the United States are—as they must be—vastly different today from what they were fifteen or more years ago. As we have remarked, the pre-war susceptibility of some Americans to Communist blandishments was born chiefly of the great economic depression and the rise of Mussolini and Hitler. Today the popular front is a distant memory, and the Soviet and satellite governments are seen as corrupted and brutalized by many of the same totalitarian vices that pervaded nazism. The Communists are well aware that their old symbols, slogans and methods are no longer effective in America, and perforce resort to other means. And it is altogether probable that one of their principal techniques today is to exploit the internal distrust, recrimination, and emotionalism which are being fomented by the very McCarthys, Reeces, Jenners and Veldes who are themselves exploiting the blind fear and hatred generated by the Communist menace.

And so it has come about that the Congressional power of investigation is being abused and misused by some committees for purposes that closely parallel the efforts of communism to subvert our political and economic structure. Militant labor unionism is a major bulwark of democracy; it was the first victim of both Communist and Nazi totalitarianism, and is anathema to the nationalist alignment. The effective exercise of our traditional liberties is dependent upon the expression of diverse and conflicting opinions by radio, television, press, pulpit, and the printed page, and upon imaginative and uninhibited educational and research processes and institutions. We know the fate of these concepts in Soviet Russia and Nazi Germany; would it be markedly different in a society dominated by Jenners and McCarrans, Reeces and Dirksens, Alfred Kohlbergs and Rabbi Schulzes?

No one who reads the history of legislative inquiries can fail to be impressed with their propensity for reversing their field, so that the investigator becomes the investigated, or vice versa. It is salutary to recall that the authorizing language under which the Un-American Activities Committee functions was drawn almost verbatim from Representative Samuel Dickstein's 1934 resolution calling for an investigation of Nazi propaganda.[17] For another example which we observed in an early chapter,[18] a century ago in both New York and Massachusetts the power of investigation was seized upon to incite and gratify the religious hatreds fanned by the Know-Nothings' outbreak of rabid and detestable anti-Catholicism. Today, in contrast, the expressions of some Catholic churchmen * have spread the im-

* *See*, for example, the remarks of Msgr. Joseph A. McCaffrey, chaplain of the New York City Police Department—the same police force that was the object of bitter attack by a Know-Nothing investigating committee a century earlier—at a communion breakfast of the Holy Name Society on April 4, 1954, at which Senator McCarthy was the principal speaker.[19] On November 7, 1954 (the day

pression, however erroneous, that Catholicism is generally sympathetic to the nationalist alignment and particularly approves of Senator McCarthy's investigative activities.[21] No doubt for this reason, the public criticism of Senator McCarthy by Bishop Bernard J. Sheil attracted unusual attention, because the speaker was a Catholic prelate.

None of the great faiths has a monopoly of anti-communism, and there are no degrees of loyalty as between Catholics, Jews and Protestants. The teaching of these past events is that abuse of the investigative power does not harm him alone who is the immediate victim. The illusion of investigative omnipotence grew most rapidly in the days of the New Deal, but its recent harvest has been a bitter one for the New Dealers.

All of which brings us back to first principles that may be learned from our experience with legislative investigations since the days of General St. Clair. Investigations are an invaluable legislative tool for detecting and diagnosing diseases of the body politic, and providing the factual basis for informed legislative policy-making. But investigating committees are totally unsuited to assume the duties of either the policeman or the judge. As detective agencies on the trail of criminal or dangerous individuals, they all too frequently prove themselves amateurish bunglers. As courts to determine the culpability of individual behavior, they are usually far too political, passionate and prejudiced to do justice.

Accordingly, in concentrating on the pursuit of accused or suspected individuals, the Congressional loyalty committees are far removed from their proper function in the field of national security. That function is to keep abreast of Communist and other subversive objectives, methods, and organizations, and to obtain the general information about these subjects which Congress needs in order to frame wise legislative policy. The information-gathering function of

---

before the opening of the Senate special session on the McCarthy censure resolution), Msgr. Edward R. Martin, addressing a communion breakfast of Catholic War Veterans,[20] recommended to his audience "the same kind of courage that McCarthy has," and declared that over $5,000,000 had been "pooled to kick Joe out of the Senate," and that "the reason is solely because of his Catholic ideals." On December 5, 1954, at the conclusion of the Senate's special session on the censure resolution, *The New York Times* carried a report from William S. White that the religious overtones of the McCarthy controversy were arousing wide concern among Senators, regardless of their religious persuasion.

the investigating committees may indeed require that they scrutinize the behavior of some individuals, whether in official or private life. But it surely does not require that the committees undertake to identify, examine and pass judgment on every individual against whom accusations have been made. These are the tasks of the executive departments and the courts, and it is the deliberate and extensive intrusion of the Congressional committees into these fields that is the basic vice of the situation that now confronts us.

Time and sad experience may eventually restore the balance by action of the voters. Today we must face the realities of investigative practices and purposes. The loyalty committees have become a sort of irregular and irresponsible security police force, operating on a mounting scale which is rapidly approaching an overt and acknowledged inquisition. They exert the power of office and the pressure of publicity to inflict severe punishment, outside the due and regular processes of criminal law, and increasingly resemble the special peoples' courts established by the Nazis to execute the "healthy feeling of the people," and in Communist countries to enforce Party standards of individual behavior and attitude.*

Perhaps the most sinister feature of these events and circumstances is that they are inducing a serious decline, even in government circles, of respect for law and the processes of justice. Senator McCarthy's tales of skunk-hunting and his open invitation to federal employees to violate the security laws are prime examples of this trend.

But Senator McCarthy is by no means the only culprit. The Communist Control Act of 1954, which in terms "outlaws" the Communist Party and strips it of all "rights, privileges, and immunities attendant upon legal bodies," was passed unanimously by the Senate, and by the House with only two negative votes.[23] The implications of this statute, and of the near-unanimity with which Congress ap-

* Shortly before this book went to press, Walter Lippmann wrote: ". . . the so-called power of investigation . . . is in fact a power not only to investigate but to put on trial and to punish. The power of investigation has become the great instrument of political warfare and bears many resemblances to the revolutionary tribunals which appear in time of great crises. The control of these tribunals is probably—on a realistic appraisal—the crux of the contest for the control of Congress." [22]

proved it, are in many respects more alarming than the excesses of individual demagogues.

It may be noted in passing that, from the standpoint of enlightened jurisprudence, it would have been hard to find a more unfortunate word than "outlaw." For outlawry was a legal procedure of medieval England which, because of its harshness and susceptibility to abuse, fell into disuse and has been almost unknown in America since Revolutionary times.* By reviving the expression, we have now succeeded in spinning the clock backwards over several centuries.

It is clear that this extraordinary bill would never have graced the statute books but for the fears and pressures generated chiefly by the Congressional loyalty investigations. President Eisenhower's administration did not seek this legislation as part of its security program. Attorney General Brownell and FBI Director J. Edgar Hoover had publicly condemned outlawing the Communist Party as a poor security measure. Governor Thomas E. Dewey and many other eminent men of both major parties and many shades of thought were vigorously and publicly hostile.

In these circumstances, the overwhelmingly favorable vote in Congress proves that many, if not most, of the members were not voting their true convictions about the bill, but rather had succumbed to fear or a cheap desire to pose before the public as zealous Communist-haters. Signing the bill with obvious reluctance, President Eisenhower declared that its purpose is to suppress the Communist conspiracy to overthrow the government. In fact it is more than doubtful that the outlawry provisions will prove useful in furthering that purpose.[24]

However, our chief concern here is not with the merits or demerits of the law as a police measure. It is, rather, with the disastrous effect of the investigations on Congress' conception and discharge of its law-making responsibilities. In the heat and haste of this Congressional stampede, vital considerations of law, morals, and public security were overlooked or even treated with contempt by Republicans and Democrats alike.

The principal effect of the new law will be to ban the public and non-conspiratorial activities of the Party, and especially to strike its

---

* *See* Appendix III, An Historical Note on Outlawry, *infra,* pp. 301-05.

name and candidates from the ballot in all future elections; already this has been the result in New Jersey.[25] Yet, ever since World War I, the keystone of American foreign policy has been to support the right of nations and peoples to determine their own political future by free elections. Since World War II, in Germany, Korea, and elsewhere we have stood forth as the champions of national self-determination by popular vote. We have staked our principles and our prestige on the proposition that, given a free and unintimidated choice at the ballot box, democracy will be the victor over Communist totalitarianism.

What is left of all this, once we abolish free elections ourselves? It is only too easy to envisage the propaganda use to which the "outlaw law" may now be put by Communists all over the world. Has it now come to this, that East Germans and North Koreans and Vietnamese may be expected to vote for democracy and reject communism, but that Americans cannot be trusted to make the choice? Surely it was worth much for us to be seen as a land where the Communist Party is not suppressed by the long arm of the police, but is rejected by the long heads of the people.

These are not abstruse considerations, and would have been readily grasped by the legislators had they paused to reflect on the outlawry proposal in its world-wide context.* But reflection was not the order of the day. No more did the grave questions of constitutionality, with which the new law abounds,[26] arouse discussion, for discussion was not the order of the day. As a result this legislation, embodying far-reaching and indeed revolutionary changes in national policy, unwanted by the Administration and condemned by a formidable array of public figures, was enacted in a fit of selfish and unseemly panic, and so hastily that there was great difficulty in ascertaining the precise language that Congress had adopted.[27] The irony is that it was no Rankin or Dies or Jenner, but the liberal Senator Humphrey who—whether like the Pied Piper or Orestes pursued by the Furies—"led" the rout. "Fear is never a wise counsellor," admonished the great German General Von Seeckt, and it would be hard to find a better example of the truth of his teaching.

---

* According to *The New York Times* for November 22 and December 2, 1954, the West German government is finding its proposal to outlaw the Communist Party embarrassing for these very reasons.

This legislative disaster is the harvest of soil cultivated by the loyalty investigations. It is bound to step up the tempo of the cold civil war, and exacerbate the bitterness with which our political life is already poisoned. More than that, it is a most ominous symptom of decay in the legal institutions upon which our American way of life is based. In the manner no less than in the fact of its passage, Congress debased the legislative process.

Freedom as we know it can exist only under law. That is why nothing is more dangerous to our traditions, or more helpful to our enemies, than that high officials, elected or appointed, should openly display their contempt for law. Nothing, that is, unless it be the failure of other officials and of the citizenry to insist upon the law's vindication. Therefore, the issues and abuses with which this book is concerned are in no way partisan. When we are talking of the basic social verities such as respect for law and regard for truth, there is no room for any outlook but conservatism. Republicans and Democrats, conservatives and liberals, must all stand on conservative ground, and set their faces squarely against the radical and destructive mischief of these latter-day Know-Nothings, of whatever party, who sow suspicion and fear in our land at a time when foreign perils urgently require that we be of one mind on the fundamentals of our way of life.

Congressional investigations can and should be a powerful shield to our free institutions, and it is the task of everyone—judges, legislators, government officials and all foresighted citizens—to join in restoring them to the beneficial fulfillment of this task, under the leadership of able, moderate and responsible members of the House and the Senate. Such leadership has never been so needed as it is today, and its reassertion would be the best way to resolve and dissolve the problems which have given rise to this book.

APPENDIX I

A NOTE FOR LAYMEN ON BRITISH PARLIAMENTARY INVESTIGATIVE PRACTICE

The differences between Parliamentary and Congressional investigative practices have been largely determined by fundamental differences of governmental *structure* and *tradition.* The former have tended to prevent the recurrence in Britain of such violent struggles between Parliament and the Government as the Walpole investigation of 1742, described in Chapter I, which in the parallel form of Congressional-Executive strife has been a more or less constant feature of American governmental history. The latter have totally prevented the use of investigations for police, inquisitorial, and punitive purposes, as is now the frequent practice in the United States.

The basic architecture of American government is trinitarian: three separate and distinct though interlocked segments of power, the operations of which are guided by a written document, the Constitution. Admirable in many respects, this nevertheless induces an arm's-length, often jealous, and sometimes hostile relation between the three branches, especially between the legislative and executive. As we have seen, Congress constantly uses its investigative power not only as a tool but also as a weapon in its shifting and uneasy dealings with the executive branch.

The British Government, in the course and as a result of the long struggle for power among Crown, Church, Lords, and Commons, has developed an essentially unitarian structure based upon legislative—*i.e.* Parliamentary—supremacy under a constitution which is not a single document but is an agglomeration of traditions, written and unwritten. The Crown endures as a potent symbol and touchstone of these traditions, but the executive power is exercised under a government which is responsible to Parliament, and which is formed by and actually a part of the Parliamentary majority.*

* In coalition governments members of the opposition may serve as ministers, but this does not alter the fundamental concept of majority responsibility.

Therefore, the relations between Parliament and the Government are far closer than between Congress and the Executive. Indeed, the leaders of the Government are likewise the leaders of the Parliamentary majority. They sit in Commons on the front bench, shape the legislative program, lead in the debates, and are the target of constant questioning on the state of the realm and their conduct of its affairs. In this setting, Parliament can readily obtain such information as it needs from the Government without resort to its investigative power.

Now, of course Congress is not entirely without means, short of formal investigation, of obtaining information from the Executive. Congress, either House, committees, and even individual Congressmen can simply request that information be furnished. The power to complain and criticize publicly on the floor of Congress, and even more the power of the purse, are usually a sufficient stimulus to the Executive so that the desired information will be forthcoming. Nevertheless, this falls far short, in terms of intimacy, identity, and responsibility, of the actual presence as members in Parliament of the Government ministers. And the result is that Congress continually turns to its power of investigation, to extract information from or put pressure on the executive branch, under circumstances which in Parliament are dealt with on the floor by question and debate in which the Government is obliged to disclose and defend its policies and actions.

Indeed, special Parliamentary procedures have been evolved, the specific purpose of which is to lubricate the Parliament-Government relationship in these very respects. The most important device of this type is the famous "question time" four days a week, during which all members of the Commons have the right to ask questions of the Government ministers. Fifty to a hundred questions are asked and answered at each question time, some of which are followed up by oral cross-questioning of the ministers; these constitute, in effect, a host of miniature investigations. Another such device is the motion for debate "on a matter of definite and urgent public importance," which may be used at any time to precipitate a prompt floor debate. The prophylactic effect of this procedure has been pungently expressed by the Right Honorable Herbert Morrison: [1]

> It is perfectly proper and indeed to the public advantage that Parliament should jump in; a short sharp vigorous debate on the adjournment, even for only half an hour in which the government is thoroughly exposed and knocked about, will have a far more rapid, beneficial effect than a number of meetings of a select committee, the result of which may be that the department may become demoralized waiting for the select committee's report, and it might, indeed, slow up the procedure of disposal. . . . But I do say on the point of exposing a scandal, that a row on the floor in my judgment is quicker and the execution by the axe against the minister is sharper than in the case of the necessarily more leisurely investigation of a select committee. . . . Sometimes party bias—a sharp

vigorous attack—is in the public interest, and if a Minister is slipping up or something is badly going wrong, the quicker he is knocked about with all the bias, vigor and energy of which the critics are capable the better.

When it comes to gathering information not already in the Government's hands—as, for example, when considering legislation in a new field—once again, Parliament and Congress behave quite differently. Most notably, the standing committees of Parliament are far less important than those of Congress. It is the House of Commons, itself, not its committees, that shapes the basic features of legislation in full debate. The standing committees of the Commons are little more than minor adjuncts of the House, set up to save its time by handling technical and relatively non-controversial features of proposed legislation. They cannot, as Congressional committees often do, give birth to laws or put bills to death by way of the pigeonhole. The chairmen of Parliamentary standing committees are chosen from a panel, and acquire none of the power that accrues to the senior committee chairmen in Congress. Nor do the Parliamentary committees hold hearings, call witnesses, or conduct investigations. When information is needed, it is obtained by inquiry to the expert civil servants in the various Government departments.

The Parliamentary standing committees, therefore, bear little practical resemblance to their nominal opposites in Congress. The principal Congressional permanent committees of either House—for example Appropriations, Government Operations, Judiciary and Interstate Commerce—are semi-autonomous concentrations of great power. It is through them that the majority of investigations are carried on today, although special investigating committees are still and not infrequently appointed, especially in the House of Representatives.

But in England the legislative investigative process has gone through great changes during the last hundred years. Its original and almost exclusive agent—the Parliamentary select committee—is still employed from time to time, but increasingly seldom since the middle of the nineteenth century. Its historic monopoly of investigative power is a thing of the past, and the function is now shared with the Royal Commissions of Inquiry and, since 1921, with the Tribunals of Inquiry. And so we must examine each of these three institutions in order to get a full and clear view of the investigative pattern in Britain today.

Select Committees. In Chapter I, we examined the origin of the Commons' select committee investigations, and traced their development down to the middle of the eighteenth century. Their legal nature has not changed significantly since that time.

For an American, accustomed to read of the prosecution of recalcitrant Congressional committee witnesses in the courts, the most important thing to remember is that in Britain the courts do not come into the enforcement picture at all. As long as the Commons is in session, the courts simply will not inquire into the reasons for an individual's imprisonment for contempt of the House. For this reason—and quite independent of the absence in Britain of a written, judicially enforceable Constitution embodying a separation of powers—there are no British court decisions limiting the scope of the Commons' power of inquiry. In legal theory that power is unlimited, and anyhow the courts will not scrutinize its exercise. For this same reason, the question of a parliamentary committee witness' right to invoke a legal privilege, such as that against self-incrimination, never has arisen in the British courts. Whether or not the privilege is to be recognized is a matter entirely in the control of the Commons itself, and the courts have nothing to say about it.

The one thing the British courts have done and would do again is to order a witness, or anyone else imprisoned for contempt of the Commons, to be released if he were to be detained after the Parliamentary session is "prorogued" (finally concluded as distinguished from temporarily "adjourned"). In practice, this limitation on the Commons' contempt power never seems to have proved awkward; at all events, there has never been any effort or suggestion that a statute should be enacted (as was done by Congress in 1857) to authorize imprisonment between the sessions. If the Commons consider that an offender has not yet or sufficiently purged himself, he is recommitted during the next session; this has happened as recently as 1880.[2]

A false statement before a Commons committee is a contempt and can be punished as such. If given under oath, the offender can also be prosecuted in the courts for perjury, but in practice this is seldom done. Interestingly enough, the House of Commons has never claimed or exercised the inherent power to administer oaths. In the seventeenth and eighteenth centuries, when the Commons considered it necessary for a witness to be sworn, they accepted the dubious expedient of having him sworn at the bar of the Lords, or before a judge of the King's Bench, or before members of the Commons who happened also to be Justices of the Peace of the County of Middlesex! Beginning in 1770, certain select committees were given by statute the authority to administer oaths, and in 1871 a general statute was enacted giving that authority to the Commons and its select committees.

As we observed in Chapters I and VII,[3] the Commons has never recognized the right of a witness to decline to answer any question under a claim of privilege, whether against self-accusation or of any other type. By 1742, when Nicholas Paxton invoked it before the Walpole investigating committee, the privilege against self-accusation was nearly a century old and well established in the British courts. Yet neither Paxton nor any one since has found the Commons disposed to recognize the efficacy of any claim of privilege before a select committee. In 1828, for example, a committee required a solicitor to disclose matters pertaining to his client, and [4] in 1947, when a newspaper editor refused to disclose to the Committee on Privileges the name of a Member of Parliament who had "leaked" certain information to him, the editor was brought before the bar of the House of Commons by the Serjeant-at-Arms, where he apologized for his contumacy and revealed the name of the Member concerned. As a result of this episode, the House then unanimously adopted a resolution that: ". . . the refusal of witnesses before a Select Committee to answer any question which may be put to them is a contempt of this House, and an infringement of the undoubted right of this House to conduct any enquiry which may be necessary in the public interest."

In actual effect, however, the practice is not as harsh as all this would suggest. In 1818, the Commons adopted a resolution [5] "That all witnesses examined before this House or in Committee thereof are entitled to the protection of the House in respect of anything that may be said by them in their evidence." Under this resolution, it is impossible to introduce in court any testimony before a select committee without the consent of the House, which would probably not be given.

Furthermore, in every case in modern times when a serious problem of self-incrimination has arisen, before committees of the Lords or the Commons, a statute has been introduced to give the witness complete immunity (or "indemnity," as the British say) against subsequent prosecution. As we saw in Chapter I, this was attempted even in Paxton's case in 1742, but failed by a narrow margin in the Lords. Since that time, however, there have been a number of such enactments.[6]

Originally, the House of Lords had wider power than the Commons to punish contempts. This was because, when the separation of the two Houses took place (about 1344), the Lords, and not the Commons, retained and exercised the judicial powers of the High Court of Parliament. The Lords, therefore, had authority to administer oaths to witnesses, and to imprison them, if recalcitrant, even beyond the duration of the session.[7] However, as the power of the Lords dwindled and the Commons attained supremacy, the Lords' investigative activities sank into relative insignificance. Upon occasion, however, the Lords participate in important joint select committees.[8]

Indeed, to a degree the same is now coming true of the Commons' investigative functions as exercised through its select committees. Historically, the select committees attained their greatest importance during the first half of the nineteenth century, when a great many abuses—for example, the conditions in debtors' prisons so graphically described by Dickens in *The Pickwick Papers*—were exposed and ameliorated. Increasingly, however, this sort of function has been taken over by the Royal Commissions.

In fact, since World War II there have been only a few select committees appointed to conduct special inquiries.* At the present time, a matter is not normally referred to a select committee unless it somehow involves Parliament's procedures, or its relations with the ministries or other agencies, and there is no discernible prospect that the select committees will regain the wider functions and importance that they formerly possessed.

Royal Commissions of Inquiry. This is the British governmental institution which most closely corresponds, in function though *not* in structure or method, to our Congressional investigating committees. Such famous inquiries as the Pujo and Pecora banking and finance investigations and the many New Deal studies in aid of new social and economic legislation would undoubtedly have been conducted in Britain by Royal Commissions. And if the responsible ministers should conclude that Communist infiltration and subversion in Britain, whether in or outside the government, presented a threat to British security and liberty which called for special study and exposure, almost certainly the task would be given to a Royal Commission, insofar as it related to general conditions rather than the loyalty of particular individuals.

But if the functions of Congressional committees and Royal Commissions are roughly parallel, their natures are strikingly different. Technically, the House of Commons has nothing to do with the establishment of a Royal Commission, which is actually an order of commission issued by the Crown, appointing the members of the Commission and specifying (by what are called the Terms of Reference) the subject and scope of the inquiry. The members of the Commission are not ordinarily members of Parliament, although there have been a very few exceptions. In practical effect, however, a Parliamentary suggestion that a Commission be appointed produces the desired result, and important Commissions are very unlikely to be established without the Government's approval.

The members of Royal Commissions serve without pay; qualified persons regard their service as both an opportunity and a civic duty. When the inquiry deals with a pressing issue to which some prompt solution must be found, and especially when large, diverse, and conflicting interests are at stake, the membership must be representative; the Commission on Liquor Licensing, for example, comprised representatives of trade unions, temperance societies, the liquor interests, and social workers, as well as government experts. If the Commission is engaged in a long-range study of broad trends and enduring problems—good illustrations are the recent Commissions on Population, and Marriage and Divorce—cultural and scientific qualifications and civic achievements are likely to be stressed. †

* Examples are the Select Committee on Budget Disclosure in 1947-48 to inquire into the Chancellor of the Exchequer's (Mr. Hugh Dalton) disclosure of the proposed Budget to a newspaperman a few minutes before he made the Budget statement in Commons, and the Select Committee on Nationalized Industries in 1951-52, to consider methods of ensuring the nationalized industries' responsibility to Parliament without unduly hampering their business initiative.

† The extent and scope of current use of Royal Commissions may be gauged

Another monumental difference between the Commissions and Congressional inquiries is that proceedings before the former are entirely *voluntary*. A Royal Commission has no power to summon witnesses and administer oaths. Problems of contempt and recalcitrancy, therefore, do not arise, and the temper of the proceedings is quiet and decorous. Ordinarily, however, the method of inquiry is searching and thorough and the witnesses' statements and views are carefully tested and explored.

How are the Royal Commissions able to function effectively without the subpoena power which is the "massive retaliation" of Congressional committees against unwilling witnesses? In part, no doubt, it is because the Royal Commissions are careful not to concern themselves with questions of individual guilt or unworthy conduct, except to the extent really necessary to illuminate the public issues they are considering. The members are not interested in sensational exposures. Then, too, the British people are pervaded with the tractability and feelings of mutual responsibility induced by a settled and successful governmental system and a relatively homogeneous population. Consequently, they are innately responsive to Lord Chancellor Harwicke's observation [9] that "the public has a right to every man's evidence." Very likely, this responsiveness is facilitated by awareness that, in the long run, concealment of any matter deemed of real importance to the government is impossible, as Parliament can always resort to its compulsory power of inquiry.

Tribunals of Inquiry. We have now covered, in British terms, a large part of the field of activity of Congresional investigations, finding some parts of it occupied by the Royal Commissions, others by the select committees, and still others by Parliamentary procedures such as question time. But we have not yet encountered the type of American legislative activity which precipitates the most controversial practices with which this book deals—the summoning of individuals who are accused or suspected of criminal, subversive, or otherwise dangerous or undesirable inclinations and proclivities, for cross-questioning before a legislative committee, in order to achieve the "exposure" which Judge Wyzanski and David Lawrence have prescribed as the great specific for whatever ails the body politic.[10]

Does this kind of investigative activity find any counterpart in Britain? In substance the answer is "no." It may safely be declared, for example, that an inquiry such as the Senate "interstate crime" (Kefauver) investigation could not possibly occur in Britain. If there were evidence of slackness

---

from the following representative list of Commissions established since 1945: On Awards to Inventors (1946); On Justices of the Peace (1946); On the Press (1947) (to enquire into the control and ownership of newspapers and periodicals and press agencies, including financing and monopolistic tendencies); On Capital Punishment (1949); On Betting, Lotteries and Gaming (1949); On Taxation of Profits and Income (1951) (dismally self-explanatory); On Marriage and Divorce (1951); On Scottish Affairs (1952); On Land and Population in East Africa (1953); On the Civil Service (1953); On the Law Relating to Mental Illness and Mental Deficiency (1954).

or corruption in criminal law enforcement, the responsible ministers would be severely "knocked about" (Mr. Morrison's phrase) in the House, and if matters were not soon put right, would be relieved of their posts. As for the colorful assortment of underworld witnesses that shared the television screen with Senators Kefauver and Tobey and Mr. Rudolph Halley, they would have long since been brought to trial, and either acquitted or put behind bars.

And yet the matter is not quite so simple. Suppose, in the situation just described, it began to appear that a minister or other official were involved in these laxities of law enforcement in a way which was indiscreet or even reprehensible, and yet the available evidence did not warrant a criminal indictment? Until 1921, this sort of mess probably would have been the occasion for a select committee. But in that year Parliament passed the Tribunals of Inquiry Act,[11] and it is such a Tribunal that would be constituted today under the supposed circumstances.

In fact, a very parallel situation arose in 1948, when it was rumored that a junior minister of the Labor Government had accepted presents or rewards in connection with the issuance of government licenses and other official actions. Judge G. J. Lynskey of the High Court and two prominent barristers were appointed as a Tribunal of Inquiry to sift the charges, and so conducted the proceedings on an issue with potentially explosive political angles that the Opposition was completely satisfied of its fairness and impartiality. As a result of the Tribunal's report, two ministers resigned.

The Tribunal of Inquiry is an unprecedented British institution and quite unlike anything known in the United States. Very roughly, it might be compared to the special board recently appointed to examine the charges against Dr. Robert Oppenheimer, which, if deemed in Britain serious enough, would surely have been heard by a Tribunal of Inquiry.

But these Tribunals are much more formal and judicial in nature than the Oppenheimer board. They can be established only by joint resolution of Parliament, and the members are designated by the Crown. The Tribunal has all the powers of the High Court with respect to oaths, subpoenas, and testimony. Contumacious witnesses may be brought before the High Court or the Scottish Court of Session and, after opportunity to justify their conduct, may be punished as for contempt of the Court.* The privilege against self-accusation, and other privileges recognized by the courts, may be claimed by witnesses before the Tribunals. At the conclusion of its proceedings, the Tribunal makes a report of its findings and minority reports are permitted. As Professor Finer has put it: [13]

> The Tribunal of Inquiry in British law and practice is an attempt to find a procedure that fits such situations—removing a quasi-political

---

* In this respect, the procedure is similar to the instances where Congress has authorized a joint investigating committee or an executive agency to enforce its testimonial process by obtaining a federal court order.[12]

misdemeanor from the political arena because the proof should be quasi-judicial, but not taking the case to a law court because the problem is quasi-political. A "political" charge is submitted to the procedure of what is almost a court of law.

During the debate in 1921 . . . it was argued that an investigatory body was needed which would give: (a) public satisfaction; (b) judicial proceedings; (c) public proceedings; and (d) evidence on oath . . . the inquiry ought to rest on five principles: speed of getting to work, impartiality, thorough and skillful investigation, full publicity, and absence of temptation to make political capital.

Interestingly enough, the Tribunals of Inquiry Act seems to have been precipitated by a select committee proceeding in which were manifested some of the intemperate and partisan characteristics of certain notorious Congressional investigations. From 1912 to 1915 a Commons select committee investigated charges that several Government ministers financially interested in the Marconi telegraph enterprises had used their influence to obtain a contract from the Postmaster General. Anti-Semitic and other passionate overtones and heated wrangles tainted the inquiry, and the upshot was totally unsatisfactory, for the exoneration of the principal subject of the inquiry, Sir Rufus Isaacs (later Foreign Minister, Lord Chief Justice, and Viceroy of India) was had only by a strict party vote of eight to six in his favor.

It should also be observed that the Tribunal of Inquiry may come into play * in sequence with Parliament's other investigative instruments. In 1928, for example, question time in the Commons disclosed that a woman had been subjected to the "third degree" and other abuses while being interrogated on a morals charge. After debate on the affair as a matter of urgent public importance, a Tribunal of Inquiry was appointed. After full hearings, the Tribunal split, but both of its reports were highly critical of Scotland Yard, and dismissals resulted. Thereafter, a Royal Commission was appointed to study police methods, and its recommendations resulted in desirable reforms. In another situation (1924), a Royal Commission on Lunacy and Mental Disorder found it necessary to investigate an individual case. To enable this, the members were constituted a Tribunal of Inquiry with subpoena powers, and the inquiry thus proceeded under "two sets of hats."

For all that British governmental practice has developed a flexible and variegated array of instrumentalities and procedures of legislative inquiry,

---

* In all, eleven Tribunals have been established under the 1921 law. In addition to the Lynskey Tribunal, these included the 1936 Budget Disclosure, involving a cabinet member's (the Rt. Hon. J. H. Thomas) premature revelation of Budget details to financiers who thereby made speculative profits, and the 1939 inquiry into the sinking, with heavy loss of life, of the submarine *Thetis*.

none of them has so far been utilized for inquiries into subversion and disloyalty. There have been no legislative inquiries of this sort in Britain.

Such a striking contrast with American practice is worth more than a moment's reflection. Without undertaking here to adjudge the issue thus suggested, and indulging the charitable and probable assumption that much might be said on both sides, it behooves us at least to comprehend the British attitude. Essentially, it is the viewpoint recently expressed by Sir Hartley Shawcross and Justice Rand before the Association of the Bar of the City of New York, which we noted in the first chapter.[14] Even more authoritative statements are not lacking. Here is Prime Minister Clement Attlee speaking in the Commons in March, 1948: [15]

> . . . I have said that there are certain duties of such secrecy that the State is not justified in employing in connection with them anyone whose reliability is in doubt.
>
> Experience, both in this country and elsewhere, has shown that membership of, and other forms of continuing association with, the Communist Party may involve the acceptance by the individual of a loyalty, which, in certain circumstances, can be inimical to the State.
>
> It is not suggested that in matters affecting the security of the State all those who adhere to the Communist Party would allow themselves thus to forget their primary loyalty to the State . . . the only prudent course to adopt is to ensure that no one who is known to be a member of the Communist Party, or to be associated with it in such a way as to raise legitimate doubts about his or her reliability, is employed in connection with work, the nature of which is vital to the security of the State . . .
>
> I should emphasize that this action is being taken solely on security grounds. The State is not concerned with the political views, as such, of its servants, and as far as possible alternative employment on the wide range of non-secret Government work will be found for those who are deemed for the reason indicated to be unsuitable for secret work.

And here is Prime Minister Sir Winston Churchill in the same place six years later: [16]

> SIR W. SMITHERS asked the Prime Minister if he will set up a Royal Commission to inquire into Communist activities and propaganda in Great Britain.
>
> THE PRIME MINISTER: No, Sir. There can be few countries in the world where communism has more difficulty in making headway than in this island, with our free institutions and long experience. The security aspect can well be dealt with under our established laws, the vigilant administration of which is under constant Parliamentary attention.
>
> SIR W. SMITHERS: Is the Prime Minister aware that Mr. Casey is reported to have said that the spy rings which have caused so much trouble in Australia are active in all countries, including Britain? Will he make an appeal to the British public relentlessly to combat Communist activi-

ties everywhere? Will he also tell the British public that there is no difference in principle between communism and socialism?

THE PRIME MINISTER: I really do not think that that would be a helpful suggestion for me to act upon.

Now, it is very easy to say, as some Americans do, that these statements reflect a nonchalant and slipshod attitude, as a result of which the British security services have been victimized and hoodwinked, and the security of the free nations jeopardized, by Klaus Fuchs, Pontecorvo, Burgess and McLean, and other spies and renegades. It is easy, too, for others to ridicule the entire security system in the United States as unnecessary, ineffective, and the product of fear, hate, and the jitters. But these blanket indictments, in whichever direction they are turned, are either thoughtless, superficial, and emotional reactions, or the deliberate sowing of distrust and suspicion for dangerous if not traitorous ends.

Much of the British investigative pattern is not at all applicable to conditions in the United States, because it grows out of basic governmental differences of such magnitude that it is academic to discuss their composition. Perhaps we should abandon separation of powers and the written constitution, and switch to the cabinet form of government. However that may be, it is in fact most unlikely, and we must proceed on the basis that our investigative methods and principles will continue to reflect, as they must, the fundamentals of our form of constitutional government. It is highly desirable that we know about the Royal Commissions, and appropriate that we grasp their advantages and admire their accomplishments. But it is futile to imagine that we can or should slavishly copy them, or that they could be imported and used in place of Congressional investigations.

Yet there are lessons to be learned on both sides of the Atlantic, and if we will take pains to learn ours, perhaps the British will do likewise. The principal lesson for us is that there are better ways and methods than Congressional committee inquiries for the determination of highly controversial issues of fact, especially when questions of individual character and conduct are at stake. It is a lesson that has been staring us in the face ever since the St. Clair inquiry in 1792.[17] The British long ago discovered that quasi-judicial matters cannot suitably or safely be committed for decision to persons whose principal affiliations and activities are avowedly political.

It is high time that we grasped and acted on this elementary principle of law and politics. And if it be said that we are of the New World and should not be confined by the traditions of the old, let it be remembered that Romans were not ashamed to learn from Greeks, and that therein lay much of their greatness.

APPENDIX II

A NOTE FOR LAWYERS ON THE NEW FEDERAL "IMMUNITY" STATUTE

The core of the new statute, insofar as it applies to Congressional investigations, is the provision that no witness shall be excused from giving evidence, on the ground of self-incrimination:

> . . . when the record shows that—
>
> (1) in the case of proceedings before one of the Houses of Congress, that a majority of the members present of that House; or
>
> (2) in the case of proceedings before a committee, that two-thirds of the members of the full committee shall by affirmative vote have authorized such witness to be granted immunity under this section with respect to the transactions, matters or things concerning which he is compelled, after having claimed his privilege against self-incrimination, to testify or produce evidence by direction of the presiding officer and—
>
> that an order of the United States district court for the district wherein the inquiry is being carried on has been entered into the record requiring said person to testify or produce evidence . . .

It may be noted that, in all probability, the clause numbered (2) should have ended after the words "of the full committee," and that the ensuing language from "shall by affirmative vote" to "presiding officer and" must be read as applicable to both clauses (1) and (2). Otherwise clause (1) is left both verbless and senseless. Beyond such linguistic defects, however, the statute raises at least five fundamental questions of meaning, policy, and constitutionality, each of which is briefly discussed hereinbelow.

First, can the witness who has invoked the privilege appear before the court and oppose the grant? The statute does not say so, and the committee report [1] does not so indicate. It is doubtful that a witness has any legal right to be granted or denied immunity. Nor would he ordinarily be qualified to speak on the value, for legislative purposes, of the evidence requested by the committee and withheld by him under claim of privilege.

Nevertheless, if the witness has no right to be heard, the non-adversary character of the proceeding before the district court is emphasized, and this may further prejudice the statute's constitutionality, discussed under the third point, below.

Second, does the district court review the *power* of the committee to compel the witness to answer the question? The wording of the statute in the portion quoted above would seem to indicate that it does, for it is stated that the court order is one "requiring said person to testify or produce evidence." Presumably, the court would not want to do this if it were made to appear that the committee lacked constitutional or other authority to compel the evidence to be given. This, too, would suggest that the witness should be allowed to appear to contest the committee's authority. But this, in turn, leads to the anomalous result that a witness who pleads the privilege gets an opportunity to challenge the committee's authority before encountering the risk of contempt or criminal prosecution, whereas a witness who does not invoke the privilege gets no such opportunity.

Furthermore, in the next paragraph (b) of the statute, the court's action is not described as an order directing the witness to testify, but as an order granting the court's "approval" of the Congressional grant of immunity. This would suggest that the issue of the committee's authority cannot be raised before the court. But if this is so, then, once again, the non-judicial character of the court's participation is underlined, and the constitutional question clearly emerges.

Third, therefore, is the statute constitutional insofar as it calls upon the federal courts to participate in the immunity-granting process? It has been settled since the early days of the Republic that, since the Constitution vests "judicial" power in the federal courts, and "legislative" and "executive" power in the other two branches, the courts can constitutionally discharge only "judicial" functions.[2] Congressional statutes undertaking to impose non-judicial functions on the courts have been declared unconstitutional.[3]

When Congress created the Interstate Commerce and Pacific Railway Commissions in 1887, and provided for enforcement of the Commission's testimonial powers by federal court order, it was at first held by a three-judge federal court, headed by Supreme Court Justice Field, that the law was unconstitutional because the courts could not act as a mere enforcement arm of the executive branch.[4] This decision was later overruled by the Supreme Court, and the enforcement procedure upheld as constitutional; but this ruling was expressly based on an interpretation of the statute whereby the courts would in each case review the Commission's legal authority to require the evidence, and decline to order the evidence to be given if the authority was found wanting.[5] On this basis, the courts' participation in the enforcement process was plainly judicial, in that there was a "case or controversy" before the courts which they could finally determine.

In line with these decisions, if the new immunity statute is construed as not calling for court review of the committee's authority, and as not contemplating the presence of the witness as an opposing litigant, its constitutionality is dubious indeed. Yet, as we have seen under the first two points, the statute does not lend itself readily to contrary interpretation.

These doubts are enhanced if we envisage the posture of events in the district court if the Attorney General does not agree with the proposed immunity grant. Under paragraph (b) of the new statute the Attorney General is to be notified when the Congressional representatives apply for the court order, and he "shall be given the opportunity to be heard with respect thereto" before the court acts. If the Attorney General opposes the application, the federal judge will face the task of deciding a dispute between the legislative and executive branches, involving no legal issues, but only considerations of legislative and executive policy. In terms of public interest, does Congress' need for the information outweigh the Attorney General's legal duty to prosecute the crime, if crime there was? This, it would seem, is not a judicial question.

It might be urged that the power of the courts to issue search warrants offers an analogy. But the juridical basis of a search warrant has nothing to do with *evidence;* it is issued to obtain stolen goods or other wrongfully-held property which the State or a private person is rightfully entitled to. Although by its very nature an application for a search warrant must be handled by the court on an *ex parte* basis in the first instance, so as not to put the alleged wrongful possessor on notice of the incipient search, the proceeding may become a controversy if the possessor subsequently challenges the application and seeks to recover the goods on his own allegedly rightful claim. Such a process, therefore, is entirely different from and lends no support to the proceeding contemplated by the new immunity statute.

It appears, therefore, that the new statute is vulnerable to constitutional attack. Apart from these legal aspects, it is hard to see any practical reasons of government policy for bringing the courts into the situation. One may hazard a guess that this provision was hastily written into the statute as a compromise between those who, like Congressman Keating, wanted the Attorney General's consent to be absolutely essential, and those who resented this as an unwarranted "veto" on the power of Congress.

Fourth, does the statute undertake to give the witness immunity from prosecution under state laws? If so, is it constitutional; if not, is the immunity from federal prosecution alone sufficient to remove the basis for the plea of self-incrimination? On these questions, the pertinent language of the statute reads:

> . . . no . . . witness shall be prosecuted or subjected to any penalty or forfeiture for or on account of any transaction, matter, or thing concerning which he is so compelled, after having claimed his privilege against self-incrimination, to testify or produce evidence, nor shall testimony so com-

pelled be used as evidence in any criminal proceeding . . . against him in any court.

The prohibition against prosecution is broad enough to include state prosecutions, although they are not explicitly comprehended. The House committee report makes it plain [6] that its members intended the prohibition to embrace state prosecutions "if it be determined that Congress has the power to do so."

The decisions of the Supreme Court on this point are by no means clear. In *Brown* v. *Walker* [7] the five majority justices declared that Congress, in the Interstate Commerce Act, had granted immunity from state as well as federal prosecution. However, this point was not necessary to the decision and three of the dissenting justices rejected this conclusion. Furthermore, in other cases the Supreme Court has said that the Fifth Amendment protects only against self-incrimination under federal law, on the theory that the risk of state prosecution is too remote.[8] But however that may be when the inquiry is exclusively federal in nature, it is quite a different matter where federal and state sovereignty overlap. For example, the Kefauver crime investigating committee questioned witnesses about violations of state law, and it was held that under these circumstances witnesses could plead the Fifth Amendment on the basis of possible incrimination under state law.[9] It would be absurd if federal and state guarantees against compulsory self-incrimination could be evaded by the device of questioning individuals about violations of state laws before federal tribunals or committees, and vice versa.

At all events, the question has now become crucially important, since Communist activities are punished or penalized not only under federal laws like the Smith and McCarran Acts, but also under state statutes, as in Texas, Massachusetts, Pennsylvania and other states.[10] Under present circumstances, I believe that any federal statute effective to overcome the privilege, when claimed by witnesses before Congressional committees inquiring into matters of loyalty, must accord immunity from state as well as federal prosecution. It seems probable that, in the field of security to which the new statute is exclusively applicable, Congress' power to do this would be upheld.

Very recently the Supreme Court went part way to this conclusion in holding that Congress may prohibit a state from *using as evidence* for a prosecution, testimony previously given by the defendant before a Congressional committee.[11] This provision has been carefully retained [12] in the new immunity statute but, under the rule of *Counselman* v. *Hitchcock*,[13] it does not furnish sufficient immunity to remove the basis for the claim of privilege.

Fifth and finally, what reason is there for restricting the statute to matters pertaining to national defense and security? I can see none. Once again, it appears that this restriction was written into the bill in the hope of making it less unpalatable to its opponents. But there does not appear to be any logical or practical justification for this limitation. There are countless other vitally important actual and potential subjects of legislation, and Congress may, in these other fields, have just as much need for information withheld under claim of privilege, as in connection with loyalty and security matters.

APPENDIX III

AN HISTORICAL NOTE ON OUTLAWRY

Outlawry is a judicial declaration that an individual is outside the protection of the law. James Bryce refers to it [1] as "the oldest of all legal sanctions," and it is known to have been in use in England before the time of King Alfred (871-901) and probably as early as 600 A.D. From the earliest times, it appears to have been reserved as a punishment for the worst offenses against the community, i.e., felony and, later, treason. As Dean Harold Potter puts it: [2]

> Primitive law could not measure its blows; he who defied it was outside the law. An outlaw was treated as a wild beast, a wolf's head whom any man might slay. He had ceased to be a member of the community because he failed to observe its laws. Such a punishment represents an early stage in the life of a community. The State is too weak to compel obedience among its members but can only threaten and execute loss of membership as a penalty for grave wrongs . . .

Gradually, as the authority of the community and the realm grew and criminal processes became less crude, outlawry ceased to be used as a punishment for those adjudged guilty of crime; rather the threat of outlawry became the means of compelling those accused to appear before the courts, and outlawry itself was imposed as the punishment for refusing to appear and submit to the court's adjudication.

Outlawry thus developed, essentially, into a punishment for contempt of the courts, but it was exceedingly severe in that the outlawry was equivalent to conviction of the felony charged. The outlawed individual's lands and chattels were all forfeited to the Crown, and, if he was thereafter apprehended, he was summarily executed without any trial to determine his actual guilt of the offense charged. No one might harbor or aid an outlaw, wherefore he was commonly referred to as a "friendlesman." Anyone might kill an outlaw with impunity, as if he were no more than a wolf, and this gave rise to the expression "wolf's head" (*caput gerat lupinum*) to describe an outlaw. In the Exchequer rolls for the seventh year of the reign of Richard I (1196) there is an allowance of two marks to one Thomas de Prestwude, for bringing to Westminster the head of William de Elleford, an outlaw.[3]

As early as the thirteenth century, a few steps began to be taken to mitigate the harshness of outlawry and prevent its abuse. In Magna Carta (1215) it was declared in the 39th clause that "No freeman shall be taken or imprisoned or disseised, or outlawed, or exiled, or anyways destroyed . . . unless by the lawful judgment of his peers, or by the law of the land." Early in Edward III's reign (1327–77) a statute was enacted providing that no one but the sheriff should put an outlaw to death, unless he were slain during an attempt to capture him.[4]

At about the same time, outlawry began to be used in civil as well as criminal proceedings. Dean Potter tells us [5]—

> In the local Courts threat of outlawry had for centuries represented the normal means of compelling a reluctant defendant to appear before the Court. In the King's Courts, however, this rule was being only tentatively applied to civil proceedings as late as the time when Bracton wrote his treatise *de Legibus* in the thirteenth century. Bracton himself argued in favor of the introduction of outlawry as a method of process by way of the Writ of Trespass, which was at least quasi-criminal in character, and with which he regarded outlawry as compatible provided that it did not involve a judgment of life or limb but only forfeiture of goods and chattels. It was in this form that civil outlawry was gradually introduced into civil process and was extended to other actions besides trespass.

Criminal or civil, outlawry remained a crude device, dangerously susceptible to abuse. A man might be away traveling or hunting, and return home to find that powerful enemies or avaricious creditors had accused or sued him in his absence and had already obtained a judgment of outlawry. Indeed, by some accounts this is exactly what happened to that most famous of all outlaws, the legendary hero Robin Hood. But the precise reason for Robin's outlawry—even whether it was criminal or civil—remains, like most of the details of his life, wrapped in the mystery of a vague and often contradictory balladry.[6]

However that may be, outlawry as a legal institution continued to flourish for several centuries after Robin Hood's time. To prevent its abuse, new requirements were developed by the courts to ensure adequate notice to persons accused or sued, so that they would not be outlawed without their knowledge. A legal writ called the *exigent* required the sheriff to *demand* the defendant in the various surrounding county courts, and no proclamation of outlawry could be made until a certain number of exactions had been issued without results.

In the meantime, however, other and more modern forms of process were developed to bring persons before the courts. There was less need for the outlawry process; the judges disliked it, and surrounded it with the most elaborate technical requirements, in order to make it easy to rule that all these had not been complied with, and that therefore grounds for outlawry did not exist. By the seventeenth century, criminal outlawry was falling into disuse, although in civil cases it continued to be used with sufficient frequency so that in 1779 one Thomas Legge was moved to publish a short treatise on the subject.[7]

At about the same time, the last famous case of criminal outlawry occurred. The subject was that prototype of the modern "controversial character," John Wilkes, who was outlawed after he fled to Paris and refused to appear at his trial and conviction for seditious libel. Upon his return to England, Wilkes was committed to jail to serve his sentence on conviction for seditious libel, but his outlawry was set aside by Lord Mansfield, who seized on the most picayune "defects" in the proceedings.[8]

A century later, outlawry breathed its last in England. The Forfeiture Act, 1870,[9] referred to outlawry as an extant legal process, but in 1879, by statute,[10] it was formally abolished in all civil proceedings. In criminal proceedings it has never been formally abolished and the county courts, theoretically, are still capable of declaring outlawries, but there has been no instance of its use since 1859.[11]

It will be seen, accordingly, that outlawry was already a dying institution in England at the time the American colonies were being settled. According to Professor Julius Goebel, early in the eighteenth century (1702-1710) there were abortive attempts made in New York to introduce the process of outlawry.[12] But in 1774 an act of the state legislature declared that outlawry "is not used in this colony."

In Virginia [13] and Pennsylvania, outlawry appears to have gained a stronger foothold, and its history in the latter state is indeed interesting. A Pennsylvania statute of 1718 prescribed the requirements for process of outlawry in the colony, and as late as 1785, one Robert Steele was outlawed on a charge of robbery, and upon being apprehended was summarily executed.[14] But at that same time, another case of outlawry attracted anxious attention in the highest quarters. One Aaron Doan was outlawed for robbery, apprehended, and sentenced to execution by the Supreme Court of Pennsylvania. The President and Supreme Executive Council, upon receipt of the record, declined to issue a warrant for Doan's execution, and a lively correspondence ensued between the President (John Dickinson) and the justices.[15] The latter defended their action with vigor, but the idea of execution without trial was so repugnant to the President and Council that, in the end, highly technical if not veritably concocted defects in the outlawry proceedings were seized on by the Council to justify their refusal to issue the warrant. President Dickinson in his memorandum of reasons referred to outlawries as "vindictive supplements to a severe code of criminal jurisprudence."

Since these few flickerings of Revolutionary times, outlawry has been a totally obsolete and discarded legal institution in the United States.[16]

So far as I have been able to determine, the word "outlaw" has only once before been used in a statute prior to the Communist Control Act of 1954. In Alabama during the turbulent reconstruction years, Ku Klux Klan and other mob murders, whereby the widows and children of the victims were often left destitute and the identity of those responsible could not be determined, led to the enactment in 1868 of a statute prescribing that the spouse or next of kin could recover damages from the county in which the killing occurred. The law applied "whenever . . . any person shall be assassinated or murdered by any outlaw, or person or persons in disguise, or mob, or for past or present party affiliation or political opinion."

The following year one W. T. Gunter was shot and killed from ambush while he was herding cattle, and his widow sued the county under this statute, claiming that the assassin was an "outlaw." This required the court to determine the meaning of the word as used in the statute. The opinion of the Supreme Court of Alabama, by Chief Justice Peck, is the most recent (1871) judicial analysis of the subject: [17]

> The word "outlaw," as used in that act, does not mean an "outlaw" in the common law sense of that term. If it does, then I am prepared to hold that there is, and can be, no such outlawry in this State. . . .
>
> Outlawry by the common law, if not inconsistent with the letter of our Bill of Rights, is so with its spirit. 1. It not only puts a man out of the protection of the law, but also renders him incapable to bring an action for redress of injuries. This is in conflict with the 15th section of the Bill of Rights, which declares that "all courts shall be open, that any person for any injury done him in his lands, goods, person or reputation, shall have a remedy by due process of law; and right and justice shall be administered without sale, denial or delay." 2. It works forfeiture of goods, and in case of treason or felony, of lands also. This is repugnant to the 21st section of the Bill of Rights, which says that "no person shall be attainted of treason by the general assembly," and that "no conviction shall work corruption of blood, or forfeiture of estate." If there can be no forfeiture of estate on a conviction for treason, certainly there cannot be on conviction for any less offense. . . .
>
> In England there are statutes, and an ancient and well settled practice of the courts, according to which a man may be outlawed; but where, in this country, do we find any statutes or practice of the courts, by which a man in either a civil or criminal case, can be outlawed according to the law of the land? I know of none. The English common law and statutes, on this subject of outlawry, have never been recognized, or in any wise adopted in this State, and the whole system is inconsistent with our institutions, and repugnant to our constitution and laws, and is without any force among us.

Accordingly, Chief Justice Peck was obliged to look for some other meaning of the word. He was able to find "a very untechnical, loose and indeterminate sense," covering disguised persons committing crimes and outrages, i.e., the Klan. He concluded that the legislature had probably inserted the word "outlaw" without "any very definite idea or comprehension of its true meaning."

No doubt the same might be said of Congress' use of the expression in the new Communist Control Act of 1954. Professor Goebel refers to outlawry as "this grimmest of all common law processes" and, as we have seen, it has been dead in the United States for over a century. Supporting the bill to outlaw the Communist Party, Representative Hyde of Maryland declared: [18] "We cannot permit the forces of evil to thrust us back into the Dark Ages." True enough, but there is the less reason for us to start in that direction without being pushed.

NOTES

CHAPTER I

1. *The New York Times,* November 6, 1953, p. 13.
2. Professor Furry testified that he had been employed in "secret radar development work" at the Massachusetts Institute of Technology from 1943 to 1945. See *The New York Times,* January 16, 1954, pp. 1 and 6.
3. *The New York Times,* January 17, 1954, p. 1.
4. *The New York Times,* January 16, 1954, p. 6.
5. Woodrow Wilson, *Congressional Government* (1901), at pp. 297-303.
6. The English origins of legislative investigations were skillfully explored and exposed by James M. Landis, later Dean of the Harvard Law School, in an article entitled "Constitutional Limits on the Congressional Power of Investigation," and published in volume 40 of the *Harvard Law Review,* at pp. 153-226 (1926). That article is the principal source of the account herein.
7. Records of *Sir Francis Godwin's Case* in 1604 survive which show that the Commons authorized an officer to search for records that might throw light on the contested facts. See Hale, *Original Institution, Power and Jurisdiction of Parliaments* (1707), p. 105.
8. In 1621 Randolph Davenport was imprisoned for misinforming a committee inquiring into a disputed election, and there were numerous similar cases thereafter until 1868, when Parliament by statute delegated the determination of contested elections to the Court of Common Pleas. See Landis, *op. cit. supra,* at pp. 160-61.
9. Landis, *op. cit supra,* p. 161.
10. *Stockdale* v. *Hansard,* 9 Adolphus & Ellis 1, at p. 114, decided by the Court of Queen's Bench in 1839. The quotation is from the opinion of Chief Justice Lord Denman.
11. Book 4 of Coke's *Institutes,* p. 11.
12. Vol. XIII of Richard Chandler's *Common Debates* at p. 172. For the other matters arising out of the Walpole investigation and mentioned in the text, see pages 139, 190, 243, 248, and the Appendix, pages 1-9 and 44-45, of the same.
13. The colonial and early state history of legislative investigations and contempts is set forth in a valuable article by Charles S. Potts, entitled "Power of Legislative Bodies to Punish for Contempt," and published in Vol. 74 of

the *University of Pennsylvania Law Review,* at pp. 691 and 780 (1926). This article is the source of the material in the text.

14. Potts, *op. cit. supra,* p. 714.

14a. *The Works of James Wilson* (Andrews Edition, 1896), p. 29.

15. *Howard* v. *Gossett,* 10 Queen's Bench 359, at 379-80, decided in 1845.

16. The last judicial decision on the subject appears to be *Lines* v. *Russell,* reported in 19 *Law Times* 364, and decided at *nisi prius* by Sir Frederick Pollock in 1852.

17. There were, however, very powerful and far-reaching investigations carried on by the Committee of Public Safety, during the French Revolution, but these can hardly be regarded as "legislative" investigations in any contemporary sense.

18. See the useful description of French and German experience with legislative investigations in an article by Henry W. Ehrmann, entitled "The Duty of Disclosure in Parliamentary Investigation: A Comparative Study," and published in volume 11 of the *University of Chicago Law Review,* at p. 1 (1943). The material in the text is largely drawn from this article.

19. *The Nemesis of Power,* by John W. Wheeler-Bennett (1953), at p. 66.

20. *Infra,* pp. 180-81.

CHAPTER II

1. The account of St. Clair's career, defeat, and subsequent tribulations is drawn from *The St. Clair Papers* (2 volumes, 1882), edited by William Henry Smith; Frazer E. Wilson, *Arthur St. Clair, Rugged Ruler of the Old Northwest* (1944); Arthur St. Clair, *A Narrative of the Manner in Which the Campaign Against the Indians Was Conducted in the Year 1791 Under the Command of Major General St. Clair* (Phila. 1812); and Calvin M. Young, *Little Turtle, The Great Chief of the Miami Nation* (1917).

2. *Annals of Congress* (2nd Cong., 1st Sess.), pp. 490-93.

3. On February 2 in the House, Steele of North Carolina had laid on the table a motion for a committee of inquiry, but with no clause empowering it to send for persons and papers. This motion never came up for discussion.

4. Jefferson's record is set forth in full in *The Complete Anas of Thomas Jefferson* (1903), at pp. 70-71. See also *Jefferson's Writings* (P. L. Ford, Federal Edition, 1904), volume 2, pp. 213-14; *Writings of Washington* (U. S. Govt. Printing Office, 1944), volume 32, page 15, footnote 41.

5. 3 Hinds' *Precedents,* at p. 80.

6. The committee reports are set forth in *The St. Clair Papers* and St. Clair's own *Narrative, supra* note 1, as well as in the *Annals of Congress.*

7. Irving Brant, *James Madison, Father of the Constitution, 1787–1800,* at p. 367.

8. The first select committee consisted of seven Members; the second consisted of five Members, of whom four had served on the first.

9. See his *Narrative,* at pp. 172-73.
10. I.e., as part of the volume comprising his *Narrative.*
11. *Annals of Congress* (15th Cong., 1st Sess.), at pp. 831 and 842-866.
12. *Infra,* pp. 47-50.

CHAPTER III

1. *The Federalist,* No. 78; Charles Evans Hughes, *The Supreme Court of the United States* (1928), pp. 79, 84.
2. *Van Horne's Lessee* v. *Dorrance,* 2 Dallas 304, 308-09 (1795).
3. *Marbury* v. *Madison,* 1 Cranch 137, 175-76 (1803).
4. Examples include the proceedings in the House of Representatives against Randall and Whitney in 1795 and against John Anderson in 1818. See Ernest J. Eberling, *Congressional Investigations* (1928), pp. 37-42, and 66-85.
5. Such cases included the publication in 1800 of derogatory statements about the Senate as a whole in the *Aurora;* disclosure by the *New York Herald* in 1848 of provisions of the Mexican treaty discussed in a secret session of the Senate; and a charge of corruption against certain Representatives published in *The New York Times* in 1857. There also were contempt proceedings involving reporters for the *New York Evening Post* in 1870 and the *New York Tribune* in 1871.
6. See, e.g., the speech of Senator Charles C. Pinckney of South Carolina, quoted in Eberling, *op. cit. supra* at pp. 45-46 and reported in *Annals,* 6th Cong., 1st Sess., pp. 70-74.
7. *Anderson* v. *Dunn,* 6 Wheaton 204 (1821). This decision established the power of the House of Representatives to arrest and punish by imprisonment for (at pp. 224-25) "contempts committed against themselves," whether within or without the walls of the House. This power, it was stated (at pp. 230-31), must be exercised in accordance with the principle "the least possible power adequate to the end proposed." Likewise, the British rule that the imprisonment could in no event extend beyond the Commons' adjournment was declared (at p. 231) applicable to Congress.
   It has often been said that this case held that the legislature's determination that a punishable contempt had been committed is conclusive and not subject to judicial review. See, e.g., Eberling, *Congressional Investigations* (1928), pp. 209, 345, 353. There are superficial implications to this effect in the opinion (6 Wheaton at 234): ". . . there is nothing on the face of this record from which it can appear on what evidence this warrant was issued. And we are not to presume that the House of Representatives would have issued it without duly establishing the fact charged on the individual." However, Anderson had challenged the warrant on the ground of total lack of power in the House to punish contempts committed outside its presence, not the validity of the exercise of the power in the particular case (which,

from other sources, appears to have arisen out of Anderson's attempt to bribe a member). Carefully read, it is clear that the case holds only that the legislature's warrant will be *presumed* to be based on valid grounds unless those grounds are challenged, and does not hold that such a presumption is conclusive.

There appear to be no relevant judicial decisions in the United States prior to *Anderson* v. *Dunn*. It was followed, in a case where the Senate's power was in question, in *Ex parte Nugent*, Fed. Cas. No. 10,375 (C.C.D. Col. 1848). The powers of legislative investigating committees do not appear to have been directly dealt with in any American judicial decision before 1855.

8. That is to say, the question was laid to rest *judicially*. In Congress, there continued to arise, from time to time, strong opposition to the exercise of the investigative power. See, e.g., the remarks of Senator Sumner of Massachusetts in 1860, quoted in Eberling, *op. cit. supra*, pp. 163-64.

9. James Schouler, *History of the United States under the Constitution, 1783–1865*, Vol. III, p. 258 (Washington, 1880–91).

10. 4 Cong. Debates 872 (1827); Landis, *op. cit. supra* Chapt. I, footnote 6, at pp. 177-78.

11. Eberling, *op. cit. supra* note 4, pp. 298-300, and compare the British experience, *infra*, p. 288.

12. 1 Stat. 554, 3 May 1798, now 2 U.S.C.A. 191.

13. *Supra*, pp. 7-8. This restriction appears to have been uniformly observed by both House and Senate except in the case of Patrick Woods, who had assaulted a Representative in the city of Richmond, and who was (in 1868) imprisoned by the House for contempt for a period of three months beginning July 7. Woods served out his term even though the House adjourned July 15. Eberling, *op. cit. supra*, at pp. 180-84.

14. Eberling, *op. cit. supra*, pp. 150-54 and 302-318; 11 Stat. 155, 24 Jan. 1857, now 2 U.S.C.A. 192.

15. Eberling, *supra*, at pp. 424-431.

16. Ray W. Billington, *The Protestant Crusade* (1938), p. 289.

17. Billington, *supra*, at p. 387.

18. The resolution did not empower the committee to send for persons and papers.

19. Billington, *supra*, p. 414.

20. H. J. Desmond, *The Know-Nothing Party*, quoted in Whipple, *The Story of Civil Liberty in the United States* (1927), at p. 59.

21. Charles Hale, *A Review of the Proceedings of the Nunnery Committee of the Massachusetts Legislature; and especially their conduct . . . on Occasion of the Visit to the Catholic School in Roxbury* (Boston, 1855).

22. *The New York Times* for July 21 and August 25, 1954.

23. Augustine E. Costello, *Our Police Protectors—History of the New York Police* (1885).

24. James W. Gerard, *London and New York: Their Crime and Police* (N.Y. 1853), originally published in the *Journal of Commerce*, Feb. 1853.

25. Act of February 9, 1855.
26. Board of Councilmen Documents 1855, Doc. No. 45; Board of Aldermen Documents 1855, Doc. No. 20.
27. See the account of Poole's death and its aftermath in John Lardner, *The Martyrdom of Bill the Butcher*, in *The New Yorker* magazine for March 20 and 27, 1954.
28. *Briggs* v. *Mackellar*, 2 Abbott's Practice Reports 30 (N.Y. Com. Pl. 1855); Board of Councilmen Doc. No. 45, *supra*.
29. Doc. No. 45, *supra*, pp. 56-57 and 66.
30. Id. at pp. 63-64.
31. See his biography, *A Commoner's Judge*, by Harold Earl Hammond (Christopher, 1954), and the many references to Judge Daly in *The Diary of George Templeton Strong* (Macmillan, 1952).
32. *Briggs* v. *Mackellar*, *supra*, at pp. 56 *et seq.*
33. Curiously enough, Judge Daly seems to have been unaware of the precedent-making character of his decision, as his collected papers, on deposit in the New York Public Library, contain no reference to it.
34. Id. at p. 62.
35. Id. at pp. 68-69.
36. *Briggs* v. *Matsell*, 2 Abbott's Practice Reports 156 (N.Y. Com. Pl. 1855).
37. *In re Falvey*, 7 Wisconsin 630 (1858); *Burnham* v. *Morrissey*, 14 Gray 226 (Mass. 1859); *Sanborn* v. *Carleton*, 15 Gray 399 (Mass. 1860); *Wickelhausen* v. *Willett*, 10 Abbott's Practice 164 (N.Y. Superior Ct. 1860), affirmed *Wilckens* v. *Willett*, 1 Keyes 521 (N.Y. 1864); *Emery's Case*, 107 Mass. 172 (1871); *People* v. *Learned*, 5 Hun 626 (N.Y. Sup. Ct. 1875). In cases not involving investigations, the legislature's power to punish contempts was upheld in *State* v. *Matthews*, 37 N.H. 450 (1859), and *Ex Parte McCarthy*, 29 Cal. 395 (1866).
38. *Burnham* v. *Morrissey*, *supra*, at p. 238.
39. Eberling, *op. cit. supra*, pp. 175-209.
40. *Stewart* v. *Blaine*, 1 McArthur 453 (S. Ct. Dist. Col. 1874).
41. The record of *Irwin*'s case and Judge McArthur's opinion are set forth in the *Congressional Record*, 43rd Cong., 2d Sess., pp. 707-27. The Court of Claims also upheld the power of Congress "to require the personal attendance before its committees, as a witness or otherwise, of any citizen in the country" in *Lilley's Case*, 14 Ct. of Cls. 539 (1878).
42. Eberling, *op. cit. supra*, at pp. 210-26, 329-33, and 350-55.
43. *Supra*, p. 35.
44. Senate Misc. Doc. vol. xii, p. 552 (53rd Cong., 2d Sess.).
45. *Kilbourn* v. *Thompson*, 103 U.S. 168 (1880).
46. *Supra*, pp. 5-10.
47. E.g., Landis, *op. cit. supra* at pp. 159-64; Morgan, *Congressional Investigations and Judicial Review*, 37 *California Law Review* 556 (1949); Cousens, *The Purposes and Scope of Investigations under Legislative Authority*, 26 *Georgetown L. J.* 905 (1938).
48. *Supra*, pp. 31-32.

49. Indeed, Mr. Justice Miller quoted with approval from Judge Hoar's decision in *Burnham* v. *Morrissey, supra.* See *Kilbourn* v. *Thompson,* at p. 199, and *supra,* p. 44.
50. *Record,* 44th Cong., 1st Sess., pp. 2013, 2017.
51. *Kilbourn* v. *Thompson,* 103 U.S. at 195.
52. *In re Pacific Railway Commission,* 32 Fed. 241, 253 (Cir. Ct. N.D. Cal. 1887).
53. Dean Landis in his article on investigations contends (*op. cit. supra* at pp. 216-17) that the investigation could have been supported, as within Congress' legislative power, if viewed as a general inquiry into government policy in determining how and where to deposit its funds. This is reasonable enough in theory, but in fact no such general purpose appears to have been in mind; the remarks of Hoar and Kasson on the floor of the House indicate that it was indeed the single real estate pool and the Jay Cooke failure that piqued Congressional curiosity.
54. *Infra,* pp. 53-55.
55. Charles Fairman, *Mr. Justice Miller and the Supreme Court* (1939), p. 332.
56. *Supra,* p. 34.
57. *Supra,* p. 39.
58. The enforcement provisions of the Pacific Railway Commission Act were held unconstitutional on the ground that the federal courts could not be made to serve as a mere enforcement arm of an administrative body. *In re Pacific Railway Commission,* 32 Fed. 241 (Circuit Court for the Northern District of California, 1887). The opinion was written by Justice Field of the Supreme Court, who served as one of the three members of the Circuit Court. This part of his ruling was overruled by the *Brimson* case, *infra* note 59.
59. *Interstate Commerce Commission* v. *Brimson,* 154 U.S. 447 (1894). The opinion was written by Justice Harlan. Justice Field, who had written the *Pacific Railway* opinion, took no part in the *Brimson* decision. There was a dissenting opinion by Justice Brewer, in which Chief Justice Fuller and Justice H. E. Jackson concurred.
60. Federal Trade Commission Act, Sections 6 and 9, 15 USCA Sections 46 and 49.
61. *Interstate Commerce Commission* v. *Brimson,* 154 U.S. 447, 478 (1894).
62. *In re Chapman,* 166 U.S. 661 (1897).
63. *Harriman* v. *Interstate Commerce Commission,* 211 U.S. 407, 417 (1908).
64. *Marshall* v. *Gordon,* 243 U.S. 521, 541 (1917).
65. Chief Justice White quoted and adopted this phrasing from *Anderson* v. *Dunn, supra,* p. 33, note 7.
66. *Federal Trade Commission* v. *American Tobacco Co.,* 264 U.S. 298, 306 (1924).
67. *Ex parte Daugherty,* 299 Fed. 620 (Dist. Ct. Ohio 1924).
68. *McGrain* v. *Daugherty,* 273 U.S. 135 (1927).
69. *McGrain* v. *Daugherty, supra,* at pp. 173-74.
70. *Sinclair* v. *United States,* 279 U.S. 263 (1929).

CHAPTER IV

1. The principal state court decisions during the fifty years following the *Kilbourn* case include *People ex rel. McDonald* v. *Keeler*, 99 N.Y. 463, 2 N.E. 615 (1885); *Matter of Barnes*, 204 N.Y. 108, 97 N.E. 508 (1912); *In re Battelle*, 207 Cal. 227, 277 Pac. 725 (1929); *Greenfield* v. *Russel*, 292 Ill. 392, 127 N.E. 102 (1920); *Attorney General* v. *Brissenden*, 271 Mass. 172, 171 N.E. 82 (1930).
2. "The Army at Bay," in *The Reporter* for March 30, 1954, page 11.
3. *Infra*, pp. 97-135.
4. "Shall Senatorial Power Be Curbed," in the magazine section of *The New York Times*, March 21, 1954.
5. "This case [*Kilbourn* v. *Thompson*] will stand for all time as a bulwark against the invasion of the right of the citizen to protection in his private affairs against the unlimited scrutiny of investigation by a congressional committee." *In re Pacific Ry. Commission*, 32 Fed. 241, 253 (Circ. Ct. N.D. Cal. 1887).
6. "Neither branch of the legislative department . . . possesses, or can be invested with, a general power of making inquiry into the private affairs of the citizen." *Interstate Commerce Commission* v. *Brimson*, 154 U.S. 447, 478 (1894).
7. "The enormous scope of the power asserted for the commission . . . to . . . summon witnesses before it and require them to disclose any facts, no matter how private, no matter what their tendency to disgrace the person whose attendance has been compelled . . . no such unlimited command over the liberty of all citizens ever was given, so far as we know, in constitutional times, to any commission or court." *Harriman* v. *Interstate Commerce Commission*, 211 U.S. 407, 417-418 (1908).
   "Any one who respects the spirit as well as the letter of the Fourth Amendment would be loath to believe that Congress intended to authorize one of its subordinate agencies to sweep all our traditions into the fire . . . and to direct fishing expeditions into private papers . . . in the hope that something will turn up." *Federal Trade Commission* v. *American Tobacco Co.*, 264 U.S. 298, 305-06 (1924).
8. "The [contempt] power is therefore but a force implied to bring into existence the conditions to which constitutional limitations apply. It is a means to an end and not the end itself." *Marshall* v. *Gordon*, 243 U.S. 521, 541 (1917).
9. ". . . a witness rightfully may refuse to answer where the bounds of the [investigative] power are exceeded or the questions are not pertinent to the matter under inquiry." *McGrain* v. *Daugherty*, 273 U.S. 135, 176 (1927).
10. ". . . the power of inquiry . . . must be exerted with due regard for the rights of witnesses . . . few if any of the rights of the people guarded by

fundamental law are of greater importance to their happiness and safety than the right to be exempt from all unauthorized, arbitrary or unreasonable inquiries and disclosures in respect of their personal and private affairs." *Sinclair* v. *United States,* 279 U.S. 263, 291-92 (1929).

11. "It is true that the scope of the [contempt] power is narrow. No act is so punishable unless it is of a nature to obstruct the performance of the duties of the legislature. There may be lack of power, because, as in *Kilbourn* v. *Thompson* . . . there was no legislative duty to be performed; or because, as in *Marshall* v. *Gordon* . . . the act complained of is deemed not to be of a character to obstruct the legislative process. . . . The ground for . . . fears has . . . been effectively removed by the decisions of this court which hold that assertions of congressional privilege are subject to judicial review. . . ." *Jurney* v. *MacCracken,* 294 U.S. 125, 147-48, 150 (1935).
12. "The citizen, when interrogated about his private affairs, has a right before answering to know why the inquiry is made; and if the purpose disclosed is not a legitimate one, he may not be compelled to answer . . . The philosophy that constitutional limitations and legal restraints upon official action may be brushed aside upon the plea that good, perchance, may follow, finds no countenance in the American system of government." *Jones* v. *Securities Commission,* 298 U.S. 1, 26-27 (1936).
13. "An investigation instituted for the mere sake of investigation, or for political purposes, not connected with intended legislation, or with any of the other matters upon which the house could act, but merely intended to subject a party or body investigated to public animadversion, or to vindicate him or it from unjust aspersions, where the legislature had no power to put him or it on trial for the supposed offenses . . . would not, in our judgment, be a legislative proceeding, or give to either house jurisdiction to compel the attendance of witnesses or punish them for refusing to attend." *People ex rel. McDonald* v. *Keeler,* 99 N.Y. 463, 485 (1885).
14. ". . . a State legislature . . . cannot violate the constitutional rights of any institution or of any individual by conducting a public and judicial investigation of any charges made against such person or institution under the pretense or cloak of its power to investigate for the purpose of legislation." *Greenfield* v. *Russel,* 292 Ill. 392, 400 (1920).
15. 19 Illinois Law Review 452 (1925).
16. "Hands Off the Investigations," in the *New Republic* for May 21, 1924.
17. Landis, "Constitutional Limitations on the Congressional Power of Investigation," 40 *Harvard Law Review* 153 (1926); Potts, "Power of Legislative Bodies to Punish for Contempt," 74 *Univ. of Pennsylvania Law Review* 691, 780 (1926).
18. "Congressional Inquiries and the Constitution," by Howard Lee McBain, in *The New York Times* (Section IX, page 6) for March 11, 1928.
19. *Supra,* p. 51. See *Investigation of Fiscal and Monetary Conditions in the United States* under House Resolutions 429 and 504 (62nd Cong., 3d Sess.).
20. Winkler, *Morgan the Magnificent* (1930), at pp. 297-301; Corey, *The House of Morgan* (1930), at pp. 397-409.
21. *Investigation,* etc., *supra* note 19, at pp. 1061-62.
22. *Henry* v. *Henkel,* 235 U.S. 219 (1914).

23. There is a good summary of the Stock Exchange hearings and their significance in Charles and Mary Beard, *America in Midpassage* (1939), at pp. 158-91.

24. Hearings of the Senate Committee on Banking and Currency, 73 Cong. 1st Sess. (1933), *Stock Exchange Investigation*, pp. 148-49, 175, and 180.

25. *Pacific Refining Co.* v. *Ryan*, 293 U.S. 388 (Jan. 7, 1935; "hot oil" provisions of National Industrial Recovery Act of 1933, held unconstitutional; Justice Cardozo dissented); *Perry* v. *United States*, 294 U.S. 330 (Feb. 18, 1935; Joint Resolution of June 5, 1933 held unconstitutional insofar as it repudiated "gold clause" in government bonds); *Railroad Retirement Board* v. *Alton R.R. Co.*, 295 U.S. 330 (May 6, 1935; retirement provisions of Railroad Retirement Act of 1934, held unconstitutional; Chief Justice Hughes and Justices Brandeis, Stone and Cardozo dissented); *Schechter Corp.* v. *United States*, 295 U.S. 495 (May 27, 1935; National Industrial Recovery Act held unconstitutional; unanimous decision); *Louisville Joint Stock Land Bank* v. *Radford*, 295 U.S. 555 (May 27, 1935; Frazier-Lemke amendments to Bankruptcy Act held unconstitutional; unanimous decision); *United States* v. *Constantine*, 296 U.S. 287 (Dec. 9, 1935; special excise tax on liquor dealers violating state laws, held unconstitutional; Justices Brandeis, Stone and Cardozo dissented); *Hopkins Federal Savings & Loan Association* v. *Cleary*, 296 U. S. 315 (Dec. 9, 1935; certain provisions of Federal Home Owners' Loan Act of 1933, held unconstitutional; unanimous decision); *United States* v. *Butler*, 297 U.S. 1 (Jan. 6, 1936; "processing tax" provisions of Agricultural Adjustment Act of 1933 held unconstitutional; Justices Brandeis, Stone and Cardozo dissented); *Rickert Rice Mills* v. *Fontenot*, 297 U.S. 110 (Jan. 13, 1936; unconstitutionality of "processing tax" held not cured by 1935 amendment to AAA); *Carter* v. *Carter Coal Co.*, 298 U.S. 238 (May 18, 1936; Bituminous Coal Conservation Act of 1935 held unconstitutional; Chief Justice Hughes concurred in part, and Justices Brandeis, Stone and Cardozo dissented); *Ashton* v. *Cameron Country Water Improvement District*, 298 U.S. 513 (May 25, 1936; 1934 amendments to Bankruptcy Act held unconstitutional; Chief Justice Hughes and Justices Brandeis, Stone and Cardozo dissented).

26. *Jurney* v. *MacCracken*, 294 U.S. 125, 150 (1935).

27. Kenneth G. Crawford, *The Pressure Boys: The Inside Story of Lobbying in America* (1939), p. 112.

28. The precursors of the Dies Committee, and that Committee's activities from 1938 to 1944, are excellently described in August Raymond Ogden, *The Dies Committee* (Catholic University Press, 1945).

29. *Investigation of Communist Propaganda*, Report No. 2290, 71st Cong., 3rd Sess., pp. 67-99 quoted in Ogden, *op. cit. supra*, at pp. 28-29.

30. 78 Cong., Dec. 4934, March 20, 1934.

31. Ogden, *op. cit. supra*, at page 296.

32. The vote was 207 to 186, with 40 not voting. For the creation and history of the post-Dies, permanent committee see Robert K. Carr, *The House Committee on Un-American Activities, 1945–1950* (Cornell Univ. Press, 1952).

33. *Infra*, pp. 147-73.

34. *Infra,* pp. 148 *et seq.*
35. *Infra,* pp. 149 *et seq.*
36. Robert H. Jackson, *The Supreme Court and Judicial Review* (1941), at p. 321.
37. See, e.g., Collins, "The Power of Congressional Committees of Investigation to Obtain Information from the Executive Branch," 39 *Geo. L. J.* 563 (1951); Ehrmann, "The Duty of Disclosure in Parliamentary Investigation: A Comparative Study," 11 *Chi. L. Rev.* 1, 117 (1943); Herwitz and Mulligan, "The Legislative Investigating Committee," 33 *Col. L. Rev.* 1 (1933); Morgan, "Congressional Investigations and Judicial Review: Kilbourn & Thompson Revisited," 37 *Calif. L. Rev.* 556 (1949).
38. James A. Wechsler, *The Age of Suspicion* (1953), p. 279. The other quotations are from the chapters of this book (pp. 266-325) dealing with Mr. Wechsler's appearance before Senator McCarthy's subcommittee.
39. Wechsler, *op. cit. supra,* at pp. 290 and 304.
40. See his speech before the New York Chamber of Commerce on April 2, 1953, printed in the Chamber's *Monthly Bulletin* for April, 1953 at pp. 370-77. The same sentiments were expressed by Mr. McCloy on February 16, 1954, in his speech before the Chamber of Commerce of Greater Philadelphia.
41. See, e.g., Coudert, "Congressional Inquisition vs. Individual Liberty," 15 *Va. L. Rev.* 537 (1929).
42. Carr, *The House Committee on Un-American Activities* (1952), at p. 409.
43. Carr, *Democracy and the Supreme Court* (1936), at p. 124.
44. Nelson McGeary, *The Developments of Congressional Investigative Power* (Columbia Univ. Press, 1940), pp. 86-87: "The personal effacements which befell Messrs. Mitchell, Harriman, and Wiggin following the committee's disclosures served to demonstrate that the results of an investigation may extend beyond the enactment of legislation."
45. *Infra,* pp. 196-99.
46. *Infra,* pp. 241-42.
47. *Supra,* p. 35.
48. *Infra,* pp. 260-62.
49. *Tenney* v. *Brandhove,* 341 U.S. 367, 378 (1951).

CHAPTER V

1. *The Federalist* No. 47, February 1, 1788.
2. *People ex rel. McDonald* v. *Keeler*, 99 N.Y. 463, 2 N.E. 615 (1885). In *People* v. *Sharp*, 107 N.Y. 427, 14 N.E. 319 (1887) an investigation of the Broadway Surface Railway Co. was upheld.
3. *Attorney General* v. *Brissenden,* 271 Mass. 172, 171 N.E. 82 (1930). The

General Court of Massachusetts instructed the Attorney General to carry out the inquiry. Brissenden was an employee of Policeman Garrett's wife, who operated a milk distributing concern, and it was charged that exorbitant prices for milk embodied payments for "protection" of vice of various kinds.

4. *People* v. *Webb*, 5 N.Y. Supp. 855 (N.Y. Sup. Ct. 1889).
5. *John Alexander Dowie and the Christian Catholic Apostolic Church in Zion*, by Rolvix Harlan (1906).
6. *The Theocrat*, vol. 6, no. 11 (April 26, 1919); see also *Leaves of Healing*, vol. XLVI, p. 111 (May 8, 1920).
7. *Greenfield* v. *Russel*, 292 Ill. 392, 127 N.E. 102 (1920).
8. *People ex rel. McDonald* v. *Keeler*, 99 N.Y. 463, 2 N.E. 615 (1885).
9. As Judge Rapallo observed in the Keeler case, *supra*, at p. 487: "We are bound to presume that the action of the legislative body was with a legitimate object, if it is capable of being so construed . . ."
10. *New York Herald Tribune*, November 26, 1953, p. 34, col. 5.
11. Senator McCarthy defended the question on the ground that "we had 140,000 casualties because of the treason of sleazy characters like you."
12. *Opinion of the Justices*, 96 N.H. 530, 73 A.2d 433 (1950).
13. In his excellent article *Standards for Congressional Investigations*, in 3 N.Y. Bar Ass'n Record 75 (1948) at p. 99, Judge Charles E. Wyzanski has written: "Where the secret is a judicial secret such as the proceedings of a judicial conference preparatory to writing an opinion, it may be that there is a privilege belonging to the judiciary, but that has not been decided, and might turn on whether the investigations were with a view to legislation or to impeachment."
14. See *The New York Times* for June 2, 1953, and Fortas, "Outside the Law," 192 *Atlantic Monthly* 42 (August, 1953). Federal Judge Goodman appeared before the Committee, and read a letter signed by all seven of the federal district judges of California, containing the following: "The Constitution does not contemplate that such matters be reviewed by the legislative branch, but only by courts . . ."
15. *Totten, Administrator* v. *United States*, 92 U.S. 105 (1875).
16. *Appeal of Hartranft*, 85 Pa. 433 (1877). See also *Boske* v. *Commingore*, 177 U.S. 459 (1900); *United States* v. *Ragen*, 340 U.S. 462 (1951); *Ex parte Sackett*, 74 F. 2d 922 (9th Circ. 1935); *United States* v. *Smith*, 27 Fed. Cas. No. 16, 342 (C.C.D.N.Y. 1806); 25 Ops. Att'y. Gen. 326 (1905); 40 Ops. Att'y. Gen. 45 (1941). In *United States* v. *Keeney*, 111 Fed. Sup. 233 (C.C.D.C. 1953), Judge Holtzoff stated (at p. 235) that: "There is a well-recognized privilege in respect to certain official documents, as well as a privilege accorded to law enforcement officers to decline to reveal confidential sources of information."
17. *Opinion of the Justices*, 328 Mass. 655, 661, 102 N.E. 2d 79, 85, 86 (1951).
18. *Supra*, pp. 17-29.
19. The history of Congressional demands for executive papers is set forth at

length in Wolkinson, *Demands of Congressional Committees for Executive Papers*, in Vol. 10, *Federal Bar Association Journal*, pp. 103, 223, and 319 (1949).

20. The request came from the House, because it was necessary to implement the treaty with an appropriation which the House was called upon to approve.
21. Taft, *Our Chief Magistrate and His Powers* (1916), p. 129.
22. The majority and minority reports are in Senate Misc. Documents, vol. 7, 52nd Cong. 2nd Sess., at pp. 232-72.
23. Federal Register, Mar. 16, 1948.
24. *Supra*, pp. 23-24.
25. H. J. Res. 342, 80th Cong., 2nd Sess.; see 94 Cong. Rec. 2224, 2279 (March 5, 1948).
26. 94 Cong. Rec. 5708 (May 12, 1948).
27. "Constitutional Limitations on the Congressional Power of Investigation," 40 *Harv. Law Rev.* 153, 196.
28. Corwin, *The President, Office and Powers* (1941), pp. 281-82.
29. Collins, "The Power of Congressional Committees of Investigation to Obtain Information from the Executive Branch: The Argument for the Legislative Branch," 39 *Georgetown L. J.* 563, 580-81.
30. To be sure, the executive departments are not all alike, and some are more closely related to or dependent upon Congress than others. These differences arose in the very first year of constitutional government; in establishing the Treasury Department in 1789, it was stipulated (and this was not done in the contemporaneous statutes creating the State and War Departments and the offices of the Attorney General and Postmaster General) that the Secretary of the Treasury should "make report . . . in person or writing (as he may be required) respecting all matters referred to him by the Senate or House of Representatives . . . which shall appertain to his office. . . ." (1 Stat. 66; 5 U.S.C. Sec. 242). Alexander Hamilton, the first Secretary of the Treasury, called this provision to the attention of Washington's Cabinet during the consideration of the House of Representatives' demand for the St. Clair papers in 1792, but expressed the opinion that this did not require him "to produce all the papers they might call for" (*supra*, p. 23).

    The modern "independent" agencies embody legislative (insofar as they promulgate rules and regulations to carry out Congressional policies) and both executive and quasi-judicial (insofar as they pass on applications for broadcasting licenses, e.g., Federal Communications Commission, or adjudicate complaints of unfair trade practices, e.g., Federal Trade Commission, unfair labor practices, e.g., National Labor Relations Board, etc.) characteristics. But they are nonetheless part of the executive branch, and subject to the President's administration.

    There is an extensive "gray area" between legislative, executive, and judicial functions. Private bills, for example, are dispensations from the law to take care of "hard cases," executive-judicial in a sense because they are by nature individual rather than general, but traditionally reserved for action by the legislature. But if Congress should itself undertake to enter into treaties, issue orders to the Army, issue patents, or discharge other distinctively executive functions, surely these acts would be held invalid as outside the bounds of legislative power, and usurpations of executive functions.

31. Richardson's *Messages and Papers of the Presidents,* vol. 1, p. 412.
32. Hinds' *Precedents of the House of Representatives* (1907), vol. 3, p. 181.
33. For an argument in favor of unlimited Congressional access to executive information see Philip R. Collins, "The Power of Congressional Committees of Investigation to Obtain Information from the Executive Branch: The Argument for the Legislative Branch," in 39 *Georgetown Law Journal* 563 (1951). Mr. Collins argues that because the President has often complied with Congressional requests for information, the occasions on which he has refused are of no weight as precedents. This seems to mistake the nature of the issue. No one contends that the President is under no obligation to furnish information to Congress; the only question is whether he may refuse when, in his opinion, the public interest so requires.
34. Testimony of Col. Kenneth BeLieu, in Hearings of Special Subcommittee on Investigations (83rd Cong., 2nd Sess.), *Charges and Countercharges involving Secretary of the Army Stevens, Senator Joe McCarthy, et al.* (May 25, 1954), at pp. 1432-45.
35. S. Rept. 1400, 79th Cong., 2d Sess., May 31, 1946, and 92 Cong. Rec. 6441-47.
36. 92 Cong. Rec. 6555.
37. *The New York Times Magazine,* May 2, 1954, p. 66.
38. "Malmedy Massacre Investigation"—Hearings of a Subcommittee of the Senate Armed Services Committee (81st Cong. 1st Sess.) pursuant to S. Res. 42 (1949) p. 839. The conclusions of the subcommittee, composed of Senators Baldwin, Kefauver, and Hunt did not support these violent charges against the Army. See *Malmedy Massacre Investigation,* Report of the Subcommittee of the Armed Services Committee, 81st Cong., 1st Sess. (Oct. 13, 1949).
39. *America's Retreat from Victory,* Devin-Adair, 1951.
40. *Communist Infiltration in the Army,* Hearings of the Permanent Subcommittee on Investigations, 83rd Cong., 1st Sess., September 21 and 28, 1953, at pp. 85-86.
41. Id. at pp. 93-94.
42. Id. at p. 105.
43. *Infra,* pp. 266-270.
44. Martin Merson, *My Education in Government,* in *The Reporter* for October 7, 1954.
45. *Supra,* p. 102.
46. *Communist Infiltration in the Army,* Hearings of the Permanent Subcommittee on Investigations, 83d Cong., 2d Sess., pp. 134, 137, and 143.
47. Id. at pp. 146-52.
48. Id. at pp. 152-53.
49. *New York Herald Tribune,* February 19, 1954.
50. *The New York Times,* February 22, 1954.

51. *The New York Times,* February 22, 1954.
52. *Supra,* p. 59.
53. *The New York Times,* February 26, 1954.
54. *The New York Times,* March 4, 1954.
55. *The New York Times,* February 24, 1954.
56. *Army Signal Corps—Subversion and Espionage,* Hearings of the Permanent Subcommittee on Investigations, 83rd Cong., 2nd Sess. (March 11, 1954), pp. 443-470.
57. *Charges and Countercharges, supra* note 34. The record of the executive session at which the inquiry was voted is printed in the record of the inquiry, at pp. 1-26.
58. See 4 *World Liberalism* (Summer, 1954), p. 16.
59. *The New York Times,* May 5, 1954; *Charges and Countercharges, supra* note 34, at pp. 703-10.
60. Id. pp. 769-70.
61. Id. pp. 759-60; *The New York Times,* May 6, 1954.
62. See 18 U.S. Code Annotated Section 793 (d):
"Whoever, lawfully having possession of, access to, control over, or being entrusted with any document, writing, code book, signal book, sketch, photograph, photographic negative, blueprint, plan, map, model, instrument, appliance, or note relating to the national defense, or information relating to the national defense which information the possessor has reason to believe could be used to the injury of the United States or to the advantage of any foreign nation, willfully communicates, delivers, transmits or causes to be communicated, delivered, or transmitted or attempts to communicate, deliver, transmit or cause to be communicated, delivered or transmitted the same to any person not entitled to receive it, or willfully retains the same and fails to deliver it on demand to the officer or employee of the United States entitled to receive it; . . . Shall be fined not more than $10,000 or imprisoned not more than ten years or both."
63. In his dissenting opinion in *Schneiderman* v. *United States,* 320 U.S. 118, 181 (1943).
64. See 18 U.S. Code Annotated Section 793 (e):
"Whoever having unauthorized possession of, access to, or control over any document, writing, code book, signal book, sketch, photograph, photographic negative, blueprint, plan, map, model, instrument, appliance, or note relating to the national defense, or information relating to the national defense which information the possessor has reason to believe could be used to the injury of the United States or to the advantage of any foreign nation, willfully communicates, delivers, transmits or causes to be communicated, delivered, or transmitted, or attempts to communicate, deliver, transmit or cause to be communicated, delivered, or transmitted the same to any person not entitled to receive it, or willfully retains the same and fails to deliver it to the officer or employee of the United States entitled to receive it; . . . Shall be fined not more than $10,000 or imprisoned not more than ten years, or both."
65. *The New York Times,* May 18, 1954. The President's letter and the Attorney General's memorandum are printed in XIV *The Federal Bar Journal* at pp. 18-20, 73-86 (Jan.-Mar. 1954).

66. Subsequently the Army publicly declared, on the basis of long investigation, that Senator McCarthy had not obtained the document from any source within the Army.
67. *The New York Times,* December 3, 1954, p. 12, col. 5.

CHAPTER VI

1. *Supra,* pp. 95-96.
2. *The Federalist,* No. 81 (Hamilton).
3. Warren, *The Making of the Constitution* (1928), pp. 506-10, 769.
4. Warren, *New Light on the History of the Federal Judiciary Act of 1789,* 37 *Harvard Law Rev.* 49, 111-32 (1923).
5. *Schenck* v. *United States,* 249 U.S. 47 (1919).
6. *Gitlow* v. *New York,* 268 U.S. 652 (1925).
7. *Fiske* v. *Kansas,* 274 U.S. 380 (1927) (free speech); *Near* v. *Minnesota,* 283 U.S. 697 (1931) (free press).
8. *American Communications Association* v. *Douds,* 339 U.S. 382 (1950) and *Osman* v. *Douds,* 339 U.S. 846 (1950).
9. *Dennis* v. *United States,* 341 U.S. 494.
10. *Garner* v. *Los Angeles Board,* 341 U.S. 716 (1951); *Adler* v. *Board of Education,* 342 U.S. 485 (1952).
11. 3 Hinds' *Precedents* 87 (May 14, 1832); see also Landis, *op. cit. supra* in 40 *Harvard Law Review* 153, at pp. 179-80.
12. See also *United States* v. *Lovett,* 328 U.S. 303 (1946).
13. Driver, "Constitutional Limitations on the Power of Congress to Punish Contempts of its Investigating Committees," 38 *Virginia Law Review* 887, 888 (1952).
14. *Bulletin* of the American Association of University Professors, vol. 39, No. 1 (1953), p. 12.
15. H. Res. 298 (81st Cong., 1st Sess.), adopted August 12, 1949.
16. H. R. Rep't. No. 3024, 81st Cong., 2d Sess.
17. 96 Cong. Rec. 13883-93.
18. *Rumely* v. *United States,* 197 F. 2d 166 (C.A.D.C. 1952).
19. These were Justices Burton and Minton. In accordance with custom, the reasons for their non-participation were not announced, but it may be conjectured that Justice Burton withdrew because of a family connection with one of the prosecuting attorneys, and Justice Minton because, when a Senator, he had once investigated Rumely.
20. *United States* v. *Rumely,* 345 U.S. 41 (1953).
21. *Supra,* p. 61.
22. *Supra,* pp. 53-54.
23. Wilson, *Congressional Government* (1901), p. 303.

24. *Supra*, pp. 75-77.
25. *United States* v. *Josephson*, 165 F. 2d 82 (C.A. 2d, 1948).
26. *Barsky* v. *United States*, 167 F. 2d 241 (C.A.D.C. 1948).
27. *Lawson* v. *United States*, 176 F. 2d 49 (C.A.D.C. 1949). Lawson, Trumbo and eight others contested the Committee's power on substantially identical grounds.
28. *Lawson* v. *United States, supra*, at p. 52. This case was decided unanimously by two judges of the Court of Appeals for the District of Columbia (Clark and Wilbur K. Miller) and District Judge Sweeney, temporarily sitting with the Court of Appeals. Judge Clark had previously participated in the *Barsky* case, concurring with Judge Prettyman.
29. Circuit Judges Chase and Swan in the Second Circuit, Circuit Judges Prettyman, Bennett Champ Clark, Wilbur K. Miller, and District Judge George C. Sweeney, Chief Judge of the District Court of Massachusetts, designated to sit as a visiting judge in the "Hollywood Ten" case.
30. *In re Falvey*, 7 Wisconsin 630, 642 (1858).
31. *Dennis* v. *United States*, 341 U.S. 494, 501 (1951).
32. *United States* v. *Dennis*, 183 F. 2d 201, 212 (C.A. 2d 1950).
33. *Supra*, p. 137.
34. Judge Prettyman subsequently took pains to limit the *Barsky* decision to the specific and single danger of Communism. In his opinion reversing Rumely's conviction, he distinguished the *Barsky* case on the ground that: "In that case it was shown that the President and other responsible government officials had, with supporting evidentiary data, represented to the Congress that Communism and the Communists are, in the current world situation, potential threats to the security of this country. For that reason, and for that reason alone, we held that Congress had the power, and a duty, to inquire into Communism and the Communists." See *Rumely* v. *United States*, 197 f. 2d 166, 173.

    Judge Bazelon, dissenting in the *Rumely* case, thought that trousers to fit the "left" leg (Barsky) should also fit the "right" leg (Rumely).
35. See his dissenting opinion in *National Maritime Union of America* v. *Herzog*, 78 F. Supp. 146, 177-78 (D.D.C. 1948).
36. Charles P. Curtis, "Wringing the Bill of Rights," II *The Pacific Spectator*, at pp. 371-73 (1948).
37. *Supra*, pp. 81-82.
38. Whittaker Chambers, "What Is a Communist?" in *Look* magazine for July 28, 1953.
39. In Section 4(f).
40. *Permit Communist-Conspirators to be Teachers?* by Hamilton A. Long, H. Doc. 213, 83d Cong., 1st Sess. (1953).

40a. *The New York Times*, June 10, 1954.

41. *DeJonge* v. *Oregon*, 299 U.S. 353, 363 (1937).

41a. *The New York Times*, Oct. 1 and 2, 1954.

42. Wechsler, *The Age of Suspicion*, p. 279 (1953).
43. *Millar* v. *Taylor*, 4 Burr. 2303, 2379, 98 Eng. Rep. 201, 242 (1769).
44. Published in 4 *Harvard Law Review* 193 (1890).

45. See, e.g., *Pavesich* v. *New England Life Insurance Co.*, 122 Georgia 490, 50 S.E. 68 (1905).
46. *Entick* v. *Carrington*, 19 Howell's State Trials 1029 (Court of Common Pleas, 1765).
47. *Boyd* v. *United States*, 116 U.S. 616, 630-31 (1886).
48. *Olmstead* v. *United States*, 277 U.S. 438 (1928). Thereafter Congress passed the Communications Act of 1934, under Section 605 of which wire-tapped evidence cannot be used in court. *Nardone* v. *United States*, 302 U.S. 379 (1937).
49. Justices Holmes, Butler, and Stone also wrote dissenting opinions.
50. 17 Howard's State Trials 675 (N.Y. 1735).
51. Curtis, "Wringing the Bill of Rights," II *Pacific Spectator* at pp. 368-69: "The First Amendment says simply, 'Congress shall make no law . . . abridging the freedom of speech . . .' The Supreme Court, with all it has had to say on the subject, has never, I think, said that this included privacy of opinion. . . . We have a right to be secure in our persons, houses, papers, and effects against unreasonable searches and seizures. This is the Fourth Amendment. I do not believe this goes far enough to make our political opinions secure against interrogation. If so, surely it is another improvement upon what our forefathers bequeathed to us. We have the right to speak. Have we equally a right to choose when to speak? Perhaps we should have. Constitutionally we have not got it yet."
52. In the *Josephson* case, Judge Chase dismissed the contention that the First Amendment protects "privacy in speaking" as "a fallacy essentially based upon the idea that the Constitution protects timidity." 165 F. 2d at page 92.
53. *Supra*, pp. 136-37.
54. *Supra*, p. 49.
55. In the *American Tobacco* case in 1924, Justice Holmes expressly referred to the Fourth Amendment as limiting the investigative power of the Federal Trade Commission.
56. *Jones* v. *Securities Commission*, 298 U.S. 1, 28 (1936).
57. *Board of Education* v. *Barnette*, 319 U.S. 624, 642 (1943).
58. In principle, the same result had previously been reached in the Pennsylvania state courts, but since the investigating committee's subpoenas in the Pennsylvania cases were for documents rather than testimony, the courts relied on the Fourth rather than the First Amendment. The leading case is *Annenberg* v. *Roberts*, 333 Pa. 203, 2 A. 2d. 612 (1938), in which a dragnet subpoena was disallowed as an unreasonable search, abridging the "right of personal privacy as against unlimited and unreasonable legislative and other governmental investigations." In the earlier case of *Shelby* v. *Second National Bank*, 19 Pa. D. & C. 202 (1933), the judge based his decision on a "constitutional right of privacy," remarking that "The right to privacy in the conduct of one's personal and private affairs is a right derived from natural law."
59. Judge Prettyman, writing the opinion in the *Barsky* case, commented on but did not come to a conclusion on the scope of the First Amendment with respect to privacy and silence. See 167 F. 2d at pp. 249-50. But in the

Rumely case he came down strongly on the affirmative side, declaring that "the realistic effect of public embarrassment is a powerful interference with the free expression of views." See 197 F. 2d at p. 174.

60. See 167 F. 2d at p. 246, and *supra,* pp. 152-53.
61. *The New Yorker* magazine, May 29, 1954, p. 20.
62. Loyalty Certificate for Personnel of the Armed Forces, Form DD-98, approved 1 February 1954.
63. Chambers, "What Is a Communist?" in *Look* magazine for July 28, 1953, at page 31.
64. See 165 F. 2d at p. 99.
65. The decisions of the federal court of appeals in the District of Columbia have approached this idea of "laying a foundation" for Congressional inquiry, but have relied on *ex parte* statements to Congress in advance of the inquiry rather than evidence developed at the hearing itself. Furthermore, in at least one case the information relied on by the court was something less than compelling. See *Marshall* v. *United States,* 176 F. 2d 473, 475 (1949): "We agree . . . that the Committee had reasonable cause to investigate the Federation, this cause being in the nature of information given to it by Congressman Martin Dies on the floor of the House when he was Chairman of the predecessor to the present Un-American Activities Committee. Any reference to this and other speeches of Congressman Dies would readily convince any reasonable person that this Committee acted properly in conducting the investigation."
66. *Supra,* p. 54. The issue whether a particular question was *necessary* is also involved in the current proceedings involving Mr. Owen Lattimore, and was dealt with in Judge Edgerton's dissenting opinion in the Court of Appeals for the District of Columbia, June 8, 1954. *United States* v. *Lattimore,* 215 F. 2d 847.
67. Similarly, Congressional investigations are more likely to be sustained when they are close to the domain of federal power than when they appear to be delving into matters that are the proper concern of the state governments. This question is discussed in Chapter VIII, *infra.*
68. *Infra,* pp. 205-10.
69. *Supra,* pp. xv to xviii and 70-79.
70. *Supra,* pp. 38-45.
71. Syndicated column of April 23, 1954.
72. Resort to the courts to enjoin or otherwise control legislative investigative abuses has met with little success. See *Tenney* v. *Brandhove,* 341 U.S. 367 (1951).
73. De Tocqueville, *Democracy in America,* pp. 405-06.
74. Wyzanski, *Standards for Congressional Investigations,* 3 *N.Y. Bar Association Record* 93, 101-102 (1948).
75. *The New York Times,* May 26, 1954, p. 17, col. 6.
76. *Supra,* pp. 14-16.
77. Ehrmann, "The Duty of Disclosure in Parliamentary Investigation: A Comparative Study," 11 *Chicago Law Review* 1 (1943). This article was cited by Judge Wyzanski in support of the position taken in his own article.

78. See *Tenney* v. *Brandhove*, 341 U.S. 367, 381 (1951); *The New York Times*, March 16 and 17, 1951; *Editor & Publisher* for March 31, 1951.
79. American Civil Liberties Union Weekly Bulletin No. 1670, November 1, 1954.
80. *Supra*, pp. 3-4.
81. *Hudson County Water Co.* v. *McCarter*, 209 U.S. 349, 355 (1908).

CHAPTER VII

1. Hearings before the Permanent Subcommittee on Investigations of the Committee on Government Operations, U.S. Senate, 83d Cong., 1st Sess., pursuant to S. Res. 40 (*State Department Information Program—Information Centers*), part 1, pp. 84 *et seq.*
2. *Supra*, pp. 1-5.
3. *Annual Report of the Senate Permanent Subcommittee on Investigations*, Report No. 881, 83d Cong. 2d Sess., Jan 25, 1954.
4. Quoted with approval by Professor Sidney Hook in "The Fifth Amendment—A Moral Issue," in *The New York Times Magazine*, November 1, 1953.
5. Elmer Davis, *But We Were Born Free* (1954), p. 63.
6. Edward S. Corwin, "The Supreme Court's Construction of the Self-Incrimination Clause," 29 *Michigan Law Rev.* 1, in footnote 3 (1930).
7. The foregoing account of the origin of the privilege is based upon the accounts in Corwin, *op. cit. supra*; Wigmore, "Nemo Tenetur Seipsum Prodere," 5 *Harvard Law Rev.* 71 (1891); Thayer, " 'Law' and 'Fact' in Jury Trials," 4 *Harvard Law Rev.* 155 (1890); Thayer, "The Older Modes of Trial," 5 *Harvard Law Rev.* 45 (1891); 8 Wigmore, *Evidence* (3d ed. 1940), pp. 286-317. Wolfram, "John Lilburne: Democracy's Pillar of Fire," 3 *Syracuse Law Rev.* 215 (1952).
8. Pittman, "The Colonial and Constitutional History of the Privilege Against Self-Incrimination in America," 21 *Virginia Law Rev.* 763 (1935).
9. It also served to protect an accused's papers from compulsory disclosure.
10. Pittman, *op. cit. supra*, at pp. 283-88.
11. The others were Pennsylvania (September, 1776); Maryland (November, 1776); North Carolina (December, 1776); Vermont (1777); Massachusetts (1780); and New Hampshire (1784).
12. In these two states, the privilege is nevertheless taken as part of the common law.
13. Chandler, *American Criminal Trials*, vol. II, p. 168 (1844).
14. The other such provisions are trial only by presentment or indictment, no double jeopardy, and due process (Fifth); speedy and public trial, trial by jury, revelation of nature of charge, confrontation of accusers, right to summon witnesses, and right to counsel (Sixth); reasonable bail, and no cruel or unusual punishments (Eighth).

15. "No person shall be held to answer for a capital, or otherwise infamous crime, unless on a presentment or indictment of a Grand Jury. . . ." except in military service.

16. Following a similar reform in several of the states, in 1878 Congress enacted a statute (20 Stat. 30) providing that in criminal trials and courts-martial the accused "shall, at his own request, but not otherwise, be a competent witness."

17. *Supra,* pp. 8-10; Cushing, *Law and Practice of Legislative Assemblies,* Sec. 1011.

18. *Borough of Boston,* 1 Peckwell 437-38 (1802); *Sudbury* and *Southampton,* Barron & Austin's Election Cases 250-51, 384-85 (1842).

19. H. R. Report No. 481, 23d Cong., 1st Sess., Serial No. 263 (May 22, 1834). The majority wrote that "It is a humane rule to be found in criminal law, which declares that no man shall be compelled to criminate himself, and one which this committee would be unwilling under any circumstances to deny." The minority expressed the same view.

20. H. R. Rep. No. 194, 24th Cong., 2d Sess., Serial No. 307 (March 3, 1837); see also the subsequent reference to Jackson's invocation of the privilege in the *Congressional Record,* 45th Cong., 3d Sess., p. 2014 (Feb. 27, 1879).

21. *Briggs* v. *Mackellar, supra,* pp. 38-45. But the Wisconsin Supreme Court expressed itself to the contrary, relying on British Parliamentary practice. *In re Falvey,* 7 Wis. 630, 642 (1858). Judge Daly, on the contrary, cited in support of his view the British precedents of committees hearing contested election cases.

22. 2 Abbott's Practice Reports at p. 62.

23. *Emery's Case,* 107 Massachusetts 172 (1871). The same conclusion was reached in *People* v. *Sharp,* 107 N.Y. 427, 14 N.E. 319 (1887).

24. The court ruled that the British practice afforded no guide, because the privilege was guaranteed by the Constitution, saying (107 Mass. at 184):

    "But the rule of the common law did not control parliamentary inquiries, for the simple and obvious reason that the authority of parliament was more potent than the common law, and might change, annul or suspend its restrictions, as that body should determine. . . . It is because the Constitution of Massachusetts is more potent and above, not only the common law, but the legislature also; controlling all tribunals and all departments of the government alike, as well as all inhabitants of the Commonwealth; that this safeguard of individual rights cannot be suspended or invaded, either by general laws, or the special order of the legislative body, or of any of its branches."

25. Eberling, *Congressional Investigations* (1928), pp. 250-54.

26. *Emspak* v. *United States,* 203 F. 2d 54 (D.C. Cir. 1952). Two other cases, likewise involving the Fifth Amendment, are also pending before the Supreme Court and will be reargued at the same time, pursuant to the Court's order of June 7, 1954. These are *Bart* v. *United States,* 203 F. 2d 45 and *Quinn* v. *United States,* 203 F. 2d 20 (both D.C. Cir. 1952).

27. See, e.g., *United States* v. *Doto,* 205 F. 2d 416 (C.A. 2, 1953); *Aiuppa* v. *United States,* 201 F. 2d 287 (C.A. 6, 1952). The Supreme Court, by a

series of decisions beginning in 1886, has held the privilege applicable to civil suits and grand jury proceedings, and has said that the privilege applies "wherever the answer might tend to subject to criminal responsibility him who gives it." See *McCarthy* v. *Arndstein*, 266 U.S. 34 (1924); *Counselman* v. *Hitchcock*, 142 U.S. 547 (1892); *Boyd* v. *United States*, 116 U.S. 616 (1886). In *United States* v. *Bryan*, 339 U.S. 323, at 335-38 and 346-47 (1950), the availability of the privilege to witnesses before Congressional committees was assumed.

28. *Blau* v. *United States*, 340 U.S. 159, 161 (1950).
29. 3 Hinds, *Precedents of the House of Representatives* (1907), p. 188; VII Richardson, *Messages and Papers of the Presidents*, p. 362.
30. *The New York Times*, May 4, 1876.
31. Justice Byles, in *Bartlett* v. *Lewis*, 12 C.B. (N.S.) 249, 265 (1865).
32. Fortas, "The Fifth Amendment," 25 *Cleveland Bar Association Journal* 91 (April, 1954) in which, despite the quoted phrase, Mr. Fortas defends the policy underlying the privilege.
33. Hook, "The Fifth Amendment—A Moral Issue," in *The New York Times Magazine*, November 1, 1953.
34. See Professor Wigmore's excellent analysis in volume 8 of his *Evidence*, at pp. 307-08.
35. *Annual Report* of the Permanent Subcommittee on Investigations, 83d Cong., 2d Sess., Rept. No. 881 (January 25, 1954).
36. See, e.g., *Interlocking Subversion in Government Departments*, Report of the Internal Security Subcommittee of the Senate Judiciary Committee, 83d Cong., 1st Sess. (1953).
37. *Rogers* v. *United States*, 340 U.S. 367, 373 (1951).
38. *Foster* v. *People*, 18 Michigan 266, 276 (1869). See also *East* v. *Chapman*, M. & M. 46 (1827), wherein Lord Chief Justice Abbott said to a witness: "You might have refused to answer at all; but having partially answered, you are now bound to give the whole truth."
39. *Rogers* v. *United States*, *supra*, at p. 378. This case dealt with testimony before a grand jury, but the principles are equally applicable to legislative committees.
40. See, e.g., *Army Signal Corps—Subversion and Espionage*, Hearings of the Permanent Subcommittee on Investigations, 83d Cong., 1st Sess., pp. 138, 249, 302.
41. Hearings, *supra*, at pp. 42-43.
42. See, e.g., Redlich and Frantz, "Does Silence Mean Guilt?" in *The Nation* (June 6, 1953) at p. 475: ". . . he may simply disapprove of the investigation itself and the methods by which it is conducted so strongly that he feels he cannot conscientiously give it any more cooperation than the bare minimum legally demanded of him."
43. *Emery's Case*, 107 Mass. 172, 184 (1871).
44. *School* v. *Bell*, 125 Kentucky 750, 102 S.W. 248 (1907).
45. *New York Herald Tribune*, Oct. 26, 1953, p. 14, cols. 3-5.
46. However, if a truthful answer would disclose the basis for a perjury charge based on testimony given on a prior occasion, the privilege may be claimed.

47. Printed in *The Harvard Law School Record,* March 25, 1954.
48. Public Law 831, 81st Cong., "Internal Security Act of 1950," Sec. 4(a). Violations are punishable by ten years' imprisonment or $10,000 fine. The constitutionality of this vague and sweeping criminal statute is dubious at best. To the best of my knowledge, there have as yet been no prosecutions instituted under its provisions.

48a. *Infra,* pp. 280-81.
49. *Supra,* p. 64.
50. Quoted in Westin, "Do Silent Witnesses Defend Civil Liberties?" in *Commentary* for June 1953, p. 541.
51. See, e.g., Redlich and Frantz, "Does Silence Mean Guilt?" in *The Nation* for June 6, 1953, pp. 473-74.
52. *Rogers* v. *United States,* 340 U.S. 367, 371 (1951).
53. Quoted in Westin, *supra* note 50, at p. 543.
54. *Ex parte Irvine,* 74 Fed. 954 (C.C. Ohio 1896); see also *United States* v. *St. Pierre,* 128 F. 2d 979 (C. A. 2d 1942).
55. *Infra,* pp. 210-15.
56. *Supra,* pp. 1-5. A similar course of action was followed by Mr. Irving Goldman, an instructor at Sarah Lawrence College, appearing before the Jenner Committee in April, 1953.
57. It is strenuously argued in Mr. Westin's article in *Commentary, supra* note 50, that witnesses before Congressional committees should always reveal the past associations of others. It seems to me that this analysis totally overlooks the question of the legal authority of the committees, and is further deficient in that it is concentrated entirely on present or former membership in the Communist Party, when actually the questions put by the committees often involve much less questionable associations and many matters of sheer opinion.
58. It should be noted that there is no problem of "waiver" when it is the committee's authority, rather than a personal privilege such as that against self-accusation, which is in question. In other words, a witness may voluntarily answer some questions which he believes the committee has no authority to demand answers to, and then decline to answer other unauthorized questions. See *Bowers* v. *United States,* 202 F. 2d 447, 452 (D.C. Cir. 1953).
59. As reported in the *New York Post* for May 4, 1954, covering Judge Rifkind's address that day, before the Philadelphia Chapter of the American Jewish Committee.
60. See the series of articles on Howe & Hummel in *The New Yorker,* November 23 and 30 and December 7 and 14, 1946.
61. *Matter of Kaffenburgh,* 188 N.Y. 49, 80 N.E. 570 (1907). Kaffenburgh was, however, disbarred for continuing to practice under the name Howe & Hummel, although Howe was dead and Hummel disbarred.
62. *Matter of Grae,* 282 N.Y. 428, 26 N.E. 2d 963 (1940).

62a. *The New York Times,* September 4, 1954.
63. UAW-CIO press release dated May 2, 1954, reported in *The New York Times* on that date.

64. *Supra*, p. 9.
65. *Supra*, p. 35.
66. *Congressional Globe*, 34th Cong., 3d Sess., p. 433.
67. *Congressional Globe*, 37th Cong., 2d Sess., pp. 364, 428-31.
68. In a recent decision, the Supreme Court has held that this provision bars the use of the evidence in state as well as federal courts. *Adams* v. *Maryland*, decided March 8, 1954.
69. *Counselman* v. *Hitchcock*, 142 U.S. 547, 585 (1892). The same result had earlier been reached in *Emery's Case*, discussed above, pp. 194 and 202.
70. *Brown* v. *Walker*, 161 U.S. 591 (1896).
71. *United States* v. *Monia*, 317 U.S. 424 (1943), wherein the administrative immunity statutes are tabulated.
72. None, that is, since 1876, when the House passed a bill substantially re-enacting the 1857 immunity provision. This bill died in the Senate, when the bad experience with the 1857 Statute was recalled. See Eberling, *Congressional Investigations* (1928), at pp. 336-39.
73. S. 16, 83d Cong., 1st Sess. (January 7, 1953). Senator McCarran had introduced a comparable bill in the 82nd Congress on May 31, 1951 (S. 1570), which was reported favorably by the Committee on the Judiciary, but died on the Senate floor.
74. The debate on and passage of the bill are reported in 99 *Congressional Record* 8646-63 (July 9, 1953). It has been held that, in the absence of a statute of this type, legislative committees do not have the power to grant immunity from prosecution. *Doyle* v. *Hofstader*, 257 N.Y. 744, 177 N.E. 489 (1931).
75. This provision had been suggested in my letter to Senator Harley Kilgore of May 11, 1953, printed in 99 *Congressional Record* 8650 (July 9, 1953).
76. It passed without a record vote, but Senators Magnuson, Kerr, McClellan, Lehman, Jackson, Stennis, Hennings, Murray, Cooper and Hayden asked to be recorded as opposed.
77. Public Law 600, 83d Cong., 2d Sess. The Senate concurred in the House amendments, so that the bill never went to conference.
78. The statute also includes separate provisions for granting immunity to witnesses in grand jury and court proceedings, the merits of which lie outside the scope of this book.
79. The problem is discussed in Berman and Hoffman, "Lawmakers as Judges," in *The Reporter*, February 17, 1953 and King, "Immunity for Witnesses," in 40 *American Bar Association Journal* 377 (May, 1954).
80. If necessary, Congress could delegate the immunity power to trustworthy committees dealing with matters affecting the national security, such as the Joint Committee on Atomic Energy, but as yet there appears to be no urgent necessity for such action.
81. Under S. 16 as amended and passed by the Senate, the proposed grant would be authorized if the committee and the Attorney General agree that it should be made; if the Attorney General disagrees, the proposal would go to the House or Senate. This would interject the Attorney General directly into the legislative process, in a manner analogous to the President's veto. Pressures and frictions would inevitably arise which seem unnecessary and

which could be mitigated by restricting the Attorney General's role to the traditional one of advice in legislative matters.

82. *The New York Times*, September 14, 1954.
83. See, e.g., *Interlocking Subversion in Government Departments*, Report of the Internal Security Subcommittee of the Senate, 83d Cong., 1st Sess. (July 30, 1953), at pp. 45-46.

CHAPTER VIII

1. *Supra*, pp. 103-04.
2. Extracts from Governor Byrnes' telegram to the Velde Committee were printed in *The New York Times* for November 12, 1953.
3. Governor Byrnes' view was anticipated in 1951 by Governor Fuller Warren of Florida, who rejected a subpoena of the Kefauver crime investigating committee, on the ground that it threatened state sovereignty.
4. See, e.g., *Hammer* v. *Dagenhart*, 247 U.S. 251 (1918), and other cases cited *supra* Chapter IV, note 25.
5. In fact it was an even two-to-two division, but under the Australian system, in these circumstances, the vote of the Chief Justice determines the outcome.
6. *Attorney General for the Commonwealth of Australia* v. *The Colonial Sugar Refining Co.* [1914] A.C. 237 (P.C. 1913).
7. Wyzanski, "Standards for Congressional Investigations," 3 *N.Y. Bar Association Record* 93, 96 (1948).
8. *Supra*, p. 3.
9. The same is true of the argument sometimes advanced that the legislative investigative power is unbounded because it may be used to inquire into the desirability of constitutional amendments. This argument is self-defeating, for it would apply to state as well as federal inquiries, and would enable federal and state investigating committees to roam at will and uninhibited through each other's pastures. This argument was advanced and explicitly rejected in the *Colonial Sugar* case, *supra* note 6.
10. The idea is by no means fanciful. A California statute requires everyone claiming certain exemptions from state taxes to file a statement under oath denying that he advocates the violent overthrow of government.
11. *United States* v. *Owlett*, 15 Fed. Supp. 736 (M.D. Pa. 1936).
12. In *United States* v. *DiCarlo*, 102 Fed. Supp. 597, 601 (N.D. Ohio 1952) the court stated that Congress cannot investigate matters lying exclusively within the reserved powers of the states "except as they may affect matters within the scope of the powers granted to the federal government."
13. *The New York Times*, May 19, 1953.
14. *Adler* v. *Board of Education*, 342 U.S. 485 (1952).
15. *United States* v. *Cohen Grocery Co.*, 255 U.S. 81 (1921).

16. The Fifth Amendment, applicable only to the federal government, provides that "No person shall . . . be deprived of life, liberty, or property without due process of law." The Fourteenth Amendment extended this limitation to the states.
17. *Lanzetta* v. *New Jersey,* 306 U.S. 451 (1939); see also *Herndon* v. *Lowry,* 301 U.S. 242 (1937).
18. *Musser* v. *Utah,* 333 U.S. 95 (1948), wherein the case was remanded to the Utah courts to see whether a more specific meaning could be spelled out of the statute.
19. *Lanzetta* v. *New Jersey, supra* at p. 453; see also *Kraus & Bros.* v. *United States,* 327 U.S. 614 (1946).
20. *Supra,* pp. 147-59.
21. *Supra,* pp. 72-73. It is presently embodied in the Legislative Reorganization Act of 1946, Sec. 121(b)(1)(q), 60 Stat. 828 (1946).
22. The majority of the court that decided the *Josephson* case held that Josephson could not raise the issue of vagueness, since he had declined to answer any questions at all, and it could not be determined that no questions whatever would have been pertinent.
23. *United States* v. *Josephson,* 165 F. 2d 82, at 96.
24. *Barsky* v. *United States,* 167 F. 2d 241, at 261-63.
25. See Potts, "Power of Legislative Bodies to Punish for Contempt," 74 *U. of Penn. Law Rev.* 691, at 716 (1926).
26. 60 Stat. 814 (1946).
27. *State* v. *James,* 36 Wash. 2d 882, 221 Pac. 2d 482 (1950).
28. *Infra,* pp. 258-59.
29. *Bowers* v. *United States,* 202 F. 2d 447 (D.C. Cir. 1953); *United States* v. *Barry,* 29 F. 2d 817 (2d Cir. 1928), reversed on other grounds, 279 U.S. 597 (1929); *United States* v. *DiCarlo,* 102 F. Supp. 597 (N.D. Ohio 1952); *United States* v. *Seymour,* 50 F. 2d 930 (D. Neb. 1931); *In re Battelle,* 207 Cal. 227, 277 Pac. 725 (1929); *People* v. *Foster,* 236 N.Y. 610, 142 N.E. 304 (1923); *Matter of Barnes,* 204 N.Y. 108, 97 N.E. 508 (1912); *Shelby* v. *Second Nat. Bank,* 19 Pa. D. & C. 202 (1933).
30. *Bowers* v. *United States,* 202 F. 2d 447, 452 (1953); see also the opinion of the Court of Appeals for the District of Columbia in the *Lattimore* case, issued June 8, 1954, 215 F. 2d 847.
31. *Supra,* pp. 53-54 and 140-47.
32. See Carr, *The House Committee on Un-American Activities* (1952), p. 301.
33. Mr. Braverman was subsequently called as a witness, and declined to answer questions, basing his refusal on the attorney-client privilege and the First and Fifth Amendments.
34. Parliamentary Debates 1828, vol. 18, col. 968.
35. *Jurney* v. *MacCracken,* 294 U.S. 125, 144 (1935), wherein Justice Brandeis expressly stated that "the claim of privilege hereinafter referred to is no longer an issue."
36. Eberling, *Congressional Investigations* (1928), pp. 349-50. This episode involved the Credit Mobilier frauds. Mr. Joseph B. Stewart, an attorney,

declined to answer questions which he claimed related to confidential communications from his client, and was committed for contempt. The ensuing litigation was inconclusive upon the point of privilege. *Stewart* v. *Blaine*, 1 MacArthur 453 (D.C. 1874).

37. See *In re Falvey*, 7 Wis. 630, 642 (1858). *Cf.* also *Ex parte Parker*, 74 S.C. 466, 55 S.E. 122 (1906); *Sullivan* v. *Hill*, 73 W. Va. 49, 55, 79 S.E. 670, 672 (1913).

38. *Powell* v. *Alabama*, 287 U.S. 45 (1932).

39. See, e.g., *Ex parte Chin Loy You*, 223 Fed. 833 (D. Mass. 1915).

40. See, e.g., *Glasser* v. *United States*, 315 U.S. 60 (1942).

41. *Coplon* v. *United States*, 191 F. 2d 749, 757 (D.C. Cir. 1951).

42. *United States* v. *Louisville & Nashville R.R. Co.*, 236 U.S. 318, 336 (1915); see also *Connecticut Mutual Life Insurance Co.* v. *Schaefer*, 94 U.S. 457 (1876); *Securities & Exchange Commission* v. *Harrison*, 80 Fed. Supp. 226 (D.C. D.C. 1948); *International Ry. Co.* v. *Mahoney*, 271 App. Div. 283, 64 N.Y. Supp. 2d 854 (1946).

CHAPTER IX

1. *Special Senate Investigation of Charges and Countercharges*, etc., Hearings of the Special Subcommittee on Investigations pursuant to S. Res. 189, 83d Cong., 2d Sess., p. 29 (April 22, 1954).

2. *Barry* v. *Cunningham*, 279 U.S. 597, 613 (1929); *Walker* v. *Baker*, 145 Tex. 121, 196 S.W. 2nd 324 (1946); Wrisley Brown, *The Impeachment of the Federal Judiciary*, 26 *Harv. L. Rev.* 684 (1913).

3. *Supra*, p. 7, Note 8. The last impeachment in Britain was that of Lord Melville in 1806; an unsuccessful effort to impeach Lord Palmerston was made in 1848.

4. *Trial of Andrew Johnson* (G.P.O. 1868), vol. I, pp. 11-12.

5. *People ex rel. McDonald* v. *Keeler*, 99 N.Y. 463, 2 N.E. 615 (1885); *In re Falvey*, 7 Wis. 630 (1858).

6. See St. Clair, *A Narrative of the Manner in Which the Campaign Against the Indians Was Conducted in the Year 1791 Under the Command of Major General St. Clair* (Phila. 1812). For other examples, see H. R. Rep. No. 460, 22d Cong., 1st Sess. 153, 292 (1832); H. R. Rep. No. 502, 22d Cong., 1st Sess. 48-49 (1832); Sen. Rep. No. 205, 36th Cong., 1st Sess. 39 (1860).

7. *Hearings Before Select Committee on Investigation of Attorney General* under S. Res. 157, 68th Cong., 1st Sess. (1924), pp. 6 and 233.

8. Frankfurter, "Hands Off the Investigations," 38 *New Republic* 329, 331 (May 21, 1924).

9. *United States* v. *Orman*, 207 F. 2d 148, 158 (C.A. 3d, 1953).

10. The hearings were held in secret, and the testimony was "censored" by military experts prior to its release to the press.
11. In *In re Leach*, 197 App. Div. 702, 189 N.Y. Supp. 52 (1st Dept. 1921) it was held that a legislative committee has no power to take testimony *in camera*. This ground of the decision, however, was not affirmed by the Court of Appeals, 232 N.Y. 600, 134 N.E. 588 (1922), and there is, to the best of my knowledge, no other judicial support for such a restriction.
12. *Annual Report* (83d Cong., 2d Sess., Report No. 885, of January 25, 1954), states (at p. 10) that 215 witnesses gave 5,671 pages of public testimony, while 331 witnesses gave 8,969 pages of testimony in executive session.
13. *Supra*, pp. 159-73.
14. *The New York Times*, February 20, 1954.
15. See the press accounts of the "executive" hearings of the Senate Permanent Investigating Subcommittee concerning alleged espionage at Fort Monmouth, N.J., and at the General Electric Co.'s plants, reported in *The New York Times*, e.g., on October 17, 18, 21, 24, 28 and 31, and November 7, 13, 14, 17 and 19, 1953.
16. See, e.g., Thurman Arnold, "Trial by Television," 187 *Atlantic Monthly* 68 (June, 1951).
17. Much of this subsection is based on my article entitled "The Issue Is Not TV, but Fair Play," in *The New York Times Magazine*, April 15, 1951, page 12.
18. See Gen. Sarnoff's article in *Radio Age* for October, 1954, at p. 32, and Dr. Stanton's *CBS Editorial*, August 26, 1954.
19. *United States* v. *Kleinman*, 107 F. Supp. 407, 408 (D.D.C. 1952).
20. *The New York Times*, June 19, 1954, p. 7.
21. Wyzanski, "Standards for Congressional Investigations," 3 *N.Y. Bar Association Record* 93, 106-08 (1948).
22. Published in 192 *Atlantic Monthly* 42 (August, 1953).
23. Indeed, Congressman Frelinghuysen, in announcing his proposed investigative reforms on November 21, 1953, declared that he wished to develop "a code outlining the rights of witnesses and assuring them protections similar to those they would receive in a court of law."
24. Keating, "Code for Congressional Inquiries," *The New York Times Magazine* for April 5, 1953, at page 10. See also his proposal to amend the House rules, embodied in H. Res. 29, 83d Cong., 1st Sess. (1953).
25. Hearings before the Senate Committee on Interstate Commerce on S. Res. 71 (Railroad Financing), 74th Cong., 1st Sess. (March, 1935).
26. *Supra*, pp. 232-33.
27. *Supra*, pp. 38-45.
28. *United States* v. *Murdock*, 290 U.S. 389, 397 (1933); see also *Eisler* v. *United States*, 170 F. 2d 273, 280 (D.C. Cir. 1948): "A person summoned to appear before a Congressional committee may refuse to answer questions and submit to a court the correctness of his judgment in doing so, but a mistake of law is no defense, for he is bound to rightly construe the statute involved."

29. No doubt this is one reason so many witnesses have pleaded the privilege against self-incrimination.
30. *Ex parte Young*, 109 U.S. 123 (1908); see Frankfurter, "The Federal Courts," 58 *New Republic* 273 (April 24, 1929).
31. *United States* v. *Owlett*, 15 F. Supp. 736 (M.D. Pa. 1936); *Annenberg* v. *Roberts*, 333 Pa. 203, 2 A. 2d 612 (1938); *Shelby* v. *Second Nat. Bank*, 19 Pa. D. & C. 202 (1933); cf. *Brown* v. *Brancato*, 321 Pa. 54, 61, 184 Atl. 89, 92 (1936). The same has been held, and injunctions issued, when the legislative investigative power was exercised through an executive agency. *FTC* v. *Claire Furnace Co.*, 285 Fed. 936 (D.C. Cir. 1923); *Attorney General for the Commonwealth of Australia* v. *The Colonial Sugar Refining Co.*, [1914] A.C. 237 (P.C. 1913). And injunctions have been granted to restrain a witness from responding to committee process. *Strawn* v. *Western Union Tel. Co.*, 3 U.S.L. Week 646 (D.C. March 11, 1936); *cf. United States* v. *Groves*, 18 F. Supp. 3 (W.D. Pa. 1937).
32. Such were the circumstances in *United States* v. *Owlett*, 15 F. Supp. 736 (M.D. Pa. 1936).
33. *Hearst* v. *Black*, 87 F. 2d 68 (D.C. Cir. 1936); *cf. Tenney* v. *Brandhove*, 341 U.S. 367 (1951); *Myers* v. *Bethlehem Shipbuilding Corp.*, 303 U.S. 41 (1938). In some New York State investigatory proceedings the witness may move to quash the subpoena. *Carlisle* v. *Bennett*, 268 N.Y. 212, 197 N.E. 220 (1935). Such an action was recently but unsuccessfully attempted in a federal district court in San Francisco. *The New York Times*, Nov. 28, 1953, p. 9, col. 4.
34. The process was held unconstitutional, on the ground that judicial functions were not involved, in *In re Pacific Ry. Comm'n*, 32 Fed. 241 (C.C.N.D. Cal. 1887), but was upheld, on the ground that the court would review the agency's legal authority to obtain the information, in *ICC* v. *Brimson*, 154 U.S. 447 (1894). Such proceedings were involved in the *Harriman, American Tobacco,* and *Jones* cases, *supra* Chapter IV, notes 7 and 12.
35. In the absence of express authorization, Congressional committees have no power to institute legal proceedings. *Reed* v. *County Commissioners*, 277 U.S. 376 (1928); *cf. Ex parte Frankfeld*, 32 F. Supp. 915 (D.D.C. 1940); *In re Davis*, 58 Kan. 368, 49 Pac. 160 (1897).
36. H. J. Res. 237, 68th Cong., 1st Sess., 43 Stat. 461-62 (1924), to investigate land grants to the Northern Pacific Railroad; H. J. Res. 103, 61st Cong., 2d Sess., 36 Stat. 871-72 (1910), to investigate the Departments of Interior and Agriculture.
37. See his speech of May 15, 1953, before the Cornell Law Association. The enormous expansion of this type of litigation underlines the desirability of the change; from 1857 to 1949 there were 113 prosecutions under the criminal statute; from 1950 to June, 1952 there were 117. See *Quinn* v. *United States*, 203 F. 2d 20, 37 n. 100 (D.C. Cir. 1952). Substantially the same proposal as the one advanced in the text above and by Congressman Keating, was made in 1930 by John T. Flynn in his article "Senate Inquisitors and Private Rights," 161 *Harper's* 357 (Aug. 1930); see also King, "Immunity for Witnesses," in 40 *A.B.A. Journal* 377, 379-80 (1954).

Judge Wyzanski has opposed this or "any other broadening of judicial review" as "ill-advised." See Wyzanski, "Standards for Congressional Investigations," 3 *N.Y. Bar Ass'n Record* 93 (1948). His principal objection is that "a witness in a trial court is not allowed thus to interrupt the progress of a case by appealing a ruling on evidence or procedure." But a legislative investigation is not a trial court, is not empowered to decide "cases," and has no appellate superstructure. The critical difference is that a witness in court who objects to a question does get an immediate judicial (though not appellate) determination of his rights. And if the witness thereafter is recalcitrant, the judge's sentence for contempt is primarily intended to induce the witness to purge himself by answering, whereas the criminal proceeding under the 1857 statute has no such effect. With all respect, I think that Judge Wyzanski's objections are unconvincing.

CHAPTER X

1. *The New York Times,* July 20, 1954.
2. *Supra,* p. 177.
3. *Supra,* pp. 175-77.
4. *Supra,* pp. 114-15.
5. See *Fort Monmouth Security Investigations* (April 25, 1954), published by the Committee on Loyalty and Security of the Federation of American Scientists; Phelps and Pollard, "Fort Monmouth," 190 *Scientific American* 29 (June, 1954).
6. *Army Signal Corps—Subversion and Espionage,* Hearings of the Permanent Subcommittee on Investigations, 83d Cong., 1st Sess., pp. 40-42, 304-06.
7. See the articles cited *supra,* note 5, as well as the newspaper articles by Peter Kihss, Walter Millis and Murray Marder, printed respectively in *The New York Times* (January 11-January 13, 1954), the *New York Herald Tribune* (December 8 and December 15, 1953) and the *Washington Post* (November 9-November 12, 1953).
8. Phelps and Pollard, *supra,* at p. 31.
9. *Ibid.*
10. See Mr. Woltman's articles in the *New York World-Telegram and Sun* (July 12-16, 1954), and the editorial in *Life* magazine for July 26, 1954, at p. 20; Mr. Martin Merson's article "My Education in Government" in *The Reporter* for October 7, 1954; *The New York Times* for October 31 and November 2, 1954.
11. See *V-2,* by Walter Dornberger (Viking Press, N.Y. 1954).
12. Id. at pp. 201-03.
13. Id. at pp. 204-05.
14. *Organization and Administration of the Military Research and Development Programs,* 24th Intermediate Report of the House Committee on Government Operations, H. Rept. No. 2618, 83d Cong., 2d Sess. (August 4, 1954), at page 37; Dr. Bush's remarks are reported in *The New York Times* for October 19, 1954.

15. See *The New York Times* for January 17, 1954, reporting the statement of former Ambassadors Norman Armour, Robert Woods Bliss, Joseph C. Grew, William Phillips, and G. Howland Shaw.
16. *Supra,* pp. 73-74.
17. *Supra,* pp. 72-73.
18. *Supra,* pp. 35-45.
19. Reported in *The New York Times* for April 5, 1954, page 12. For the police department's troubles in 1855, see *supra,* pp. 38-45.
20. *The New York Times,* November 8 and 9, 1954.
21. See Cardinal Spellman's speech in Brussels, reported in *The New York Times* for October 25, 1953, page 20: "No American uncontaminated by communism has lost his good name because of Congressional hearings on un-American activities . . . The anguished cries and protests against 'McCarthyism' are not going to dissuade Americans from their desire to see Communists exposed . . ." With all respect to the eminent speaker, the accuracy of the first sentence is open to serious challenge, and the second is hard to square with the teaching that "the most honorable end can never justify the use of evil means." See the letter of Donald McDonald, Editor of *The Catholic Messenger,* published in *The New York Times* for June 21, 1954.
22. The *New York Herald Tribune,* September 28, 1954.
23. The act (Public Law 637, August 24, 1954) is entitled "An Act to Outlaw the Communist Party" and for other purposes, and Section 2, entitled "Findings of Fact," concludes: "Therefore, the Communist Party should be outlawed." The operative sections carry out this purpose by means of the "rights, privileges, and immunities" language quoted in the text. The two Representatives who cast negative votes were Abraham L. Multer (a Brooklyn Democrat) and Usher L. Burdick (a North Dakota Republican).

    The language depriving the Communist Party of the "rights, privileges, and immunities attendant upon legal bodies" appears to have been derived from the Pennsylvania Act of December 21, 1951 (Public Law 1712, Purdon's Pennsylvania Statutes Annotated, Sec. 3811), which provides that the Communist Party "and all other organizations, no matter under what name, whose object or purpose is to overthrow the Federal or State government by force and violence, are hereby declared illegal and not entitled to any of the rights, privileges and immunities attendant upon legal bodies" created under the laws of Pennsylvania. This statute, unlike the new federal law, also makes it a felony to be a member of the Party with knowledge of or participation in its revolutionary purposes.
24. Other laws which have been on the statute books for many years make it a crime to conspire to overthrow the government, or to advocate or conspire to advocate such overthrow. The Internal Security Act of 1950 requires members of "Communist-action" organizations to register with the Attorney General, and debars them from holding any non-elective federal position and from holding a passport. A proceeding by the Subversive Activities Control Board declaring the Communist Party such an organization is under court review. The new Communist Control law undertakes to visit these penalties immediately upon members of the Party. But these provisions are

of even more dubious constitutionality than those of the Internal Security Act, and will surely be challenged. All in all, the new "outlawry" provisions add nothing but confusion and constitutional problems.

25. The Communist candidate for Freeholder of Mercer County lost his place on the ballot because of the new "outlawry" statute, and this action was sustained by the Supreme Court of New Jersey on October 11, 1954. See *The New York Times* for September 30, 1954, and the ACLU monthly publication *Civil Liberties* for October, 1954.

26. So far as the Party organization is concerned, the principal intended effect of the statute is to make unlawful various activities—especially activities as a political party—which are not intrinsically criminal, and are not unlawful when carried on by other organizations. Likewise, it substitutes a legislative finding of the Party's illegal character for the administrative-judicial finding envisaged by the Internal Security Act of 1950. The attempted accomplishment of these ends by legislative rather than judicial means is of very dubious constitutionality. See the interesting discussion in *Dale County* v. *Gunter*, 46 Alabama 118, 141 (1871).

Likewise, the new statute prescribes (in Section 5) a series of fourteen indicia of "membership or participation in the Communist Party" which the jury "shall" consider in proceedings against accused individuals. Some of these are extremely general and sweeping, e.g.:

"(8) Has written, spoken, or in any other way communicated by signal, semaphore, sign, or in any other form of communication, orders, directives, or plans of the organization; . . .

"(11) Has advised, counseled, or in any other way imparted information, suggestions, recommendations to officers or members of the organization or to anyone else in behalf of the objectives of the organization;

"(12) Has indicated by word, action, conduct, writing, or in any other way a willingness to carry out in any manner and to any degree the plans, designs, objectives, or purposes of the organization;

"(13) Has in any other way participated in the activities, planning, actions, objectives, or purposes of the organization. . . ."

The constitutionality of provisions such as these should be considered especially in the light of *DeJonge* v. *Oregon*, 299 U.S. 353 (1937), in which the Supreme Court held unconstitutional under the First Amendment the Criminal Syndicalism Law of Oregon, insofar as it sought to proscribe mere participation in meetings called under the auspices of the Communist Party. In the opinion, Chief Justice Hughes wrote (at pp. 362-363 and 365):

". . . However innocuous the object of the meeting, however lawful the subjects and tenor of the addresses, however reasonable and timely the discussion, all those assisting in the conduct of the meeting would be subject to imprisonment as felons if the meeting were held by the Communist Party. . . . Thus if the Communist Party had called a public meeting in Portland to discuss the tariff, or the foreign policy of the Government, or taxation, or relief, or candidacies for the offices of President, members of Congress, Governor, or state legislators, every speaker who assisted in the conduct of the meeting would be equally guilty with the defendant in this case, upon the charge as here defined and sustained. The list of illustrations might be indefinitely extended to every variety of meetings under the auspices of the Communist Party although held for the discussion of political issues or to adopt protests and pass resolutions of an entirely innocent and proper character. . . .

"... consistently with the Federal Constitution, peaceable assembly for lawful discussion cannot be made a crime. The holding of meetings for peaceable political action cannot be proscribed. Those who assist in the conduct of such meetings cannot be branded as criminals on that score. The question, if the rights of free speech and peaceable assembly are to be preserved, is not as to the auspices under which the meeting is held but as to its purpose; not as to the relations of the speakers, but whether their utterances transcend the bounds of the freedom of speech which the Constitution protects. If the persons assembling have committed crimes elsewhere, if they have formed or are engaged in a conspiracy against the public peace and order, they may be prosecuted for their conspiracy or other violation of valid laws. But it is a different matter when the State, instead of prosecuting them for such offenses, seizes upon mere participation in a peaceable assembly and a lawful public discussion as the basis for a criminal charge."

27. See "Congress Doesn't Yet Know What It Passed," Arthur Krock's column in *The New York Times,* August 27, 1954.

APPENDIX I

1. Quoted in Finer, "The British System," 18 *Univ. of Chicago Law Review* 521, 530-31 (1951), from the Third Report of the Select Committee on House of Commons Procedure, No. 189-91 (1946), at pp. 123, 127. Mr. Finer's article is the basis of much of the material in this Appendix.
2. See the case of Grissell, in the Commons Journals (1880), pp. 73, 77.
3. *Supra,* pp. 9-10 and 192-93.
4. Vol. 18 Parliamentary Debates (1828), column 968; Commons Journals (1946–47), at p. 378.
5. Resolution of May 26, 1818, Commons Journals (1818), p. 389.
6. E.g., Election Compromises (1842), 5 & 6 Vict. c. 31; Sudbury Disfranchisement (1843), 6 & 7 Vict. c. 11; Gaming Transactions (1844), 7 & 8 Vict. c. 7.
7. See the Lords' Journals 1767–70 at p. 575, and 1850 at 478. In *Lord Shaftesbury's Case,* 6 State Trials 1296, however, two of the judges opined that if the Lords committed a witness for an uncertain rather than a fixed term, he should be discharged at the end of the session.
8. E.g., twice in 1938, in inquiries into frauds in quasi-charitable solicitations, and into food and drug inspection methods.
9. Quoted in Justice Frankfurter's dissenting opinion in *United States* v. *Monia,* 317 U.S. 424 (1943).
10. *Supra,* pp. 176-83.

11. The Tribunals of Inquiry (Evidence) Act, 11 & 12 Geo. V, c. 7 (1921).
12. *Supra,* pp. 260-62.
13. Finer, *supra,* note 1, at pp. 562-63.
14. *Supra,* pp. 3-4.
15. 448 Hansard cols. 1703-04 (March 15, 1948).
16. 526 Hansard cols. 1784-85 (April 29, 1954).
17. *Supra,* Chapter II.

APPENDIX II

1. H. R. Rept. No. 2600, 83d Cong., 2d Sess. (August 3, 1954).
2. *Hayburn's Case,* 2 Dallas (U.S.) 409 (1792).
3. See, e.g., *Gordon* v. *United States,* 117 U.S. 697 (1864); *Muskrat* v. *United States,* 219 U.S. 346 (1911).
4. *In re Pacific Railway Commission,* 32 Fed. 241 (C.C.N.D. Cal. 1887).
5. *Interstate Commerce Commission* v. *Brimson,* 154 U.S. 447 (1894).
6. H. R. Report, *supra,* note 1, at p. 7.
7. 161 U.S. 591, at 606-07 (1896).
8. *United States* v. *Murdock,* 284 U.S. 141 (1931); see also the converse holding in *Jack* v. *Kansas,* 199 U.S. 372 (1905).
9. *United States* v. *DiCarlo,* 102 F. Supp. 597 (N.D. Ohio 1952).
10. However, the constitutionality of some of these state statutes is dubious. See the note on this question in 66 *Harvard Law Review* 327 (1952); also Gellhorn, *The States and Subversion* (1952); Emerson and Haber, *Political and Civil Rights in the United States* (1952).
11. *Adams* v. *Maryland,* 347 U.S. 179 (1954).
12. H. R. Report, *supra,* note 1, at p. 7.
13. 142 U.S. 547 (1892).

APPENDIX III

1. Bryce, Vol. II, *Studies in History and Jurisprudence* (1901), p. 642.
2. Potter, *An Historical Introduction to English Law and Its Institutions* (London 1932), pp. 296-97.
3. See Joseph Ritson's *Robin Hood* (Universal Library, London 1853), pp. 10-11, citing Madox' *History of the Exchequer,* p. 136. The learned barrister Mr. Ritson comments, "Such was the humane policy of our enlightened ancestors!"

4. Taswell-Langmead, *English Constitutional History* (1896), p. 108. For an example of outlawry in operation just after Magna Carta, see *Page* v. *Godman*, 2 Bracton's Note Book 115, pl. 135 (Common Pleas, 1222).
5. Potter, *op. cit. supra*, pp. 253-54.
6. Ritson's *Robin Hood, supra.* The old sources most commonly have it that Robin Locksley became the Earl of Huntingdon, after which he lived prodigally, squandered his substance, and that consequently "sutes were commenced against him whereunto he answered not, that by order of lawe he was outlawed." The old ballad *A True Tale of Robin Hood* (c. 1631), included in Ritson's compilation, embodies this version, and likewise explains why Robin, after he became an outlaw, was forever picking on abbots and other high churchmen:

   At last, by his profuse expence,
   He had consum'd his wealth;
   And, being outlaw'd by his prince,
   In woods he liv'd by stealth.

   The abbot of Saint Maries rich,
   To whom he money ought,
   His hatred to the earl was such
   That he his downfall wrought.

   So being outlaw'd (as 'tis told)
   He with a crew went forth
   Of lusty cutters stout and bold
   And robbed in the North.

   But this version is not overly suitable for the young, and most modern stories of Robin Hood prefer to enlarge upon the account in *Robin Hood's Progress to Nottingham*, another ballad in the Ritson compilation. Robin as a youth is on his way to Nottingham for an archery tournament, and is taunted by a group of the King's foresters. Upon a wager to prove his skill to them, he shoots a hart at a great distance, and becomes technically guilty of poaching. The foresters refuse to pay the wager and drive him off with threats, and one sends an arrow after him, which misses. In a rage, Robin turns and shoots one or many of the foresters. Realizing that he will be accused of murder as well as poaching, he flees into Sherwood Forest, and is soon proclaimed an outlaw.
7. Legge, *The Law of Outlawry* (London, 1779).
8. In 1762 Wilkes had commenced publication of his polemic periodical, the *North Briton*. The following year in the famous "issue number 45," Wilkes (then a member of Parliament) wrote a savage attack on the King's speech, which George III regarded as a personal insult. Shortly thereafter, Wilkes's obscene parody (*Essay on Woman*) on Alexander Pope's *Essay on Man* was read aloud to a scandalized House of Lords. The Commons then declared "number 45" to be a seditious libel. Faced with trial on that charge, Wilkes fled to Paris; he was expelled from the Commons, tried and convicted *in absentia*, and, after his continued failure to appear, he was out-

lawed by the coroners of the Middlesex County Court on November 1, 1764.

In 1768 he returned to England, surrendered himself to the sheriff, and sought reversal of his conviction and outlawry in the Court of King's Bench. *Rex* v. *Wilkes*, 4 Burrow 2527 (K.B. 1770). In deference to the old process, Lord Mansfield declared that (p. 2551) "Outlawry is an essential part of the criminal law," but observed (p. 2545): "The Court, in all cases . . . leans to the reversal of outlawries, because the punishment of outlawry is often greater than the punishment of the offense itself." In the upshot, the Court set aside the outlawry because, in one of the exactions, the words "for the County of Middlesex" had been omitted. The conviction for seditious libel was affirmed, and Wilkes was fined and sentenced to 22 months' imprisonment, which he served while crowds gathered daily at the prison gates to do him honor.

9. 33 & 34 Vict. c. 33.
10. 42 & 43 Vict.
11. See the note in 4 Halsbury's *Statutes of England* at p. 648.
12. Goebel and Naughton, *Law Enforcement in Colonial New York* (1944), pp. 442-46.
13. *Commonwealth* v. *Hale*, 2 Virginia Cases 241 (1821). It is an intriguing reflection of the old "wolf's head" concept that outlawry was actually pronounced, not by the court, but by the coroner. This and two contemporaneous Virginia cases (two involving assaults and the other larceny) are the last instances of American use of the outlawry procedure that I have been able to find. See also *Commonwealth* v. *Hagerman*, 2 Virginia Cases 244 (1821) and *Commonwealth* v. *Andersen*, 2 Virginia Cases 245 (1821). It is apparent from the opinions in all three cases (by Judge Bouldin of the General Court, then the highest criminal court of Virginia) that the outlawry procedure was so obsolescent as to be very unfamiliar.
14. *Respublica* v. *Steele*, 2 Dallas 92 (1785).
15. *Respublica* v. *Doan*, 1 Dallas 86, 495 (1784–85).
16. See *Hall* v. *Lanning*, 91 U.S. 160, 166 (1875), and 37 *Harvard Law Review* 799 (1924).
17. *Dale County* v. *Gunter*, 46 Alabama 118, 138-140 (1871).
18. *Congressional Record* for August 16, 1954, at page 13838.

SOURCES AND ACKNOWLEDGMENTS

The investigative power of legislatures has been the subject of innumerable expositions and critiques in law review articles and in periodical literature. But there are, so far as I know, only three books dealing exclusively with this general subject: Eberling, *Congressional Investigations* (1928); Dimock, *Congressional Investigating Committees* (1929); and McGeary, *The Developments of Congressional Investigative Power* (1940). All three are competent works and valuable to the student. None of the three, however, is recent enough or presented in such a manner as to meet the needs of the general reader today.

There are two excellent and very readable books on the House Un-American Activities Committee: Ogden, *The Dies Committee* (1945); and Carr, *The House Committee on Un-American Activities, 1945–1950* (1952). State loyalty investigating committees in California, Washington, and New York, respectively, are the subjects of Barrett, *The Tenney Committee* (1951); Countryman, *Un-American Activities in the State of Washington: The Work of the Canwell Committee* (1951); and Chamberlain, *Loyalty and Legislative Action: A Survey of Activity in the New York State Legislature, 1919–1949* (1951). The recent Army-McCarthy hearings have been excellently described and analyzed in Michael Straight's *Trial by Television* (1954), and a recent critical analysis of the loyalty investigations is Gillmor's *Fear, the Accuser* (1954).

Three legal periodicals have each devoted one or more complete issues to a symposium on Congressional investigations: *Congressional Investigations—A Symposium*, 18 University of Chicago Law Review No. 3 (Spring, 1951); *Legislative Investigations: Safeguards for*

Witnesses, 29 Notre Dame Lawyer No. 2 (Winter, 1954); and *A Symposium on Congressional Hearings and Investigations,* 14 The Federal Bar Journal Nos. 1 and 2 (1954). The single articles that I have found most useful are cited in the notes; the basic historical studies by Landis and Potts are, of course, indispensable. Useful bibliographies have been compiled by Mr. George B. Galloway of the Library of Congress, whose own articles on the subject are among the best.

My friends Walter Gellhorn and Charles Lyon have been generous and helpful in reading and commenting on the text. My wife has made the transition from German generals to Congressional committees with admirable serenity, and the book owes much to her help as critic, researcher, and indexer. I am grateful to my secretary, Zelda Golden, for typing the manuscript, to my friend and former colleague Elwyn Jones, M.P., for his aid in obtaining the information on Parliamentary investigations, and to the many others in Washington who have generously assisted in collecting legislative material.

INDEX

A

Acheson, Dean, 152, 166
Adams, Dr. Arthur S., 226
Adams, John (president), 26
Adams, John (counsel to Department of the Army), 116, 117, 120, 124, 125, 132, 239
Adams, John Quincy, 139
Advisory Commission on Universal Training, 230
Agricultural Adjustment Act, 68, 69, 72, 224
Air Force, United States, 124, 167
Alabama, Supreme Court of, 304
Alfred, King, 301
Allegheny Corporation, 66
Allen, Charles B., 36
American Association of University Professors, 140
American Bar Association, Special Committee on Communist Tactics and Strategy of, 210, 211
American Civil Liberties Union, 143
American Council on Education, 226
American Federation of Labor, 71
American Labor Party, 156, 165, 267
American League for Peace and Democracy, 175
American Legion, 273
"American" Party; *see* Know-Nothing Movement
American Society of Newspaper Editors, 81
American Telephone & Telegraph Company, 67
American Tobacco case, 54, 143, 151, 235
American Tobacco Company, 54
American Veterans' Committee, 273
Amherst, Jeffrey, 19
Amtorg Trading Corporation, 71, 72
Anderson, John, 33
André, Major John, 191
Andrews, Paul Shipman, 202, 203, 213
Argentina
  Committee on Anti-Argentine Activities, 180, 181
  Congress, 16, 180, 181
Army, Department of the, 58, 59, 104, 112-134, 176, 242, 266-269
Army Dental Corps, 116
Army Intelligence (G-2), 113, 114, 129, 131, 275
Army-McCarthy Hearings; *see* Senate, Committees and Investigations
Army Signal Center at Fort Monmouth, 95, 107, 114, 124, 127, 128, 178, 246, 258, 266-269, 270, 272, 273, 274, 275
Army Signal Corps, 1, 2, 113, 209
Association of the Bar of the City of New York, 3, 181, 294
Atomic Energy Commission, 107

Attlee, Clement, 294
Australia
High Court, 225
Parliament, 224, 225
Royal Commissions Act, 224, 225

B

Baker, George F., 63, 64
Baldwin, Hanson, 122
Baldwin, Senator Raymond E., 175
Baldwin, Roger, 71
Bank of the United States, 33, 193
Barker, James W., 38
Barsky, Dr. Edward K., case of, 75, 76, 77, 148, 149, 151, 152, 154, 163, 230, 231
Barth, Allen, 140
Bennett, Senator Wallace F., 252
Benson, Governor Elmer, 74
Bentham, Jeremy, xv
Bentley, Elizabeth, 77, 78
Bergin, General William E., 120, 121, 126
Berthélémy (French jurist), 15
Bevan, Aneurin, 166
Biddle, Nicholas, 193, 196
Bismarck, Otto von, 15
Bituminous Coal Conservation Act, 68
Black, Justice Hugo, 67, 69, 80, 138, 143, 145, 149, 151, 153, 195, 200
Blaine, James G., 45
Blue Jacket, Chief, 18, 19
Bolling, General Alexander R., 128
Bowdoin, Governor James, 19
Boy Scouts, 73
Bracton, Henry de, 302
Bradford, William, 190
Braddock, General Edward, 19
Bradley, General Omar, xiv, 103
Bradley, Justice Joseph P., 161
Brady, James T., 41, 43, 139
Brandeis, Justice Louis D., 3, 60, 68, 69, 70, 161, 162, 179
Brant, Joseph, 18
Braun, Dr. Werner von, 271, 272
Braverman, Maurice, 235, 236, 237
Breshkovskaya, Catherine, 71
Bricker Amendment, 110
Bridges, Harry, 94, 95
Brookhart, Senator Smith W., 60
Brooks, Representative Preston, 33
Brown, John, 34
Brownell, Herbert, 79, 104, 130, 133, 221, 281
Bryce, James, 301
Budenz, Louis, 94, 95, 113, 165
Buckongahelas, Chief, 18
Bureau of Standards, 101, 168
Bureau of the Census, 165
Burgess, Guy, 295
Burgoyne, General John, 20, 122
Burnett (Federal attorney), 101, 106
Burr, Aaron, 106, 192
Bush, Senator Prescott, 252
Bush, Dr. Vannevar, 274
Butler, Representative Benjamin, 105
Butler, Justice Pierce, 30, 56, 60, 68, 229
Butler, General Richard, 18, 21
Byrnes, James F., 63, 223, 224, 229

C

Caldwell, William J., 35
California State Senate Fact-Finding Committee on Un-American Activities, 181
Camden, 1st Earl of, 161
Campfire Girls, 73
Canada, Supreme Court of, 4
Capp, Al, 241
Cardozo, Justice Benjamin N., 68
Carnegie Foundation, 277
Carr, Francis P., 124, 127, 132, 242

Carr, Professor Robert K., 83
Catholic Association for International Peace, 73
Catholic War Veterans, 279
Celler, Representative Emanuel, 252
Central Intelligence Agency, 107, 133, 275
Chamber of Commerce, United States, 66
Chambers, Whittaker, 77, 155, 156, 166, 176, 235, 240
Charles I, King (England), 188
Charles II, King (England), 189, 205
Chase, Chief Justice Salmon P., 242
Chase National Bank, 65, 66, 82
Cherner Motor Company, 235
Cherokee Indians, 106
Chiang Kai-shek, 159, 166
Christian Catholic Apostolic Church in Zion, 92
Churchill, Sir Winston, 294, 295
Civil Service Commission, 100
Clark, Judge Charles E., 148, 149, 152, 153, 168, 230
Clark, Justice Thomas C., xiv
Clay, Henry, 27, 40, 44
Cleveland, Grover, 62, 99, 100, 101, 103, 106
Clinton, Sir Henry, 191
Cochran, Judge Andrew, 55, 61, 62
Cohn, Roy, xiii, 107, 113, 115, 124, 125, 127, 132, 178, 239, 242
Coke, Sir Edward, 8, 61, 188, 189
Coleman, Aaron, 129
Coleridge, Lord Justice, 13
Columbia Broadcasting System, 79
Committee for Constitutional Government (CCG), 140-147
Communist Control Act of 1954, 155, 174, 280, 281, 304, 305
Communist Party, 2, 77, 123, 138, 148, 149, 152, 155, 157, 158, 159, 164-166, 174, 177, 184, 195, 198, 207, 214, 235, 280, 281, 282, 294, 305
Condon, Dr. Edward U., 101, 102
Congress
  Joint Committee on Atomic Energy, 131, 259
  Joint House-Senate Committee, 34, 261, 334
  proposed Joint Committee on Internal Security, 259
Congress of Industrial Organizations, 71
Connecticut, Supreme Court of, 176
Constitution
  Bill of Rights, xv, 83, 85, 136-150, 163, 171, 182, 191, 222, 223, 238, 257, 304
  First Amendment, 130-183, 195, 230, 231
  Fourth Amendment, 136, 139, 160, 161, 162, 231
  Fifth Amendment, 1, 2, 4, 9, 77, 86, 116, 117, 118, 147, 148, 160, 173, 184-221, 226, 229, 235, 239, 267, 268, 299
  Sixth Amendment, 191, 238
  Eighth Amendment, 191
  Fourteenth Amendment, 138, 229, 238
  Twenty-Second Amendment, 110
Cooke, Jay, 46, 48, 91, 94
Coolidge, Calvin, 60, 66, 100, 179
Coplon, Judith, 238
Cornwallis, General Charles, 122
Corwin, Edward S., 104
Costello, Frank, 240, 247
Coughlin, Father Charles E., 71
Court-packing Plan, 70
Cox, Eugene, xii
Crawford, Kenneth, 71
Credit Mobilier, 45
Cromwell, Oliver, 188
Cumberland, Duke of, 19
Cushing, Justice Luther S., 3
Custer, General George A., 19

D

Dalton, Hugh, 290
Daly, Judge Charles Patrick, 40-45, 49, 52, 139, 194, 260, 261
Daugherty, Harry, 54-57, 104, 244
Daugherty, Mally S., 54-57, 61, 62
Daugherty case; *see McGrain* v. *Daugherty*
Davis, Elmer, 185, 197
Day, Justice William R., 239
Defense, Department of, 123, 124
Delaware Indians, 18
Del Monte, John F., 98, 99
Democratic National Committee, 66
Dennis, Eugene, 76
Dewey, Thomas E., 174, 281
Dickens, Charles, 289
Dickey, John, 185
Dickinson, John, 303
Dickstein, Representative Samuel, 72, 73
Dies, Representative Martin, xii, 71-75, 80, 83, 111, 174, 175, 177, 181, 263, 282
Dies Committee; *see* House, Committees and Investigations
Dirksen, Senator Everett, 121, 127, 178, 278
District of Columbia
  Court of Appeals, 143, 149, 238
  District Court, 46, 47, 49
Dmytryk, Edward, 77
Doan, Aaron, 303
Dodd, William S., 72
Donnell, Senator Forrest C., 109
Dooley, Mr. (Finley Peter Dunne), 146
Dornberger, General Walter, 270-273
Doughton, Representative Robert L., 63
Douglas, Senator Paul H., 72, 175, 252
Douglas, Justice William O., 138, 143, 145, 146, 149, 151, 153, 163
Dowie, John Alexander, 92
Dred Scott case, 32, 224
Duguit (French jurist), 15
Duncan, Justice Warren W., 60, 93
Durocher, Leo, 128
Duskin (Federal attorney), 101, 106

E

Earle, George H., 227
Eastman, Max, 152
Edgerton, Judge Henry W., 149, 153, 163, 230
Edward III, King (England), 302
Einstein, Dr. Albert, 182
Eisenhower, Dwight D., 60, 111, 112, 113, 116, 122, 131, 132, 133, 135, 170, 281
Eisler, Gerhart, 76, 148
Eisler, Hanns, 76, 148
Elizabeth I, Queen (England), 187
Elleford, William de, 302
Elliott, Captain J. D., 33
Emery, Henry, 194
Emspak, Julius, 195
Espionage Laws, 131, 132, 133

F

Fast, Howard, 170
Federal Bureau of Investigation, 2, 100, 102, 129, 132, 134, 238, 265, 266, 267, 281
Federal Communications Commission, 67, 217
Federal Reserve System, 62
Federal Trade Commission, 53, 54, 62, 139
Feinberg Law, New York State, 138
Ferguson, Senator Homer, 78
Field, Justice Stephen J., 60, 297
"Fifth Amendment Communists," xiv, 3, 4, 5, 86, 117, 122,

159, 185, 196-199, 202, 210, 213, 225, 226, 267
Fillmore, Millard, 99, 100
Finer, Professor Herman, 292
First National Bank, 63
Fish, Representative Hamilton, 72, 73, 78
Fish, Hamilton, 91
Fitzsimmons, Representative, 22
Flanders, Senator Ralph, 123, 134
Flanagan, Hallie, 80
Flynn, John T., 141, 142, 145, 178
Food Control Act of 1917, 229, 233
Ford Foundation, 277
Foreign Operations Administration, 275
Forfeiture Act of 1870, 303
Fortas, Abe, 197, 255, 256
Fort Monmouth; *see* Army Signal Center at Fort Monmouth
Foster, William Z., 71
France
  Chamber of Deputies, 14
  Legislative Inquiries, 14-15
Francis, David, 71
Franco, General Francisco, 166, 175
Frank, Judge Jerome, 72
Frankfurter, Justice Felix, 3, 58, 61, 62, 87, 143, 144, 146, 149, 151, 173, 244
Franklin, Benjamin, xv
Frazier-Lemke, Amendments to Bankruptcy Act, 68
Frelinghuysen, Representative Peter, 252, 259
Frey, John P., 71, 73
Fuchs, Klaus, 295
Fulbright, Senator James W., 134
Furry, Wendell H., 1-5, 94, 95, 185, 199, 206, 208

G

Gannett, Frank, 141
Garrett, Oliver B., 91
Gary, Judge Elbert H., 61
General Electric Company, 3, 4, 5, 79, 212, 246
General Land Office, 51
George, Senator Walter, 56
George II, King (England), 10
George III, King (England), 340
Gerard, James W., 39
Germany
  Army Ordnance, 270-273
  Gestapo, 271
  legislative inquiries, 15
  Reichstag, 14, 15
  Schutzstaffel (SS), 271
  Weimar Constitution, 15
Girty, Simon, 18
Glatis, James W., 265
Goebel, Professor Julius, 303, 305
Gomez, Lefty, 265
Government Printing Office, 113
Grant, Ulysses S., 99, 100, 196, 197
Gray, Justice Horace, 3
Green, William, 71
Greene, General Nathanael, 20, 191
Greenville, Treaty of, 19
Gregory IX, Pope, 187, 188
Griswold, Erwin, 203
Gunter, W. T., 304

H

Hague, Frank, 133
Haldane, Viscount, Lord Chancellor, 225
Halleck, Representative Charles A., 142
Halley, Rudolph, 240, 292
Hamilton, Alexander, 23, 25, 26, 28, 30, 137, 150, 162, 178
Hammett, Dashiell, 170, 184, 185
Hand, Judge Learned, 151, 152, 168, 170, 182
Harding, Warren G., 60-62, 179
Hardwicke, Lord Chancellor, 291
Harlan, Justice John M., 53, 60
Harmar, General Josiah, 18, 20

Harriman, E. H., 53, 54
Harriman v. *Interstate Commerce Commission,* 54, 56, 143, 151, 235
Harris, Reed, 167
Hart, Henry T., 72
Harvard Law School, 3, 61, 104, 211
Harvard University, 1, 3, 5, 79, 185, 225
Hayes, Rutherford B., 99
Hellman, Lillian, 206, 207, 208
Hendrickson, Senator Robert C., 259
Henry, George, 64, 205, 237
Hensel, Struve, 239
High Commission, Court of, 187, 188, 189
High Court of Parliament, 289, 292
Hill, James J., 63
Hillman, Sidney, 72
Himmler, Heinrich, 270-273
Hindenburg, Field Marshall Paul von, 15
Hiss, Alger, 77, 176, 235, 240
Hiss, Joseph, 37, 38
Hiss Committee; *see* Nunnery Committee
Hitler, Adolf, 15, 72, 158, 270-273, 277
Hoar, Representative George F., 48
Hodgdon, Samuel, 21, 24, 25, 244
Hoffman, Representative Clare, 103, 104, 108
Hoffman Resolution, 102, 103, 104
Hollywood motion picture industry, xiii, 77, 149, 158, 170
"Hollywood Ten," 77, 149, 151, 153
Holmes, Justice Oliver Wendell, 3, 54, 60, 138, 139, 143, 144, 151, 182, 186
Hood, Robin, xiv, 302
Hook, Sidney, 197
Hoover, Herbert, 100
Hoover, J. Edgar, 79, 128, 129, 131, 152, 265, 281
Hopkins, Harry L., 227
Hopkins, William, 10
House, Committees and Investigations
  Banking and Currency Committee, 63; Money Trust Investigation (Pujo Hearings), 51, 63-65, 290
  Buchanan Committee (investigation of lobbying), 141, 142, 144
  Fish Committee (investigation of Communist propaganda), 71
  Government Operations Committee, 274
  Judiciary Committee, 105, 195, 218
  King Committee (investigation of Bureau of Internal Revenue), 79
  Real Estate Pool and Jay Cooke Financial Indebtedness Committee, 46, 205
  Reece Committee (investigation of tax-exempt foundations), 38, 156, 226, 277
  Un-American Activities Committee, xiii, 71-80, 83, 104, 110, 141, 148, 149, 152, 176, 195, 202, 207, 213, 214, 219, 223, 230, 232, 235, 236, 237, 240, 245, 259, 265, 277, 278
House of Commons, 5, 6, 7, 8, 9, 13-15, 23, 91, 187, 215, 220, 285-295
House of Lords, 9, 215, 220, 288, 289
Houston, Samuel, 33
Howe, Fred, 72
Howe & Hummel, 211
Hughes, Chief Justice Charles Evans, 63, 157
Hughes, Archbishop John, 36
Humphrey, Senator Hubert, 282
Hunter College, 158

Hyde, Representative DeWitt S., 305
Hyman, Harry, 267, 268
Hyman, Sidney, 59

I

Ickes, Harold, 74
Illinois, Supreme Court of, 60, 93
Immunity Bill of 1954, 217-221, 296-300
Ingraham, Judge, 43
Innocent III, Pope, 187
Institute of Pacific Relations, 78, 243
Interior, Department of the, 56, 216
Internal Revenue, Bureau of, 34
Internal Security Act of 1950, 155, 156, 174, 175, 204, 299
Internal Security Committee; *see* Senate, Committees and Investigations
International Information Administration, 80, 115, 270
International Monetary Fund, 223
Interstate Commerce Act, 52, 53, 62, 217, 299
Interstate Commerce Commission, 52, 53, 62, 139, 217, 238, 297
Irwin, R. B., 46
Isaacs, Sir Rufus, 293

J

Jackson, Andrew, 34, 99, 100, 193, 196
Jackson, Justice Robert H., 80, 136, 163
Jacques, Moses, 35
James I, King (England), 186
Jansen, Dr. William, 228
Javits, Representative Jacob K., 38, 252
Jefferson, Thomas, xv, 23, 24, 27, 99, 106, 178
Jeffreys of Wem, Baron, 61
Jenkins, Ray, xiii, 241
Jenks, Francis, 205
Jenner, Senator William, xii, 5, 79, 80, 83, 164, 165, 166, 175, 199, 202, 228, 264, 278, 282
Johnson, Andrew, 45, 242
Johnson, Dr. Robert L., 270
Joint Anti-Fascist Refugee Committee, 75, 148
Josephson, Leon, case of, 76, 77, 148, 151, 152, 153, 154, 168, 230, 231
Judicial Committee of the Privy Council, 225
Justice, Department of, 54, 130, 153, 176, 227, 244
Juvenal (Decimus Junius Juvenalis), 108

K

Kaffenburgh, Abraham, 211
Kaghan, Theodore, 167
Kahn, Otto, 53, 54, 66
Kasson, Representative John A., 48
Kazan, Elia, 206
Keating, Representative Kenneth B., 252, 256, 262, 298
Kefauver, Senator Estes, 79, 124, 218, 240, 252, 254, 292
Keitel, Field Marshal Wilhelm, 271
Kilbourn, Hallett, 46-49, 91, 92, 205, 260
Kilbourn v. *Thompson*, 47-50, 53, 55, 56, 59, 91, 163
Killian, Dr. James, 274
King's Bench, Court of, 288
Kinsey, Dr. Alfred C., 172
Knowland, Senator William F., 134
Know-Nothing Movement, 35-45, 70, 139, 174, 260, 278, 283
Knox, General Henry, 23, 24, 25, 28, 99, 244
Kohlberg, Alfred, 278

Kuhn, Loeb & Company, 63, 66
Ku Klux Klan, 304, 305

L

Lafayette, Marquis de, 191
La Follette, Robert M., Jr., 67, 69, 80, 109
Lamont, Corliss, 113, 154, 206, 208, 209
Lamont, Thomas W., 65
Landis, James M., 61, 62, 72, 104, 108
Landis, Judge Kenesaw Mountain, 92
La Prensa (newspaper), 181
Lardner, Ring, Jr., 77
Lattimore, Owen, 167, 243, 255
Lawrence, David (journalist), 176, 291
Lawrence, David (mayor), 227
Lawson, John Howard, 77, 149
Lawton, General Kirke B., xiv, 115, 267
Lee, General Robert E., 109
Legge, Thomas, 303
Legislative Reorganization Act of 1946, 78, 108, 232, 233, 258, 259
Leo XIII, Pope, 156
Lerner, Max, 167, 267
Lewis, Fulton, Jr., 273
Lilburne, Freeborn John, 188, 189, 190, 205
Lilienthal, David, 70
Lincoln, Abraham, 97, 99, 100, 109, 178
Lindbergh, Representative Charles A., 63
Lippmann, Walter, 122, 178, 280
Little Turtle (Me-She-Kin-No-Quah), 18, 19, 20, 28
Livingston, Representative Edward, 34
Locke, John, xv
Long, Hamilton, 156
Ludendorff, General Erich, 15
Lynskey, Judge G. J., 292, 293
Lyons, Eugene, 152

M

MacArthur, General Douglas, 103, 245
McArthur, Judge, 46
McCaffrey, Msgr. Joseph A., 278
McCann, Michael, 40, 41, 43
McCarran, Senator Patrick, xii, 78, 79, 111, 174, 175, 181, 217, 218, 221, 243, 278
McCarran Act; *see* Internal Security Act of 1950
McCarthy, Senator Joseph R., xii, xiii, xiv, 1-5, 38, 58, 59, 78-83, 86, 87, 95, 107, 109, 111, 112-135, 164, 174, 175, 176, 184, 185, 196, 197, 201, 202, 206, 208, 225, 239, 242, 245, 246, 253, 258, 264-268, 275-279, 280
McClellan, Senator John L., 109
McCloy, John J., 82
McCormack, Representative John, 73
McCormack Act of 1938, 73
McCracken, William P., Jr., 69, 237
McDonnell, Representative John, 76
McDougall, Captain Alexander, 11
McGill, Dr. V. Jerauld, 158
McGrain v. *Daugherty*, 55-57
Mackellar, William, 40, 43
McLean, Donald, 295
Madden, J. Warren, 70
Madison, James, 22, 25, 26, 27, 30, 89, 90, 137, 151
Magna Carta, 186, 188, 302
Mallary, Representative, 34
"Malmédy Massacre," 112, 115, 176
Manhattan District Project, 270
Mansfield, William Murray, 1st Earl of, 303

Marlowe, Christopher, 80
Marshall, General George, 112, 115, 152
Marshall, Chief Justice John, 31, 32, 47, 192
Martin, Msgr. Edward R., 279
Martin, Representative Joseph, 233, 259
Marx, Karl, 123
Massachusetts, Supreme Judicial Court of, 44, 98-99, 194, 202
Massachusetts "Body of Liberties," 189
Matsell, George W., 38-41, 260
Matthews, Francis P., 112, 114
Matthews, J. B., 74, 79
Mead, William, 189
Melchior, Isaac, 12
Mellon, Andrew, 100
Menjou, Adolphe, 77
Messersmith, George, 76
Metal Trades Department, A.F.L., 71
Miami Indians, 17, 18, 20
Michigan, Supreme Court of, 200
Mikhailovitch, Draja, 166
Mill, John Stuart, 269
Miller, Justice Samuel F., 47-50, 55, 91, 162, 163
Millikin, Senator Eugene D., 134
Millis, Walter H., 122
Mitchell, Charles, 65, 66, 84
Monroe, James, 99, 100
Monroney, Senator A. S. Mike, 134
Montesquieu, Charles de Secondat, Baron de, xv, 50, 90
Moore, Judge William, 11
Morgan, Arthur E., 70
Morgan, J. P. (the elder), 63, 64
Morgan, J. P. (the younger), 65, 66
Morrison, Right Honorable Herbert, 286, 287, 292
Morrissey, John, 40
Morse, Senator Wayne, 134, 218, 259
Moss, Annie Lee, 123
Mueller, SS General Heinrich, 271, 272
Mundt, Senator Karl, 76, 121, 124, 125, 127, 129, 241
Murphy, Justice Frank, 69, 74, 79
Mussolini, Benito, 277

N

Nash, A., 40
National City Bank, 65, 66
National Labor Relations Board, 70
National Recovery Act, 68, 69, 224
Navy, Department of the, 56, 91, 104, 124
Nazis, 72, 73, 147, 180, 273, 278, 280
Nelson, Representative, 72
New Deal, 57, 65, 67-70, 73, 80, 82, 83, 84, 110, 135, 141, 279, 290
New Hampshire
  Public Service Commission, 96
  Public Service Company, 96
  Supreme Court, 96
New York City
  Court of Common Pleas, 39, 40, 43, 49
  Department of Public Works, 91
  Police Department, 38-45, 139, 165, 278
New York Post, 60, 80
New York State
  Court of Appeals, 60, 94, 211
  Supreme Court, 39
New York Times, 1, 35, 60, 74, 125, 215, 246
New York Tribune, 60
Nixon, Richard M., 76, 77, 123
Noyes, William Curtis, 40, 41
Nunnery Committee (Massachusetts), 37, 38
Nuremburg Trials, 166, 250
Nye, Senator Gerald, 67, 69

O

O'Connor, Harvey, 154
Ogden, Father August R., 74
Oppenheimer, Dr. Robert, 272, 273, 275, 292
Order of the Star-Spangled Banner, 36
Ordinance of 1787 (Northwest Ordinance), 20
Otis, James, 161
Outlawry, xiv, xv, 301-305

P

Pacific Gas and Electric Company, 181
Pacific Mail Steamship Company, 45
Pappas, Theodore, 3, 4
Parliament, British, xv, 7, 8, 9, 10, 13-15, 24, 25, 31, 47, 188, 193, 215, 220, 237, 242, 285-295; Committee on Privileges, 289; investigative practices of, 13-15, 193, 194, 220, 237, 239
Partridge, General Richard C., 113-115, 117, 275
Paterson, Justice William, 30
Paxton, Nicholas, 9, 192, 215, 288, 289
Peck, Judge, 304, 305
Pecora, Ferdinand, 63, 65, 66, 67, 83, 84
Peenemuende, 270-273
Pegler, Westbrook, 167
Penn, William, 189
Pennsylvania, Supreme Court of, 97-98, 303
Pepper, Senator George Wharton, 61
Peress, Dr. Irving, 116-119, 121, 122, 126
Pericles, 178
Permanent Subcommittee on Investigations; *see* Senate, Committees and Investigations
Perón, Juan Domingo, 16, 181
Peterson, Representative, 76
Pinkerton Detective Agency, 51
Pitt, William (the elder), 9, 28
Pius XI, Pope, 156
Polk, James K., 99, 103
Pontecorvo, Bruno, 295
Poole, Bill, 40
Potter, Senator Charles, 121
Potter, Dean Harold, 301, 302
Potts, Charles S., 61, 62
Prestwude, Thomas de, 301
Prettyman, Judge E. Barrett, 152, 163, 165, 230
Progressive Party, 156
Public Utility Holding Company Act of 1935, 67
Public Works Administration, 72
Pugh, Senator, 216
Pujo, Representative Arsène, 63
Pujo Hearings; *see* House, Committees and Investigations
Pusey, Nathan M., 3, 4

R

Radio Free Europe, 169
Railroad Retirement Act, 68
Rand, Justice Ivan C., 4, 294
Randall, Robert, 13
Randolph, Edmund, 23
Rankin, Representative John, 75, 76, 282
Rapallo, Judge, 60, 94
Raskob, John J., 66
Rayburn, Representative Sam, 233, 259
Reece, Representative Carroll, xii, 38, 278
Reece Committee; *see* House, Committees and Investigations
Reed, John, 71
Reed, Justice Stanley, 69

Regulation of Lobbying Act of 1946, 141, 145
Remington, William, 77, 78
Reuther, Walter P., 213, 214
Reynaud, Paul, 15
Richard I, King (England), 301
Rifkind, Judge Simon, 210, 213
Roberts, Justice Owen J., 63
Rochette-Caillaux scandal, 15
Rockefeller Foundation, 277
Rogers, Mrs. Leila (mother of Ginger), 77
Rooke, Thomas, 10
Roosevelt, Mrs. Eleanor, 76
Roosevelt, Franklin D., xvi, 68, 70, 100, 110, 111
Roosevelt, Theodore, 62, 100
Rosen, Mr. and Mrs. William, 235, 237
Rosenberg, Julius and Ethel, 95, 96, 114, 201
Royal Commissions of Inquiry (British), 287, 290-291, 295; on Liquor Licensing, 290; on Lunacy and Mental Disorder, 293; on Population, and Marriage and Divorce, 290
Rumely, Edward A., case of, 140-147, 149, 151, 154, 163, 173, 188, 206, 208, 209, 235
Russell, Senator Richard, 175

S

St. Clair, General Arthur, 17-29, 32, 91, 99, 191, 243, 244, 258, 279, 295
Salomon Brothers, 64, 205, 237
Saltonstall, Senator Leverett, 124, 175
Sarnoff, General David, 248
Schiff, Jacob, 63
Schine, G. David, 115, 123, 125, 127, 132
Schulz, Rabbi Benjamin, 278
Schweinhaut, Judge Henry A., 249
Scotland Yard, 293
Scott, Adrian, 77
Scott, Representative Hugh D., Jr., 252
Scottish Court of Session, 292
Scoville, John W., 141
Screen Writers Guild, 149, 165
Scroggs, Sir William, 61
Scroop, Adrian, 189
Scrope, John, 9, 10
Securities Act of 1933, 67
Securities and Exchange Commission, 67, 217
Securities Exchange Act of 1934, 67
Seeckt, General Hans Von, 263, 282
Select Committees, British, 287-290; on Budget Disclosure (1947), 290; on Nationalized Industries (1951–52), 290
Senate, Committees and Investigations
- Armed Services Committee, 124, 232
- Banking and Currency Committee, 65; Stock Exchange Investigation, 65-67, 290
- Brookhart-Wheeler Select Committee, 62, 244
- Education and Labor Committee, 67
- Expenditures in the Executive Department, Committee on, 78, 103
- Government Operations Committee, 113, 133, 184, 185, 258; Permanent Investigating Subcommittee, xiii, 1, 2, 3, 38, 78, 80, 89, 113-124, 159-160, 199, 208, 209, 225, 233, 241, 242, 245, 258, 259; Army-McCarthy Hearings, xiii, 124-134, 239, 240, 241, 242, 252

Senate—*Continued*
Interstate and Foreign Commerce Committee, 232, 258
Judiciary Committee, 78, 101, 232; Internal Security Subcommittee, xiii, 5, 78, 79, 164, 165, 199, 211, 218, 219, 227, 228, 233, 243, 245, 255, 259, 265, 266, 277
Kefauver (Interstate Crime) Hearings, 79, 240, 247, 249, 251, 252, 291, 292, 299
Labor and Public Welfare Committee, 232
Munitions Investigation, 82
National Defense Program, Special Committee to Investigate (Truman Committee), 70, 109
Ocean and Air Mail Contracts, Special Committee to Investigate, 237
Public Lands, Committee on, 56
Watkins Committee (McCarthy Censure Resolution), 134, 237, 242, 248
Seward, George F., 105, 194, 195
Shawcross, Sir Hartley, 3, 4, 5, 14, 181, 294
Shawnee Indians, 17, 18, 20
Sheil, Bishop Bernard J., 279
Signal Corps of the Army; *see* Army Signal Corps
Sinclair, Harry F., 56, 104
Sinclair v. *United States,* 56, 57
Slamm, Levi, 35
"Smelling Committee"; *see* Nunnery Committee
Smith, Gerald L. K., 267
Smith Act of 1940, 138, 151, 155, 156, 174, 176, 195, 203, 204, 299
Smithers, Sir W., 294, 295
Sokolsky, George, 273
Spanish Loyalists, 158, 159, 175
Spellman, Francis Cardinal, 152
Stalin, Josef, 72
Stanbery, Representative, 33
Stanton, Frank, 248
Star Chamber, Court of, 187, 188, 189, 190, 205
Starnes, Representative Joe, 80
Stassen, Harold E., 275
State, Department of, 78, 79, 112, 113, 176, 194, 275, 276
Statute of 1857 (Congressional Investigations), 35, 53, 56, 64, 69, 76, 87, 142, 148, 194, 215, 216, 218, 229, 230, 231, 233, 288
Stavisky scandals, 179
Steele, Robert, 303
Steele, Walter, 73
Stepinac, Archbishop, 166
Steuben, Baron Friedrich Wilhelm von, 191
Stevens, Robert T., xiv, 114, 115, 116, 117, 121-28, 239
Stewart, Joseph B., 45
Stockholm Peace Appeal, 159
Stone, Chief Justice Harlan F., 68, 131
Story, Justice Joseph, 3
Strawn, Silas, 66
Stripling, Robert, 76, 235
Subversive Activities Control Board, 175, 265
Sumner, Senator Charles, 33
Supreme Court of the United States, 29, 30-35, 45, 48, 52, 53-57, 58, 60, 61, 62, 68, 69, 70, 83, 84, 90, 97, 138-140, 143-147, 149, 150, 154, 161-163, 168, 171, 173, 195, 200, 206, 207, 217, 224, 228, 229, 230, 234, 237, 238, 239, 260, 297, 299
Sutherland, Justice George, 60, 68, 163

Sweezy, Paul, 154
Symington, Senator Stuart, 121

T

Taft, Senator Robert A., 175
Taft, Justice William H., 62, 100, 144, 161, 207
Taft-Hartley Act, 110, 138, 141
Taylor, Robert, 77
Teapot Dome, 56, 57
Temple, Shirley, 74, 79
Tennessee Valley Authority, 70
Tenney, Jack, xii, 175, 264
Theocrat (newspaper), 93
Thetis (submarine), 293
Thomas, Senator Elbert, 67
Thomas, Right Honorable J. H., 293
Thomas, Representative J. Parnell, xii, 73, 76, 77, 240, 242, 244
Time (magazine), 251
Times, The (of London), 122
Tito, Marshal (Josip Broz), 166
Tobey, Senator Charles, 240, 292
Tocqueville, Alexis de, 177, 178
Toledo, Lady from, 140-147
Treasury, Department of the, 33
Tribunals of Inquiry, British, 287, 291-294
Truman, Harry S., xiv, xvi, 70, 100, 102, 103, 109, 111, 133, 152, 223,
"Truman Directive," 102-104, 116, 130, 131
Trumbo, Dalton, 77, 149, 165
Tugwell, Rexford Guy, 72
Tydings, Senator Millard, 175
Tyler, John, 99, 100, 104, 106

U

Un-American Activities Committee; *see* House, Committees and Investigations
Union League Club, 91
Union Pacific Railroad, 45
United Automobile Workers, 213, 214
United Electrical, Radio & Machine Workers of America, 195
United Nations, 79, 211
United States Bank, 139
Untermyer, Samuel, 63, 64, 205

V

Vail, Representative Richard, 76
Van Devanter, Justice Willis, 55, 56, 60, 68
Van Sweringen, Oris P., 65
Velde, Representative Harold, xii, 78, 79, 80, 166, 202, 223, 224, 278
Vinson, Chief Justice Frederick M., 151
Virginia
  House of Burgesses, 10
  House of Delegates, 231
Virginia Declaration of Rights of 1776, 191
Voice of America, 79, 107, 113, 127, 169, 269, 275, 276
Voliva, Wilbur Glenn, 92-95
Voorhis, Representative Jerry, 74

W

Wage and Hour Law of 1938, 70
Wagner Labor Relations Act, 68
Wallace, Henry, 156
Walpole, Sir Robert, 8, 9, 23, 91, 192, 215, 285, 288
Walsh, Father Edmund, 71, 152
Walsh, Senator Thomas, 56, 60, 61
War, Department of, 33, 79
Warren, Samuel, 161
Washington, George, 20-24, 26-29, 86, 99, 100, 102, 133, 135

Washington (state)
  Joint Legislative Fact-Finding Committee on Un-American Activities, 232
  Supreme Court, 232
Washington Post, 140
Wayne, General "Mad Anthony," 19, 28
Webster, Daniel, 40
Webster, Timothy, 40, 41, 43
Wechsler, James, 80-82, 155, 159, 160, 166, 167, 179, 206, 208, 209
Welch, Joseph, xiii, 129, 239, 241
Welles, Sumner, 76
West, Edward, 10
Western Union, 91
Whalen, Grover, 71
Wheeler, Senator Burton K., 60, 61, 62, 67, 69, 80, 258
White, Chief Justice Edward D., 54, 60
White, Harry Dexter, 77, 79, 104, 223
White, Theodore H., 59, 122
Whitgift, John, Archbishop of Canterbury, 187
Whitney, George, 65, 66
Whitney, Richard, 66
Wiggin, Albert H., 65, 84
Wigmore, Dean J. H., 60, 61
Wilde, Oscar, 170
Wilkes, John, 161, 303
Wilkinson, General James, 33
Williamson, Hugh, 22
Wilson, Charles Erwin, 123
Wilson, Woodrow, 6, 51, 62, 143, 144, 177
Winchell, Walter, xiv, 237
Wirt, Dr. William, 72
Wolfe, General James, 19
Wolman, Leo, 72
Woltman, Frederick, 270
Wood, Fernando, 38, 39
Wood, Representative John, 76, 77
Woods, Patrick, 310
Works Progress Administration, 227, 229
World Bank, 82
Wyzanski, Judge Charles E., Jr., 178-180, 182, 225, 254, 256, 291

Y

Young Communist League, 81, 175

Z

Zenger, John Peter, 162
Zion City, 92-94
Zwicker, General Ralph, xiv, 59, 87, 89, 116-121, 126, 127, 134

NOTE ABOUT THE AUTHOR

TELFORD TAYLOR *is one of the more versatile of contemporary Americans, having already had noteworthy careers as lawyer, writer and government administrator. His knowledge of Congressional investigations was acquired at first hand from his experience between 1935 and 1939 as counsel to the inquiry into railroad finance headed by Senators Burton K. Wheeler and Harry S. Truman. During the war he served with distinction in the Army intelligence service and in 1946 he was named chief of counsel for the prosecution of war criminals at Nuremberg with the rank of brigadier general. From his war and postwar activity he wrote* Sword and Swastika, *the first volume of a major study of the German General Staff in Hitler's Third Reich. Mr. Taylor has also been general counsel of the Federal Communications Commission and, more recently, Small Defense Plants Administrator. He now practices law in New York City and writes and speaks frequently on political, legal, and military subjects.*